British culture after empire

Manchester University Press

STUDIES IN IMPERIALISM

General editors: Andrew S. Thompson and Alan Lester
Founding editor: John M. MacKenzie

When the 'Studies in Imperialism' series was founded by Professor John M. MacKenzie more than thirty years ago, emphasis was laid upon the conviction that 'imperialism as a cultural phenomenon had as significant an effect on the dominant as on the subordinate societies'. With well over a hundred titles now published, this remains the prime concern of the series. Cross-disciplinary work has indeed appeared covering the full spectrum of cultural phenomena, as well as examining aspects of gender and sex, frontiers and law, science and the environment, language and literature, migration and patriotic societies, and much else. Moreover, the series has always wished to present comparative work on European and American imperialism, and particularly welcomes the submission of books in these areas. The fascination with imperialism, in all its aspects, shows no sign of abating, and this series will continue to lead the way in encouraging the widest possible range of studies in the field. 'Studies in Imperialism' is fully organic in its development, always seeking to be at the cutting edge, responding to the latest interests of scholars and the needs of this ever-expanding area of scholarship.

To buy or to find out more about the books currently available in this series, please go to: https://manchesteruniversitypress.co.uk/series/studies-in-imperialism/

British culture after empire

Race, decolonisation and migration since 1945

Edited by

Josh Doble, Liam J. Liburd
and Emma Parker

MANCHESTER UNIVERSITY PRESS

Copyright © Manchester University Press 2023

While copyright in the volume as a whole is vested in Manchester University Press, copyright in individual chapters belongs to their respective authors, and no chapter may be reproduced wholly or in part without the express permission in writing of both author and publisher.

Published by Manchester University Press
Oxford Road, Manchester M13 9PL

www.manchesteruniversitypress.co.uk

British Library Cataloguing-in-Publication Data
A catalogue record for this book is available from the British Library

ISBN 978 1 5261 5974 8 hardback
ISBN 978 1 5261 8254 8 paperback

First published 2023
Paperback published 2024

The publisher has no responsibility for the persistence or accuracy of URLs for any external or third-party internet websites referred to in this book, and does not guarantee that any content on such websites is, or will remain, accurate or appropriate.

Typeset by Newgen Publishing UK

Contents

List of figures   vii
List of contributors   viii
Foreword: Living in the bush of ghosts
   Elleke Boehmer   xi
Acknowledgements   xvii

Introduction: Rhodesia and the 'Rivers of Blood'
   Josh Doble, Liam J. Liburd and Emma Parker   1

Part I: Institutions of empire

1 'Bloomsbury bazaar': Daljit Nagra at the diasporic museum
   John McLeod   29
2 Anthropology at the end of empire: Turning a 'colonial science' on Britain itself
   Katherine Ambler   46
3 'He is not a "racist" but should not be appointed director of LSE': The impact of colonial universities on the University of London
   Dongkyung Shin   65

Part II: Writing identity, conflict and class

4 Beyond experience: British anti-racist non-fiction after empire
   Dominic Davies   87
5 Empire, war and class in Graham Swift's *Last Orders* (1996)
   Ed Dodson   106

Part III: Racial others, national memory

6 White against empire: Immigration, decolonisation and Britain's radical right, 1954–1967
   Liam J. Liburd   127

7 Racism, redistribution, redress: The Royal Historical Society and *Race, Ethnicity & Equality in UK History: A Report and Resource for Change*
  Shahmima Akhtar — 147
8 Exemplar empires: Battles over imperial memory in contemporary Britain
  Astrid Rasch — 166

Part IV: At home in postcolonial Britain

9 Empire, security and citizenship in Arab British fiction
  Tasnim Qutait — 189
10 Black, beautiful and essentially British: African Caribbean women, belonging and the creation of Black British beauty spaces in Britain (c. 1948–1990)
  Mobeen Hussain — 207
11 Convivial cultures and the commodification of otherness in London nightlife in the 1970s and 1980s
  Steve Bentel — 230
12 Tribe Arts, Tribe Talks
  Josh Doble, Liam J. Liburd, Emma Parker, Samran Rathore and Tajpal Rathore — 248

Afterword: Disorder and displacement
  Bill Schwarz — 259
Index — 267

Figures

0.1	'Southern Rhodesia Memorial Avenue' in Southrepps, Norfolk (2018)	1
3.1	Sir Walter Adams by Godfrey Argent, 1 July 1969, © National Portrait Gallery, London	68
10.1	'Perma STRATE', *The West Indian Gazette*, December 1959, p. 4 © British Library Board, Mic.B.967	210
10.2	'Carmen Skinlite Bleach Cream', *The West Indian Gazette* February 1962, p. 12 © British Library Board, Mic.B.967	216

Contributors

Shahmima Akhtar is a historian of race, migration and empire at Royal Holloway, University of London. She is interested in constructions of whiteness and the intersections between display and the visual in identity making. Shahmima is currently working on her monograph *Exhibiting Irishness: Empire, Race and Identity, 1851–1970* and her next project is provisionally titled ' "Longing for Home": Voices of History, Citizenship and Identity in British Bangladeshi Communities'.

Katherine Ambler is completing a PhD at the Centre for the History of Science, Technology and Medicine (CHoSTM) at King's College London. Her work focuses on the 'Manchester School' and the development of social anthropology in postwar Britain. Katherine's research is funded by the London Arts and Humanities Partnership (LAHP).

Steve Bentel is a contemporary urban historian with a focus on race and popular culture. He recently completed a PhD at Queen Mary University of London focusing on white, middle-class responses to London's changing racial landscapes. He currently teaches at Queen Mary University of London and the American Institute of Foreign Studies.

Elleke Boehmer is Professor of World Literature in the English Faculty, University of Oxford, and Director of the Oxford Centre for Life-Writing at Wolfson College. She is a founding figure in the field of colonial and postcolonial studies in English, and her recent work includes *Postcolonial Poetics* (2018) and *Indian Arrivals* (2015), which won the ESSE Book Award for 2015–2016. Boehmer's recent fiction includes *To the Volcano* (2019) and *The Shouting in the Dark* (2015), winner of the EASA Olive Schreiner Prize for Prose in 2018.

Dominic Davies is Senior Lecturer in English at City, University of London. He is the author of two monographs and several articles in the field of colonial and postcolonial literature, writing and visual culture. His forthcoming trade book, *Infrastructures of Feeling*, explores the ideologies of global supremacy and imperial nostalgia that are built into the levelling-up agenda in Britain today.

Josh Doble is a social researcher and a historian of twentieth-century Africa. He has previously worked at the Universities of Edinburgh and Leeds and at the Institute of Historical Research. His research focuses on histories of animals, settler colonialism and race, largely within the decolonising territories of East and Central Africa. He has published work on 'racist dogs' in *History Workshop Journal* and has forthcoming work on colonial pidgin languages in the *Journal of Southern African Studies*.

Ed Dodson completed his PhD in English at the University of Oxford. He has previously published articles on Alan Hollinghurst and Julian Barnes in the *Journal of Postcolonial Writing* and the *Journal of Modern Literature*.

Mobeen Hussain is an early-career historian of the British Empire researching race, caste, gender, medicine and corporeal consumption in South Asia. She is currently a postdoctoral research fellow on Trinity College Dublin's Colonial Legacies project. She is also working on her first monograph on race, colourism and skin lightening in colonial India.

Liam J. Liburd is Assistant Professor of Black British History at Durham University. His research focuses broadly on the ongoing impact of the legacies of empire and decolonisation in modern Britain. His current research focuses on Black radical analyses of fascism and on the question of how historians might use these to transform our understanding of the relationship between British fascism and the British Empire, as well as, more broadly, of the politics of race in modern Britain. He is currently in the process of trying to turn his thesis 'The Eternal Imperialists: Empire, Race and Gender on the British Radical Right' (University of Sheffield, 2019) into a book.

John McLeod is Professor of Postcolonial and Diaspora Literatures at the University of Leeds. His books include *Postcolonial London: Rewriting the Metropolis* (2004), *Beginning Postcolonialism*, 2nd ed. (Manchester University Press, 2010) and *Life Lines: Writing Transcultural Adoption* (2015). He is the co-editor of Ohio University Press's book series 'Formations: Adoption, Kinship, and Culture'.

Emma Parker is Lecturer in Postcolonial Literature at Keele University. She has previously worked as a postdoctoral researcher at the Oxford Centre for

Life Writing, and at the University of Leeds. She is the author of numerous articles on autobiography, the afterlives of colonialism and graphic life narratives. Her monograph *Contemporary Life Writing and the End of Empire* is out in 2023.

Tasnim Qutait is a lecturer in English Literature at Uppsala University. Her research interests are in translation studies and world literature, with a focus on North Africa and Southwest Asia. She is the author of *Nostalgia in Anglophone Arab Literature: Nationalism, Identity and Diaspora* (2021). Currently, she is working on a monograph on security and diaspora culture during the long War on Terror.

Astrid Rasch is Associate Professor of English at the Norwegian University of Science and Technology (NTNU). Her research examines memory culture at the end of the British Empire, with a particular focus on memoirs from Zimbabwe, Australia and the Caribbean, and the postimperial memory politics of contemporary Britain. She is editor of the anthologies *Life Writing After Empire* (2017), *Embers of Empire in Brexit Britain* (with Stuart Ward, 2019) and a special issue of the *Journal of Southern African Studies* called 'Writing Repression in Zimbabwe' (with Minna Niemi and Jocelyn Alexander, forthcoming, 47.5).

Samran Rathore is Associate Director of Tribe Arts, as well as an actor and writer. He is a published poet and a graduate of BBC Writersroom and also studied at the Manchester School of Acting.

Tajpal Rathore worked across the BBC in various roles for twenty years before transitioning to the arts and theatre sector, and is now Artistic Director and Executive Producer of Tribe Arts, as well as being an actor.

Bill Schwarz is the author of *White Man's World* (2011) and a member and editor of *History Workshop Journal*.

Dongkyung Shin is a PhD candidate in History at King's College London. Her doctoral research, entitled ' "Partnership in Universities": British Strategies for New Universities at the End of Empire', explores the activities of the Inter-University Council for Higher Education in the Colonies from 1942 to 1981. Prior to her time at King's, Dongkyung Shin taught history for a decade at high school level in South Korea.

Foreword:
Living in the bush of ghosts

Elleke Boehmer

The phrase 'after empire', which forms half of this book's title, embraces several different provocative and convergent meanings, not least in relation to 'British culture', the title's other half. At an immediate level, the phrase denotes 'following from empire', which is linked to the strict chronological sense of 'the next phase' or 'the historical time following empire itself'. But this reference straightaway brings in an undertone of 'merely carrying on' – as in, time flows forward but there is little to distinguish the postimperial now from the imperial then. Such suggestions of homogeneous continuation then mesh with other 'after empire' connotations of copying, including miscopying, and belatedness. Hence, too, the word-cluster includes senses of diminution and tailing off, and, withal, disappointment and denial at the loss of former imperial confidence and power.

The chapters in this book consider these varied meanings in the context of 2020s Britain, not leaving aside the often-volatile intersections between them. From their different perspectives, the contributors explore the uneasy and sometimes violent repetition upon the not-yet-truly-postcolonial present of the imperial past. And, in so doing, they demonstrate conclusively the importance and timeliness of the book they have produced. As we see in the many reassertions of Britain's so-called 'global' (read: 'imperial') status in the media, government and other areas of public life, wherever 'after-ness' or belatedness is refused, imperial nostalgia repeatedly recharges itself, often with divisive consequences. Together, these chapters confront and expose how there is almost no subject that is more disputed in the UK today than national self-image backlit by the faint yet still persistent light of empire. How does the nation (country, kingdom, archipelago, union?) see itself after, with, through and beyond empire? Depending on demographic, context and region, there are many different unsettled and unsettling answers to this question.

At the end of the last century, in the 1990s, the decade in which postcolonial studies became established in the Anglo-American academy, colonialism after Edward Said was studied first and foremost as a *discourse* – as power relations made manifest through forms of social and cultural knowledge.[1] That meant that colonial experience could be critically interrogated at the levels of language, representation, image and expression – though in practice this interrogation happened more in the classroom and on the pages of scholarly journals than on the street or in Parliament. Now, post-Brexit, as the third decade of the twenty-first century settles into its stride, empire may still express as forms of power-knowledge, such as in educational infrastructures, but it also remains an immediate, pressing and day-to-day concern, perhaps as never before. It is not a closed subject; it is not codified in literary writing alone. It is ongoing in the form of debates and conflict over statues, museum collections, syllabuses, power structures, institutions, histories of slavery, reputations, identities – debates which take place in the street as well as in the classroom. And which almost always involve that other pressing subject of our time, race.

As scholars of imperial discourse such as Anne McClintock and others long ago pointed out, empire is not 'elsewhere – a disagreeable fact of history external to Western identity', but woven into the very fabric of public and domestic life.[2] Today, a greater number of people in Britain recognise this to be the case perhaps than ever before, even in the breach, in the vehemence of their denial. To this extent, contemporary Britain presents to me as something akin to the haunted bush in Nigerian novelist Amos Tutuola's perennially salient and remarkable *My Life in the Bush of Ghosts* (1954).[3] The novel follows the pathway of a young boy into a dense African forest where he encounters terrifying composite beings drawn from Yoruba myth, Christian allegory, illusory colonial modernity and the writer's own fantasy. The structure is episodic; the boy spends twenty-four years wandering through the forest and, eventually, after meeting the 'television-handed ghostess', finds his way out. By then, however, his life has itself become phantasmagoric. Reminiscent of Wole Soyinka and Ben Okri, Tutuola's forest has often been read as an allegory of postcolonial Africa but, I suggest, it also oddly resembles Britain today. Like Tutuola's bewitched 'bush', the 2020s UK is a shadowy and confusing place in which nothing is quite as it seems, clown-politicians spread distorting and dangerous tales, and unchecked and weird voices, presences and irruptions continually catch off-guard anyone trying to make their way through it.

In the public sphere, the ghostly haunting of the UK by empire is perhaps never so starkly evident as when the status of former heroes of pre-1945 British history is called into question. Foremost among these now less-than-gilded heroes in recent times has been the 'greatest Briton of them all', Winston Churchill, with his dubious curriculum vitae of war hero, on the one hand, and white supremacist and racist, on the other. Former prime minister

Boris Johnson's rhetoric undergirds the former interpretation, the attested numbers of 1942–1943 Bengal famine dead the latter.[4] In the aftermath of the 2017 Grenfell fire in London, and the mid-2020 George Floyd and Breonna Taylor murders in the United States, it is now almost surprising to recall the predominantly positive ways in which the prime minister of 'the darkest hour' was seen as recently as 2014, when Johnson's hagiography was published, and to contrast that image with how he is seen in many circles today. As with debates over school curricula, the fury generated across 2020–2021 around discussions of Churchill's reputation conclusively demonstrates once again how very unresolved imperial legacies remain, and how unappeased is Britain's imperial memory. In Britain, it truly is the case that the imperial past is not over – it isn't even past, to adapt William Faulkner's often-cited phrase.

In another example of continuing turbulence, from the realm of my own experience, in December 2020 *Prospect Magazine* invited ancient world historian Tom Holland and I to engage in one of their monthly 'duels'.[5] The objective was to debate in writing, across three 300-word rounds, the question 'Are Empires Always Bad?' I spoke for the motion, Holland against. Interestingly for a book entitled *after empire*, we independently approached the question in comparative terms, without an explicit focus on Britain. I, for my part, argued that 'everyone in the modern world is a product of empire in some way'. However, I went on to say, while we cannot 'unthink the processes of our ... making', this should not release us from the obligation to confront 'the destructive consequences of empire and [think] critically and ethically about the empires of which we are a part and whose legacies we partake in'.

On his side, Holland pursued an argument of imperial inevitability and necessity worldwide, and, consequently, that for empires to flourish cultural reprogramming was essential: 'Empires tend to endure, not by imposing obedience at the point of a sword, but by bringing subject peoples to embrace the ideological self-justifications of their rulers.' The duel was, in a nutshell, a case of postcolonial critique pitched against a universalising apologia for colonial mimicry. And it was, in effect, all about Britain. As is customary for the magazine, the outcome of the duel was published in the following issue. Readers deemed the case against empire (or for the motion) to have won by a healthy margin, with 68 per cent of the vote.[6] However, when the debate was first published, and then publicised on social media, the criticism was for the most part levelled *against* that same side. If I had believed the responses, I might have thought that I had resoundingly lost. My arguments were called out by hundreds of commentators as weak. I was repeatedly told that mine was evidently the losing side and that Holland was clearly winning. Without even factoring in the gender differences at stake, the duel over empire had clearly encouraged turbulent ghosts to irrupt.

The imperial past intervenes ceaselessly and fretfully in the only seemingly postimperial present, as this example suggests. The legacies of empire do not rest quiet. The chapters below interweave historical, literary, visual and political analysis to examine that restlessness, and expose lingering imperial disparities and injustices. Yet they also carry out a second, equally valuable task, which is to model, by way of the exchanges and convenings *between* chapters, how we properly deal with that restlessness, how we process the 'strange relations' that pertain between nation, empire and self. How do we navigate the British bush of ghosts? Not by evading it – that is impossible, the bush is all-surrounding – but by analysis and collaboration; not by polarisation but by tacking between 'the jagged dimensions of the postcolonial present';[7] not by shouting at each other from opposite sides of the field but by recognising the areas we hold in common, and by educating and re-educating ourselves about each other's seemingly opposed standpoints.[8]

No question of empire is easily – or even ever – decided for good and for all. Too many people have died and too much wealth has been stolen for that to be the case. Four hundred years of conquest and looting have 'seeped into every part of the culture', Salman Rushdie said of Britain in *Imaginary Homelands*, published three decades ago this year.[9] When it comes to empire, there will always be other stories and countervailing ways of looking. Or, as the philosopher Achille Mbembe puts it, in the world today, the signs of race and empire remain 'unfinished', their meanings still unresolved, perhaps irresolvable.[10] 'After empire', therefore, remains for the most part an aspiration. We are postcolonial in the finely provocative sense of that disruptive, non-hyphenated term; we are still sailing in empire's long wake. Or, as Stephen Best writes in a richly suggestive essay on Toni Morrison's aesthetics, 'On Failing to Make the Past Present', while some histories may be recoverable, not least through the imaginative work of fiction, we may have to accept that others must remain forever unforthcoming, unamenable to reanimation.[11] Consciously refusing to make the past present is therefore a valid way of doing difficult history.

In confronting the legacies of empire, it is clear that the more that areas of difference are treated as single-issue stand-offs, the more division can break out. Conversely, the best and most effective way in which a multiplicity of different meanings can be respected is through ceaseless conversation and mutual exploration, what John McLeod, discussing poet Daljit Nagra, describes as reconstellating social and cultural relations from a diasporic vantage-point (Chapter 1). His mention in the same commentary of the 'fortuitous and future-facing' possibilities that are thereby released reminds me of the always future-facing Nelson Mandela playing chess on Robben Island, during his twenty-seven and a half years of incarceration. Among the other political prisoners, Mandela was famous for the slowness with which he played the game, as he liked to look at the chessboard from many different 'constellated' perspectives in order to decide how to move – a similar approach to the one he used in working towards the 1994 negotiated settlement in South Africa.

Mandela's chessboard is akin to Hannah Arendt's table around which she conceived human discourse as taking place. As she wrote in *The Human Condition*: 'To live in the world means essentially that a world of things is between those who have it in common, as a table is located between those who sit around it; the world, like everything in between, relates and separates meanings at the same time.'[12] *Reading* is another concise but charged way of describing this process of separation *and* relationship – that is, if we define reading as a process of seeing things anew, and, in Ngũgĩ wa Thiong'o's words, generating 'new possibilities of thinking'.[13] Or, as Barbara Harlow powerfully suggested in her early postcolonialist study *Resistance Literature* (1986), literature convenes an arena of struggle in which debate can be held.

As I come to pulling open the curtains on this excellent collection, I touch in closing on a composite image that presses many of the pulse-points of the book's achievement. The image is drawn from Zimbabwean writer Petina Gappah's *Out of Darkness, Shining Light*, a fictional account of the epic 1873–1874 trek undertaken by sixty-nine Africans to convey the body of the Scottish missionary David Livingstone from Chitambo in present-day Zambia to Bagamoyo on the East African coast, now in Tanzania.[14] Retelling the famous story in which the imperial hero is reduced to an eviscerated and dried-out corpse, then toted like so much extra baggage through thousands of miles of bush, Gappah brilliantly dramatises the demanding collaborative effort that went into the making of the Livingstone myth. We see that the story of one often-confused white explorer depended on and was shaped by the medical and navigational skills, ingenuity and courage of a large group of Africans, foremost among them Halima the talkative cook, and Jacob Wainwright the Indian-trained African missionary. Without Halima's near-scientific expertise in curing perishable flesh, it would have been impossible to transport a dead body for over 200 days through the tropics. Meanwhile, Jacob's diasporic story equates to Livingstone's own in the depth of its disillusionment and the level of its emotional complexity.

Gappah's novel reminds us that the still-dominant history of the single, dead white man masks so much else – multiple cross-ocean pathways, painful feats of endurance, many divers forms of local knowledge, as well as jokes, passions, intrigues, longings and entreaties. The novel joins with the chapters here to show that it is by reading with forward-looking yet 'after-empire' eyes, from different constelled angles, that these other stories can at last come to the fore and be celebrated – not only in Zambia and Tanzania, but also in contemporary Britain.

Notes

1. Elleke Boehmer and Alex Tickell, 'The 1990s: An Increasingly Postcolonial Decade', *Journal of Commonwealth Literature* 50:3 (2015), pp. 315–352.
2. Anne McClintock, *Imperial Leather* (London: Routledge, 1995), p. 5.
3. Amos Tutuola, *My Life in the Bush of Ghosts* (London: Faber, 1954).
4. See Boris Johnson, *The Churchill Factor: How One Man Made History* (London: Hodder and Stoughton, 2014); Madhusree Mukherjee, *Churchill's Secret War: The British Empire and the Ravaging of India during World War II* (New York: Basic Books, 2010). Winston Churchill was voted 'Greatest Briton' in a viewer poll held at the end of the 2002 BBC television series 'Great Britons', in which the achievement of ten Britons (two women, eight men) was comparatively assessed.
5. Elleke Boehmer and Tom Holland, 'Are Empires Always Bad?', *Prospect Magazine* (December 2020), pp. 16–17.
6. 'Are Empires Always Bad?' Duel result, *Prospect Magazine* (January/February 2021), p. 7.
7. To draw in a phrase from my December 2018 'After Empire?' conference keynote, also cited by the editors in their Introduction to this volume.
8. See Matthew D'Ancona, *Identity, Ignorance, Innovation: Why the Old Politics is Dead* (London: Hodder and Stoughton, 2020); Charlotte Henry, 'Time for a Culture War Truce', *Times Literary Supplement* (2 April 2021), p. 8.
9. Salman Rushdie, *Imagining Homelands: Essays 1981–91* (London: Granta Books, 1992). The quotation was cited with powerful effect by Corinne Fowler in her inaugural lecture 'Rewriting History? Heritage, Rurality and Empire' (Centenary inaugural lecture), University of Leicester (29 April 2021), www.youtube.com/watch?v=oIUljLIZZ_g [accessed 24 May 2021]. See also: Corinne Fowler, *Green Unpleasant Land: Creative Responses to Rural England's Colonial Connections* (Leeds: Peepal Tree, 2020).
10. Achille Mbembe and Homi Bhabha, with Ato Quayson, 'The Planetary Library' (*Into the Dark Night* book discussion), WiSER online talk (28 April 2021), https://wiser.wits.ac.za/event/planetary-library-achille-mbembe-and-homi-bhabha-conversation-28-april-6pm-sa-time [accessed 24 May 2021].
11. Stephen Best, 'On Failing to Make the Past Present', *Modern Language Quarterly* 73:3 (2012), pp. 453–474.
12. Katherine Adams, 'At the Table with Arendt: Toward a Self-Interested Practice of Coalition Discourse', *Hypatia* 17:1 (2002), pp. 1–30.
13. For more on reading as working with relevance and exercising epistemic vigilance, see Elleke Boehmer, *Postcolonial Poetics: 21st-Century Readings* (Cham: Palgrave, 2018), especially, pp. 37–62.
14. Petina Gappah, *Out of Darkness, Shining Light* (London: Faber, 2020).

Acknowledgements

Josh Doble, Liam J. Liburd and Emma Parker

This book began as a series of private conversations about Enoch Powell and Rhodesia's legacies within Britain, and later developed into a conference hosted at the University of Leeds during December 2018. 'After Empire: The Contested History of Decolonisation, Migration and Race in Modern Britain' brought together scholars, public researchers and practitioners in the fields of history, English literature, sociology, politics and heritage studies. The range of submissions, and attendees, testified not only to the vibrancy of colonial and postcolonial studies within Britain, but also the ongoing political and social urgency of the issues which we sought to delve into. The vital conversations and interventions made over the two days, not only from our panelists but also from our keynote speakers – Elleke Boehmer, Bill Schwarz and Gary Younge – underpin the arguments and themes which run throughout this book. For this reason, we start by thanking all of those who attended and presented at 'After Empire'; your intellectual engagement and willingness to contribute are the foundation of all the chapters contained here.

Each contributor to this book has patiently and diligently worked in dialogue with our editorial team, in some cases over several years. We thank each of them for their forbearance, critical insights and good will. In addition to our contributors, we also acknowledge all those who spoke, listened and shared ideas in Leeds during 2018, including: Emma Barnes, Jade Bentil, Benjamin Bland, Rachel Bower, Nikki Bullock, Chloé Germaine Buckley, Daniel Burdsey, Robert Burroughs, Christine Checinska, Lara Choksey, Taous R. Dahmani, Fiona Farnsworth, Corinne Fowler, Sam Goodman, Rachel Gregory Fox, Cathie Jayakumar-Hazra, Chris Jeppesen, Amber Lascelles, Itay Lotem, Churnjeet Mahn, Kristine Mitchell, Peter Mitchell, Bharti Parmar, Benjamin Poore, James Reay Williams, Elliot Ross, Jiyi Ryu, Jean Smith, Kate Spowage, Paul Stocker, Jason Todd, Hayley Toth and Matthew Whittle. Thank you to Bethan Hughes for designing our beautiful conference posters and to John McLeod for providing support and sage advice throughout 2018 and beyond. Thank you also to Pam Rhodes and Lindsey English.

We are grateful to the institutions and collectives who provided generous funding and enthusiastic support for this project: the White Rose College of the Arts and Humanities, the Royal Historical Society, the Economic History Society, the Imperial Afterlives research group at the White Rose Universities and the University of Leeds's Institute for Colonial and Postcolonial Studies.

Finally, our thanks to Manchester University Press and in particular to Tom Dark and Paul Clarke for getting the ball rolling. Thank you to our anonymous reviewers for their clear and supportive feedback which helped shape the book into its final form.

Introduction: Rhodesia and the 'Rivers of Blood'

Josh Doble, Liam J. Liburd and Emma Parker

Figure 0.1 'Southern Rhodesia Memorial Avenue' in Southrepps, Norfolk (2018).

The quiet East Anglian countryside surrounding Southrepps Hall might seem, at a glance, to be a landscape far removed, both geographically and temporally, from the legacies of the British Empire. And yet, flying from the estate's flagpole is the Rhodesian flag, symbol of a renegade state and former white settler colony that broke with the British Commonwealth in 1965. The flag's startling presence (witnessed by one of our editors on a summer's day in 2018) illustrates perfectly Corinne Fowler's warning that although 'the [English] countryside is widely viewed as having everything to do with whiteness and little to do with empire', the colonial roots of historic, rural England run deep.[1] Set in its own 'Southern Rhodesia Memorial Avenue', close to the North Norfolk coast, the flag displayed at the eighteenth-century Southrepps Hall was at the centre of yearly local celebrations of 'Pioneer's Day', an old Rhodesian public holiday marking the arrival of white settlers in Salisbury in 1890.[2] This event, enacted annually in East Anglia, was attended not only by the gentry who owned the site and country house, but also by local clergy and a brass band.

It is important to be clear. Past and present, the Rhodesian flag has served as a potent symbol of white supremacy. Doris Lessing, who spent the first thirty years of her life in southern Rhodesia, insisted that the country 'was never anything but the modern version of a slave state'.[3] For decades in Britain, the political right regarded Rhodesia as the romantic landscape of 'white Africa',[4] while in the twenty-first century the Rhodesian flag has been used internationally as a rallying symbol for white supremacists and alt-right murderers.[5] More locally, the memorial at Southrepps Hall, established in 1990, attracted the support of two right-wing establishment groups, the Rhodesian Christian Group and the Constitutional Monarchy Association.[6]

Rhodesia, and the legacies of this settler colony in Britain, was a common thread of interest that brought together three researchers engaged in very different projects: white life writing at the end of empire (Emma Parker), the history of the British white supremacist movement (Liam J. Liburd) and the history of settler colonialism in Africa (Josh Doble). The Southrepps flag, marking the corner of a country field that is forever Rhodesia, speaks to Britain's uneasy relationship with its imperial past. 'Rhodesia Memorial Avenue' is both a commemorative space and a site that reveals wider contestations within Britain's national life regarding the memories and legacies of empire. It may have once been possible for many in Britain to pass flags, statues and memorials to colonialism – 'shards' of Britain's imperial past, as John MacKenzie once put it – almost absent-mindedly.[7] However, as the post-Brexit era of nostalgic and resurgent nationalism has been met with renewed struggles against racial injustice, this is no longer possible. Discussions surrounding the entangled histories of empire, colonialism, racial violence and decolonisation have become topics of national interest and public debate in Britain.

In the years since our 2018 sighting of the Southrepps flag, a statue of Cecil Rhodes at the University of Oxford's Oriel College, another monument to Rhodesia, was approved for removal following the sustained efforts of Rhodes Must Fall activists. However, in 2021 Oriel College backtracked on this initial decision, citing costs and regulatory challenges as the cause of its prevarication. Rhodes Must Fall retorted that this move 'is a slap in the face with the hand of white supremacy'.[8] On the one hand, from provincial Norfolk to Parliament Square, activists and researchers are working to expose and exorcise Britain's colonial ghosts.[9] Not even the obscure memorial avenue in East Anglia has escaped the notice of organisations seeking, in the aftermath of Edward Colston's toppling in Bristol, to decolonise and reshape Britain's imperial monuments.[10] On the other, institutions such as Oriel have hidden behind bureaucratic processes in order to resist the calls of decolonisation movements. Such organisations are, perhaps unsurprisingly, unwilling to critique and reassemble the frameworks of British higher education.

The year 2018 also witnessed national events marking fifty years since Enoch Powell's 'Rivers of Blood' speech, a now-infamous anti-immigrant and racist tirade given by the then Conservative Party MP at the Midland Hotel in Birmingham. The anniversary reignited national conversations on Powell's argument that Britain was 'literally mad, as a nation', to permit immigration from Commonwealth countries and that elderly white women in his Wolverhampton constituency were 'trapped' inside their own homes for fear of these new arrivals.[11] Powell's warnings of embattled whiteness attempted to resist an increasingly multiracial society. His speech transported the language of colonial white supremacy into a perceived crisis in the metropole, an event visualised by the presence of people of colour in Britain. As Bill Schwarz demonstrates, colonies like Rhodesia sustained postwar British imaginaries of whiteness such as those articulated by Powell in 1968.[12] This context informs Liam J. Liburd's discussions, in Chapter 6, of shared beliefs among the British 'radical right' that the combined impact of postwar decolonisation and immigration rendered Britain comparable to a white settler colony. These groups drew direct inspiration from white settler regimes – like Rhodesia – to ferment their own brand of ethnic populism. The radical right (often dismissed as 'un-British') are, in fact, a vital component of postwar British history precisely *because*, as Liburd demonstrates, of 'their obsession with the Empire and their fretful fears of decolonisation'.

Such arguments speak to our contention that the lingering potency of Rhodesia – and the ideological leftovers of the white settler experience – informed postimperial racism in Britain. Fears, such as those of the Wolverhampton widow evoked in Powell's speech, of being overrun and outnumbered in one's own homes, on one's own streets and within one's own country resembled a metropolitan reworking of the paranoia at the heart of white Rhodesian identity. As Schwarz has outlined, old colonial anxieties informed postcolonial British nativist racism. When Powell delivered his infamous speech, he spoke in unambiguously racist terms, yet it seems important to note that by the end of his career, he had been rehabilitated as a scholarly and venerable old Parliamentarian. His 1989 appearance on *Desert Island Discs* saw his transformation into a subject for genteel broadcasting rather than for critical, national introspection.[13] In the twenty-first century, the memories of Powell's poisonous arguments continue to reverberate, albeit in new, subverted forms. In Zadie Smith's *White Teeth* (2000) the British-Bangladeshi Alsana remembers sheltering in her own Whitechapel basement, hiding from violent youths in steel-capped boots after 'that madman E-knock someoneorother gave a speech'.[14] Alsana dryly summarises that it was all 'Rivers of blood silly-billy nonsense', submitting Powell to comic derision while memorialising the terrible consequences of his words for many immigrant communities across Britain.[15]

Clearly, the contributors to this collection do not limit themselves to a discussion of Powell and his legacy. His name appears only infrequently, yet as a political figure Powell is nevertheless emblematic of the intersection between memory, forgetting, race and the postimperial legacy of empire that fascinated us and led to the 'After Empire' conference at the University of Leeds in late 2018. As Stuart Hall wrote back in 1978:

> … the development of an indigenous British racism in the post-war period begins with the profound historical forgetfulness – what I want to call the loss of historical memory, a kind of historical amnesia, a decisive mental repression … [T]he native, home-grown variety of racism begins with this attempt to wipe out and efface every trace of the colonial and imperial past. Clearly, that is one effect of the traumatic adjustment to the very process of bringing Empire to an end.[16]

It is not so much that Powell inaugurated this process as that he was one of its most eloquent and sincere articulators. Beyond scholarly studies of Powell, the imperial context to his infamous and provocative interventions into debates around immigration, asylum and citizenship rarely feature in public discussions of his 'Rivers of Blood' speech.[17] Powell's journey from a bookish, young imperial soldier with dreams of becoming viceroy of India to a cynical Tory minister issuing apocalyptic prophecies about a multi-racial England in decline involved the deliberate memorial discarding of empire. The mixture of selectively forgetting and remembering the history of the British Empire, and the way that these lapses and inconsistencies have fuelled a renewed racial prejudice, were not peculiar to Powell's personal response to imperial decline. As Robert Saunders recently explored in relation to debates and campaigns over Britain's membership of the European Union, they characterise a broader and ongoing predicament.[18] Nigel Farage's infamous citations of Powell as a personal hero who inspired his 'awestruck silence' during their early encounters reveals the ongoing impact of Powell on the politics of Brexit.[19] 'E-knock someoneorother' may have been a half-remembered figure of derision in Smith's 2000 novel, yet by 2016 his spirit was clearly revived in renewed anti-immigration policies across the British political spectrum.[20] In this sense, then, the researchers, journalists, artists and community practitioners who came together back in December 2018 – many of whom are now contributors to this book – attempted to exorcise the haunting spectre of Powell which continues to plague post-Brexit Britain.

While our speakers utilised numerous disciplines and methodologies, we shared the collective starting point – to borrow the phrase of one participant – that the culture and politics of late-twentieth-century Britain were underwritten by 'unappeased memories of the imperial past'.[21] In the wake of national events such as Brexit and the Windrush scandal, we extended this thesis on apparent imperial forgetfulness to examine empire's resurgent memory-traces in the twenty-first century. Ed Dodson, writing in Chapter 5, articulates a question central to our collective concerns: 'what happens … when tenacious imperial mythologies outlast the material reality of empire and linger as afterlives?' Our wide-ranging discussions contend that the cultural afterlives of colonialism in Britain can and must be addressed through intersecting inquiries in literary, historical, cultural and sociological studies. Both during our initial conference and here we explicitly reject politically charged attempts to view empire as a positive or somehow laudable endeavour.[22] In the words of Priyamvada Gopal, we resist the celebratory, elided imperial histories that suggest that 'violence, slavery and famine' were 'passing unfortunate occurrences', rather than integral components of Britain's colonial past.[23] Such simplistic renderings of Britain's history since decolonisation, largely shorn of nuance and complexity, have distorted public debates and understandings of colonial history.

Moreover, and as conference speaker Gary Younge has argued, two dimensional understandings which unequivocally celebrate British imperial power mask the nation's specific, complex and often uneven colonial histories. Younge states that mythologised stories of the British Empire continue to convince readers 'that the reason we are at the centre of most world maps is because the Earth revolves around us, not because it was us who drew the maps'.[24] *British culture after empire* expands upon Younge's challenging vision to rethink and challenge myths of imperial might. Rather than proposing a totalising narrative, we focus on seemingly disparate elements – from gig venues and institutions such as the British Museum, to archival documents and prize-winning novels. These suggest that the colonial past is both firmly embedded in modern British culture and continues to shape its parameters. Our focus encompasses the postwar and contemporary eras, spanning the five decades after Powell's speech. As a community of scholars, teachers and creators, we argue that the afterlives of empire are a fluid and constructive force within contemporary Britain, shaping our cultural, social and political spheres. While these inquiries were urgently felt during our collective discussions in 2018, the years between the conference and this publication have seen a shift in public conversations surrounding the legacy of empire in Britain. What began as the subject of scholarly debate and the preoccupation of activist circles is fast becoming a new front in the 'culture wars', with tabloids and politicians viciously attacking scholars and weaponising history in their baseless claims about 'biased' research into Britain's colonial legacy.[25]

Empire, Britain and 'imperial history wars'

The public debate over post-Brexit Britain's relationship with its imperial past did not begin with the high-profile Black Lives Matter (BLM) protests in the summer of 2020, nor with the increasingly vitriolic news coverage discussing slavery and empire that followed these events.[26] The rise of the Rhodes Must Fall (RMF) movement at the University of Oxford in late 2015 marked a key moment when questions about Britain's imperial legacy began to take on national significance. Inspired by a previous campaign mounted by students at the University of Cape Town in South Africa, hundreds of Oxford students demanded the removal of Cecil Rhodes's statue from Oriel College's Rhodes Building. The students did not just object to architecture but sought to interrogate their institution's colonial past. As Dalia Gebrial has suggested, many viewed the statue of Rhodes, which stood raised above the city's high street, as an emblem of how empire's legacies continue to operate – both invisible and hyper-visible, hovering just out of eyesight, but nevertheless exerting a powerful, shaping force on the institution and the community below.[27] These calls to dislodge the continuing authority of empire have gained pace, resulting in efforts to 'Decolonise the Curriculum' at universities throughout the UK. Yet it has become clear that decolonisation, which looks to fundamentally reshape the university, is all too frequently (and perhaps deliberately) confused with diversifying curricula and staff hiring practices. The vaunting of decolonised curricula is evident in university prospectuses and in the recruitment drives of open days across the UK. In the face of such widespread institutional manoeuvres, Gurminder K. Bhambra, Kerem Nişancıoğlu and Gebrial presciently remind us that decolonisation is about reframing 'power, *not* about public relations'.[28] As higher-education management teams across the UK appear eager to issue the enlightened last word on decolonising and decolonisation, we look forward to the radical potential of a conversation that has only just begun. To paraphrase the saying coined by Romain Rolland and popularised by Antonio Gramsci, when it comes to decolonisation, it may be useful to keep in mind the tempering pessimism of the intellect while valuing the essential optimism of the will.[29]

Several chapters within this collection – including those by Katherine Ambler (Chapter 2) and Dongkyung Shin (Chapter 3) – mobilise historical case studies to challenge the epistemological authority claimed by Western universities as 'privileged site[s] of knowledge production'.[30] These suggest how the consequences of formal, mid-twentieth-century decolonisation as experienced (and often forgotten) in Britain now shape contemporary decolonial movements. Ambler investigates how anthropology, that 'colonial science', was brought home to postwar Britain before being repurposed to study so-called 'peripheral', working-class communities in Wales. This discussion of class, race and national identities intersects with Shin's arguments that 'university systems in former colonies were a means to maintain Britain's soft power at the end of empire'. Whether by trawling the university archives (Shin) or scrutinising mid-twentieth-century anthropological studies (Ambler), these interlocking conversations map the local coordinates of Britain's unfinished relationship with both formal decolonisation and its former colonies.

Returning briefly to the RMF movement in Britain, one of the Oxford academics who had spoken and written in defence of Rhodes and his legacy was Professor Nigel Biggar. In 2017, Biggar's new project 'Ethics and Empire' was announced at the university's McDonald Centre, seeking 'to develop a nuanced and historically intelligent Christian ethic of empire' by bringing 'morally sophisticated' nuance to debates over 'military intervention for humanitarian purposes in culturally foreign states, the cohesion of multicultural societies, and [the] settling [of] imperial pasts'.[31] While the project looked at empires throughout history, Biggar – a moral theologian – criticised the 'dominant' (he claimed) perception of the British Empire as irredeemably oppressive, exploitative and racist. In reality, Biggar and his project have been described by Rhodes Professor of Imperial History Richard Drayton as underpinned by 'a lack of rigour and shallow learning', attempting only to 'tell moralising stories about the nation'.[32] As Astrid Rasch suggests in Chapter 8, which critiques both Biggar's project and Niall Ferguson's bestselling *Empire: How Britain Made the Modern World* (2003), 'contemporary British memory culture is marked by a singularisation of the imperial past' in which 'emblematic images and episodes are seen as representative of the whole'. Building on recent debates in memory studies, Rasch's scrutiny of populist and popular discussions of empire argues for the necessity of discussing a multiplicity of British empires, rather than a singular, exemplary organisation. This volume seeks to move beyond the 'exemplar empires' Rasch rightly critiques by demonstrating the myriad ways in which empire operated and how Britain's imperial legacies now manifest.

The stark contrast between Oxford's Rhodes Must Fall movement and Biggar's 'Ethics and Empire' project represents two opposing positions in the latest phase of what Dane Kennedy terms 'the Imperial History Wars'.[33] Kennedy rightly exposed how the contested public memory of the British Empire was intimately connected to anxieties around the ongoing viability of the nation, a tension exemplified in the Scottish independence referendum of 2014 but made all the sharper by the Brexit vote of 2016. As Saunders argues, 'imperial modes of thought' have historically inspired *both* pro- and anti-Europe sections of political opinion. For Saunders, Brexiteers are not so much propelled by imperial nostalgia as by imperial amnesia (we would add that these two are not distinct processes). While we acknowledge that British involvement in the European Economic Community (EEC) and later European Union (EU) was often sold in terms of Britain as a 'leader' of Europe and the Commonwealth, elements of the 'Leave' campaign clearly reanimated various racist elements of Britain's imperial legacy.[34] Beyond 'Empire 2.0' in-jokes between civil servants, the Brexit vote provoked a correlating rise in hate crimes and the return of an 'ethnic populism'.[35] Identified by Bill Schwarz as a '*discontinuous presence*' in Britain's history, the ethnic populist passions which fuelled imperialism during the late Victorian period later stoked the fires of Powellism and other reactionary responses to decolonisation.[36]

The distinction between England and Britain requires some complicating in our discussions. Schwarz, among others, has reiterated the importance of discussing 'Englishness' as opposed to British identity when grappling with Britain's imperial legacy.[37] Much of the nativist, postimperial anxiety found in the right-wing vitriol of Powell's successors, from Nick Griffin to Nigel Farage, has its roots in the instability of white English identity. For the 'Celtic fringes' of the United Kingdom, imperialism, and the experience of colonialism, often meant something quite different to England. The centuries-old colonisation of Wales and Scotland has resulted in different political traditions and expressions of identity which juxtapose the dominant presence of England, as Ambler's Chapter 2 on colonial anthropologists in Wales makes clear. Ireland's experience of empire, settlement and partition has been a defining feature of its history since the first waves of English settler colonialism in the sixteenth century.[38] This has been reinvigorated as tensions over the Irish border post-Brexit have fostered sectarian violence and brought the possibility of a united Ireland closer than ever before.[39] Scottish, Northern Irish and Welsh identity stand in a strange relationship to Englishness. On the one hand, they are united in an unstable union under a banner of 'Britishness' constructed against 'the other' in the Empire and in continental Europe.[40] On the other, though they were involved in the Empire, they were not equally enriched by its wealth, nor was the whiteness inherent in imperial Britishness equally open or extended to them.

Not only were all the constituent parts of Great Britain involved in the Empire, and marked by its postcolonial legacies, but England after empire has also mobilised Britishness in defence of a fragile English nation. This fragility is refracted through Tasnim Qutait's suggestion, in Chapter 9, that contemporary Arab British writing by Leila Aboulela, Selma Dabbagh, Jamal Mahjoub and Robin Yassin-Kassab confronts the ideal of security and the phenomenon of securitisation in Britain. This raises the question of which subjects are permitted to be securely 'at home' in an anxious, neoimperial Britain which wages 'Wars on Terror' against a homogenised, Muslim 'other'. The coordinates of Qutait's chapter, stretching from Scotland to London, reveal how and why we cannot write about postcolonial national identity in Britain and speak only of England and Englishness.

The divergent politics and identities of England, Northern Ireland, Scotland and Wales, if highlighted in the postimperial debates surrounding Brexit, have become starkly apparent in the varying responses of the devolved administrations to the COVID-19 pandemic. We have tried to remain attentive to slippages between 'British' and 'English' when discussing histories of empire. Tottenham MP David Lammy's eloquent defence of his identity as a Black Englishman in March 2021, against the racist claims denying his access to this recognition, is one of many examples in which an enduring notion of a racialised 'Englishness' stands distinct from a more amorphous 'British' identity.[41] These attempts to deny that people of colour could also be British has sharp resonances with the kind of embattled white England evoked in Powell's 1968 speech, but also with the broader legacies of empire in Britain.[42] As Shahmima Akhtar's Chapter 7 on racism in the historical academy suggests, the elision of 'early settlement, colonialism and slavery' from national curricula 'creates a false idea that Black and minority ethnic people have no history in Britain prior to mid-twentieth-century migration'. Akhtar connects the sustained racial and ethnic inequalities inbuilt within British universities to a broader unwillingness to teach the entangled histories of empire, migration and slavery in Britain. We further suggest that racialised understandings of British identity, imbued with the legacies of empire, continue to inform the increasingly inhumane tone and actions of the Conservative government's immigration policy. This extends across Theresa May's 'Hostile Environment' to the Windrush scandal, and the tragic deaths of twenty-seven people, largely from Iraqi Kurdistan, who drowned in the English Channel during November 2021 while attempting to seek refuge in Britain. Many British reactionaries – including former home secretary Priti Patel, whose policies contributed to the aforementioned tragedy – display a fondness for a 'tough' Australian-style immigration system. This is connected to the longer, punishing history of Antipodean penal transportation and to a longstanding British admiration for the perceived racial rectitude of (former) colonial 'white man's countries'.[43]

The chapters within *British culture after empire* are, to a large extent, tackling 'Englishness' after empire, rooted as they are in the politics, institutions and literature of England. This is, perhaps, exemplified in Dodson's reading of Graham Swift's *Last Orders* (1996) in Chapter 5 as representative of 'the breaking from and clinging to imperial ideas and desires in postwar England'. More broadly, however, Britain, or an imagined idea of Britain, remains an important lynchpin for postimperial Englishness, and indeed England's Unionist politics. England remains preoccupied with an elusive quest for 'the restoration of British greatness' by means of a bigger cultural and political unit.[44] As other critics have demonstrated, there is a 'discontinuous' political tradition whose adherents looked to the 'Empire as the antidote to a collapse of the centre, to England itself'.[45] Successive generations of politicians have tried again and again to inflate an economically and regionally divided England, ill at ease with its past and present, and uncertain about its future. This expanded England once took the form of an imperial 'Greater Britain'. In the early postwar years, Britain's political class transferred their imperial ambitions onto the unstable shoulders of the 'New' Commonwealth.[46] As several scholars have recently commented, active support or lingering nostalgia for the Empire/Commonwealth has historically motivated *both* proponents of European integration and Eurosceptic 'Little Englanders'.[47] This is most evident among a section of Brexit supporters who have presented various schemes for an Anglospheric alliance between an independent Britain, its Commonwealth partners and the United States of America, all reminiscent of nineteenth-century racial fantasies of 'Greater Britain', Anglo-Saxon alliances and unions of (white) 'English-speaking peoples'.[48]

In the context of these increasingly public conversations, our chapters follow Elleke Boehmer's opening invitation to trace those colonial legacies which are 'woven into the very fabric of [British] public and domestic life', investigating the local sites where these manifest. These locations and interests range from Steve Bentel's discussions of performers, punters and venue management at the Brixton Academy (Chapter 11) to Mobeen Hussain's case study of Black British beauty salons as spaces 'for engendering Black female solidarity' (Chapter 10). Our closing interview with Leeds-based theatre group Tribe Arts (Chapter 12) explores how their decolonial artistic practice looks to challenge Britain's dominant modes of cultural production. Whether on the dancefloor, the stage, or in the salon chair, these discussions scrutinise individual subjects and specific social coordinates which unexpectedly reveal empire's afterlives. We therefore interrogate the specifics of, to borrow a phrase from Boehmer, 'the jagged dimensions of the postcolonial present'.⁴⁹ In our insistence on remembrance, we aim to resist the nativist dangers unleashed by an improper and incomplete understanding of the past, answering Kennedy's call to scrutinise the 'social and ideological forces' which shape the study of imperial Britain.⁵⁰

'The UK is not innocent'

Since the first publication of his argument, Kennedy's 'Imperial History Wars' have moved from the pages of scholarly journals to the streets and even (as John McLeod explores in Chapter 1) to Britain's museums. In the summer of 2020, debates over statues and the legacy of the Empire in Britain spread far beyond an effigy of Rhodes at the University of Oxford, propelled by the murder of George Floyd, a forty-six-year-old African American man killed by Minneapolis police officers on 25 May 2020. Though the Black Lives Matter (BLM) movement originated in the USA in 2013, Floyd's murder and its intersection with the COVID-19 pandemic (an event which emphasised longstanding, interrelated issues of racism and social and economic inequality) led to BLM's international expansion. Its slogan and hashtags now adorned walls, windows and social media pages from Baltimore to Belgium. In Britain, the murder of Floyd accelerated several (small-'p') political currents and developments, including the movement to 'decolonise' Britain's public spaces and institutions (especially universities), along with the growing interest in Britain's own Black history and associated histories of racism and colonialism. As Gary Younge wrote in in early June 2020, 'Europe has every bit as vile a history of racism as the Americas – indeed, the histories are entwined.'⁵¹ Floyd's murder sprang from a uniquely American social and political context but it was not the product of a uniquely American problem. Both in the sense of historical legacies and present social injustices, the United Kingdom too, as the protestors' slogan went, is not innocent. Indeed, as Dominic Davies's discussion in Chapter 4 on the renewed tradition of anti-racist non-fiction suggests, prior to the BLM protests of 2020, a plethora of best-selling contemporary texts had foregrounded British imperial history and institutional racism through a combination of autobiographical narrative and structural analysis. The importance of understanding how the BLM movement has travelled across the Atlantic, and been both anticipated and remobilised within a British context, remains all too urgent. On the one-year anniversary of transport worker Belly Mujinga's death from COVID-19 in April 2020, her grieving relatives protested that no charges had been pressed against Mujinga's assailant, who claimed he had the disease and spat on her during her shift at Victoria Station.

The Black Lives Matter protests that swept across the UK during June 2020 were a response to the long histories of white supremacy and racialised violence which Black and minority ethnic communities in Britain have endured both before, during and since formal 'decolonisation' in the 1960s.[52] The BLM movement provided the social momentum to name and challenge the oppressive system under which they have been living. However, these protests also resulted in renewed scrutiny of researchers examining the legacies of colonialism in Britain, particularly of scholars involved in University College London's Centre for the Study of the Legacies of British Slavery and the National Trust's 'Colonial Countryside' project. Our colleagues involved in these projects have been subjected to sustained attacks from both politicians and the right-wing press. While their intellectual work has prompted much-needed conversations about the relationship of Britain's stately homes, museum collections and memorials to empire, the resulting backlash reflects ongoing, institutional attempts to curtail public conversations surrounding colonialism in the UK.[53] This was clearly articulated in the 2021 UK government-commissioned report on 'Race and Ethnic Disparities', chaired by Tony Sewell, that denied the existence of institutional racism in Britain.[54] It publicised this outrageous claim despite citing documents, submitted by organisations such as the Runnymede Trust, evidencing institutional racism as 'the intersectional driving force' for inequalities experienced by Black and minority ethnic communities.[55] By cherry-picking research and selectively citing experts, the report argued that decolonising curricula across the UK would lead to 'the banning of White authors', distorting decolonial methodologies while championing what it called 'Commonwealth history and literature'.[56] Sewell's report recommended new teaching resources on 'the making of modern Britain', suggesting that by returning to the Commonwealth, educators could tell an upbeat story of the British Empire which is 'not solely one of imperial imposition'.[57]

The field of 'Commonwealth literature' referenced in Sewell's report enjoyed institutional backing in Britain for several decades from the mid-1950s and utilised a liberal, humanist approach to literary texts.[58] So why would a government-backed investigation of race and ethnic disparities in 2021 cite the mid-twentieth-century predecessor of modern postcolonial studies?[59] The report gestures towards Commonwealth history and literature not to reawaken a largely dormant discipline, but to obscure both the extractive violence of empire and the resistance to colonial order that developed 'at home' in Britain and across colonial territories worldwide.[60] It looks to the Commonwealth in order to sidestep the recalcitrant, anticolonial ideas which form the bedrock of many postcolonial syllabuses, attempting instead to enforce 'political neutrality' by teaching colonial history 'in an impartial way'.⁶¹ The report's conclusions – including that the slave trade was not just about profit – are neither neutral nor impartial judgements. This should go without saying. As Akhtar and others within this book suggest, it is true that Britain's national school curriculum can and should offer a better understanding of colonialism and its ongoing legacies.⁶² Yet the Sewell report and the coordinated press attacks on academic research into slavery and colonialism look to keep the physical and ideological architecture of imperial Britain intact. In so doing, they respond to the particular British translations of the BLM movement, looking to quash public conversations on racial injustice reignited by campaigns like Justice for Belly Mujinga, and to counteract the surging sales of anti-racist non-fiction. Between the lines of Sewell's report and the innumerable printed newspaper columns attacking projects like 'Colonial Countryside' is an anxious response to BLM which looks always to obscure Britain's complicity in violent colonial projects.⁶³

Britain's imperial history is evidently political, bound up with national self-image and self-esteem, and wider questions of the UK's place in the world, most notably post-Brexit. If, as postcolonial critics have argued, nations are narrations, then the narratives discussed in this collection provide conflicting accounts which trouble the boundaries of the British nation.⁶⁴ As Bill Schwarz's Afterword concludes, each chapter in this book reveals how 'the familiar spatial properties of the colonial system no longer hold', dismantling the once-settled distinctions between metropole and colony. These reveal a series of often-concealed colonial histories which exert pressure upon the postimperial present. The editors and contributors to this volume therefore first insist that the legacies of British colonialism have persisted after the end of the Empire. But, second, we contend that empire's aftermath can only be satisfactorily traced by marshalling a series of cross-disciplinary inquiries. The legacies of colonialism have shaped the identities of white Britons and the ways that both state and society view Black and brown citizens alike. This has conditioned many areas of British politics, from rhetoric about immigration, to Britain's relationship with continental Europe. We refuse recent attempts to rewrite Britain's history as an innocent island story or as the tale of a benevolent builder of roads, railways and public health systems for poor, unfortunate people of colour. Such efforts efface more than they explain, subordinating rigorous academic research to feelings of forgetful imperial nostalgia or to a more resentful 'postcolonial melancholia'. The case studies of British culture in this collection, examining sites from novels to nightclubs, contribute to wider, public conversations about the UK as 'a shifting entity, a historically configured archipelago', rejecting the notion of a self-contained or singular island.⁶⁵

Beyond the myth kitty: Local cultures after empire

In Daljit Nagra's *British Museum* (2017), the poet roams through the famous domed entrance hall in the heart of Bloomsbury, challenging the calcifying narratives of 'the museum as nation' and instead beckoning the reader to stray 'beyond the comfort zone of our myth kitty'.[66] While Nagra forms McLeod's primary focus in Chapter 1, the poet's scepticism towards national, collective cultures extends across many of the conversations within this book. Rejecting the comfort zone of a mythologised and homogeneous 'British culture', these intersecting discussions seek instead the granular details of local sites across the UK. Nagra's questioning gaze confirms how the galleries of Britain's national museums are, as Sumaya Kassim and others have noted, showcases for 'the loot of former colonies'.[67] Yet McLeod's readings of Nagra prompts us to ask: can and should such emblematic establishments of empire be reimagined, and even rewritten, in the twenty-first century? More broadly, might local case studies allow us to move beyond the 'myth kitty' of hoarded national stories? Whether in relation to the sprawling, institutional cultures of universities, or the more enclosed, subcultural spaces of nightclubs, such questions animate our engaged, if necessarily uneven, concerns with British culture after empire.

From the opening explorations of empire's institutions to the closing discussions of decolonial performance with Tribe Arts, our conversations confirm that British imperialism was not simply about the prerogatives of high politics or the foreign policy concerns of the 'official mind'. Imperialism was instead woven into the fabric of everyday life for Britons living in both colonies and the metropole across the nineteenth, twentieth and twenty-first centuries. As Catherine Hall has demonstrated, empire as a cultural project was 'visible in innumerable ways' across Britain at the turn of the twentieth century, manifesting in adventure stories, the lyrics sung in music halls and the organisation of museum collections.[68] Yet, following the dismantlement of Britain's imperial power, the modern English novel has been especially prized by literary and cultural critics for its power to reveal 'the impact of the end of empire on the culture of the metropole'.[69] This collection's cross-disciplinary inquiries look beyond the novel to other literary forms, including poetry (McLeod, Chapter 1), plays (Tribe Arts, Chapter 12), newspaper articles (Hussain, Chapter 10) and life writing (Davies, Chapter 4).[70] If Britain's culture was, as Hall and others point out, permeated with colonialism, then these textual debates explore why imperialism did not and could not simply dissipate following the dismantling of the Empire. As, in the words of the late Stuart Hall, we all remain empire's 'inheritors, still living in its terrifying aftermath', this book explores the unexpected narratives, histories and locales where our imperial inheritances continue to manifest.[71]

This volume operates with a working definition of 'culture' that builds on the work of Catherine Hall, who approaches the term 'as a set of *practices*' rather than merely 'as a set of *things*'.[72] Culture is therefore about the production and exchange of meanings – it is a means of making sense of, ordering and regulating the world around us. It is about the language, signs and symbols that shape our world and our identities. We are guided by Stuart Hall's development of cultural studies, exemplified in his questions to postgraduate students at the University of Birmingham during the 1970s: 'what really bugs you ... in the terrible interconnection between culture and politics? What is it about the way in which British culture is now living through its kind of postcolonial, posthegemonic crisis that really bites into your experience?'[73] Hall's prescient, demystifying inquiries began an ongoing debate regarding social and cultural change in Britain that we aim to continue. In this conversation, the term 'culture' cannot be limited to the elevated forms which Matthew Arnold once described as 'the best which has been thought and said'.[74] Instead, we follow both Hall's and Edward Said's focus on culture as a set of practices subject to historical and political contexts, including those created by imperialism. Culture, in Said's words, cannot be 'antiseptically quarantined from its worldly affiliations'.[75] This book is therefore concerned with culture as part of everyday life, not as removed from or beyond daily concerns. It is through this broad conception of culture that the meaning of empire and of the imperial identities constructed by the coloniser and foisted on the colonised were defined and enforced. As the 'after empire' of our title suggests, many of our contributors draw on Paul Gilroy's arguments that the afterlives of imperialism operate on both visible and subterranean levels of British culture, from contemporary novels to the reverberating chant of 'two world wars and one World Cup'.[76]

The size and scope of the imperial project left a diffuse legacy at the end of empire that is best understood through an interdisciplinary lens. This volume is inspired by the intersecting work of historians, literary critics and cultural theorists, and particularly by John MacKenzie's 'Studies in Imperialism' series. As these collective efforts have demonstrated that imperialism constituted a 'core ideology' in British society from the 1880s to the 1950s, we now extend this to include the twenty-first century.[77] As scholars such as MacKenzie, Schwarz, Stuart Ward and Wendy Webster have critiqued British society's apparent insulation from the politics of empire,[78] this volume continues in the same spirit, replying to Ward's important claim in *British Culture at the End of Empire* (2001) that 'the stresses and strains of imperial decline [in Britain] were not safely contained within the realm of high politics'.[79] We acknowledge our debt to Ward's collection and here assemble a new generation of researchers to continue these critical conversations. While our contributors examine the postwar histories of right-wing politics and colonial anthropology, these twentieth-century case studies raise further post-millennial concerns, from security in the post-9/11 era (Qutait, Chapter 9), to anti-racist life writing (Davies, Chapter 4) and demands to decolonise Britain's public institutions (McLeod, Chapter 1; Shin, Chapter 3; Tribe Arts, Chapter 12).

Our meeting in 2018 was prompted by a shared editorial interest in the imperial constructions and postimperial reformulations of whiteness, whether as the means of policing collective memory, a racialised expression of empire's political legacies or an unrecognised concern in contemporary literature. This interest was matched by a desire to resist the mutated imperial legacies disfiguring contemporary British politics – namely whiteness as cultural manifestation and political action. Due to a widespread lack of diversity, both in terms of demography and perspectives, academia has been slow to take these phenomena seriously. Our own sense of historical urgency was fired by that timely glimpse of a Rhodesian flag flying in the heart of the English countryside. For us, this represented an encounter with one of the 'shards' of empire that litter the landscape of postimperial Britain and which we attempt to expose and analyse in this collection. The volume that follows is an interdisciplinary and methodologically varied salvo against the misremembering of empire and the denial of its ongoing legacies, whether through discussions of curricula reform, literary texts, or historical case studies. This collection of intersecting conversations is, necessarily, non-exhaustive and we hope that it will provoke further cross-disciplinary dialogue. By rejecting the singular, nationalist myths of an island nation and examining colonialism's impact on British culture, we look forward to future debates and understandings of empire's afterlives in contemporary Britain.

Notes

1 Corinne Fowler, *Green Unpleasant Land: Creative Responses to Rural England's Colonial Connections* (Leeds: Peepal Tree, 2020), p. 22.
2 See Josh Doble, 'Rhodesia in Norfolk and the Dangers of Imperial Amnesia', *The Norwich Radical*, 21 January 2019 https://thenorwichradical.com/2019/01/21/rhodesia-in-norfolk-and-the-dangers-of-britains-imperial-amnesia [accessed 5 January 2022]. Online research suggests that at least some of the attendees of 'Pioneers Day' at Southrepps Hall were actively aware of the fraught history at play during this event. Support from the Rhodesian Christian Group and the Constitutional Monarchy Association indicates the event's ties to right-wing establishment groups.

3 Doris Lessing, *Going Home* (London: Pantha Books, 1984), p. 301.
4 *The Herald*, 'Tory Candidate Calls Racist Rhodesian Leader a Hero', 21 June 2008, www.heraldscotland.com/default_content/12767936.tory-candidate-calls-racist-rhodesian-leader-a-hero [accessed 5 January 2022]; Daniel McNeil, '"The Rivers of Zimbabwe Will Run Red with Blood": Enoch Powell and the Post-Imperial Nostalgia of the Monday Club', *Journal of Southern African Studies*, 37:4 (2011), pp. 731–745; Philip Murphy, *Party Politics and Decolonization: The Conservative Party and British Colonial Policy in Tropical Africa, 1951–1964* (Oxford: Clarendon Press, 1995), pp. 203–212; Mark Pitchford, *The Conservative Party and the Extreme Right, 1945–75* (Manchester: Manchester University Press, 2011), pp. 151–156.
5 Dylann Roof, who massacred nine black parishioners attending church in Charleston, North Carolina, was pictured wearing both the Rhodesian flag and the flag of apartheid-era South Africa shortly before his crimes in June 2015. For details, see John Ismay, 'Rhodesia's Dead – but White Supremacists Have Given It New Life Online', *The New York Times*, 4 October 2018, www.nytimes.com/2018/04/10/magazine/rhodesia-zimbabwe-white-supremacists.html [accessed 6 April 2021].
6 See www.springbk.org.uk/speech16.htm.
7 John M. MacKenzie, '"Comfort" and Conviction: A Response to Bernard Porter', *The Journal of Imperial and Commonwealth History*, 36:4 (2008), p. 665.
8 Michael Race, 'Cecil Rhodes: Refusal to Remove Oxford Statue a "Slap in the Face"', BBC News, 20 May 2021, www.bbc.co.uk/news/uk-england-oxfordshire-57189928 [accessed 5 January 2022].
9 Following Colston's removal by a crowd in the city of Bristol, Topple the Racists unveiled a crowdsourced map of UK statues and monuments that celebrate slavery and racism to 'shine a light on the continued adoration of colonial icons and symbols'. See www.toppletheracists.org.
10 Simon Parkin, 'Why is this Village Memorial being Targeted by "Topple the Racists"?', *Eastern Daily Press*, 13 June 2020, www.edp24.co.uk/lifestyle/heritage/southrepps-south-rhodesia-memorial-targeted-by-topple-the-racists-1556440 [accessed 5 January 2022].
11 Bill Schwarz, '"The Only White Man in There": The Re-Racialisation of England, 1956–1968', *Race & Class*, 38:1 (1996), pp. 76–78.
12 The apartheid states of Rhodesia and South Africa served, in Schwarz's words, 'as the idyll of fantasised white homes' in Britain, 'uncompromised by the complexities and chaos of modern life'. See Bill Schwarz, *The White Man's World* (Oxford: Oxford University Press, 2011), p. 56.
13 Shirin Hirsch suggests Powell's anti-immigration arguments echo even 'within sections of the Labour Party that had campaigned most vigorously to remain within the European Union'. Shirin Hirsch, *In the Shadow of Enoch Powell: Race, Locality and Resistance* (Manchester: Manchester University Press, 2018), p. 106.
14 Zadie Smith, *White Teeth* (London: Penguin, 2001), p. 62.
15 Smith, *White Teeth*, pp. 62–63.

16 Stuart Hall, 'Racism and Reaction', in *Selected Political Writings: The Great Moving Right Show and Other Essays*, ed. by Sally Davison, David Featherstone, Michael Rustin and Bill Schwarz (Durham, NC: Duke University Press, 2017), p. 145.
17 For thorough examinations of Powell's life and legacy, see Camilla Schofield, *Enoch Powell and the Making of Postcolonial Britain* (Cambridge: Cambridge University Press, 2013) and Hirsch, *In the Shadow of Enoch Powell*.
18 Robert Saunders, 'Brexit and Empire: "Global Britain" and the Myth of Imperial Nostalgia', *The Journal of Imperial and Commonwealth History*, 48:6 (2020), pp. 1140–1174.
19 Nigel Farage, *Fighting Bull* (London: Biteback, 2010), p. 23.
20 Smith, *White Teeth*, p. 62.
21 Schwarz, *The White Man's World*, p. 32.
22 Tony Sewell, Maggie Aderin-Pocock, Aftab Chughtai, Keith Fraser, Naureen Khalid, Dambisa Moyo, Mercy Muroki, Martyn Oliver, Samir Shah, Kunle Olulode and Blondel Cluff, *Commission on Race and Ethnic Disparities: The Report*, March 2021, https://assets.publishing.service.gov.uk/government/uploads/system/uploads/attachment_data/file/974507/20210331_-_CRED_Report_-_FINAL_-_Web_Accessible.pdf [accessed 6 January 2022], p. 8; p. 91.
23 Priyamvada Gopal, *Insurgent Empire: Anticolonial Resistance and British Dissent* (London: Verso Books, 2019), p. viii.
24 Gary Younge, 'Britain's Imperial Fantasies Have Given Us Brexit', *The Guardian*, 3 February 2018, www.theguardian.com/commentisfree/2018/feb/03/imperial-fantasies-brexit-theresa-may [accessed 20 June 2019].
25 Danyal Hussain, 'National Trust Accused of Bias', *Daily Mail*, 16 December 2020, www.dailymail.co.uk/news/article-9058475/National-Trust-accused-bias-team-investigating-ties-properties-slave-trade.html [accessed 4 January 2022]; Jessica Murray, 'Politicians Should Not Weaponise UK History Says Colonialism Researcher', *The Guardian*, 22 February 2021, www.theguardian.com/culture/2021/feb/22/politicians-should-not-weaponise-uk-history-says-colonialism-researcher [accessed 6 January 2022].
26 The National Trust's 'Colonial Countryside' project stands as an ongoing example of the negative, even hysterical, news coverage discussing the histories of slavery and empire during 2020. Conservative MP Andrew Bridgen stated that the project 'confirms our worst fears that they've [the Trust] been overtaken by divisive Black Lives Matter supporters. In what way do they feel that is attractive to the average person who wants to visit a National Trust property?' Hussain, 'National Trust Accused of Bias'.
27 Dalia Gebrial, 'Rhodes Must Fall: Oxford and Movements for Change', in *Decolonising the University*, ed. by Gurminder K. Bhambra, Dalia Gebrial and Kerem Nişancıoğlu (London: Pluto Press, 2018), pp. 19–37.
28 Gurminder K. Bhambra, Kerem Nişancıoğlu and Dalia Gebrial, 'Decolonising the University in 2020', *Identities* 27:4 (2020), 509–516, p. 514.
29 Gramsci borrowed the slogan 'Pessimism of the intelligence, optimism of the will' from Rolland, using it in his articles for the Italian socialist magazine

L'Ordine Nuovo as early as 1919. See *Selections from the Prison Notebooks of Antonio Gramsci*, ed. by and trans. Quintin Hoare and Geoffrey Nowell Smith (New York: International Publishers, 1971), p. 257.

30 Gurminder K. Bhambra, Dalia Gebrial and Kerem Nişancıoğlu, 'Introduction: Decolonising the University?', in *Decolonising The University* (London: Pluto Press, 2018), pp. 1–19, p. 3.

31 McDonald Centre, 'Ethics and Empire', www.mcdonaldcentre.org.uk/ethics-and-empire [accessed 16 December 2021].

32 Richard Drayton, 'Biggar vs Little Britain', in *Embers of Empire in Brexit Britain*, ed. by Stuart Ward and Astrid Rasch (London: Bloomsbury, 2019), pp. 143–156, p. 150.

33 Dane Kennedy, 'The Imperial History Wars', *Journal of British Studies*, 54:1 (2015), pp. 5–22.

34 For further details on Brexit's relationship to the colonial past, see Stuart Ward and Astrid Rasch, 'Introduction: Greater Britain, Global Britain', in *Embers of Empire in Brexit Britain* (London: Bloomsbury, 2019), pp. 1–14; Danny Dorling and Sally Tomlinson, *Rule Britannia: Brexit and the End of Empire* (London: Biteback, 2019).

35 See Joel Carr, Joanna Clifton-Sprigg, Jonathan James and Suncica Vujic, *Love Thy Neighbour? Brexit Hate Crime* (Bonn: Institute of Labor Economics, 2000).

36 Bill Schwarz, 'Forgetfulness: England's Discontinuous Histories', in *Embers of Empire in Brexit Britain*, ed. by Stuart Ward and Astrid Rasch (London: New York: Bloomsbury, 2019), pp. 55–57.

37 Bill Schwarz, 'Introduction', in *End of Empire and the English Novel*, ed. by Rachael Gilmour and Bill Schwarz (Manchester: Manchester University Press, 2015), pp. 1–37.

38 Kevin Kenny, *Ireland and the British Empire* (Oxford: Oxford University Press, 2005); Keith Jeffrey (ed.), *'An Irish Empire'? Aspects of Ireland and the British Empire* (Manchester: Manchester University Press, 2017).

39 Adam Fleming, 'What is Brexit doing to Northern Ireland?', BBC News, 9 April 2021, www.bbc.co.uk/news/uk-politics-56678489 [accessed 4 January 2022].

40 Linda Colley, *Britons: Forging the Nation, 1707–1837* (New Haven, CT: Yale University Press, 3rd ed., 2008), pp. 6–7.

41 Fiona Jones, 'David Lammy Schools Caller who Tells Him He's "Not English"', *LBC*, 29 March 2021, www.lbc.co.uk/radio/presenters/david-lammy/david-lammy-schools-caller-who-tells-him-hes-not-english [accessed 5 January 2022].

42 R. A. Huttenback, 'The British Empire as a "White Man's Country": Racial Attitudes and Immigration Legislation in the Colonies of White Settlement', *Journal of British Studies*, 13:1 (1973), pp. 108–137; Laura Tabili, *'We Ask for British Justice': Workers and Racial Difference in Late Imperial Britain* (Ithaca, NY; London: Cornell University Press, 1994); Kathleen Paul, *Whitewashing Britain: Race and Citizenship in the Postwar Era* (Ithaca, NY; London: Cornell University Press, 1997).

43 Marilyn Lake and Henry Reynolds, *Drawing the Global Colour Line: White Men's Countries and the International Challenge of Racial Equality*

(Cambridge: Cambridge University Press, 2008); Elise Klein and China Mills, 'Islands of Deterrence: Britain's Long History of Banishing "Undesirables"', openDemocracy, 1 April 2021), www.opendemocracy.net/en/opendemocracyuk/islands-of-deterrence-britains-long-history-of-banishing-undesirables [accessed 6 January 2022].

44 Paul Gilroy, *After Empire: Melancholia or Convivial Culture?* (Abingdon: Routledge, 2004), p. 109.
45 Schwarz, *White Man's World*, p. 103; Schwarz, 'Forgetfulness: England's Discontinuous Histories', p. 55.
46 Saunders, 'Brexit and Empire', pp. 1149–1150.
47 David Thackeray and Richard Toye, 'Debating Empire 2.0', in *Embers of Empire in Brexit Britain*, ed. by Stuart Ward and Astrid Rasch (London; New York: Bloomsbury, 2019), pp. 15–35; Duncan Bell and Srdjan Vucetic, 'Brexit, CANZUK, and the Legacy of Empire', *British Journal of Politics and International Relations*, 21:2 (2019), pp. 367–382; Saunders, 'Brexit and Empire', pp. 1147–1149.
48 Bell and Vucetic, 'Brexit, CANZUK, and the Legacy of Empire', p. 368.
49 Elleke Boehmer, *Postcolonial Poetics: 21st-Century Critical Readings* (London: Palgrave Macmillan, 2018), p. 7.
50 Kennedy, 'Imperial', p. 6.
51 Gary Younge, 'What Black America Means to Europe', *The New York Review of Books*, 6 June 2020, www.nybooks.com/daily/2020/06/06/what-black-america-means-to-europe/ [accessed 13 January 2022].
52 As Patricia Francis and others have documented, the June 2020 protests were by no means the first to be organised by Black Lives Matter UK, who led initial 'shutdown' protests during 2016 to highlight Black deaths in police custody, along with racism and climate change. According to BBC coverage these protests were met with 'some confusion' during the 2010s, although Nesta McGregor's 2016 report for Newsbeat explained the impetus behind the growing BLM UK movement. Patricia Francis 'Black Lives Matter: How the UK Movement Struggled to be Heard in the 2010s', The Conversation, 7 June 2021, https://theconversation.com/black-lives-matter-how-the-uk-movement-struggled-to-be-heard-in-the-2010s-161763 [accessed 4 January 2022]; Nesta McGregor, 'That Black British Feeling', BBC News, 31 October 2016, www.bbc.co.uk/news/newsbeat-37715090 [accessed 4 January 2022].
53 Corinne Fowler, who discussed her groundbreaking child-led 'Colonial Countryside' project at our 2018 conference, has been repeatedly singled out for criticism and abuse in Britain's right-wing press. Critics have claimed her aims are 'anti-British' and questioned whether Fowler, a well-respected literary scholar, should be permitted to discuss Britain's colonial past as she 'is not a historian'. See Charles Moore, 'The National Trust is Trapped in Hostility to Britain's Heritage', *The Telegraph*, 2 April 2021, www.telegraph.co.uk/news/2021/04/02/national-trust-trapped-hostility-britains-heritage-now-way [accessed 14 April 2021].
54 In the report's foreword, the Commission's chair Tony Sewell states that 'we no longer see a Britain where the system is deliberately rigged against ethnic minorities' and that 'geography, family influence, socio-economic background background, culture and religion have more significant impact on life chances than

racism'. Tony Sewell et al., *Commission on Race and Ethnic Disparities: The Report*, p. 9.

55 The Runnymede Trust, 'CORE Submission to Commission on Race and Ethnic Disparities', November 2020, www.runnymedetrust.org/uploads/pdfs/CORE%20submission%20to%20Commission%20on%20Race%20and%20Ethnic%20Disparities.pdf [accessed 14 April 2021].
56 *Commission on Race and Ethnic Disparities: The Report*, p. 8.
57 *Commission on Race and Ethnic Disparities: The Report*, p. 91.
58 John McLeod provides an account of Commonwealth literature in *Beginning Postcolonialism* (2000), noting that one of the fundamental differences between modern postcolonial critics and their Commonwealth predecessors was that Commonwealth literature did not challenge 'the Western criteria of excellence used to read [literary texts]'. John McLeod, *Beginning Postcolonialism* (Manchester: Manchester University Press, 2000), p. 15.
59 By 1983 Salman Rushdie famously argued that Commonwealth literature does not exist on the grounds that the term allowed publishers and institutions 'to dump a large segment of English literature into a box and then more or less ignore it'. See Salman Rushdie, 'Commonwealth Literature Does Not Exist', in *Imaginary Homelands: Essays and Criticism 1981–1991* (London: Granta Books, 1991), pp. 61–71, p. 66.
60 Gopal, *Insurgent Empire*.
61 *Commission on Race and Ethnic Disparities: The Report*, p. 92.
62 Kimberley McIntosh, Jason Todd and Nandini Das, *Teaching Migration, Belonging and Empire in Secondary Schools* (London: TIDE and the Runnymede Trust, 2019).
63 Charlie Parker, 'National Trust Accused of Bias in Study of Colonial History', *The Times*, 16 December 2020, www.thetimes.co.uk/article/national-trust-accused-of-bias-in-study-of-colonial-history-xknc6tvks [accessed 3 January 2022].
64 Edward Said's suggestion (articulated elsewhere by Homi K. Bhabha) that 'nations themselves *are* narrations' responds to Benedict Anderson's famous formulation of the nation as 'an imagined political community'. Edward Said, *Culture and Imperialism* (London: Chatto and Windus 1993), p. xiii; Benedict Anderson, *Imagined Communities: Reflections on the Origins and Spread of Nationalism* (London: Verso, 1983), p. 6.
65 David Reynolds, *Island Stories: Britain and Its History in an Age of Brexit* (Glasgow: William Collins, 2019), p. 5.
66 Daljit Nagra, 'Meditations on the British Museum', in *British Museum* (London: Faber and Faber, 2017), pp. 49–53, pp. 50–51.
67 Sumaya Kassim, 'The Museum is the Master's House: An Open Letter to Tristram Hunt', *Medium*, 29 July 2019, https://medium.com/@sumayakassim/the-museum-is-the-masters-house-an-open-letter-to-tristram-hunt-e72d75a891c8 [accessed 7 January 2021].
68 Catherine Hall, 'Culture and Identity in Imperial Britain', in *The British Empire: Themes and Perspectives*, ed. Sarah Stockwell (Oxford: Blackwell, 2008), p. 202.
69 Schwarz, 'Introduction', pp. 1–38, p. 5.

70 For discussions of the English novel and the end of Empire, see Graham MacPhee, *Postwar British Literature and Postcolonial Studies* (Edinburgh: Edinburgh University Press, 2011); John McLeod, 'The Novel and the End of Empire', in *The Oxford History of the Novel in English, Volume Seven: British and Irish Fiction since 1940*, ed. by Peter Boxall and Bryan Cheyette (Oxford: Oxford University Press, 2016), pp. 80–93; Matthew Whittle, *Postwar British Literature and the 'End of Empire'* (London: Palgrave Macmillan, 2016).
71 Stuart Hall with Bill Schwarz, *Familiar Stranger: A Life Between Two Islands* (London: Penguin, 2018), p. 21.
72 Hall, 'Culture and Identity in Imperial Britain', p. 202.
73 Stuart Hall, 'The Emergence of Cultural Studies and the Crisis of the Humanities', *October*, 53 (1990), pp. 11–23, p. 17.
74 Matthew Arnold, 'Preface', in *Culture and Anarchy* (Oxford: Oxford University Press, 2006), p. 5.
75 Said, *Culture and Imperialism*, p. xv.
76 Gilroy, *After Empire*, p. 117.
77 John MacKenzie, *Propaganda and Empire* (Manchester: Manchester University Press, 1984), p. 11.
78 See Wendy Webster, *Englishness and Empire* (Oxford: Oxford University Press, 2005), p. 2.
79 Stuart Ward, 'Introduction', in *British Culture at the End of Empire*, ed. Stuart Ward (Manchester: Manchester University Press, 2001), pp. 1–20, p. 6.

Bibliography

Anderson, Benedict, *Imagined Communities: Reflections on the Origins and Spread of Nationalism* (London: Verso, 1983).

Arnold, Matthew, 'Preface', in *Culture and Anarchy* (Oxford: Oxford University Press, 2006).

Bell, Duncan and Srdjan Vucetic, 'Brexit, CANZUK, and the Legacy of Empire', *British Journal of Politics and International Relations*, 21:2 (2019), pp. 367–382.

Bhambra, Gurminder K., Kerem Nişancıoğlu and Dalia Gebrial, 'Decolonising the University in 2020', *Identities*, 27:4 (2020), 509–516.

Bhambra, Gurminder K., Dalia Gebrial and Kerem Nişancıoğlu, 'Introduction: Decolonising the University?' in *Decolonising The University* (London: Pluto Press, 2018), pp. 1–18.

Boehmer, Elleke, *Postcolonial Poetics: 21st-Century Critical Readings* (London: Palgrave Macmillan, 2018).

Carr, Joel, Joanna Clifton-Sprigg, Jonathan James and Suncica Vucic, *Love Thy Neighbour? Brexit Hate Crime* (Bonn: Institute of Labor Economics, 2000).

Colley, Linda, *Britons: Forging the Nation, 1707–1837* (New Haven, CT: Yale University Press, 3rd ed., 2008).

Doble, Josh, 'Rhodesia in Norfolk and the Dangers of Imperial Amnesia', *The Norwich Radical*, 21 January 2019, https://thenorwichradical.com/2019/01/21/rhodesia-in-norfolk-and-the-dangers-of-britains-imperial-amnesia/ [accessed 5 January 2022].

Dorling, Danny and Sally Tomlinson, *Rule Britannia: Brexit and the End of Empire* (London: Biteback, 2019).

Drayton, Richard, 'Biggar vs Little Britain', in *Embers of Empire in Brexit Britain*, ed. by Stuart Ward and Astrid Rasch (London: Bloomsbury, 2019), pp. 143–155.

Farage, Nigel, *Fighting Bull* (London: Biteback, 2010).

Fleming, Adam, 'What is Brexit doing to Northern Ireland?', BBC News, 9 April 2021, www.bbc.co.uk/news/uk-politics-56678489 [accessed 4 January 2022].

Fowler, Corinne, *Green Unpleasant Land: Creative Responses to Rural England's Colonial Connections* (Leeds: Peepal Tree Press, 2020).

Francis, Patricia, 'Black Lives Matter: How the UK Movement Struggled to be Heard in the 2010s', The Conversation, 7 June 2021, https://theconversation.com/black-lives-matter-how-the-uk-movement-struggled-to-be-heard-in-the-2010s-161763 [accessed 4 January 2022].

Gebrial, Dalia, 'Rhodes Must Fall: Oxford and Movements for Change', in *Decolonising the University*, ed. by Gurminder K. Bhambra, Dalia Gebrial and Kerem Nişancıoğlu (London: Pluto Press, 2018), pp. 19–36.

Gillmore, Graham, 'Fly the Flag Day: Rhodesian Pioneer Day 2016', The Springbok Club, www.springbk.org.uk/speech16.htm [accessed 30 August 2022].

Gilroy, Paul, *After Empire: Melancholia or Convivial Culture?* (Abingdon: Routledge, 2004).

Gopal, Priyamvada, *Insurgent Empire: Anticolonial Resistance and British Dissent* (London: Verso Books, 2019).

Gramsci, Antonio, *Selections from the Prison Notebooks of Antonio Gramsci*, ed. and trans. by Quintin Hoare and Geoffrey Nowell Smith (New York: International Publishers, 1971).

Hall, Catherine, 'Culture and Identity in Imperial Britain', in *The British Empire: Themes and Perspectives*, ed. by Sarah Stockwell (Oxford: Blackwell, 2008), pp. 199–217.

Hall, Stuart, with Bill Schwarz, *Familiar Stranger: A Life Between Two Islands* (London: Penguin, 2018).

Hall, Stuart, 'Racism and Reaction', in *Selected Political Writings: The Great Moving Right Show and Other Essays*, ed. by Sally Davison, David Featherstone, Michael Rustin and Bill Schwarz (Durham, NC: Duke University Press, 2017), pp. 142–157.

Hall, Stuart, 'The Emergence of Cultural Studies and the Crisis of the Humanities', *October*, 53 (1990), pp. 11–23.

The Herald, 'Tory Candidate Calls Racist Rhodesian Leader a Hero', 21 June 2008 www.heraldscotland.com/default_content/12767936.tory-candidate-calls-racist-rhodesian-leader-a-hero [accessed 5 January 2022].

Hirsch, Shirin, *In the Shadow of Enoch Powell: Race, Locality and Resistance* (Manchester: Manchester University Press, 2018).

Hussain, Danyal, 'National Trust Accused of Bias', *Daily Mail*, 16 December 2020, www.dailymail.co.uk/news/article-9058475/National-Trust-accused-bias-team-investigating-ties-properties-slave-trade.html [accessed 4 January 2022].

Huttenback, Robert Arthur, 'The British Empire as a "White Man's Country": Racial Attitudes and Immigration Legislation in the Colonies of White Settlement', *Journal of British Studies*, 13:1 (1973), pp. 108–137.

Ismay, John, 'Rhodesia's Dead – but White Supremacists Have Given It New Life Online', *The New York Times*, 4 October 2018, www.nytimes.com/2018/04/10/magazine/rhodesia-zimbabwe-white-supremacists.html [accessed 6 April 2021].

Jeffrey, Keith (ed.), *'An Irish Empire'? Aspects of Ireland and the British Empire* (Manchester: Manchester University Press, 2017).

Jones, Fiona, 'David Lammy Schools Caller who Tells Him He's "Not English"', LBC, 29 March 2021, www.lbc.co.uk/radio/presenters/david-lammy/david-lammy-schools-caller-who-tells-him-hes-not-english/ [accessed 5 January 2022].

Kassim, Sumaya, 'The Museum is the Master's House: An Open Letter to Tristram Hunt', *Medium*, 29 July 2019, https://medium.com/@sumayakassim/the-museum-is-the-masters-house-an-open-letter-to-tristram-hunt-e72d75a891c8 [accessed 7 January 2021].

Kennedy, Dane, 'The Imperial History Wars', *Journal of British Studies*, 54:1 (2015), pp. 5–22.

Kenny, Kevin, *Ireland and the British Empire* (Oxford: Oxford University Press, 2005).

Klein, Elise and China Mills, 'Islands of Deterrence: Britain's Long History of Banishing "undesirables"', openDemocracy, 1 April 2021, www.opendemocracy.net/en/opendemocracyuk/islands-of-deterrence-britains-long-history-of-banishing-undesirables [accessed 6 January 2022].

Lake, Marilyn and Henry Reynolds, *Drawing the Global Colour Line: White Men's Countries and the International Challenge of Racial Equality* (Cambridge: Cambridge University Press, 2008).

Lessing, Doris, *Going Home* (London: Pantha Books, 1984).

McDonald Centre, 'Ethics and Empire', www.mcdonaldcentre.org.uk/ethics-and-empire [accessed 16 December 2021].

McGregor, Nesta, 'That Black British Feeling', BBC News, 31 October 2016, www.bbc.co.uk/news/newsbeat-37715090 [accessed 4 January 2022].

McIntosh, Kimberley, Jason Todd and Nandini Das, *Teaching Migration, Belonging and Empire in Secondary Schools* (London: TIDE and the Runnymede Trust, 2019).

MacKenzie, John, '"Comfort" and Conviction: A Response to Bernard Porter', *The Journal of Imperial and Commonwealth History*, 36:4 (2008), pp. 659–668.

MacKenzie, John, *Propaganda and Empire* (Manchester: Manchester University Press, 1984).

McLeod, John, *Beginning Postcolonialism* (Manchester: Manchester University Press, 2000).

McLeod, John, 'The Novel and the End of Empire', in *The Oxford History of the Novel in English, Volume Seven: British and Irish Fiction since 1940*, ed. by Peter Boxall and Bryan Cheyette (Oxford: Oxford University Press, 2016), pp. 80–93.

McNeil, Daniel, '"The Rivers of Zimbabwe Will Run Red with Blood": Enoch Powell and the Post-Imperial Nostalgia of the Monday Club', *Journal of Southern African Studies*, 37:4 (2011), pp. 731–745.

MacPhee, Graham, *Postwar British Literature and Postcolonial Studies* (Edinburgh: Edinburgh University Press, 2011).

Moore, Charles, 'The National Trust is Trapped in Hostility to Britain's Heritage', *The Telegraph*, 2 April 2021, www.telegraph.co.uk/news/2021/04/02/national-trust-trapped-hostility-britains-heritage-now-way [accessed 14 April 2021].

Murphy, Philip, *Party Politics and Decolonization: The Conservative Party and British Colonial Policy in Tropical Africa, 1951–1964* (Oxford: Clarendon Press, 1995).

Murray, Jessica, 'Politicians Should Not Weaponise UK History Says Colonialism Researcher', *The Guardian*, 22 February 2021, www.theguardian.com/culture/2021/feb/22/politicians-should-not-weaponise-uk-history-says-colonialism-researcher [accessed 6 January 2022].

Nagra, Daljit, 'Meditations on the British Museum', *British Museum* (London: Faber and Faber, 2017), pp. 49–53.

Parker, Charlie, 'National Trust Accused of Bias in Study of Colonial History', *The Times*, 16 December 2020, www.thetimes.co.uk/article/national-trust-accused-of-bias-in-study-of-colonial-history-xknc6tvks [accessed 3 January 2022].

Parkin, Simon, 'Why is this Village Memorial being Targeted by "Topple the Racists"?', *Eastern Daily Press*, 13 June 2020, www.edp24.co.uk/lifestyle/heritage/southrepps-south-rhodesia-memorial-targeted-by-topple-the-racists-1556440 [accessed 5 January 2022].

Paul, Kathleen, *Whitewashing Britain: Race and Citizenship in the Postwar Era* (Ithaca, NY; London: Cornell University Press, 1997).

Pitchford, Mark, *The Conservative Party and the Extreme Right, 1945–75* (Manchester: Manchester University Press, 2011).

Race, Michael, 'Cecil Rhodes: Refusal to Remove Oxford Statue a "Slap in the Face"', BBC News, 20 May 2021, www.bbc.co.uk/news/uk-england-oxfordshire-57189928 [accessed 5 January 2022].

Reynolds, David, *Island Stories: Britain and Its History in an Age of Brexit* (Glasgow: William Collins, 2019).

Runnymede Trust, 'CORE Submission to Commission on Race and Ethnic Disparities', November 2020, www.runnymedetrust.org/uploads/pdfs/CORE%20submission%20to%20Commission%20on%20Race%20and%20Ethnic%20Disparities.pdf [accessed 14 April 2021].

Rushdie, Salman, 'Commonwealth Literature Does Not Exist', in *Imaginary Homelands: Essays and Criticism 1981–1991* (London: Granta Books, 1991), pp. 61–70.

Said, Edward, *Culture and Imperialism* (London: Chatto and Windus, 1993).

Saunders, Robert, 'Brexit and Empire: "Global Britain" and the Myth of Imperial Nostalgia', *The Journal of Imperial and Commonwealth History*, 48:6 (2020), pp. 1140–1174.

Schofield, Camilla, *Enoch Powell and the Making of Postcolonial Britain* (Cambridge: Cambridge University Press, 2013).

Schwarz, Bill, 'Forgetfulness: England's Discontinuous Histories', in *Embers of Empire in Brexit Britain*, ed. by Stuart Ward and Astrid Rasch (London: New York: Bloomsbury, 2019), pp. 55–57.

Schwarz, Bill, 'Introduction', in *End of Empire and the English Novel*, ed. by Rachael Gilmour and Bill Schwarz (Manchester: Manchester University Press, 2015), pp. 1–37.

Schwarz, Bill, '"The Only White Man in There": the Re-Racialisation of England, 1956–1968', *Race & Class*, 38:1 (1996), pp. 65–78.

Schwarz, Bill, *The White Man's World* (Oxford: Oxford University Press, 2011).

Sewell, Tony, Maggie Aderin-Pocock, Aftab Chughtai, Keith Fraser, Naureen Khalid, Dambisa Moyo, Mercy Muroki, Martyn Oliver, Samir Shah, Kunle Olulode and Blondel Cluff, *Commission on Race and Ethnic Disparities: The Report*, March 2021, https://assets.publishing.service.gov.uk/government/uploads/system/uploads/attachment_data/file/974507/20210331_-_CRED_Report_-_FINAL_-_Web_Accessible.pdf [accessed 6 January 2022].

Smith, Zadie, *White Teeth* (London: Penguin, 2001).
Tabili, Laura, *'We Ask for British Justice': Workers and Racial Difference in Late Imperial Britain* (Ithaca, NY; London: Cornell University Press, 1994).
Thackeray, David and Richard Toye, 'Debating Empire 2.0', in *Embers of Empire in Brexit Britain*, ed. by Stuart Ward and Astrid Rasch (London: Bloomsbury, 2019), pp. 15–35.
Topple the Racists, website, www.toppletheracists.org [accessed 30 August 2022].
Ward, Stuart, 'Introduction', in *British Culture at the End of Empire*, ed. by Stuart Ward (Manchester: Manchester University Press, 2001), pp. 1–20.
Ward, Stuart and Astrid Rasch, 'Introduction: Greater Britain, Global Britain', in *Embers of Empire in Brexit Britain* (London: Bloomsbury, 2019), pp. 1–14.
Webster, Wendy, *Englishness and Empire* (Oxford: Oxford University Press, 2005).
Whittle, Matthew, *Postwar British Literature and the 'End of Empire'* (London: Palgrave Macmillan, 2016).
Younge, Gary, 'Britain's Imperial Fantasies Have Given Us Brexit', *The Guardian*, 3 February 2018, www.theguardian.com/commentisfree/2018/feb/03/imperial-fantasies-brexit-theresa-may [accessed 20 June 2019].
Younge, Gary, 'What Black America Means to Europe', *The New York Review of Books*, 6 June 2020, www.nybooks.com/daily/2020/06/06/what-black-america-means-to-europe [accessed 13 January 2022].

Part I

Institutions of empire

1

'Bloomsbury bazaar': Daljit Nagra at the diasporic museum

John McLeod

>   Each allegorical
> or tantric form shorn of its origin and tribal worship lauds
>   itself
>
> before its mild god, the British Museum.
>   (Daljit Nagra, 'Meditations on the British Museum', 2017)[1]

In June 2011 I found myself at the Yushukan military and war museum in the heart of Tokyo, before a glass case containing a *hanayome ningyo* or 'bride doll'. The Yushukan museum is not without controversy. Attached to the infamous Yasukuni Shrine, it commemorates those who died fighting for Japan in the early decades of the twentieth century, including the *tokkotai* or Special Attack Corps who flew the fatal 'kamikazi' missions during the Second World War. Bride dolls were made by the mothers or sisters of the *tokkotai* as a means of memorialising their lost lives as well as providing the souls of the departed with a symbolic companion for the afterlife.[2] I spent a long time before the glass case, deeply moved – not because of any particular investment on my part in the terrible fate of the *tokkotai* or those they killed, or due to the more general upset I had been feeling during my visit about the glorification of imperialism and militarism. Rather, in an unexpected encounter with an image of filial severance, one which often marked the broken and unrecoverable relations between mother and son, I had chanced upon an object which seemed to frame and capture something of my own consciousness of maternal severance as an adoptee. As the product of a 'closed' adoption in the UK in 1970, I had (at that point) never known my Irish birth-mother and possessed very little information about her. Representations of adopted life and personhood at large remain thin on the ground, so chancing upon cultural resources with which to think through adoption is unusual. In the museum, and just for a moment, the *hanayome ningyo* acted as a surrogate symbol of my birth-mother's spectral selfhood and her enforced surrender of me, however unlikely or disproportionate these disaggregated contexts might appear on a warm June morning in Tokyo. My reframing of the museum's object did not elide, erase or simplify the doll's morbid provenance or embeddedness in Japanese imperialism and nationalism; indeed, my unsettled responses to it modulated turbulently across such divergent and emotionally various matters. But neither did the object's primary provenance constrain entirely my reactions. It also enabled me to consider a little of the unregulated affective cost of Japanese nationalism suffered by its people otherwise unrecognised in the queasily celebratory display, with which my ongoing reflections on adoption's emotional damage struck a strange relation. It was, in the sharpest and richest sense of the term, a museum encounter characterised in terms of unscripted and fecund *curiosity*.

According to Nicholas Thomas, curiosity empowers a vital capacity to strike important new relations (cultural, political, ethical) when we encounter unfamiliar human creativity. The museum is a distinctive location where curiosity can do its generative work. In *The Return of Curiosity* (2016), Thomas reminds us that, unlike other aesthetic fora such as theatres or cinemas, the museum is a distinctly itinerant site where we wheel or walk a peculiar route through culture: 'a special sort of walk through a building of a singular kind, punctuated by encounters with objects, yet with no fixed focus on any single centre of attention'.[3] One is tempted here to cast the museum visitor in terms of Michel de Certeau's urban wanderer, whose innovative passages suggest a new ambulant grammar that rewrites the concept-city planners' imperious script.[4] At the same time, Thomas in no way advocates a *laissez-faire* vision of the museum as an arena of amiable contact. As an experienced curator and scholar of South Pacific material culture, he is keenly aware of the politics of display and curation, the colonial histories which frame collections and acquisitions, the habitus which moulds the attitudes and privileges which visitors inevitably bring with them, and the highly charged contemporary debates concerning object repatriation raging at large.[5] The evolution of metropolitan museums, their possessions and popularity, is inseparable from colonial materiality. The discursive domains that have converted selective things into select objects, and which inevitably structure every encounter between the varied visitors and encased artefacts, cannot and should not be sidestepped. Yet, if the ongoing politics of possession are inerasable in museums, museums may also become sites where they could come curiously undone.

Such undoing is not easy, and not least because the politics of museum possession is entangled with the thorny issue of object provenance, its true or proper domain. Thomas counsels caution over, in his phrase, the 'naturalism of heritage' that sometimes animates attitudes to museums' collections – that is, the perception of an object's primary provenance always in terms of its perceived national or cultural origins.[6] The assumption of an organic attachment between source communities and objects, one that often animates debates about object repatriation, is in danger of vacating the complexity and historicity of such relations as well as bypassing the complex and often variable conditions under which each object is collected. While the pursuit and protection of 'heritage' can become politically progressive for once-colonised cultures after empire whose artefacts have been rebranded abroad, the pursuit of originary attachment in organic terms (rather than as an invention of tradition) risks sustaining modernity's means of imagining community in terms of biotic kindred relations. In this biocentric episteme, clear guidance is fixed concerning who and what really belongs where, which cultural activities are legitimately one's issue. Curiosity opens up possible new relations beyond the predetermined or organically hallowed. It empowers unscripted opportunities for imagining and materialising uncommissioned relations that certainly recognise natal provenance and face the enduring politics of possession, but also source progressive affiliations that confront the Manichean misnomers mandated by modernity. Thomas proposes that 'objects can be related to a host of people', not exclusively 'those creators' descendants',[7] before clinching his point powerfully a few pages later: 'communities and individuals *adopt* and appropriate things; they may sense connection with things, and value things, that are not part of "their" heritage in a refined cultural, ethnic or national sense'.[8] Here the mystified realm of filial attachment gives way to the unguessed bearings of adoptive relations that might guide us to new possibilities of rapport, intimacy and community beyond modernity's incurious prejudices. Neither persons nor things are fated forever to be vessels of *patria*, a term which entangles ancient matters of ancestry, heredity, family, fathers and fatherlands, sustained in the contemporary signage of 'repatriation'. In the museum, new *kinds* of, as well as new occasions for, relations can be struck – adoptively.

In this chapter I want to consider a recent significant literary exploration of curiosity's adoptive possibilities, Daljit Nagra's 'Meditations on the British Museum', the longest poem in his collection *British Museum* (2017). As I shall demonstrate in due course, in seeking to imagine the museum as both complicit in coloniality *and* as a transgressive site of postcolonial curiosity, Nagra ultimately reconceives the phenomenology of museum objects from a distinctly diasporic vantage and in a manner which replaces the certainties of natal nativism with critical opportunities born from reconstellated relations.

As scholars of critical adoption studies know all too well, adoption's bracing critique of the myth of origins has unnerving consequences far beyond the primary context of kinship. The relocation of those affected by the legal mechanism of adoption is always a consequence of inequality and underwritten by asymmetrical power relations between birth-parents and adopting families that continue to structure the childcare economy. The attempt on the part of adoptees to recover the natal provenance from which they were transported can never engender the delivery of lost origins, even if one discovers biogenetic kin. Yet, from these often-painful circumstances, transgressive ways of thinking have emerged. For some, adoption productively challenges the assumption that natal provenance best explains, reveals or exhausts the definitive bearings of being that adoptees are schooled to think they forever lack when, for example, information about their birth-parents or place of birth is legally withheld in so-called 'closed' adoptions. As Margaret Homans's work brilliantly shows, an adoptee's quest to (re)discover their origins in their perceived 'birth culture' ultimately defamiliarises, first, the notion of 'birth culture' itself as an homogenising fiction unloosed from the material dimensionality of all cultural provenances, and, second, the very idea of origins themselves as wholly explanatory and fully retrievable retrospectively rather than *always* invented and imposed after the fact. As Homans states, 'the quest for literal origins ultimately gives way to an understanding of the figurative – indeed, fantasmatic – nature of origins'.[9] It is impossible to return to one's origins even if one 'goes home' because origins can never be fully captured by or coincident with the perceptions we craft about them. And even if they could, the precise conditions of the perceived moment of origin no longer exist. As adoption studies proposes for adopted and non-adopted persons alike, quests for the natal are forever fated to terminate at the navel – the attenuated evidence of severance that stumps all fantasies of fluent filial reconnection.

When such quests engage objects and artefacts rather than people, modernity's myth of origins – ever hallowed but always hollow – conspicuously holds fast. Both Thomas's advocacy of curiosity and Nagra's poetic reflections upon museums and objects inevitably happen within and cannot avoid current debates and controversies raging in the heritage sector that are highly sensitive and explosively charged: the metropolitan possession and display of objects made by colonised peoples, calls for object repatriation and reparations, the pressurised politics of public art and architecture. In June 2020, the toppling in Bristol by protesters of John Cassidy's 1895 statue of the slave-trading merchant Edward Colston (1636–1721) symbolised the widespread and growing anger about extant public celebrations of colonial-age capitalists in heroic terms triggered by the outcry over by the appalling killing of George Floyd in Minneapolis the previous month, which prompted the Black Lives Matter protests worldwide. A few months later, the literary and cultural critic Corinne Fowler found herself subject to condemnation in Parliament and by sections of the British press for her contribution to the National Trust's 'Colonialism and Historic Slavery Report' (2020) and her book *Green Unpleasant Land* (2020).[10] The report dared to trace the undisputable connections between the evolution of Britain's rural spaces, including its grand architecture, and the sordid business of empire. Amid today's clashes concerning the heritage industries, often escalated by populist politicians and the popular press into the latest 'culture wars', perceptions of ancestry, provenance and origin have calcified. As Alice Procter has bluntly declared, the genealogy of museums as modern institutions can be traced back to violent origins; colonialism's violence 'is in their foundations, the origins of their collections. We are all living in its legacy, and this inheritance of trauma and power will not go away. Fundamentally, a museum cannot be decolonized without being completely reinvented.'[11] Procter's approach importantly insists that we always attend to the museum's 'colonial present'[12] which sustains its unpalatable past, so that, to borrow Walter Benjamin's words, we soberly reconceive of its civil display as a 'document of barbarism'.[13]

As we shall see, Nagra's poetry fully faces the barbaric bonds between colonialism and heritage made visible in the plinthing of empire's plunder and its plunderers. But just as insistently, however, it refashions the museum as a site of postcolonial curiosity, where empire's wares might be refigured adoptively with an eye as much on the future as on the past, but without allowing the violence of origins or proscriptions of genealogy to constrain fully the possibility of vital new relations beyond imperious progeniture.

It is a necessary and much-needed intervention. Both the full title and argument of Procter's book, *The Whole Picture: The Colonial Story of the Art in Our Museums & Why We Need to Talk About It* (2020), index the wider growing antipathy to museums as perceived storehouses of colonialism's loot and plunder. Her situating of the museum within enduring colonialist legacies is unquestionably necessary and valuable; the recognition of Britain's silenced colonial past should *never* be unwelcome, in any context. But we might pause to consider further Procter's assertion, cited above, that the museum *as museum* cannot broker counter-hegemonic thought due to its sorry origins: 'a museum cannot be decolonized without being completely reinvented'. Nagra's work, as we shall see, suggests otherwise, and also in a distinctly Benjaminian mood. While Benjamin was keen to rescript civilisation as a document of barbarism, as noted previously, he also famously advocated a progressive reimagining of history that did not deny the facticity of the past but sought to forge new, empowering relations between past and present. For Benjamin this entailed engaging with the past *otherwise* – blasting it out of historicism's unchanging continuum in the name of an agential, progressive historical materialism, by 'grasp[ing] the constellation which his own era has formed with a definite earlier one'.[14] The museum, let us remember, is arguably a space of constellations *par excellence*, not only by situating diverse objects in relation to each other but also in terms of the various visitors who bring into the museum's contact zone their distinctive and curious intersectional personhoods – 'variously local residents, the inhabitants of a city, migrants, tourists and others', as Thomas reminds us (and to which we might add academic adoptees ambulating curiously through the display cases of the Yushukan museum).[15] Stephen Clingman carefully reminds us that Benjamin's 'version of the constellation does not involve superimposition or equation but distance and difference: without that there could be no flash of meaning in the first place'.[16] Given these matters, and *contra* Procter, there indeed emerges the opportunity to decolonise the museum 'after empire' – and in both senses of this phrase – as a site where we go *in pursuit* of the horrific and oft-hidden colonialist preamble that continues to contribute to the museum's conditions of possibility, *and* as a space where new relations may be adopted through the mercurial ambulation of curious visitors.

This curious, transgressive, generative mobility is captured precisely in Nagra's 'Meditations on the British Museum'. The son of Sikh Punjabi migrants who spent his formative years in London and Sheffield, Nagra has long been interested in exploring in his poetry the polyglot and polycultural constellations that cluster in relation to diasporic personhood. As Andrew Green has argued, Nagra's writing is readily approachable as a distinctive example of Bakhtinian heteroglossia that challenges the usual precepts of identity: 'Nagra's work insistently worries at the different borders and boundaries he encounters as he charts his route as a poet, be they of language, of colour, or of culture.'[17] It is all the more fascinating, then, that he chooses a conspicuous location of *national* culture – the British Museum, situated at the heart of Bloomsbury in Central London – as the space where these explorations are materially and imaginatively pursued. In 'Meditations on the British Museum', the museum emerges as a crucial site for Nagra where both the pursuit of empires' sorry histories *and* the establishment of a dissident diasporic futurity can be productively adopted.

For Nagra, the British Museum convenes an occasion for diasporic curiosity rather than rests easy as the treasure-house of national imperiousness. In an interview with Green, he moots a description of the British Museum which offers pause for thought, not least due to Nagra's distinct subject position and diasporic dispensation. When asked to reflect upon 'the historical-cultural violence that is represented by such an institution',[18] Nagra acknowledges the museum's complexity in a lengthy response worth quoting in full:

> It's complicated. We only have to look at the contemporary Middle East. If we didn't have these beautiful artefacts here, what would happen to them? Take the celebrations about the destruction of the Buddhas of Bamiyan in

Afghanistan. We are now guardians, and the West needs to protect these things. I think that events in recent decades have led to a change in the argument. In the past Britain was guilty of appropriating things, but Britons are also incredible preservers. That's become increasingly important. It's too easy to say that artefacts should be returned to where they came from. I don't think that's always the case. I also think that the way the items are displayed in Western museums and the amount of people who come to see them provides huge publicity for a wealth of cultures and communities. Appropriation is where it started, but now we have to be more pragmatic. Perhaps that helps cleanse the cultural politics.[19]

There are elements of this response that would sit uneasily with Procter's strict decolonial agenda, not least the presentation of the 'Western' museum as a hub where the world's cultures are preserved, as a site of practical expediency and custodianship. Yet Nagra's 'we' is not discretely national, diasporic or transcontinental – as a diasporic subject, he is aware that the 'Britons' and 'people' of whom he speaks may combine or move between all three. While making an unequivocally clear acknowledgment of the museum's role in 'guilty' appropriation, Nagra's recognition of the complications of curation also insists upon the museum as a postcolonial technology for 'a change in the argument' where a new 'cultural politics' can be pragmatically adopted. Refusing 'easy' positions that struggle to embrace the complications of collection and curation, Nagra's response reconsiders the museum as a critical site where the colonial present might be diasporically disarticulated by relaxing (not eliding) the rhetoric of exalted origins and striking up new relations between persons and things.

'Meditations on the British Museum' consists of nineteen seven-line stanzas split into four sections. It concerns the speaker's ruminations on the diverse objects he sees as he wanders through the museum's various galleries. His contemplative, quizzical engagement with the museum's displays soberly situates many of the objects in the imperious histories of empires ancient and modern, reminding us that the museum's 'noble casket' (p. 49) has been filled to the brim with the spoils of conquest. Such tangible evidence, when framed as such, can be used to engender a wider facing-up to the definitive colonial encounters which have left their remains in the present. At the same time, the speaker's reflective meanderings also reconceive of the objects beyond conventional assumptions of provenance, as not fully the possessions of either the imperious realm in which they remain affixed or their cultures of origin. They are also figured as diasporic objects, the curious contemplation of which disrupts the enduring values that secured their current dwelling. As Paul Basu argues, diasporic objects engender new relationships even as they bear witness to the circumstances of their initial transportation. Clearly, he argues, we must always

> make explicit the 'politics' implicit in any object collected in one place and transported to another, particular in contexts of colonial domination. But the diasporic location of these collections also reminds us that such objects exist in a space between one sociocultural context and another – they mediate across the different worlds encompassed in their biographies. ... [T]he object diaspora is not only a product of historical relationships (social, spatial, and temporal), but, by dint of this historical web of relationality, it has the capacity to 'reactivate' these connections and generate new relationships.[20]

The relations born from colonial domination should not be tidied away or obscured beneath an exclusively formalist appreciation of aesthetic creativity. But these initial relations do not fully define or inhibit possible new ones from being struck. Indeed, such diasporic thinking runs parallel with recent work in critical adoption studies in daring to challenge the misnomer that the provenance of origin must take precedence over all subsequent ways of accounting for meaning or forging relations 'postpartum'.[21] Originary relations exist *as one distinctive set among others* and can themselves be revisited creatively and curiously from a displaced, disjunctive, diasporic standpoint.

Nagra's speaker is diasporic in both his subject position and his sensibility. His reflections on the objects have the capacity to reactivate relations that challenge both the enduring coloniality of the 'museum as nation' (p. 50) and an unquestioning advocacy of *patria*. The poem's construction mirrors the notion of the museum as a hub of contingent cultural confluence as it constellates and curates existing poetic achievement. Through careful referencing it collects and displays a range of poetic intertexts, not least the work of W. B. Yeats, whose writing also reflected often on museums, galleries and buildings. In recalling Yeats's 'Meditations in Time of Civil War' (1923) in its title, Nagra's poem installs high on its agenda the consideration of poetry's proximity and response to conflict, as well as the relationship between the enduring possibilities of art when set against the vicissitudes of corporeality. These concerns are upheld by further references: to Yeats's 'Sailing to Byzantium' (1933) – 'Or try to decode the spirit of Yeats's resurrection / where his singing bird of Byzantium, high on a golden bough' (pp. 51–52) – and the work of Seamus Heaney, another Irish writer who dwelt upon the relations between poetry and civil conflict, as well as W. H. Auden's 'The Shield of Achilles' (1952) and the Sanskrit epic poem the *Ramayana*. These poetic intertexts commingle with references to Shakespeare's *The Tempest* (1611) and the prose writing of George Orwell, E. M. Forster and Leonard Woolf, each of which keeps the entanglements of literature and colonialism determinedly in view. Such literary latticework also sets the scene for the poem's assemblage of museum objects amid the brutal histories they serve to materialise. Nagra draws these from a number of imperial contexts, as his poem squarely faces the documents of barbarism discovered amid the museum's 'millennia of / civilisation' (p. 49). In so doing, Nagra refuses to sanitise museum space by repressing either such contexts or the colonial-crafted attitudes towards cultural particulars. This insidious practice he exposes elsewhere in *British Museum*, in the poem 'The Museum of Archaeology and Anthropology in Cambridge', when describing a visit there by the prime minister of Fiji, who was shown 'his island's wares' (p. 25): 'I overhear our tyrant was not exposed to the "cannibal forks". / But was most impressed by the kava bowl and whale // teeth whose curves he stroked with gloveless hands' (p. 25). As poetic curators, if you will, Nagra's speakers-as-museum-visitors pursue a fuller exposure to museum collections' dimensionality in order to avoid the glibly sweet confection of Fijian objects presented to the prime minister and symbolised by the 'apple strudel slice' (p. 25) he is reverently served by museum staff.[22]

Yet lest it appear that Nagra wishes to posit a highly determinist and enduring relation between museums, conflict and empire – culture *as* imperialism, if you will – 'Meditations on the British Museum' commences with an epigraph comprising the sixth and seventh lines of Louis MacNeice's early poem 'Museums' (1933), in which the museum appears as a space of imaginative curiosity and witty self-invention: *'Mirrors himself in the cases of pots, paces himself by marble lives, / Makes believe it was he that was the glory that was Rome ...'* (p. 49, italics in the original). This sense of the museum as a curious site of creative indulgence where one might 'make believe' contrasts with a view of it as firmly and forever alien or alienating, where reflection (visual, imaginative) remains unavailable to the visitor who wanders unmirrored and unrecognised through its monumental imperium.[23] While Nagra refuses to uncouple the British Museum from its colonial entanglements and proximity to matters of uncivil strife – like Achilles's decorative shield, his poem also exposes civilisation's barbarity in its casting – his speaker's choice of intertextual references also hints at the museum as a place (akin to a poem) where other possibilities are available. Elsewhere in MacNeice's poem the museum appears as a 'centrally heated refuge' for those keen to escape the cold, unappealing grind of daily life, 'running from among buses', so that the imagination can be replenished and rejuvenated, ready to face again the world: 'And then returns to the street, his mind an arena where sprawls / any number of consumptive Keatses and dying Gauls'.[24] For Nagra, the British Museum does not simply display the spoils of colonialism but also importantly makes available a contemplative opportunity to requisition material culture that helps fashion *that which might come after*, and for those who come after. In the museum, we do not exclusively encounter culture as imperialism – the one the product of the other – but also culture *and* imperialism, in Edward Said's famous conceptualisation of this phrase.[25] Said's *Culture and Imperialism* (1993) determinedly explored these terms as hinged rather than bolted together, when thinking through literary culture as contributing to imperialism's critique as well as its continuation, either nonchalantly in the fiction of Jane Austen or in a more revolutionary vein, as in the poetry of Aimé Césaire or W. B. Yeats. In a parallel manoeuvre, Nagra considers how the counterpointing of culture and imperialism perceived in the British Museum sparks the possibility of progressive thought where one might regard critically the legacies of empires ancient and modern. This critical approach to the museum's objects negotiates between past and present diasporically, in Basu's sense of this term, so that new constellations of meaning can be illuminated due to the specifics of uncommissioned ambulation.

Nagra's British Museum curates a dissident poetics of diaspora rather than shores up the 'pre-loaded' politics of *patria*, by facing rather than fighting shy of the colonial present within which all institutions, not just museums, continue to exist.[26] At the beginning of 'Meditations on the British Museum', the museum appears simultaneously in two guises, at once cadaverous and revitalising. Held at the 'dead centre' of the Great Court, 'the treasure core of our crowning jewels', the speaker yet perceives 'a back street open-ended Bloomsbury bazaar / where every marvel / migrant, in the four-wing three-floor stone, is guarded quaint' (p. 49). The core of this British institution is distinctly diasporic and demotic, more bustling marketplace than bulwark of morbid obeisance, where 'every marvel migrant' may signify both the object and the visitor before it. Here, under the distinctive glass ceiling of 3,312 panes, the speaker spies a chance to 'renew / perspective' as he picks his way through this 'house / of colonnaded counter-thoughts where my propositions are jots / amidst a meandering / crowd' (p. 49). Such mobility resequences the British Museum from the standpoint of the diasporic subject whose Britishness admits – indeed, expresses – the entanglements and *unheimlich* presences of a range of other places, cultures and languages. This diasporic quest for 'counter-thoughts' and new propositions sustains vigilance towards the objects' violent origins. The speaker adopts a sceptical rather than reverential encounter with the museum's objects and artefacts that confronts the colonial cruelties of the past. In the first of the poem's four sections his peregrination takes him to plenty of objects 'shorn of … origin and tribal worship' (p. 50), as he mulls amid evidence of Cecil Rhodes's imperial conquests and the colonies' obsequiousness before Queen Victoria. By the second section, his concerns about the museum's politics rise to the surface as he worries that, like invited state dignitaries, 'we go soft // about these rooms' (pp. 50–51) in both senses – moving quietly and submissively; devoid of hardened critical attitudes – as we gaze compliantly at an 'exotic sublime' (p. 51). These concerns propel him mentally towards the cultural and intellectual resources of counter-colonial thinking sourced in his reading of novels of empire and the scholarly thinking that succeeded them: 'I feel sent packing to read between the lines a Burmese Orwell, / a Woolf in workaday Ceylon and a canon of post-colonialists' (p. 51).

In reconstellating the material conditions of the objects' past provenances in relation to the wisdom and standpoint of a disjunctive habitus, the museum's objects are readied as diasporic vehicles for another kind of thinking. In curating the objects in terms not of an imperious *patria* but demotic *diaspora*, Nagra's poem seeks to engender the possibility for new relations to be adopted in the museum, fortuitous and future-facing, that eventually set colonialist attitudes on the move. The objects' potential meaningfulness is not fully constrained by the colonial politics of their collecting. In Nagra's British Museum, objects become cultural conduits of critique as curious relations are struck at the interface of diasporic visitor and plinthed artefact. In the poem's third section, the speaker appears increasingly overwhelmed by a violence that seems inerasable from the various objects' provenances. In standing 'each object in the dock ... with my poetic grounding', he would 'have it account for the applause awarded its opulence' (p. 51). Such calling to account brings the speaker historically to repatriate the 'bare-tooth mask of Quetzalcoatl' (p. 51), bestowed by the Aztec ruler Montezuma upon the Spanish Conquistador Hernán Cortés, to the sordid history of Spanish colonialism that subdued Aztec civilisation in (modern-day) Mexico in an 'unprovoked // genocide' (p. 51). He reflects, too, on a *Ramayana* statue of Vibishana 'who betrayed his own kin to side with Rama, the foe, purely / for moral profit' (p. 52). In the *Ramayana*, Vibishana joins with the forces of Rama against his brother Ravana (after Ravana kidnaps Rama's wife Sita) and helps Rama kill him. Yet it is not just the past which is called to account here; the meditations on the objects provide leverage on the speaker's contemporaneity. The past's violence and complexities captured by the range of cultural artefacts have the capacity *critically* to reconceive the contemporary in terms of the colonial present. The 'dissonance in Forster's Marabar Cave' (p. 52) that sounded the unsettling 'ouboum' in the ears of the expatriate British in *A Passage to India* (1924) becomes imaginatively linked to the so-called 'War on Terror' in the wake of 9/11 and the conflicts fought in other caves: 'what sound // booms from these nooks summoning each child to its Tora / Bora dome, / where an ordinance drones: *home*?' (p. 52). In a similar vein, the moral complexity attached to Vibishana's pursuit of *dharma* in his killing of Ravana reframes the present, when the speaker asks, '[a]re today's Vibishanas Manning, Snowden, Assange?' (p. 52). In *this* British Museum, the artefacts' embeddedness in violence empowers a critical perspective on our current moment by arranging today's politics and conflicts in relation to a range of instructive analogues and examples.

But this is only one part of the constellation. While wondering about the 'rooms of fresh / ruin' (p. 52) that contemporary beliefs and conflicts are anticipating, Nagra persistently unsettles this grim poetic curation through his repeated deployment of the rhetorical question. There are twenty-four such questions in the poem that simultaneously assert and cast doubt on the several reflections of the museum and its objects, such as '[a]re they held by the glare / of torture?' (p. 51). This rhetorical strategy, one that also recalls Yeats's poetry, sustains the conception of the museum as an interrogative space, a site of 'meditations' (as the poem's title insists) and intellectual ambulations, rather than scripted assertions. The speaker is forever curious, constantly asking questions as he wanders. This manoeuvre also keeps open a more dimensional relationship with the museum's objects that are connected to, but not fully held, by violent provenances – what else might they mean? Especially in its closing fourth section, this poetics of interrogation sustains a curious approach to the past that keeps buoyant the adoptive creativity of thinking through object diasporas.

Remembering the speaker's initial rendition of the museum in terms of 'every marvel migrant' (p. 49), we might recognise the poem's exploration of museum space as distinctly transitive and persistently unpredictable in the encounters and relations it brokers. Here, divisions and siloings may no longer hold amid the curatorial juxtapositions of objects – which the poem itself performs in its literary curation of a bust of Plato, a statue of Vibishana, the mask of Quetzalcoatl and more besides – and also due to the unanticipated blend of visitors who combine in this Bloomsbury bazaar. 'Bring out the kids from the segregated schools', (p. 50) proclaims the speaker as he imagines cloistered classes of children now roaming adventurously and uncontrollably together through the '[o]gres, griffins, fire serpents, // manacles, gags and coins' (p. 50). In his museum the politics of segregation meet their match in the polycultural imaginative possibilities that offer other visions of engagement and value – never idealised, of course – through the creative currency of the bazaar's questioning contact zone. Dismissing the notion of the artist as exiled from the world prompted by his beholding a bust of 'our father, pure-minded Plato' (p. 53), the speaker pursues a recalcitrant and dissenting attitude towards both patriarch and *patria* by 'rebut[ting] the gods' (p. 53) of the contemporary with reference to the 'the best of our house' (p. 53). If the 'treasure core' of the past's 'crowning jewels' (p. 49) has empowered the speaker inquisitively to face the brutalities of the past, then the consciousness they engender can be brought to bear on the conflicts that scar the terrain of our uneven globalised contemporaneity. These poetic encounters value the museum as a dissident postcolonial space of recalcitrant thinking that avoids canonised forms of postcolonial critique. In the museum, beyond the merely partisan, the speaker denounces a range of contemporary criminality, including the environmental damage and petropolitics wrought by the latest 'oil giant', the 'new zealot' of the terrorist or suicide bomber, the 'victorious rebel' (p. 53) digging the death pits of the latest genocide, and the panoptical imperium of digital intelligence that serves a new century's online tyranny: 'Now Prospero's surveillance hoards our every scripted quip / for the island / of our interrogation' (p. 52). Contemptuous of imperialisms and *patria* old and new, disdainful of the fundamentalisms of American-led neoliberalism as much as the Islamist statecraft of ISIS that rejoices in filming 'statues collapsing in slow motion' (p. 53), the speaker finds *in the meditative curiosity prompted by the objects* the critical opportunity to refuse the atavism of all empires, to imagine relations otherwise, beyond nation, segregation and silo. These ideas are clinched in the poem's climactic lines:

> ... Let's praise
>
> the unconquerable climate of our cultures who find a portion
>   of their own
> safe in this fortress, in our sovereign values where Britain is
>   guardian
> of the legacy to ensure monumental mankind stay immemorial.
> We're at home, albeit lost, while roaming among our kind
> in Cuerdale, Yarlung, Shang, Ashanti, Aulong, Kush, Thule, Ur.
>
> (p. 53)

This British Museum enshrines a futurity in which a pluralised rendition of 'our cultures' makes the institution of the nation a disjunctive home for all, where loss is forever acknowledged and where 'sovereign values' are struck diasporically. Conjoined by the ambulatory opportunity to roam unscripted, this diverse affiliative citizenry – 'our kind' – encounters a polycultural domain within which heritage is only a 'portion of their own' on display amid a wider demotic. Nagra's British Museum will not succumb to nationalist proportions. Culture and imperialism remain counterpointed rather than fatally accounted, so that the 'immemorial' artefacts of 'monumental mankind' are neither blindly regarded as aloof from the violence of barbarism nor wholeheartedly condemned as the aesthetic result of colonialism's cruelty. By the poem's close, the museum's 'dead centre' has been enlivened spatially through its blurring with other locations, far away yet coincident at the museum's core. And while some might be quick to frown at the speaker's notion of the museum as a 'fortress' protecting endangered or rare cultural artefacts, I would hazard that it is rather the occasion for curious thinking – meditating, questioning, reading between the lines – that Nagra's poem commends in terms of 'sovereign values': the ethical richness of this Bloomsbury bazaar where imperious behaviours across past and present are both uncovered and come unstuck. *This* fortress of refuge contrasts significantly with those recent renditions of enclosed terrain and padlocked *patria* – 'fortress Europe', the checkpoints and walls of Brexit and Trump – that Nagra's poem unflinchingly locates in the *longue durée* of colonial modernity: 'Which dignified nation looks away despite each precious cargo / of slave and migrant being run overboard, while demigods // set themselves in stone?' (p. 53). Nagra's British Museum is closer to a more worldly diasporic domain – forever striated and uneven, never free-floating – than the nation's 'noble casket' (p. 49) through which one tiptoes reverently.

No longer 'the' British Museum – Nagra's elision of the definite article in the collection's title appears strategic – this Bloomsbury bazaar seems closer to a place of refuge than a site of exclusion, open for all comers, where to be 'home, albeit lost', marks both the diasporic subject's torment as well as their tenure. In the bazaar the illiberal vocabulary of *patria* encounters alternative opportunities for striking human relations. 'Could the museum', asks the speaker hopefully, 'help inter / our old ideas of the outsider breeding amidst/within us terms / such as *infidel, insurgent, vigilance*? Is our world now plinth'd?' (p. 52). Ultimately, 'Meditations on the British Museum' is precisely a poetic attempt to plinth our present: to use the past to confront and contest the colonial present by striking up new relations. It rewrites a national institution as facilitating a critical, curious encounter with diasporic objects, one which calls the enduring violence of empires determinedly to account while it looks forward to – indeed, enacts – desegregrated thought.

As Bassu proposes, 'diasporas of objects have the potential to play an important role for corresponding diasporas of people, acting as vehicles for cultural identity construction and expression'.[27] Nagra's poetry certainly realises this vision in a literary mode, while also taking us past the assumed cultural confluence of visitor and object presumed by Basu's phrase 'corresponding diasporas'. Like the figure of the Indian-descended Briton *curiously* contemplating the mask of Quetzalcoatl, a bust of Plato and the statue of Vibishana – like, too, an England-raised adoptee reflecting surprisingly on his Irish birth-mother before the *hanayome ningyo* of the Yushukan museum – such unsolicited occasions configure illuminating constellations which flash the way towards fresh future relations that have learned the lessons of troubled pasts. Like many a literary pursuit of postcolonial transformation, Nagra's writing asks what *else* might be sourced from the sorry resources of yesteryear. Resisting the temptations of unsubtle nativist thinking, national proprietorship and exalted natal origins, 'Meditations on the British Museum' memorably curates a significant encounter between the present's enduring coloniality and the contestatory constellations yielded by unchartered diasporic curiosity.

Notes

1 Daljit Nagra, *British Museum* (London: Faber and Faber, 2017). All subsequent references to this edition are given in parentheses.
2 For more on these and similar *imon ningyo* (comfort dolls) made during the 1930s and 1940s, see Ellen Schattschneider, 'The Bloodstained Doll: Violence and the Gift in Wartime Japan', *Journal of Japanese Studies*, 31:2 (2005), pp. 329–356.
3 Nicholas Thomas, *The Return of Curiosity: What Museums Are Good For in the 21st Century* (London: Reaktion Books, 2016), p. 45.
4 See Michel de Certeau, *The Practice of Everyday Life*, trans. by Steven Rendell (Berkeley: University of California Press, 1988), pp. 91–110.
5 Such alertness is consistently evidenced across his several publications. For example, see Nicholas Thomas, *Colonialism's Culture: Anthropology, Travel and Government* (Cambridge: Polity Press, 1994) and Nicholas Thomas, *Possessions: Indigenous Art/Colonial Culture* (London: Thames and Hudson, 1999).
6 Thomas, *The Return of Curiosity*, p. 68.
7 Thomas, *The Return of Curiosity*, p. 68.
8 Thomas, *The Return of Curiosity*, p. 96 (emphasis added).
9 Margaret Homans, *The Imprint of Another Life: Adoption Narratives and Human Possibility* (Ann Arbor: University of Michigan Press, 2013), p. 114.
10 See Corinne Fowler, *Green Unpleasant Land: Creative Responses to Rural England's Colonial Connections* (Leeds: Peepal Tree, 2020). The National Trust's report can be viewed at www.nationaltrust.org.uk/features/addressing-the-histories-of-slavery-and-colonialism-at-the-national-trust [accessed 23 January 2021]. The recently formed 'Common Sense Group', comprising fifty-nine Conservative Party MPs and seven peers, has been at the forefront of the condemnation of the National Trust's enquiry into its property's colonial connections.
11 Alice Procter, *The Whole Picture: The Colonial Story of the Art in Our Museums & Why We Need to Talk About It* (London: Cassell, 2020), p. 261.
12 I borrow this phrase from Derek Gregory's book of the same name in order to acknowledge the continuation of colonial violence and control in a period that is allegedly 'after' empire. Gregory's work explores US-led militarism in the Middle East; my renting of his phrase signifies the colonial structuring of the contemporary habitus on an often-global scale. See Derek Gregory, *The Colonial Present: Afghanistan, Palestine, Iraq* (Oxford: Wiley Blackwell, 2004).
13 Walter Benjamin, 'Theses on the Philosophy of History', in *Illuminations*, ed. by Hannah Arendt, trans. by Harry Zorn (London: Pimlico, 1999), pp. 245–255, p. 258.
14 Benjamin, 'Theses on the Philosophy of History', p. 255.
15 Thomas, *The Return of Curiosity*, p. 60.
16 Stephen Clingman, *The Grammar of Identity: Transnational Fiction and the Nature of the Boundary* (Oxford: Oxford University Press, 2009), p. 91.

17 Andrew Green, 'Moving World, Moving Voices: A Discussion with Daljit Nagra', *Journal of Commonwealth Literature*, 57:2 (2020), pp. 388–405.
18 Green, 'Moving World, Moving Voices', p. 15.
19 Green, 'Moving World, Moving Voices', pp. 15–16.
20 Paul Basu, 'Object Diasporas, Resourcing Communities', *Museum Anthropology*, 34:1 (2011), pp. 28–42, p. 37.
21 As Salman Rushdie has suggested, our departure from the womb is in essence a frontier-crossing moment that situates migration and displacement at the very core of our natal origins: 'Our own births mirror that first crossing of the frontier between the elements. As we emerge from the womb, we, too, discover that we can breathe; we, too, leave behind a kind of waterworld to become denizens of earth and air.' See Salman Rushdie, *Step Across This Line: Collected Non-Fiction 1992–2002* (London: Jonathan Cape, 2002), p. 408.
22 This poem is undoubtedly inspired by Nagra's participation in 'Thresholds', a project run by Cambridge University in 2013 that enabled ten poets to become writers-in-residence at ten of the university's museums and collections. Nagra's residency was at the Museum of Archaeology and Anthropology (MAA), where Nicholas Thomas has acted as director since 2006. Nagra spoke warmly of his experience: 'I love the Cambridge Museum of Archaeology and Anthropology! This beautifully small museum is packed full of amazing objects from the four imagined corners of the globe such as textiles, stones, paintings, sculptures, masks, weapons and skins. I suspect we would be able to construct the whole history of mankind and mankind's relationship to the planet with a few of the MAA's objects spanning hundreds of thousands of years.' See www.cam.ac.uk/research/discussion/we-ask-the-experts-why-do-we-put-things-into-museums [accessed 29 July 2020].
23 Interestingly, Nagra has confessed to such an experience when remembering his initial visits: 'when I [first] visited the British Museum, as an adult, I felt intimidated by the aloof joyless manner of the entrance. I felt there was a code of self-presentation that I needed to rapidly adopt so that I looked as though I fitted in.' See www.cam.ac.uk/research/discussion/we-ask-the-experts-why-do-we-put-things-into-museums [accessed 29 July 2020].
24 Louis MacNeice, 'Museums', in *Collected Poems*, ed. by Peter MacDonald (London: Faber and Faber, 2016 [2007]), p. 29.
25 See Edward Said, *Culture and Imperialism* (London: Chatto and Windus, 1993).
26 Thomas, *The Return of Curiosity*, p. 33.
27 Basu, 'Object Diasporas, Resourcing Communities', p. 37.

Bibliography

Basu, Paul, 'Object Diasporas, Resourcing Communities: Sierra Leonean Collections in the Global Museumscape', *Museum Anthropology*, 34:1 (2011), pp. 28–42.
Benjamin, Walter, 'Theses on the Philosophy of History', in *Illuminations*, ed. by Hannah Arendt, trans. by Harry Zorn (London: Pimlico, 1999), pp. 245–255.

Clingman, Stephen, *The Grammar of Identity: Transnational Fiction and the Nature of the Boundary* (Oxford: Oxford University Press, 2009).
de Certeau, Michel, *The Practice of Everyday Life*, trans. by Steven Rendell (Berkeley: University of California Press, 1988).
Fowler, Corinne, *Green Unpleasant Land: Creative Responses to Rural England's Colonial Connections* (Leeds: Peepal Tree, 2020).
Gregory, Derek, *The Colonial Present: Afghanistan, Palestine, Iraq* (Oxford: Wiley Blackwell, 2004).
Green, Andrew, 'Moving World, Moving Voices: A Discussion with Daljit Nagra', *Journal of Commonwealth Literature*, 57:2 (2020), pp. 388–405.
Homans, Margaret, *The Imprint of Another Life: Adoption Narratives and Human Possibility* (Ann Arbor: University of Michigan Press, 2013).
MacNeice, Louis, 'Museums', in *Collected Poems*, ed. by Peter MacDonald (London: Faber and Faber, 2016 [2007]), p. 29.
Nagra, Daljit, *British Museum* (London: Faber and Faber, 2017).
National Trust, 'Addressing the Histories of Slavery and Colonialism at the National Trust', www.nationaltrust.org.uk/features/addressing-the-histories-of-slavery-and-colonialism-at-the-national-trust [accessed 4 January 2022].
Procter, Alice, *The Whole Picture: The Colonial Story of the Art in Our Museums & Why We Need to Talk About It* (London: Cassell, 2020).
Rushdie, Salman, *Step Across This Line: Collected Non-Fiction 1992–2002* (London: Jonathan Cape, 2002).
Said, Edward, *Culture and Imperialism* (London: Chatto and Windus, 1993).
Schattschneider, Ellen, 'The Bloodstained Doll: Violence and the Gift in Wartime Japan', *Journal of Japanese Studies*, 31:2 (2005), pp. 329–356.
Thomas, Nicholas, *Colonialism's Culture: Anthropology, Travel and Government* (Cambridge: Polity Press, 1994).
Thomas, Nicholas, *Possessions: Indigenous Art/Colonial Culture* (London: Thames and Hudson, 1999).
Thomas, Nicholas, *The Return of Curiosity: What Museums Are Good For in the 21st Century* (London: Reaktion Books, 2016).
University of Cambridge Research, 'We Ask the Experts: Why Do We Put Things into Museums?', 26 November 2013, www.cam.ac.uk/research/discussion/we-ask-the-experts-why-do-we-put-things-into-museums [accessed 4 January 2022].

2

Anthropology at the end of empire: Turning a 'colonial science' on Britain itself

Katherine Ambler

In 1954, the British Department for Industrial and Scientific and Industrial Research awarded funding to the University of Manchester's Department of Social Anthropology for a series of studies of workplace behaviour in British factories. The project would send researchers into Lancashire garment factories and electrical engineering workshops where they would work alongside employees in order to determine how and why certain practices emerged, such as the tendency of workers to impose their own production quotas despite managers offering bonuses to those who produced more. The man behind this project at Manchester was Max Gluckman, an anthropologist better known for his work on ritual and custom in southern and central Africa.[1] Why was an anthropologist whose expertise lay in Africa tasked with analysing the behaviour of British industrial workers – a group whose lived experience would undoubtedly diverge significantly from that of African villagers?

Gluckman believed that the frequent depiction of workers as irrational was similar to how African ideas about witchcraft and magic had been dismissed as misguided superstitions. Just as anthropologists had previously sought to explain the logic in witchcraft, Gluckman appointed a team of researchers to discover why factory workers behaved as they did.[2] Gluckman, like many anthropologists, had established his career in the context of the British Empire – prior to joining Manchester in 1949 he had been director of the Rhodes-Livingstone Institute in Northern Rhodesia, which was funded by the Colonial Office and colonial governments in the central African region. Now in Britain, he was determined to demonstrate that this expertise and approach were applicable to an entirely new context.

This chapter seeks to connect two parallel developments in postwar Britain – the end of empire and the expansion of the social sciences – in order to argue that social scientific ideas about Britain in the 1950s and 1960s drew on ideas and practices developed to explain the social dynamics of the Empire. As colonial sources of funding dried up, and with access to many colonial research sites increasingly restricted on security grounds from the 1950s, those social scientists whose subject of research had focused on Britain's Empire were obliged to find new patrons and fields of study. During the same period, the British government committed funding to academic expansion and the development of social scientific research within the country, with industrial relations of particular concern. A number of anthropologists and sociologists therefore aimed to demonstrate how their expertise could now be applied to labour, community or social relations in Britain. This work positioned researchers as scientific observers and interpreters who could use their knowledge of different societies and cultures to provide guidance to the British government and public in a period of social change, industrial unrest and shifting ideas about national identity. While in the colonial field the subject of anthropologists' research was a racial 'other', within Britain the lens shifted to the analysis of different 'others' – industrial workers, the unemployed or minority groups within the country, such as the Welsh.

The idea that the end of empire shaped Britain itself in profound ways is now well established. As Jordanna Bailkin has argued, decolonisation was intertwined with the development of the welfare state and experts such as social scientists had a role to play in suggesting how to manage the end of empire.[3] In this sense, decolonisation was a significant opportunity for those who could position themselves effectively as navigators of change. This 'post-colonial careering', as Joseph M. Hodge has called it, enabled former colonial officers and experts to transition into new roles in academia, NGOs or other institutions, reframing their expertise as international and postimperial.[4] Paying attention to such figures and their networks points to the many continuities that existed between empire and its aftermath, revealing how expertise and knowledge derived from colonial frameworks retained its currency in new contexts.[5] Within academia, the colonial background of anthropology remains a source of much soul-searching within the discipline.[6] Yet, while anthropologists often note that the end of empire had a significant impact on the discipline, there has been little critical historical reflection on how the period of late empire and decolonisation shaped anthropological practice.[7]

In parallel to these studies detailing links between empire and academic thought and practice, there has been significant historical interest in exploring the expansion of the social sciences in Britain in the second half of the twentieth century. The growth in the social sciences in this period, argues Mike Savage, was part of the wider process of constructing Britain as a modern, rational and postimperial nation, and social scientists had a critical role in defining – and representing – new ideas about modernity. Sociology, in particular, promised a new, modern rational form of expertise that could provide objective insights.[8] Sociologists took everyday questions or concerns – such as social mobility, family life or delinquency – and developed new techniques to make them investigable, such as surveys, interviews, questionnaires and observations. Historians have demonstrated the value of re-examining such social scientific studies not only to trace the emergence of key ideas, but also as a rich resource for social histories of the period.[9] Despite their intention of studying subjects such as class, race or gender scientifically, encounters between researchers and their subjects were shaped by the ways in which all parties imagined and performed social roles. However, while the connections between these studies of Britain and influences from the 'colonial science' of anthropology have been noted by historians, what this means for our understanding of such studies – as well as how they came to be produced in the first place – has not been addressed in detail.

Creating a new kind of anthropology at the University of Manchester

In 1949, the South Africa-born anthropologist Max Gluckman was appointed as chair of the University of Manchester's newly formed anthropology department. Within the field of anthropology, the group of scholars associated with Max Gluckman in the 1950s and 1960s has come to be known as the 'Manchester School', representing a distinctive style of anthropology in the period, one that focused closely on the study of conflict and the use of specific case studies as the basis of analysis.[10] The department was peopled by staff and students who were interested in understanding the social problems and dynamics of modern societies around the world, including those close to home. This reflected a blurring of disciplinary boundaries between anthropology and sociology; the application of sociological methods to 'traditional' anthropological field sites in Africa, in parallel with more anthropological approaches to the study of 'modern' sites in Britain, was a feature of the department's work. Disciplines such as sociology appeared to offer a form of expertise that was more modern and rational, well equipped for the study of changing societies and which sought to interpret and depict the average, anonymous citizen. However, by retaining anthropological methods, such as extended participant observation and the use of personalised case studies rather than anonymised data, the Manchester scholars created a body of work somewhat at odds with the mainstreams of both anthropology and sociology, yet which nevertheless represented a significant strand of social scientific research in this period.

Before his arrival at Manchester, Gluckman had carried out fieldwork in South Africa and Northern Rhodesia (now Zambia). He hoped to continue to send students and researchers to southern and central Africa to expand his previous research on the impact of colonialism and capitalism on the region, for example, by studying trade unions in the mining regions of Northern Rhodesia. Although some of this research did continue in the 1950s, the political situation in Northern Rhodesia made such lines of investigation increasingly difficult.[11] Several of Gluckman's students at Manchester who wanted to go to Northern Rhodesia for their PhD fieldwork were refused visas by the British government in the early 1950s on the basis of their past involvement in the Communist or Socialist Parties.[12] In a period of labour unrest and militancy, and as demands for independence increased, anthropologists were now perceived by both the British and Colonial governments to be dangerously subversive – too close to local people and likely to encourage them in their demands for better working conditions and political rights.[13]

Jed Esty has argued that modernist writing about England and Englishness in the twentieth century was profoundly shaped by the experience of empire, and that the end of empire saw the 'domestication of anthropology', with modernist writers scrutinising their homeland and what they saw as its distinctive culture.[14] In contrast, while the Manchester anthropologists would indeed draw on colonial anthropology's methods to examine modern Britain, the objective was not necessarily to identify anything distinctive about British culture but rather to find parallels and continuities between both so-called modern and 'primitive' societies. Indeed, there was little interest in identifying an all-encompassing 'English' or 'British' culture. As with much of the work produced by the Manchester anthropologists, there was a belief that people adapt to the social situations and networks in which they find themselves rather than being governed by innate 'cultural' norms or values. Accordingly, the role of the social anthropologist was to focus on the social systems that can be found within any group of people, anywhere in the world. The goal was to identify and explain similarities, rather than uncover differences.

It was in this context that Gluckman and his colleagues began to think about how the new department at Manchester could reorient its anthropological research towards new areas, closer to home. While it had been envisaged from the outset that the department would also teach sociology, it seemed increasingly clear to Gluckman that anthropology itself was also equipped to interpret modern Britain. He believed that anthropological theories and methodologies could apply equally well to both what had been considered 'tribal' and 'traditional' communities and to modern and industrial ones.

Anthropology on the Home Front

Ronald Frankenberg, a postgraduate student in the Manchester anthropology department, originally planned to undertake his PhD fieldwork in the

West Indies. However, upon his arrival in January 1953, he was refused access to Jamaica, Barbados and St Vincent and forced to return to Britain. Although the specific reasoning behind this refusal was not disclosed, Gluckman and Frankenberg were told the decision had been made on security grounds, which they understood to refer to the latter's involvement in the student Socialist Society.[15] The university administration was unhappy with the embarrassment caused by the affair and reluctantly agreed that Frankenberg could continue with his PhD at Manchester, but only if he 'worked within a day's journey of Manchester under the close supervision of Professor Gluckman'.[16] In the spirit of sticking as close to the anthropological tradition of fieldwork as possible – in which language-learning was a vital part of the process – it was decided to shift his doctoral research project to Wales. The whole framework for Frankenberg's project – right down to the title of 'Unemployment and Family Structure' – was shifted to Glyn Ceiriog in North Wales.[17]

The anthropological methodology of participant observation was based on an extended period of residence in the place being studied, during which time anthropologists were expected, as much as possible, to immerse themselves in everyday life. This methodology had been largely developed in the 'colonial encounter'.[18] However, there was also a history of fieldwork undertaken in Britain itself, influenced by the colonial science of anthropology, whereby researchers spent time with working-class communities in an effort to better understand their lives. Early mass observation projects had centred on participant observation rather than the later diaries for which they are best known, while George Orwell's reportage was also shaped by anthropological studies.[19] While Wales was a new location for academic anthropology, Frankenberg's project also echoed a long history of representations of the Welsh as somehow more 'tribal' or 'traditional' than the rest of Britain – an ethnic, 'Celtic', other.[20] As Tony Ballantyne has argued, the interest in defining national origins and ethnic groups that was to be a feature of imperial rule also played out in Britain itself, with an interest in 'Anglo-Saxon' or 'Celtic' origins and influences.[21] Frankenberg, however, would come to understand the Welsh not as a mystical, ancient people defined by land and culture, but rather as another group oppressed by the British establishment for political and economic ends.

Frankenberg spent 1953 attempting to learn Welsh and become part of village life, helping the community organise a carnival, supporting the local football team and attending parish council meetings. In his dissertation based on this fieldwork, and the subsequent book, he draws on traditional anthropological concepts of the social function of ritual and of 'the stranger' to depict tensions between Welsh and English residents of the village, and to discuss how inhabitants were struggling to uphold their sense of tradition in the face of economic decline caused by the closure of local slate mines. Deploying the idea of the 'stranger', for example, Frankenberg explains that strangers 'are brought into an activity to take the responsibility and withstand the unpopularity of leadership and the taking of decisions ... Decisions are usually taken by the villagers themselves. They only *appear* to be made by strangers who are forced to shoulder the responsibility for decisions when they prove unpopular with dissident groups of villagers.'[22] Examples are drawn from village committees to illustrate, for example, that strangers help to agree how the proceeds of the village carnival should be spent.[23] He backs up this point by drawing on parallels with anthropological literature about the Nuer (of Sudan) or the Tonga (of Northern Rhodesia/Zambia).[24] However, this parallel is not exact, he acknowledges, since in the African examples, the 'stranger' providing external authority is often a spirit or oracle who provides mystical 'guidance' to particular villagers. In Wales, on the contrary, 'the stranger has no ritual power or licenced freedom to protect him'.[25] Nonetheless, the parallels were sufficient 'to establish the existence of this principle'.[26] Wales, Frankenberg argued, was not so different from Britain's African colonies both in the explanatory power of custom for shaping behaviour and in the existence of tension between the 'local' community and English outsiders.

Frankenberg would later describe how his fieldwork experience – and the resultant book *Village on the Border* – had made him and Gluckman 'pioneers in bringing British anthropology back home', demonstrating the discipline's 'theoretical thrust ... to emphasize not the exotic custom but the familiar process'.[27] Indeed, reviews of the book upon publication in 1957 made just this point. In a review entitled 'Anthropologist on the Home Front', *The Manchester Guardian* praised the book for 'demonstrating how little we really know about the people across the street' and suggested that anthropologists were well equipped to reveal to British readers just how little was actually 'normal' about their society.[28] Although the focus of Frankenberg's book was the tension between Welsh- and English-speaking residents of a Welsh town close to the border with England, both the author and reviewers felt able to extrapolate broader points about Britain from it. As Mike Savage has pointed out, there was an 'ambivalence' to Wales's position in relationship to England that offered social scientists the intellectual space to try out new ideas and approaches that implicitly critiqued English norms, while also retaining some distance.[29] In this respect, Welsh communities were both representative of Britain and also still different enough for comparisons with the Nuer or Tonga not to shock readers.

As Frankenberg pointed out in an introduction to a later edition of his book, 1953, the year of his fieldwork, was 'the year of the coronation of Queen Elizabeth II and a period of taking stock'.[30] Part of this reflection was a consideration of the nature of modern 'community' in Britain.[31] As Gluckman himself spelled out in his introduction to the first edition, 'Many people are concerned to develop community life in the new towns and housing estates that are being built. For the feeling that people get happiness out of living in communities is strong in Britain.'[32] In the case of Glyn Ceiriog, one of the challenges for the Welsh villagers was maintaining their sense of community in the face of English political and economic control. It was not made explicit in the original edition, but later Frankenberg made clear that he perceived this to be 'an openly colonial situation'.[33] For Frankenberg, this parallel with colonial society was also connected to his understanding of Britain's class structure.

In a letter to Gluckman, his supervisor, while in the field, he stated that

> Glyn, and Wales as a whole, is also in transition from Colonial rule, but the situation is a mild form of the West Indian form of Colonial Decay rather than the African one ... In a sense all working class units in our own society ... have the characteristics of a colonial society in transition ... Since coming to Glyn ... I have found it profitable to think of the village as a decayed Island Colony.[34]

This focus on class, rather than race, was a feature of much of the Manchester School work. While contemporaneous anthropologists at the University of Edinburgh, for example, were studying the lives of migrant communities in Britain and analysing the attitudes of white Britons to their new neighbours, Manchester anthropologists such as Frankenberg tended to set aside racial dynamics in favour of class-based ones.[35] This is not to say that they were not concerned with racism, but rather that they understood economic factors to be of critical importance in structuring working peoples' lives, both within Britain and in colonies such as Northern Rhodesia.[36] Some scholars have suggested that studies of working-class life in Britain could replicate the dynamics of colonial anthropology as elite visiting observers looked down on the practices of the poor,[37] or allowed their own class prejudices to shape the direction of research.[38] Frankenberg, however, was making a political statement (inspired, he later admitted, by his reading of Marx and Mao) about the importance of working-class culture. In this, he was reflecting 'the intellectual spirit of the time'[39] embodied in books such as Richard Hoggart's *The Uses of Literacy*[40] or E. P. Thompson's *The Making of the English Working Class*.[41]

Frankenberg's work has been described as 'the seminal anthropological study of a mainland British rural community ... it was unquestionably crucial to the development of an anthropology of Britain'.[42] *Village on the Border* took its place among the wave of so-called 'community studies' published in the 1950s and 1960s. Frankenberg became a prominent exponent of this new field, publishing a popular Penguin paperback on the subject in 1966 in which he reiterated the importance of anthropology for analysing Britain itself.[43] However, while the village of Glyn Ceiriog was in some respects a relatively traditional anthropological location for the study of a small community and its customs, anthropologists at the University of Manchester also believed that anthropology could be applied to a very different environment.

Anthropology on the shop floor

In 1954, Gluckman and the Manchester anthropology department won funding from the British Department for Scientific and Industrial Research (DSIR) for a programme of research into the problem of 'restriction of output' in British factories.[44] This phenomenon whereby workers appeared to collude deliberately to limit the amount they produced, despite economic incentives to the contrary, had been a factor in a number of strikes across Britain in the 1950s.[45] Productivity, in general, was a significant source of concern for the government and for employers.[46] This interest was driven in part by the influence of the US Marshall Plan, which channelled financial support in the form of 'Conditional Aid' towards European productivity bodies, as well as funding research into 'human relations in industry', partly in an attempt to mitigate the influence of the Communist Party on European trade unions.[47] The Manchester research was part of this state-directed attempt to gain insight into workers' behaviour in order to facilitate more effective interventions, a subtext that does not appear to have generated much concern on the part of Gluckman and his colleagues.

Such projects were controversial within the field of academic anthropology. As David Mills has revealed, in the same period the Royal Anthropological Institute (RAI), while initially tempted to take money from British industrialists to fund a major programme of research into factory-floor dynamics, was ultimately unwilling to fully support a programme of 'applied anthropology'.[48] This concern was particularly acute in the post-war period, when anthropology was still in the process of professionalisation. Such attempts to maintain the integrity and impartiality of research glossed over the fact that, at least since the 1930s, much anthropological research had been funded by the British state as part of its colonial development and welfare efforts.[49] Indeed, anthropologists such as Gluckman were keen to increase the amount of funding available to support anthropological research in Britain's remaining colonies through government bodies such as the Colonial Social Science Research Council (CSSRC).[50] A belief in the anthropologist's ability to act as an objective, scientific observer enabled many individual anthropologists to happily take funding from bodies such as the DSIR or the CSSRC.[51]

Researcher Tom Lupton was recruited to Manchester to work on the study as a PhD project; although this was closely directed by Gluckman, Lupton would take on responsibility for the overall planning of the project and undertook two of the three initial studies carried out in the first phase of research.[52] In 1955, additional funding was secured from the DSIR, and a further researcher, Sheila Cunnison, was added to the project team.[53] Although the Conditional Aid programme that had initially funded the DSIR's productivity studies had come to an end at the close of 1955, the grant was extended in 1956 with the DSIR's own funds, with an additional researcher, Shirley Wilson, joining the team.[54] The initial industry chosen for examination was that of waterproof-garment manufacturing. In addition to the waterproof-garment factories, research was later also undertaken in the electrical engineering industry.

Tom Lupton and Sheila Cunnison went on to work in the fields of management studies and industrial sociology. However, the methodologies of the 'Manchester shop-floor studies' they undertook in the 1950s were profoundly influenced by anthropology and in particular by the interests and approaches of Gluckman and his anthropologist colleagues. To begin with, unlike other industrial and sociological research at the time, which relied on interviews and surveys, this project was carried out on the basis of 'open participant observation'. This meant that, for the period of the research, Lupton and Cunnison were employed by the factories they were studying and worked on the production line, with their own responsibilities and targets to meet. Workers, management and union officials knew that they were there to undertake research; it had been agreed that failure to disclose their academic status was too close to spying.[55] In addition, while their research would be grounded in detailed personal experience, it would be contextualised by the kind of data – on wages, for example – that could only be obtained by working with the owners and officials of the factory.

As with Frankenberg's parallels between colonial society and working-class communities in Britain, the Manchester factory studies included reflections on class and social status. Before undertaking military service in the Second World War, Lupton had worked in an engineering workshop and, in his published work on the research project, he uses his working-class background and prior experience of manual labour to establish his credibility, as well as to justify the approach he took. In his book about the factory studies, he begins with an anecdote about his pre-academic experience of the shop floor.

> During the second day in the shop I was given a job by the foreman which completely absorbed my interest. I became oblivious to my surroundings and to the passage of time. I was disturbed by the sounding of the 'buzzer' which

announced the official finishing time, and when I looked up I found myself surrounded by a group of men who had obviously been watching me for some time. They were all ready to go home. Nothing was said but their looks made it clear that I would soon become unpopular if I persisted in observing official times. The lesson was quickly learned, and not unwillingly.[56]

Anyone who has worked in a factory, he tells the reader, knows that there are certain norms and taboos that cannot be broken, and that interactions between management and workers often amount to 'guerrilla warfare'.[57] Such statements establish that the anthropologists on the shop floor will not take the management perspective. Indeed, in the preface to the books, Lupton begins by thanking the trade unions with which he had collaborated, noting, 'I can only hope that my work will add to greater understanding of the problems which they, and others like them, face. This was its only object.'[58] Throughout the book, he reiterates how hard the work is, and draws attention to the personal difficulties of many of the workers in the factory – poverty, illness, insecurity, as well as the challenges faced by many of the women working in the factory, who had significant domestic responsibilities on top of their employment duties.

Fieldwork is a central and defining experience of anthropology and the hardship that this often entails is a rite of passage for anthropologists.[59] Accordingly, the Manchester shop-floor studies include such moments of self-exposure, as the researchers outline their struggles with the work they were undertaking. Describing his experience in a waterproof-garment factory, Lupton writes, 'I found the work hard and exhausting ... I found it difficult to adjust myself to a job which required me to stand in the same place for long hours ... I was laughed at as being a "cissie" when I mentioned how tired standing made me.'[60] Throughout the text, he emphasises his solidarity with the workers whom he had toiled alongside, while also making it clear that they possess a level of skill at their tasks which he does not.

The shop-floor studies drew directly on anthropological tools and techniques to explain the events in the factory. Apart from Max Gluckman, one of the main influences on the Manchester factory studies was anthropologist Victor Turner. Turner had undertaken his PhD research in Northern Rhodesia, where he studied ritual among the Ndembu people. He subsequently worked in the Manchester department. Turner examined the significance of various rituals to Ndembu society, developing the idea of the 'social drama', an extension of the 'extended-case analysis'. The social drama is an account of a specific ritualised process which is designed to reveal the importance of conflict for all societies. The idea of the social drama informs the work of the Manchester factory studies and in this it reflects another important element of Manchester-style anthropology: a close focus on the importance of conflict. Lupton explicitly cites Turner as an influence in his study of conflict on the shop floor, although he takes care to note that 'there are some resemblances between the mechanisms which are brought into play to handle conflict in the African society which Turner studied, and in the workshop ... but there are, of course, significant differences'.[61] Primarily, the workshop in Manchester was less bound by ritual and custom than the Northern Rhodesian society studied by Turner (although these were still present in part), while the power differential between workers and management was much greater than any equivalent social division among the African group.

Cunnison similarly credits Turner's work on social dramas as an influence on her work, and uses his techniques to evoke examples of conflict on the shop floor.[62] She details the story of a row between two workers, Edna and Lucy, who quarrelled because Edna perceived her wage packet to have been negatively affected by the poor quality of Lucy's work at an earlier stage of the production line.[63] Her account of the dispute draws on Turner's ideas about how crises make visible the contradictions that arise between the principles embodied by social norms and the experience of individuals when these norms are enforced. However, as Lupton had also found, the model did not work perfectly; unlike in Turner's examples, where communal rituals were used as a way of redressing breaches within groups, in the Manchester factory, Edna simply chose to resign and seek alternative work. Although the anthropological templates did not always fit the new field site, this focus on conflict served to highlight the many tensions that existed in the workplace, not only between management and worker, but also between workers operating in stressful and precarious economic conditions. Indeed, only by working on and observing the production lines could researchers really analyse how conflict and cooperation worked in practice.

Conclusion

Delimiting and relocating anthropological expertise to encompass modern and industrial settings in Britain seemed to offer a way for practitioners to weather challenges as the discipline's traditional practices and techniques were called into question at the end of empire. While the Manchester studies of Welsh villages and Lancashire factories could be seen to merely replace colonial anthropology's racial 'other' with a new social 'other' of the working class, the use of participant observation obliged researchers to identify with the struggles of the villagers and labourers they lived and worked alongside. Moreover, the recruitment of social scientists who themselves shared the social background of their subjects also encouraged the writing of deeply sympathetic portrayals of working-class life. However, while

Lupton, Cunnison and Wilson's work contains interesting reflections on the role of gender in the workplace and on the position of Jewish workers in the factories, the demographics of the workers at the sites chosen for these studies meant that the researchers did not need to address questions of race. Such anthropological studies undertaken in Britain were able to mitigate the 'otherness' of research subjects through the similarity between researcher and research subject, a similarity that was easier to invoke along economic lines than racial ones. Such issues lie at the heart of anthropology's ongoing efforts to grapple with its colonial past and the challenges of decolonising a discipline whose roots lie in the colonial endeavour.[64]

In the context of colonial anthropology, Helen Tilley has argued that much of the research produced in Britain's colonies subverted colonial power and ideology by challenging European perspectives and stereotypes. Anthropologists working within the system they were critiquing were able to justify their acceptance of colonial money and status because they believed that they were able to act as neutral scientific observers and that their work served to foreground the point of view of the people they were studying.[65] For Gluckman and his team, the source of the funding they received and the objectives of their funders were the object of little critical reflection. Rather, through these studies of British communities, Max Gluckman and the University of Manchester anthropology department were seeking to establish the applicability of anthropological theory to modern Britain and to demonstrate the credibility of the anthropologist applying these theories taken from fieldwork in Africa to labour, community or social relations in Britain. In doing so, this work positioned the Manchester anthropologists as scientific observers and interpreters who could use their knowledge of different societies to provide guidance to the British government and public. It also reveals how the end of empire and the loss of the privileges of 'colonial science' forced scholars to find new ways to justify their expertise and to adapt their practices to win support from new patrons. Anthropology on the home front remained imbued with the tools and techniques of the colonial field, yet by studying British communities with the same scrutiny as 'tribes' in the colonies it also served to challenge British readers' ideas of just how 'normal' they were.

Notes

1 Gluckman's major publications include: *The Judicial Process among the Barotse of Northern Rhodesia* (Manchester: Manchester University Press, 1955) and *Order and Rebellion in Tribal Africa* (London: Cohen and West, 1963).

2 For example, in an earlier research project known as the 'Hawthorne Experiments', social scientists had observed a team of US workers at an electrical

plant deliberately slowing their production rate, resulting in the loss of potential income. Higher wages did not seem to equate with higher production levels. For more on this project, which primarily interpreted such behaviour in terms of individual psychology, see Richard Gillespie, *Manufacturing Knowledge: A History of the Hawthorne Experiments* (Cambridge; New York: Cambridge University Press, 1991).

3 Jordanna Bailkin, *The Afterlife of Empire* (Berkeley: University of California Press, 2012).

4 Joseph M. Hodge, 'British Colonial Expertise, Post-Colonial Careering and the Early History of International Development', *Journal of Modern European History*, 8:1 (2010), pp. 24–46.

5 For example: Véronique Dimier, *The Invention of a European Development Aid Bureaucracy: Recycling Empire* (Basingstoke: Palgrave Macmillan, 2014); Becky Taylor, 'Good Citizens? Ugandan Asians, Volunteers and "Race" Relations in 1970s Britain', *History Workshop Journal*, 85 (2018), pp. 120–141.

6 There is extensive literature on anthropology's entanglements with colonialism, including, from a more critical perspective, James Clifford and George E. Marcus, eds, *Writing Culture: The Poetics and Politics of Ethnography* (Berkeley: University of California Press, 1986); Johannes Fabian, *Time and the Other: How Anthropology Makes Its Object* (New York: Columbia University Press, 1983); and, from a more reflective point of view, Benoit de L'Estoile, Federico G. Neiburg and Lygia Sigaud, eds, *Empires, Nations, and Natives: Anthropology and State-Making* (Durham, NC: Duke University Press, 2005); Helen Tilley and Robert J. Gordon, *Ordering Africa: Anthropology, European Imperialism and the Politics of Knowledge* (Manchester: Manchester University Press, 2007).

7 For example: Fredrik Barth, *One Discipline, Four Ways: British, German, French, and American Anthropology* (Chicago, IL: University of Chicago Press, 2005); Jack Goody, *The Expansive Moment: The Rise of Social Anthropology in Britain and Africa, 1918–1970* (Cambridge: Cambridge University Press, 1995).

8 Michael Savage, *Identities and Social Change in Britain since 1940: The Politics of Method* (Oxford: Oxford University Press, 2010).

9 For example: Helen McCarthy, 'Social Science and Married Women's Employment in Post-War Britain', *Past & Present*, 233:1 (2016), pp. 269–305; Selina Todd, 'Affluence, Class and Crown Street: Reinvestigating the Post-War Working Class', *Contemporary British History*, 22:4 (2008), pp. 501–518.

10 Literature on the 'Manchester School' includes: T. M. S. Evens and Don Handelman, eds, *The Manchester School: Practice and Ethnographic Praxis in Anthropology* (New York: Berghahn Books, 2006); Joan Vincent, *Anthropology and Politics: Visions, Traditions, and Trends* (Tucson: University of Arizona Press, 1990); on the earlier work by some of the School's members in Britain's central African colonies, see Lyn Schumaker, *Africanizing Anthropology: Fieldwork, Networks, and the Making of Cultural Knowledge in Central Africa* (Durham, NC: Duke University Press, 2001).

11 Examples of work produced by 'Manchester School' scholars on Africans societies in the 1950s include: Arnold Leonard Epstein, *Politics in an Urban African*

Community (Manchester: Manchester University Press, 1958); and Victor Turner, *Schism and Continuity in an African Society: A Study of Ndembu Village Life* (Manchester: Manchester University Press, 1957).

12 Geoffrey Gray, '"A Great Deal of Mischief Can Be Done": Peter Worsley, the Australian National University, the Cold War and Academic Freedom, 1952–1954', *Journal of the Royal Australian Historical Society*, 101:1 (2015), pp. 25–44.
13 For an examination of how anthropological research was curtailed by governments and the security services, see Grahame Foreman, 'Horizons of Modernity: British Anthropology and the End of Empire' (unpublished PhD dissertation, University of California, Berkeley, 2013).
14 Jed Esty, *A Shrinking Island: Modernism and National Culture in England* (Princeton, NJ: Princeton University Press, 2004).
15 University of Manchester Archives (hereafter UM), Vice Chancellor's Archives (hereafter VCA), VCA/7/404, Folder 1, Letter from Max Gluckman to the Vice Chancellor of the University of Manchester [Sir John Stopford], 10 February 1953.
16 Ronald Frankenberg, *Village on the Border: A Social Study of Religion, Politics and Football in a North Wales Community* (Prospect Heights, IL: Waveland, [1957] 1990), p. 171.
17 It was renamed Pentrediwaith in published material, to preserve residents' anonymity.
18 George W. Stocking Jr, ed., *Observers Observed: Essays on Ethnographic Fieldwork* (Madison: University of Wisconsin Press, 1983).
19 James Hinton, *The Mass Observers: A History, 1937–1949* (Oxford: Oxford University Press, 2013); Kristy Liles Crawley, 'George Orwell's The Road to Wigan Pier: An Experimental Ethnographic Study with a Novelist's Touch', *Prose Studies*, 38:2 (2016), pp. 137–151.
20 Pyrs Gruffudd, David T. Herbert and Angela Piccini, 'In Search of Wales: Travel Writing and Narratives of Difference, 1918–50', *Journal of Historical Geography*, 26:4 (2000), pp. 589–604.
21 Tony Ballantyne, *Orientalism and Race* (London: Palgrave Macmillan, 2001), pp. 38–41.
22 Frankenberg, *Village on the Border*, pp. 18–19 (italics in the original).
23 Frankenberg, *Village on the Border*, p. 135.
24 Frankenberg, *Village on the Border*, p. 155.
25 Frankenberg, *Village on the Border*, p. 156.
26 Frankenberg, *Village on the Border*, p. 157.
27 Frankenberg, *Village on the Border*, p. 175.
28 Roy Perrott, 'Anthropologist on the Home Front', *The Manchester Guardian*, 20 December 1957.
29 Savage, *Identities and Social Change*, 148.
30 Frankenberg, *Village on the Border*, p. 166.
31 For a wider consideration of ideas of 'community' in postwar Britain, see Jon Lawrence, *Me, Me, Me?: The Search for Community in Post-War England* (Oxford: Oxford University Press, 2019).

32 Max Gluckman, 'Introduction', in Frankenberg, *Village on the Border*, p. 7.
33 Frankenberg, *Village on the Border*, p. 180.
34 Letter from Ronald Frankenberg to Max Gluckman, 17 October 1953, cited in Frankenberg, *Village on the Border*, p. 181.
35 For the Edinburgh anthropological studies of migrant communities in Britain, see Robbie Shilliam, 'Behind the Rhodes Statue: Black Competency and the Imperial Academy', *History of the Human Sciences*, 32:5 (2019), pp. 3–27; Chris Waters, '"Dark Strangers" in Our Midst: Discourses of Race and Nation in Britain, 1947–1963', *Journal of British Studies*, 36:2 (1997), pp. 207–238.
36 Gluckman, for example, was invited to speak on the BBC about racial tensions in Britain, later published as an essay: Max Gluckman, 'How Foreign Are You?', *Race*, 4:1 (1962), pp. 12–21.
37 Peter Gurney, '"Intersex" and "Dirty Girls": Mass-Observation and Working-Class Sexuality in England in the 1930s', *Journal of the History of Sexuality*, 8:2 (1997), pp. 256–290.
38 Jon Lawrence, 'Social-Science Encounters and the Negotiation of Difference in Early 1960s England', *History Workshop Journal*, 77:1 (2014), pp. 215–239.
39 Frankenberg, *Village on the Border*, p. 179.
40 Richard Hoggart, *The Uses of Literacy* (London: Chatto and Windus, 1957).
41 E. P. Thompson, *The Making of the English Working Class* (London: Gollancz, 1963).
42 Anthony P. Cohen, 'Village on the Border, Anthropology at the Crossroads: The Significance of a Classic British Ethnography', *The Sociological Review*, 53:4 (2005), pp. 603–620, pp. 603–604.
43 Ronald Frankenberg, *Communities in Britain: Social Life in Town and Country* (Harmondsworth: Penguin, 1966).
44 UM VCA/7/404 Folder 1, Correspondence relating to DSIR grant, 1953.
45 For example, in 1955, several Rolls Royce factories in the Glasgow region went on strike because of a dispute over the status of a worker who had been exceeding production limits agreed by the union; 'Clash of Principles in the Rolls-Royce Strike', *The Manchester Guardian*, 3 December 1955.
46 Mark W. Bufton, *Britain's Productivity Problem, 1948–1990* (Basingstoke: Palgrave Macmillan, 2004); Jim Tomlinson, *Managing the Economy, Managing the People: Narratives of Economic Life in Britain from Beveridge to Brexit* (Oxford: Oxford University Press, 2017).
47 Anthony Carew, *Labour under the Marshall Plan: The Politics of Productivity and the Marketing of Management Science* (Manchester: Manchester University Press, 1987).
48 David Mills, 'Dinner at Claridge's: Anthropology and the "Captains of Industry", 1947–1955', in Sarah Pink, ed., *Applications of Anthropology: Professional Anthropology in the Twenty-First Century* (New York: Berghahn Books, 2006), pp. 55–70.
49 David Mills, *Difficult Folk? A Political History of Social Anthropology* (New York: Berghahn Books, 2008).
50 David Mills, 'British Anthropology at the End of Empire: The Rise and Fall of the Colonial Social Science Research Council, 1944–1962', *Revue d'Histoire des Sciences Humaines*, 6:1 (2002), pp. 161–188.

51 For an overview of how this belief was constructed and maintained, see Henrika Kuklick, 'Personal Equations: Reflections on the History of Fieldwork, with Special Reference to Sociocultural Anthropology', *Isis*, 102:1 (2011), pp. 1–33.
52 Sheila Cunnison, *Wages and Work Allocation: A Study of Social Relations in a Garment Workshop* (London: Tavistock, 1966), p. xvi.
53 Née Sheila Smith, she would marry Ian Cunnison, a fellow anthropologist in the Manchester anthropology department.
54 Wilson did not publish her study but her work is recorded in her PhD thesis: C. S. Wilson, 'Social Factors Influencing Industrial Output: A Sociological Study of Factories in N.W. Lancs' (unpublished PhD dissertation, University of Manchester, 1963).
55 Tom Lupton, *On the Shop Floor: Two Studies of Workshop Organization and Output* (Oxford: Pergamon Press, 1963), p. 202.
56 Lupton, *On the Shop Floor*, p. 2.
57 Lupton, *On the Shop Floor*, p. 2.
58 Lupton, *On the Shop Floor*, p. vii.
59 James Clifford, 'On Ethnographic Self-Fashioning: Conrad and Malinowski', in *The Predicament of Culture: Twentieth-Century Ethnography, Literature, and Art* (Cambridge, MA: Harvard University Press, 1988), pp. 92–113.
60 Lupton, *On the Shop Floor*, p. 36.
61 Lupton, *On the Shop Floor*, p. 75.
62 Sheila Cunnison, 'The Manchester Factory Studies', in Ronald Frankenberg, ed., *Custom and Conflict in British Society* (Manchester: Manchester University Press, 1982), p. 129.
63 Cunnison, *Wages and Work Allocation*, pp. 141–152.
64 See, for example: Andrew Sanchez, 'Canon Fire: Decolonizing the Curriculum', *The Cambridge Journal of Anthropology*, 36:2 (2018), pp. 1–6, as well as other articles in this issue; Zoe Todd, 'An Indigenous Feminist's Take on the Ontological Turn: "Ontology" is Just Another Word for Colonialism', *Journal of Historical Sociology*, 29:1 (2016), pp. 4–22.
65 Helen Tilley, *Africa as a Living Laboratory: Empire, Development, and the Problem of Scientific Knowledge, 1870–1950* (Chicago, IL: University of Chicago Press, 2011).

Bibliography

Bailkin, Jordanna, *The Afterlife of Empire* (Berkeley: University of California Press, 2012).
Ballantyne, Tony, *Orientalism and Race* (London: Palgrave Macmillan, 2001).
Barth, Fredrik, *One Discipline, Four Ways: British, German, French, and American Anthropology* (Chicago, IL: University of Chicago Press, 2005).
Bufton, Mark W., *Britain's Productivity Problem, 1948–1990* (Basingstoke: Palgrave Macmillan, 2004).
Carew, Anthony, *Labour under the Marshall Plan: The Politics of Productivity and the Marketing of Management Science* (Manchester: Manchester University Press, 1987).

Clifford, James, 'On Ethnographic Self-Fashioning: Conrad and Malinowski', in *The Predicament of Culture: Twentieth-Century Ethnography, Literature, and Art* (Cambridge, MA: Harvard University Press, 1988).
Clifford, James and George E. Marcus, eds, *Writing Culture: The Poetics and Politics of Ethnography* (Berkeley: University of California Press, 1986).
Cohen, Anthony P., 'Village on the Border, Anthropology at the Crossroads: The Significance of a Classic British Ethnography', *The Sociological Review*, 53:4 (2005), pp. 603–620.
Crawley, Kristy Liles, 'George Orwell's *The Road to Wigan Pier*: An Experimental Ethnographic Study with a Novelist's Touch', *Prose Studies*, 38:2 (2016), pp. 137–151.
Cunnison, Sheila, *Wages and Work Allocation: A Study of Social Relations in a Garment Workshop* (London: Tavistock, 1966).
Cunnison, Sheila, 'The Manchester Factory Studies', in Ronald Frankenberg, ed., *Custom and Conflict in British Society* (Manchester: Manchester University Press, 1982).
de L'Estoile, Benoit, Federico G.Neiburg, and Lygia Sigaud, eds, *Empires, Nations, and Natives: Anthropology and State-Making* (Durham, NC: Duke University Press, 2005).
Dimier, Véronique, *The Invention of a European Development Aid Bureaucracy: Recycling Empire* (Basingstoke: Palgrave Macmillan, 2014).
Epstein, Arnold Leonard, *Politics in an Urban African Community* (Manchester: Manchester University Press, 1958).
Esty, Jed, *A Shrinking Island: Modernism and National Culture in England* (Princeton, NJ: Princeton University Press, 2004).
Evens, Terence M. S. and Don Handelman, eds, *The Manchester School: Practice and Ethnographic Praxis in Anthropology* (New York: Berghahn Books, 2006).
Fabian, Johannes, *Time and the Other: How Anthropology Makes Its Object* (New York: Columbia University Press, 1983).
Foreman, Grahame, 'Horizons of Modernity: British Anthropology and the End of Empire' (unpublished PhD dissertation, University of California, Berkeley, 2013).
Frankenberg, Ronald, *Village on the Border: A Social Study of Religion, Politics and Football in a North Wales Community* (Prospect Heights, IL: Waveland, [1957] 1990).
Frankenberg, Ronald, *Communities in Britain: Social Life in Town and Country* (Harmondsworth: Penguin, 1966).
Gillespie, Richard, *Manufacturing Knowledge: A History of the Hawthorne Experiments* (Cambridge; New York: Cambridge University Press, 1991).
Gluckman, Max, *The Judicial Process among the Barotse of Northern Rhodesia* (Manchester: Manchester University Press, 1955).
Gluckman, Max, *Order and Rebellion in Tribal Africa* (London: Cohen and West, 1963).
Gluckman, Max, 'How Foreign Are You?', *Race*, 4:1 (1962), pp. 12–21.
Goody, Jack, *The Expansive Moment: The Rise of Social Anthropology in Britain and Africa, 1918–1970* (Cambridge: Cambridge University Press, 1995).
Gray, Geoffrey, '"A Great Deal of Mischief Can Be Done": Peter Worsley, the Australian National University, the Cold War and Academic Freedom, 1952–1954', *Journal of the Royal Australian Historical Society*, 101:1 (2015), pp. 25–44.

Gruffudd, Pyrs, David T. Herbert and Angela Piccini, 'In Search of Wales: Travel Writing and Narratives of Difference, 1918–50', *Journal of Historical Geography*, 26:4 (2000), pp. 589–604.
Gurney, Peter, '"Intersex" and "Dirty Girls": Mass-Observation and Working-Class Sexuality in England in the 1930s', *Journal of the History of Sexuality*, 8:2 (1997), pp. 256–290.
Hinton, James, *The Mass Observers: A History, 1937–1949* (Oxford: Oxford University Press, 2013).
Hodge, Joseph M., 'British Colonial Expertise, Post-Colonial Careering and the Early History of International Development', *Journal of Modern European History*, 8:1 (2010), pp. 24–46.
Hoggart, Richard, *The Uses of Literacy* (London: Chatto and Windus, 1957).
Kuklick, Henrika, 'Personal Equations: Reflections on the History of Fieldwork, with Special Reference to Sociocultural Anthropology', *Isis*, 102:1 (2011), pp. 1–33.
Lawrence, Jon, 'Social-Science Encounters and the Negotiation of Difference in Early 1960s England', *History Workshop Journal*, 77:1 (2014), pp. 215–239.
Lawrence, Jon, *Me, Me, Me?: The Search for Community in Post-War England* (Oxford: Oxford University Press, 2019).
Lupton, Tom, *On the Shop Floor: Two Studies of Workshop Organization and Output* (Oxford: Pergamon Press, 1963).
McCarthy, Helen, 'Social Science and Married Women's Employment in Post-War Britain', *Past & Present*, 233:1 (2016), pp. 269–305.
Manchester Guardian, 'Clash of Principles in the Rolls-Royce Strike', 3 December 1955.
Mills, David, 'British Anthropology at the End of Empire: The Rise and Fall of the Colonial Social Science Research Council, 1944–1962', *Revue d'Histoire des Sciences Humaines*, 6:1 (2002), pp. 161–188.
Mills, David, 'Dinner at Claridge's: Anthropology and the "Captains of Industry", 1947–1955', in Sarah Pink, ed. *Applications of Anthropology: Professional Anthropology in the Twenty-First Century* (New York: Berghahn Books, 2006), pp. 55–70.
Mills, David, *Difficult Folk? A Political History of Social Anthropology* (New York: Berghahn Books, 2008).
Perrott, Roy, 'Anthropologist on the Home Front', *The Manchester Guardian*, 20 December 1957.
Sanchez, Andrew, 'Canon Fire: Decolonizing the Curriculum', *The Cambridge Journal of Anthropology*, 36:2 (2018), pp. 1–6.
Savage, Michael, *Identities and Social Change in Britain since 1940: The Politics of Method* (Oxford: Oxford University Press, 2010).
Schumaker, Lyn, *Africanizing Anthropology: Fieldwork, Networks, and the Making of Cultural Knowledge in Central Africa* (Durham, NC: Duke University Press, 2001).
Shilliam, Robbie, 'Behind the Rhodes Statue: Black Competency and the Imperial Academy', *History of the Human Sciences*, 32:5 (2019), pp. 3–27.
Stocking Jr, George W., ed., *Observers Observed: Essays on Ethnographic Fieldwork* (Madison, WI: University of Wisconsin Press, 1983).
Taylor, Becky, 'Good Citizens? Ugandan Asians, Volunteers and "Race" Relations in 1970s Britain', *History Workshop Journal*, 85 (2018), pp. 120–141.
Thompson, E. P., *The Making of the English Working Class* (London: Gollancz, 1963).

Tilley, Helen, *Africa as a Living Laboratory Empire, Development, and the Problem of Scientific Knowledge, 1870–1950* (Chicago, IL: University of Chicago Press, 2011).

Tilley, Helen and Robert J. Gordon, *Ordering Africa: Anthropology, European Imperialism and the Politics of Knowledge* (Manchester: Manchester University Press, 2007).

Todd, Selina, 'Affluence, Class and Crown Street: Reinvestigating the Post-War Working Class', *Contemporary British History*, 22:4 (2008), 501–518.

Todd, Zoe, 'An Indigenous Feminist's Take on the Ontological Turn: "Ontology" is Just Another Word for Colonialism', *Journal of Historical Sociology*, 29:1 (2016), pp. 4–22.

Tomlinson, Jim, *Managing the Economy, Managing the People: Narratives of Economic Life in Britain from Beveridge to Brexit* (Oxford: Oxford University Press, 2017).

Turner, Victor, *Schism and Continuity in an African Society: A Study of Ndembu Village Life* (Manchester: Manchester University Press, 1957).

University of Manchester Archives, Vice Chancellor's Archives, VCA/7/404: Social Anthropology Department.

Vincent, Joan, *Anthropology and Politics: Visions, Traditions, and Trends* (Tucson: University of Arizona Press, 1990).

Waters, Chris, '"Dark Strangers" in Our Midst: Discourses of Race and Nation in Britain, 1947–1963', *Journal of British Studies*, 36:2 (1997), pp. 207–238.

Wilson, C. S., 'Social Factors Influencing Industrial Output: A Sociological Study of Factories in N.W. Lancs' (unpublished PhD dissertation, University of Manchester, 1963).

3

'He is not a "racist" but should not be appointed director of LSE': The impact of colonial universities on the University of London

Dongkyung Shin

In January 1967, Walter Adams, principal of the University College of Rhodesia and Nyasaland (hereafter the UCR), was appointed as the new director of the London School of Economics (hereafter LSE).[1] In an immediate response, LSE students occupied the Old Theatre building to protect what they construed as the most multiracial university in Britain from having a director they regarded as holding reactionary racial views. *The Telegraph* observed that 'his appointment as director of the LSE acted as a signal for student agitation'.[2] LSE students were concertedly against the new director's arrival in London and they openly challenged the school's governance and policymaking process.

This LSE boycott has been constructed by the British media as an image of the culmination of university students' protest in the late 1960s in the United Kingdom.[3] At the institutional level, LSE memorialises the boycott, seeking to demonstrate how LSE developed students' voices, evident in a 2019 exhibition and panel discussion commemorating 1960s student activism. These explored both anti-Vietnam War demonstrations during 1968 and LSE's closure due to the student protest in 1969.[4] As Richard Vinen considers, the 1968 British student protests clearly intersected with issues of race and empire. Vinen reveals that 'the radical left was mobilized against the government of South Africa and Rhodesia' and Adams's career in Rhodesia was 'an important *casus belli* for the protest movement at the LSE' and British student activism in the 1960s.[5] The LSE protest during this period directed significant attention to both Walter Adams's appointment and the school's relationship with the UCR. Yet very commonly overlooked in these histories is the existence of a deeper structural linkage between the University of London and colonial universities more widely, under the scheme known as 'Special Relations'. By utilising university materials for overseas policies and students' activities, this chapter introduces new postcolonial perspectives on the history of the University of London.

The continued inflow of international students and returning educators from the former colonies further shaped new communities of British and London universities in the post-1945 period. This chapter configures the LSE episode as a key example of Britain's afterlives of empire, exploring the LSE students' demonstration in the context of decolonisation.

This chapter investigates the circulation of what we might term 'a transnational race issue' between Rhodesia and London, examining both the race controversy at the UCR during Adams's incumbency from 1955 to 1967 and his appointment to LSE as provoking the students' radical demonstrations in London. Adams's career, his responses to racial issues and his university governance are inevitable themes. However, this chapter focusses on these connected histories of the UCR and LSE as institutional and societal dimensions rather than on Adams's individual biography. The continued inflow of returning staff and international students from former colonial institutions shaped new communities and cultures at the University of London (including LSE) from the late 1960s. These overseas students' radical activities within Britain helped to highlight and challenge racial issues and postcolonial outlooks within British universities and among students. Britain's 1960s student counterculture was shaped by these colonial networks, which brought the colonial empire's race and decolonisation issues 'home'. Comprehending the intertwined and previously overlooked relationships between British universities and former colonial universities requires us to appreciate the ways in which modern Britain has been transformed through higher-educational institutions throughout the colonial and postcolonial eras.

The UCR and Walter Adams

In 1945, the Asquith and Elliot Commissions reported their recommendations for the foundation and governance of universities across Britain's colonies. In line with Britain's postwar colonial development policies, new university colleges were opened in Africa, Asia and the Caribbean. The Inter-University Council for Higher Education in the Colonies (later Inter-University Council for Higher Education Overseas and hereafter IUC) was established to forge educational ties between British universities and new colonial university institutions. To teach and research in the colonies, the IUC recruited and sent over 8,000 educational experts for academic, library, administrative and technician staff positions between 1946 and 1981.[6] The University of London was affiliated with these new colleges to promote its academic standard and export the 'London-style' university system in the postwar era.[7] Their inter-institutional collaboration was principally represented in the scheme of 'Special Relations', through which eight new affiliated colonial university colleges awarded local students University of London degrees. As the UCR was the last partner university relationship to survive, it was institutionally and individually connected to the educational and cultural afterlives of empire. Amid the dying embers of the British Empire, this persistent, lasting interaction between universities exposes the lingering academic legacies of British colonialism in the era of decolonisation. The activities of the IUC and the University of London reveal how the broader implanting of British-style university systems in former colonies was a means to maintain Britain's soft power at the end of empire and in the post-independence era.[8]

In 1952, the UCR was first opened as a local college. As the government of the Union of South Africa announced that 'native' African students from outside the Union would not be permitted in its educational institutions from 1953, the Federation of (North and South) Rhodesia and Nyasaland (known as the Central African Federation) became determined to establish a joint college to offer higher education to African students. Initially, Southern Rhodesia opposed the concept of a multiracial institution but dramatically changed to appear more racially progressive due to the restrictions in apartheid South Africa. Southern Rhodesia's attitude of cooperating with the federal university ran parallel to the metropolitan government's policy for continuing British imperial ideology post-1945.[9] As Bill Schwarz outlines, the creation and failure of the Central African Federation was the story of a white settler-supremacist union desperately seeking the façade of 'multi-racial partnership'.[10] In this same context, the British Colonial Office led the setting up of the Special Committee on the Higher Education for Africans (hereafter the Committee), chaired by Alexander Carr-Saunders, director of LSE from 1937 to 1957 and chairman of the IUC from 1951 to 1956. Although the Committee stated its task was 'quite independent from the present proposals for the political federation of the Central African territories', the UCR was not totally divorced from these metropolitan and local political issues.[11] At Carr-Saunders's direct suggestion, Walter Adams joined the process of transforming the UCR into a federal and multiracial institution as secretary of the Committee.[12] Reflecting on the Carr-Saunders Committee's report, the UCR was thus redesigned to serve the regional needs of the Central African Federation's territories as a vehicle for inter-territorial and multiracial collaboration. In doing so, the UCR was granted a Royal Charter in 1955 and Walter Adams was appointed as its first principal. It applied to the scheme of 'Special Relations' during the next year, with students being registered and prepared for London degrees, except for the Faculty of Medicine, which was affiliated to the University of Birmingham. Through these, the multiracial principle was the most important and commonly held value not only for the UCR but also for the other colonial universities associated with the IUC and the University of London. It was the metropolitan initiative for local colonial colleges from the Asquith Commission. However, the UCR was thought of as a British-style university, rather than as an African higher-education institution.

Figure 3.1 Sir Walter Adams by Godfrey Argent, 1 July 1969, © National Portrait Gallery, London.

Before joining the UCR, Walter Adams was a lecturer in history at University College London. He then worked at the Academic Assistance Council from 1933, where he administered national and international universities and helped refugee European scholars. He was appointed secretary of LSE during the Second World War. In 1946, Adams held the first secretary position of both the IUC and the Colonial University Grants Advisory Committee, which enabled him to attend key meetings for operating the 'Special Relations' of the University of London.[13] Throughout his career of communicating with scholars from Britain and Europe, he was well known not only in Africa and British territories but also in the USA and Canada for his role in developing new universities. As secretary of the IUC, he played a significant role in opening many new colonial universities in Africa, South Asia and the Caribbean before becoming the principal of the UCR, operating in a politically complex situation in which the issue of 'race relations' featured prominently.

In response to an official request by the Central African Federation government, the IUC assisted in the foundation of the UCR.[14] Alexander Carr-Saunders and Walter Adams had both been working together through LSE, the IUC and the University of London and had been closely involved in setting up the UCR. As Michael Gelfand observes, despite local Europeans' reluctance in the Central African Federation, on behalf of the IUC, Carr-Saunders and Adams promoted the idea of a racially harmonious institution in line with British official policies for the colonial universities.[15] Adams was also able to maintain the UCR as a federal and independent university, despite the dissolution of the Federation of Rhodesia and Nyasaland at the end of 1963. Understanding these institutional and individual connections between London and Rhodesia provides us with a more detailed picture of how the political culture of British higher-education institutions and their educationalists shaped a 'new' Commonwealth ideal and postcolonial universities. At the same time, the multiracial principle of colonial universities transcended metropolitan politics, as it was working in support of British policy in relation to the Central African Federation. The story of the UCR reveals another level of political issues that existed in the development of colonial universities and how the Colonial Office and white settlers attempted to make multiracial institutions that maintained their imperial authority.

However, in practice the UCR used racially segregated accommodation from its inception; for European students and African and Asian/other mixed students, segregation was a feature of student life. A pioneering historian in African history, Terence Ranger recalled that during his time in the UCR from 1957, 'my powers were widely resented' as a young warden of all three halls of residence and a Rhodesian tradition of residential segregation and white supremacy was strongly maintained.[16] There were sixty-eight first-year students, including eight African students and one African woman, Sarah Chavunduka. Sarah had no accommodation as there were only three halls: for European male students, for African and other male students, and for European female students. From 1960 to 1966, almost a quarter of students at the UCR were African.[17]

Following Rhodesia's Unilateral Declaration of Independence (UDI) in November 1965, the UCR's ideals of 'a multiracial institution' and 'academic freedom' were jeopardised by the white-supremacist pariah regime. Despite colonial universities' institutional autonomy from the government, endangered academic freedom became one of the main concerns for the Inter-University Council and the University of London.[18] In the middle of this sensitive process, Walter Adams was criticised for his inaction and lack of opposition to the UDI. When Adams had been recommended for the position of principal of the UCR in 1954, Alexander Carr-Saunders was asked about Adams's views on race given that the multiracial identity was one of the most important values for the board of the UCR. He stated:

> Adams does feel very strongly that Africans should have the same educational opportunities as Europeans. ... [but he] is not the sort of man who gives expression to large views on racial policy; his attitude would find expression in and around practical questions ... Indeed, there is no fear that he would be an unjudicious propagandist for Africans at large.[19]

With hindsight, we can see that Carr-Saunders's observation was perceptive, as when Adams needed to give an official answer about racial issues, he mainly avoided doing so.

When the UDI was announced, the news was broadcast in the student hall at lunchtime while the students were having their meals in the dining room. African students were distraught, and several of them were in tears. The announcement coincided with final examinations and hence there was no immediate reaction from students.[20] It is also worth considering that, unlike their European peers, African students often relied upon Rhodesian government scholarships. Their financial reliance now upon a pariah state may also have contributed to their relatively quiet initial reaction. Soon after, several history lecturers outlined how their academic freedom was being threatened by the illegal government in a letter to *The Times*, entitled 'Academic Freedom under Pressure'.

1. Several students had been declared prohibited immigrants.
2. Students were arrested on their arrival home from long vacations.
3. A broadsheet to be issued by a member of staff was banned by the censors.
4. A pamphlet of essays, dealing with recent findings in historical research, had been banned by the Rhodesian censors.
5. A member of staff had been refused permission by the National Archives to publish documents it considered politically inexpedient.

6. Members of staff and students had had their rooms and homes raided by the police.[21]

Following the reopening of campus after the summer vacation, on 16 March 1966 demonstrations began. Students demanded that the UCR should denounce the UDI and condemn restrictions and the harassment of students by law enforcement agents. However, Adams avoided any such public announcement, instead sending a letter to the president of the Student Union which caused great resentment among African students again. Adams issued:

> a statement by the College Council pointing out that student behaviour, on and off the campus, was a matter for College discipline. This means that political activities outside the College might easily be construed as bad behaviour and perhaps cause the loss of Government grants.[22]

At the same time, the wider European population in Rhodesia became dissatisfied as both staff and students within the UCR criticised the white regime. In the end, nine lecturers and nine students were arrested and expelled from the country because of demonstrations and class boycotts.[23] This is a main reason why Adams's neutral attitude was criticised by both critics and supporters of the UDI, as well as by the UCR's staff and students. Soon after this, in June 1966, in the middle of this turmoil, the news broke that Adams had been appointed the new director of LSE.

At this stage, it is worth reiterating one point about the governance of new colonial colleges. The students in Rhodesia believed that most of the money for the UCR was coming from Britain as most members of staff were recruited by a British organisation – the IUC – and their degrees were being issued by the Universities of London and Birmingham. They felt, therefore, that the UCR was a British one, and that Britain should take action for them against the UDI. However, the UCR was largely financed by the Rhodesian government, not the United Kingdom.[24] Although the University of London acted to furnish cultural and educational capital, in reality the colonial government underpinned the institutions' recurrent finances. In this context, Walter Adams's unwillingness to condemn the ruling government in Rhodesia might be seen as an economic as well as a moral decision. As the United Kingdom government was tentative and unsure in dealing with the Rhodesian government and not supportive of the UCR or Rhodesia, the IUC and the University of London gradually ceased their assistance by 1970.

LSE's reaction

Walter Adams's move to London as the director of LSE seems somewhat surprising amid the political and racial turmoil of events in Rhodesia, notwithstanding the fact that Sydney Caine, Adams's predecessor, championed Adams's appointment vigorously. Whether his racial perspective and political career at the UCR would have been a matter for the appointment committee, or how far the board of the LSE considered the likely student response, cannot be ascertained. The LSE library has lost – or at least 'misplaced' – the critical file, Adams W/7/3, that might have shed light on this.[25] A previously published LSE documentary book, which used the material before it was lost, confirms that the consultation and preparation for Adams's appointment was an informal process and there was no student participation in decisionmaking.[26]

From the 1960s, many British expatriate staff were returning to British universities from colonial institutions due to the uncertain political, societal and academic conditions in newly independent countries. Walter Adams was not exceptional, but one of many staff returning from Rhodesia to London. In this regard, the IUC instituted new schemes and policies to assist their resettlement in British or other Commonwealth institutions funded by the Ministry of Overseas Development such as the Resettlement Fellowship Scheme from 1965 to 1975. The IUC arranged these returning staff's academic posts in British institutions and financially offered resettlement fellowships.[27]

Meanwhile, British university students were increasingly aware of racial issues, mostly due to South African apartheid policies, and LSE was a leading institution at the University of London.[28] As Sarah Stockwell points out, London was not only an imperial administrative centre, but also a nexus for ideas of anti-colonialism and radicalism, aided by the activities of overseas students before and after the Second World War.[29] According to an LSE student survey in 1967, British home students were mostly aware of majority rule in Rhodesia and legislation against racial discrimination.[30] However, the LSE demonstration did not mean that they were only discontented with the appointment of Adams and his colonial career. More broadly, the students were dissatisfied with increasingly overcrowded buildings, the quality of their lectures and a lack of accommodation and library facilities.[31] These conditions also provided fertile ground in which the student voices became radical and stronger. Some participants believed that the urban location of LSE also stimulated the movement in the 1960s. A former student, Martin Tomkinson, who studied economics and international relations from 1965 to 1969, remembers that the location of LSE in the heart of the metropolitan city helped to shape their radical ideas and give attention to postimperial and social issues of Britain and the world.[32] Fleet Street, where LSE is located, was a central location, nationally and internationally, as the historic home of the British press and of a number of embassies and offices of empire. The LSE campus was convenient and accessible for neighbouring journalists, and as a result they paid the protests more attention in comparison with those of other student movements in Britain.

As soon as Adams's appointment was announced, LSE students published critical articles addressing their new director. David Adelstein, president of the Student Union, published a letter in *The Times* on 29 October and a petition calling for the withdrawal of the appointment – signed by 1,026 students – was sent to the Academic Board. An LSE student magazine, *Agitator*, published a special report on Adams.

> The London School of Economics now has a special relationship with the University College of Rhodesia: Walter Adams, the present Principal of that College will be coming to LSE, as our new Director. The official LSE magazine ... greets this appointment with what appears to be considerable warmth. It even quotes Sir Sydney Caine: 'I found Adams', he has said, 'a very efficient administrator'. We do not share its warmth nor Sir Sydney's estimation of Adams' ability, ... it is our belief that Adams – a Principal unprepared to defend the freedom of his staff and students – is not a suitable person to be placed in charge of any centre of higher education. Nor, especially, is he suitable is the Director of a multi-racial college like L.S.E., since his belief in multi-racialism does not seem to extend to actions in its defence.[33]

The students criticised Adams on four main counts regarding the events in Rhodesia: his 'unwillingness to take a stand on the issue of academic freedom, avoidance of important decision-making, extreme isolation from staff and students, and administrative inefficiency'.[34]

In January 1967, Marshall Bloom, president of the Graduate Students' Association of LSE, booked the Old Theatre for an evening meeting titled 'Stop Adams'. In response, Adams banned the meeting. However, more than 500 students had gathered in the lobby and corridors outside of the Old Theatre. Finally, the students decided to occupy the theatre, remaining there until at least 4 am. During this turbulence, one of the porters suffered a heart attack and sadly died. Although there was no physical assault or violence by the students, the events received much critical attention from newspapers. The Academic Board then decided to bring disciplinary charges against Adelstein, Bloom and four other members of the Students' Council. As both Adelstein and Bloom were found guilty in March, students once again occupied the Old Theatre and their boycott and sit-in movements continued until the end of term. In the end, on 14 April 1967, the suspension of the penalties was removed and both students were readmitted to LSE. The first strike called by students against the authorities of a British university was over.[35]

In taking this action over Adams's appointment, the LSE students recognised that they could and should participate more in the governance and decisionmaking of the school. Before, there had been no student representatives in any of the major decisionmaking bodies at the school. However, in February 1967, a joint committee of members of the Court of Governors and of the Academic Board was set up to make recommendations for changes in the governance of LSE. In June five student members were added to this committee. A report in February 1968 contained proposals for a small number of student members on all the major policymaking and executive bodies and their subsidiary committees.[36] An LSE student survey reveals that most students desired representation for academic issues, including library improvements and university disciplinary committees. Concurrently, they strongly felt that the students should participate in staff appointments and student admissions, most especially the appointment of incoming directors.[37] Following this, as a newspaper points out, although the troubles were triggered by Adams's appointment, 'what is at stake at the LSE is the idea of a University'.[38] It said that the inevitable clash would be between the deeply rooted idea of disciplined paternalism among the administration and senior staff and the demands for a right to participate in decisionmaking from the student body. Reflecting the student voice, therefore, throughout Walter Adams's incumbency at LSE from 1967 to 1974, the school reformed its governance, especially in the relationship between the academic staff and students.

Impact on the University of London

The University of London suddenly ceased 'Special Relations' in line with the British government's policy of separating itself from the apartheid policies of Ian Smith's illegal Rhodesian government.[39] This change reduced the hopes of the expatriate staff and students in Rhodesia who were against the UDI and wished to maintain the principle of multiracial institution. Indeed, in 1967 the UCR remained the only college under the 'Special Relations' scheme after the seven other African universities and the University College of the West Indies acquired 'university' status. Thereby, London ostensibly stated that the UCR's academic growth was good enough to upgrade to university status. Nonetheless, unable to uphold the principle of a multiracial British-style university across all of the central African region as per the Royal Charter, the Universities of London and Birmingham and the IUC decided to loosen their ties to Rhodesia. London's assistance was gradually phased out by August 1970 and the UCR gained full university status on 1 January 1971, beginning to issue its own degrees.[40] The Universities of London and Birmingham continued to fulfil their obligations to local students already registered for degree courses under the 'Special Relations' scheme and the Medical School Sponsorship arrangement, respectively.

Students of the UCR and British universities alike refused to remain silent about the issue of endangered academic freedom and suppressed students in Rhodesia. In 1970, an article titled 'Plight of UCR Students' was published by Tim Matthews, an expelled history student from the UCR who became a member of the National Union of Students.[41] Matthews argued that 'British universities, especially those of London and Birmingham who have had a special relationship with the University College of Rhodesia, should think more seriously about helping Africans from Rhodesia.'[42] Jack Straw, president of the National Union of Students, law graduate of the University of Leeds and a future foreign secretary, wrote of his concern about the UCR to Christopher Cox, educational advisor of the Ministry of Overseas Development (hereafter the ODM), who had been an influential figure in colonial/overseas education at the former Colonial Office. Straw, on the behalf of the Union, suggested providing funding for 'refugee' students to cover the cost of travel from Rhodesia to the United Kingdom, tuition fees and maintenance grants for continuing study at a British university. He also suggested that the British government make a special provision for expelled Rhodesian students to legally study and remain in Britain, including full British citizenship when it was needed after finishing their study.[43]

A newsletter by Birkbeck College's Student Union dealt with the phasing out of the University of London's association with the UCR, portraying this decision as a reflection of student power and linking it together with other academic and political issues.[44] Beyond the LSE students, Rhodesia was an important and sensitive racial issue for student unions at a number of British universities, both in terms of the relationship with the Universities of London and Birmingham and as Rhodesia became a touchstone of British politics in the late 1960s. As Bill Schwarz's argument about the 're-racialisation' of Britain between 1957 and 1968 suggests, British society was more aware of politics and the sensitivity of racial relations 'at home' than ever before against the backdrop of the Notting Hill Riots and later Enoch Powell's 'Rivers of Blood' speech.[45] Following Schwarz's drawing for the conjunction of Powellism and British-right politics and the idea of 'kith and kin' in Rhodesia, the radical movements of British student unions and their reaction to the UCR issue should also be seen as part of a broader conversation regarding race and racial tensions within British universities and society.

Management of expelled students from Rhodesia was concentrated within British government departments and institutions. The University of London and the IUC, both in charge of operating the 'Special Relations' scheme for colonial universities, continued to show their 'imperial responsibility' by accepting expelled students in Britain, while UNESCO stopped finance and academic projects, following the policy of the United Nations. As Hilary Perraton comments in a discussion of international student mobility, 'ironically, the institutions of the Commonwealth grew stronger as the bonds linking its members grew slacker' in the 1960s and 1970s.[46] Although it was not part of its official responsibilities concerning student welfare, the IUC requested that other related British government departments or institutions offer practical help for expelled Rhodesian students to continue their studies in Britain. As a result, the ODM announced 'the Special Commonwealth Programmes for the education of Rhodesian Africans', seeking support for courses in British universities, which led to a large and unprecedented influx of Rhodesian African students. The United Kingdom government generally recognised 'an obligation to provide further education for any Rhodesian African students' and pursued 'Black' majority rule in Rhodesia at some point in the future, by educating potential future African leaders in Britain.[47] In 1975, the ODM granted about £52,000 to support seventy selected Black students at the University of Rhodesia. In the same year, the ODM estimated that 200 Rhodesian students were awarded funding for their study but estimated up to 1,000 still needed grants and places at British universities.[48] Other educational organisations such as the World University Service in London and the United Kingdom Council for Overseas Student Affairs (currently the UK Council for International Student Affairs) also offered scholarships for Rhodesian students after the UDI. In this context, from 1970, the Universities of London and Birmingham were asked to accept more than 400 African and Asian students from Rhodesia, causing a perceived 'influx threat' from the former colony.[49] While British institutions received individual African students from Rhodesia, their institutional associations were not easy to renew in the 1970s. For example, medical students at the University of Birmingham opposed the Senate's proposal to renew links with the Medical School in Rhodesia. The Birmingham students insisted that their academic association should be resumed 'only when majority rule is achieved in Rhodesia' and the school should implement a 'fully multi-racial' policy.[50]

More widely, the increasing number of international students from the new Commonwealth countries to British universities and their unique academic activities should not be forgotten in imperial history, nor in the history of universities.[51] Through the lens of Howe's arguments on the 'internal decolonisation' of Britain, we can see that the student protests and activities at LSE and the University of London demonstrate a process of internal decolonisation within Britain's universities.[52] Radical ideology and the colonial/overseas background of the international students helped to form consciously postcolonial cultures at London universities and in British society. By 1969, one in every three of LSE's 4,000 students came from overseas. As Student Union President Christopher Pryce explained, the school's involvement in radical social movements was 'because of international students', along with many faculty members' international roots and ideas.[53] Based on

London's transplanted university curriculum and their University of London degrees, former colonial and overseas students were academically and culturally familiar with British universities, particularly for their postgraduate study. This was part of the metropolitan initiative to maintain or strengthen the 'British Academic World' and Britain's soft power.

In turn, international students helped to strengthen the student voice in Britain in the context of radical protests in the late 1960s and early 1970s. Such students, with their varied historical and cultural backgrounds, likely awakened domestic students and academic cultures of metropolitan universities to the colonial and postcolonial realities of their institutions. These institutional and individual interactions with overseas universities, staff and students, combined with Britain's own relationship with the 'new' Commonwealth, changed the governance and cultures of metropolitan universities, moving towards postcolonial, multiracial and cosmopolitan institutions both in London and across the United Kingdom.

Conclusion

This chapter has shown the ways in which 'racial issues' migrated from Rhodesia to London through institutional connections between LSE, the University of London and the University of Rhodesia from the 1950s to 1970s. Walter Adams was a key figure in the intertwined history of British and overseas universities during decolonisation. The LSE student magazine continued to introduce the director as a 'well-known liberal racist and former principal of University College Rhodesia' in the 1970s.[54] In contrast, Adams excused himself by saying, 'in Rhodesia they called [me] nigger-lover. Here they call me Smith's lackey.'[55] Perhaps Adams was, as one journalist suggested, 'a man uniquely tossed by gale of the world'.[56] Apart from an assessment of his racial attitudes or educational career, the fact that Adams gained a controversial reputation during both his positions in Rhodesia and London reflects a historical sense of different times and places in the postcolonial culture in Britain and the afterlife of the British Empire. Adams embodied the fraught connections and contradictions of Britain's wary relationship with current and former colonies, particularly Rhodesia. LSE and British universities were, in the end, confronted by questions of colonialism, racism and the afterlives of empire.

News of Adams's sudden death in 1975 during a visit to the University of Rhodesia to receive an honorary degree after his retirement from LSE proved shocking for universities in Britain and overseas. Many academic staff and (former) students were (dis)advantaged by his activities and networks. It is perhaps a pity in the history of the development of overseas universities that such an active and chief participant left no record documenting his own perspective. However, Adams's willingness to receive the honorary degree from Ian Smith's supremacist government in the middle of the Rhodesian Bush War goes someway towards indicating his political and racial outlook.

At the institutional level, the LSE protests in the late 1960s are a good example of how London students responded to colonial university issues, including racial justice and academic freedom, particularly through London's 'Special Relations' with the UCR. The LSE student troubles were stimulated by local concerns, including Walter Adams's appointment as the school's director and recognising the importance of student voices in the school's decision. However, they also positioned themselves in an international context, understanding how Britain's national and imperial activities were complicit in the racial injustice taking place in southern Africa. Combining this with an awareness of domestic issues, including the racist riots in Notting Hill in 1958 and the far-right politics exemplified by public figures such as Enoch Powell, radical student movements among British universities sought reformed institutional governance and academic conditions, especially in the relationship between the academic staff and students.

London students' protests against endangered academic freedom and political suppression in Rhodesia created a unique culture in London universities. The University of London and British universities accepted many Rhodesian refugee students supported by financial and administrative assistance provided by the Ministry of Overseas Development and the Inter-University Council. This resulted in an increase in the number of international students and a more diverse culture within universities in the United Kingdom, which could be seen as the first wave of the movement to 'decolonise the university'. The University of London's affiliation with the University College of Rhodesia through the imperial and academic connections and its colonially influenced ideas of race, in turn, reshaped the University of London and more broadly British universities.

In current British universities, the movements to decolonise the curriculum and academia have proved controversial, particularly in their attempts to challenge and expose the legacies of empire and further embrace the voices of students from various ethnic and cultural backgrounds. The earlier activism of LSE students and student unions at British universities in the late 1960s represents the predecessor of more recent movements to 'decolonise the university'. This remains an ongoing project. This chapter has demonstrated the connections between the actions of British universities at the end of empire and LSE and British students' activism in the 1960s. These intertwined histories offer a vital precedent for comprehending twenty-first-century decolonisation movements at higher-educational institutions both in Britain and across the world.

Notes

1. The college later became the University of Rhodesia from 1971, and the University of Zimbabwe from 1980. It is located in Harare (previously known as Salisbury). The quote in the title to this chapter is from 'Dr. Adams and the London School of Economics', *Minerva*, 5:2 (1967), p. 312.
2. *The Telegraph*, 29 April 1967.
3. BBC, '1967: Protest Over Student Suspension', n.d., http://news.bbc.co.uk/onthisday/hi/dates/stories/march/13/newsid_2542000/2542639.stm [accessed 11 April 2020]; BBC, '1969, Once a Rebel', n.d., http://news.bbc.co.uk/onthisday/hi/witness/january/24/newsid_2639000/2639609.stm [accessed 11 April 2020].
4. LSE History, 'The LSE Troubles', n.d., https://blogs.lse.ac.uk/lsehistory/the-lse-troubles [accessed 11 April 2020]; LSE Alumni, 'LSE in the 1960s: Revisiting a Complex Period in the School's History', n.d., www.alumni.lse.ac.uk/s/1623/interior-hybrid.aspx?sid=1623&gid=1&pgid=252&cid=8225&ecid=8225&crid=0&calpgid=402&calcid=1389%20&utm_source=Impact Newsletter&utm_medium=email&utm_campaign=Impact0219 [accessed 11 April 2020].
5. Richard Vinen, *1968 Radical Protest and Its Enemies* (New York: HarperCollins, 2018), pp. 213–216.
6. Bodleian Library, Oxford (BLO), Mss. Afr. s. 1825 (f. 77), I. Maxwell, 'Recruitment through the Inter-University Council', 14 December 1982.
7. The term 'university college' was used as an interim title when new colonial colleges were founded but were not yet fully at the status of 'university'. In order to attain full university status, they needed to develop a high-quality teaching and examining system and legitimated autonomy as an independent university. They then could award their own university degrees for their students. So, the IUC and the University of London suggested and formed the 'Special Relations' scheme for the interim period.
8. The activities of the IUC and the University of London in the development of new colonial universities with three overseas universities in Ghana, Nigeria and the West Indies are the subject of the author's doctoral research at King's College London.
9. See Michael Collins, 'Decolonisation and the "Federal Moment"', *Diplomacy & Statecraft*, 24:1 (2013), pp. 21–40.
10. Bill Schwarz, *Memories of Empire: The White Man's World* (Oxford: Oxford University Press, 2011), pp. 341–384.
11. BLO, Mss. Perham, Box 724, File 6, *Report of Commission on Higher Education for the Africans in Central Africa* (1953), pp. 2–3.
12. The National Archives, London (TNA), BW 90/746, Under-Secretary of State for the Colonies to Adams, 6 September 1952.
13. Senate House Library, University of London, London (SHL), UoL/AC 11/19/1, Invitation to Secretary to IUC to Attend Meeting of Special Committee of the Senate, 14 May 1946.
14. TNA, BW 90/746; see, for example, the IUC, written by Walter Adams, 16 January 1952.

15 Michael Gelfand, *A Non-Racial Island of Learning: A History of the University College of Rhodesia from its Inception to 1966* (Gwelo: Mambo Press, 1978), pp. 211–212.
16 Terence Ranger, *Writing Revolt: An Engagement with African Nationalism, 1957–67* (Woodbridge: James Currey, 2013), p. 14.
17 London School of Economics, Women's Library, London (LSE), Adams W7/1 'The University College of Rhodesia, Background to the Events of March to May 1966', p. 3.
18 Colonial universities were autonomous bodies from the United Kingdom government and local governments following the ethos of British universities. For details on 'institutional autonomy' in colonial institutions, see Sarah Stockwell, 'Imperial Liberalism and Institution Building at the End of Empire in Africa', *The Journal of Imperial and Commonwealth History*, 46:5 (2018), pp. 1009–1033.
19 LSE, Adams W/3/1, Carr-Saunders to Hodson, 17 June 1954.
20 Gelfand, *A Non-Racial Island of Learning*, p. 255.
21 Gelfand, *A Non-Racial Island of Learning*, p. 258.
22 Gelfand, *A Non-Racial Island of Learning*, p. 260.
23 Blessing Makunike, 'The Zimbabwe Student Movement: Love-Hate Relationship with Government?', *Journal of Student Affairs in Africa*, 3:1 (2015), pp. 35–48.
24 Gelfand, *A Non-Racial Island of Learning*, p. 258.
25 As of February 2021, the file is listed as 'Missing', https://archives.lse.ac.uk/Record.aspx?src=CalmView.Catalog&id=ADAMS+W%2f7%2f3 [accessed 7 February 2021].
26 Tessa Blackstone, *Students in Conflict LSE in 1967* (London: London School of Economics and Political Science, 1970), p. 153.
27 I. C. M. Maxwell, *Universities in Partnership: The Inter-University Council and the Growth of Higher Education in Developing Countries 1946–70* (Edinburgh: Scottish Academic Press, 1980), p. 44.
28 See newspapers and London student magazines about racial issues from Rhodesia and South Africa, located in SHL, UoL/AC 11/15/14.
29 Sarah Stockwell, *The British End of the British Empire* (Cambridge: Cambridge University Press, 2018), p. 107.
30 Blackstone, *Students in Conflict*, p. 42.
31 Blackstone, *Students in Conflict*, p. 108.
32 LSE History, 'The LSE Troubles'.
33 LSE, Adams W7/2, 'LSE's New Director a Report on Walter Adams', *Agitator*, n.d.
34 LSE, Adams W7/2, Open Committee and LSE Socialist Society, 'LSE, What It Is: and How We Fought It', 26 April 1967.
35 Blackstone, *Students in Conflict*, p. xxi.
36 Blackstone, *Students in Conflict*, p. 134.
37 See, for example, LSE, Adams W7/2, Open Committee and LSE Socialist Society, 'LSE, What It Is and How We Fought It', 26 April 1967.
38 'Student Power', no newspaper title, n.d., clipping located in LSE, Adams W7/1.
39 In general, London remained extremely reluctant to maintain 'Special Relations' with the UCR at this time but sought a way to help discriminated students in Rhodesia. This can be seen in correspondences in SHL, UoL/AC 11/15/22.

40 SHL, UoL/AC 11/15/19, 'Resolution Regarding the IUC's Association with the University of Rhodesia', 1970.
41 Matthews was a Leeds-born United Kingdom citizen and later worked as the chair of the Zimbabwe Working Group of the UK Council on Overseas Student Affairs in 1980.
42 *Times Educational Supplement*, 14 August 1970, located in SHL, UoL/AC 11/15/14.
43 TNA, BW 90/1944, Jack Straw to Christopher Cox, 15 July 1970.
44 *Spectrum*, 3:6 (1 January 1970), located in SHL, UoL/AC 11/15/15.
45 Bill Schwarz, '"The Only White Man In There": The Re-Racialisation of England, 1956–1968', *Race and Class*, 38:1 (1996), pp. 65–78; Schwarz, *Memories of Empire: The White Man's World*.
46 Hilary Perraton, 'International Student Mobility', in *Universities for a New World, Making a Global Network in International Higher Education, 1913–2013*, ed. by Deryck Schreuder (Los Angeles, CA: Sage, the Association of Commonwealth Universities, 2013), p. 181.
47 TNA, BW 90/1935, Ministry of Overseas Development, 'To All Institutes of Future and Higher Education', 14 April 1976.
48 TNA, BW 90/1935, 'Rhodesian Students', 24 September 1975.
49 'Influx Threat from College', *The Guardian*, 7 July 1970, located in SHL, UoL/AC11/15/14.
50 Francis Hill, 'Medic Opposes Renewed Rhodesia links', *Times Higher Education Supplement*, February 1976, located in TNA, BW 90/1935.
51 Rhodesia was not a Commonwealth member at the time until Zimbabwe's independence in 1980. For more details about student movement to Britain, see Hilary Perraton, *A History of Foreign Students in Britain* (Basingstoke: Palgrave Macmillan, 2014).
52 Stephen Howe, 'Internal Decolonization? British Politics since Thatcher as Post-Colonial Trauma', *Twentieth Century British History*, 14:3 (2003), pp. 286–304.
53 Florence Mouckley, 'Upheaval among the Bookstacks', *The Christian Science Monitor*, 30 December 1969.
54 LSE Digital Library, *Beaver*, 113 (25 November 1971), p. 2.
55 Mary Kenny, 'In Rhodesia They Called Me Nigger-Lover. Here They Call Me Smith's Lackey', *Evening Standard*, 28 April 1967.
56 Peter Hennessy, 'A Man Uniquely Tossed by Gale of the World', *Times Higher Education Supplement*, 27 September 1974.

Bibliography

Primary sources

Bodleian Library, University of Oxford
    MSS. Afr. s.1825, Higher Education in Anglophone Tropical Africa
    MSS. Perham, 724, Education, miscellaneous reports

London School of Economics and Politics Library
    Adams W Adams Sir Walter (1906–1975), Knight, University Administrator
    LSE Digital Library
The National Archives, Kew
    BW 90, Inter-University Council for Higher Education
Senate House Library, University of London
    UoL/AC 11, Overseas Colleges in Special Relationships

Secondary sources

'Dr. Adams and the London School of Economics', *Minerva*, 5:2 (1967), p. 312.

BBC, '1967: Protest Over Student Suspension', n.d., http://news.bbc.co.uk/onthisday/hi/dates/stories/march/13/newsid_2542000/2542639.stm [accessed 11 April 2020].

BBC, '1969, Once a Rebel', n.d., http://news.bbc.co.uk/onthisday/hi/witness/january/24/newsid_2639000/2639609.stm [accessed 11 April 2020].

Blackstone, Tessa, *Students in Conflict LSE in 1967* (London: London School of Economics and Political Science, 1970).

Collins, Michael, 'Decolonisation and the "Federal Moment"', *Diplomacy & Statecraft*, 24:1 (2013), pp. 21–40.

Gelfand, Michael, *A Non-Racial Island of Learning: A History of the University College of Rhodesia from its Inception to 1966* (Gwelo: Mambo Press, 1978).

Hennessy, Peter, 'A Man Uniquely Tossed by Gale of the World', *Times Higher Education Supplement*, 27 September 1974.

Hill, Francis, 'Medic Opposes Renewed Rhodesia links', *Times Higher Education Supplement*, February 1976, located in TNA, BW 90/1935.

Howe, Stephen, 'Internal Decolonization? British Politics since Thatcher as Post-Colonial Trauma', *Twentieth Century British History*, 14:3 (2003), pp. 286–304.

Kenny, Mary, 'In Rhodesia They Called Me Nigger-Lover. Here They Call Me Smith's Lackey', *Evening Standard*, 28 April 1967.

Makunike, Blessing, 'The Zimbabwe Student Movement: Love-Hate Relationship with Government?', *Journal of Student Affairs in Africa*, 3:1 (2015), pp. 35–48.

LSE Alumni, 'LSE in the 1960s: Revisiting a Complex Period in the School's History', n.d., www.alumni.lse.ac.uk/s/1623/interior-hybrid.aspx?sid=1623&gid=1&pgid=252&cid=8225&ecid=8225&crid=0&calpgid=402&calcid=1389%20&utm_source=ImpactNewsletter&utm_medium=email&utm_campaign=Impact0219 [accessed 11 April 2020].

LSE History, 'The LSE Troubles', n.d., https://blogs.lse.ac.uk/lsehistory/the-lse-troubles [accessed 11 April 2020].

Maxwell, I. C. M., *Universities in Partnership: The Inter-University Council and the Growth of Higher Education in Developing Countries 1946–70* (Edinburgh: Scottish Academic Press, 1980).

Mouckley, Florence, 'Upheaval among the Bookstacks', *The Christian Science Monitor*, 30 December 1969.

Perraton, Hilary, *A History of Foreign Students in Britain* (Basingstoke: Palgrave Macmillan, 2014).

Perraton, Hilary, 'International Student Mobility', in *Universities for a New World: Making a Global Network in International Higher Education,*

1913–2013, ed. by Deryck Schreuder (Los Angeles, CA: Sage, the Association of Commonwealth Universities, 2013), pp. 176–196.

Ranger, Terence, *Writing Revolt: An Engagement with African Nationalism, 1957–67* (Woodbridge: James Currey, 2013).

Schwarz, Bill, *Memories of Empire: The White Man's World* (Oxford: Oxford University Press, 2011).

Schwarz, Bill, ' "The Only White Man in There": The Re-Racialisation of England, 1956–1968', *Race and Class*, 38:1 (1996), pp. 65–78.

Stockwell, Sarah, 'Imperial Liberalism and Institution Building at the End of Empire in Africa', *The Journal of Imperial and Commonwealth History*, 46:5 (2018), pp. 1009–1033.

Stockwell, Sarah, *The British End of the British Empire* (Cambridge: Cambridge University Press, 2018).

Vinen, Richard, *1968 Radical Protest and Its Enemies* (New York: Harper Collins, 2018).

Part II

Writing identity, conflict and class

4

Beyond experience: British anti-racist non-fiction after empire

Dominic Davies

Introduction: The rise of anti-racist non-fiction

On 10 June 2020, three days after #BlackLivesMatter protesters toppled the statue of the slave trader Edward Colston in Bristol, Reni Eddo-Lodge's *Why I'm No Longer Talking to White People about Race* topped the UK non-fiction bestseller chart, making her the first Black British woman to do so – ever.[1] The book shot into the top ten of several other international bestseller lists too, where it was included alongside influential academic studies and memoirs by prominent Black figures, as well as a number of books marketed as guides for readers – especially white readers – wishing to educate themselves about the effects of structural racism on individual lives. In the wake of the murder of George Floyd, and after a month of #BlackLivesMatter protests rocking US cities and spurring anti-racist action in Britain, the tradition of anti-racist non-fiction writing appeared finally to be drawing mainstream attention on both sides of the Atlantic.

All of the titles populating these bestseller lists place notable emphasis on the value of personal anecdote and experience, blending memoir with often detailed and cogent anti-racist critique to create a kind of anti-racist life writing that has a long history in African American literary culture.[2] One need only think of James Baldwin's *Notes of a Native Son* (1955) and Malcolm X's *Autobiography* (1965), for example – or Frederick Douglass's *Narrative of the Life* (1845) and Anna Julia Cooper's *A Voice from the South* (1892) – to see that, for Black America at least, the most enduring analyses of white supremacy have been built from the concrete specificities of individual experience. While the genre is less widely known in Britain (with some notable exceptions), I argue in this chapter that a similar suturing of individual biographies into the structural contours shaping social, cultural and institutional life in Britain after empire has been deployed by a number of Black writers in recent years, often to persuasive and powerful effect.

This pivot from experience to structure, or from one genre of knowledge to another, is encapsulated in what the Combahee River Collective, writing in their 1970s 'Statement', called 'identity politics': 'We believe that the most profound and potentially most radical politics comes directly out of our own identity', they wrote. 'We reject pedestals, queenhood, and walking ten paces behind. To be recognised as human, levelly human, is enough.'[3] For the Collective, identity politics connected their members' personal experiences as Black women to the racist systems, institutions and policies that refused to recognise their humanity. In their understanding, experience was instrumental for a properly anti-racist politics, wherein anti-racism is defined as the formation of meaningfully anti-racist policies and other concrete actions within institutions, from universities and police forces through to the state itself – Politics, that is, with a capital 'P'. What they did not endorse was the narrow fetishisation of the 'identity' in identity politics that has, in the decades since, often dovetailed with neoliberalism to endorse defensive and insular movements, rather than outward-facing, expansive and inclusive ones.[4]

In Britain, the 'anti-racist non-fiction' genre blends memoir with social and historical commentary to build similar connections between individual experiences and structural conditions, often (though not always) without conforming to the individualising inclinations of identity politics that are otherwise so pervasive in our neoliberal era. My aim in this chapter is to explore how this process works by focusing on two of the most rigorous and best-selling of Britain's anti-racist non-fiction titles. I look first at Eddo-Lodge's *Why I'm No Longer Talking to White People about Race* (2017) and discuss its implications for anti-racist work. I then offer a brief overview of a larger body of British anti-racist non-fiction, much of which is written under Eddo-Lodge's influence, before turning to a concluding discussion of Akala's *Natives: Race and Class in the Ruins of Empire* (2018). In brief moments throughout this discussion, I will link this to experiences of my own, as a postgraduate student and then academic who has worked in higher education for over a decade. My intention here is to reveal the importance of experience to analyses of institutional racism, and to undermine the rhetorical separation of 'academic' writing from individual biography. The performance of pseudo-objectivity and authorial invisibility often adopted in academic writing has long and troubling connections with the privilege of whiteness itself.[5] With these anecdotes, I want to expose the limitations of a lack of experience that academic writing on racism sometimes tries to conceal, and which Britain's rising anti-racist non-fiction amends by foregrounding experience instead.

The chapter's most basic argument is therefore disconcertingly simple. As the Combahee River Collective observed, the only way to build properly anti-racist institutions that create meaningfully anti-racist policies is to understand institutional racism from the perspective of those who experience it directly. By dwelling on this, I suggest we can reach larger conclusions about the popularity of anti-racist non-fiction in Britain today, that way considering its potential as a tool for anti-racist work while also probing its limitations. As early as 1990, Paul Gilroy suggested that the growing 'sense of the insurmountable cultural and *experiential* divisions which, it is argued, are a feature of racial difference' was bringing about 'the end of anti-racism', properly defined.[6] Three decades on, the extent to which an essentialising identity politics has thrived under neoliberalism should be cause for immediate concern.[7] Prioritising individual experiences and behaviours at the expense of concrete institutional actions, neoliberal identity politics has tended to fragment potential anti-racist solidarities along narrow, essentialising lines.[8] With this context in mind, I argue that much of Britain's anti-racist non-fiction works against such divisive formations, instead blending first-hand experience with longer histories of racist policymaking to advance an anti-racist agenda in British institutions and society more widely. As Micha Frazer-Caroll wrote of Eddo-Lodge's book on 25 June 2020: 'Reading a book won't transform you into an ally, only taking political and economic action can do that – but referring to the evidence, the record of what black people have been saying for decades, is one step towards it.'[9]

'Talking' about race is not anti-racism

Why I'm No Longer Talking to White People about Race has become the 'blueprint for the "anti-racist textbook"', observes Mishti Ali in *gal-dem*, detailing Eddo-Lodge's influence on numerous comparable titles turned out by Britain's 'trend-led' publishing industry in the space of just a few years.[10] The number of titles published in the mould of Eddo-Lodge's book is perhaps not so surprising. When it first appeared in 2017, *I'm No Longer Talking* emerged as a seemingly singular counter to the resurgent white nationalism of post-Brexit-referendum Britain, and not only in the public sphere. As an academic regularly attending conferences on everything from imperial nostalgia to postcolonial Britain, I found that Eddo-Lodge's book was often steps – sometimes leaps – ahead of conversations taking place in those rooms. In 2018, it was given precedence over a series of iconic feminist titles – including Mary Wollstonecraft's *A Vindication of the Rights of Woman* and Germaine Greer's *The Female Eunuch* – when it was awarded first place on a list of 'top 10 books by women that changed the world'.[11] Eddo-Lodge accepted this accolade with characteristic modesty ('we need a few more years to determine if it's really changed the world'), but she was understandably more disdainful of the June 2020 announcement that she had become the first Black British woman to top the UK's non-fiction bestseller list: 'Reader demand aside', she wrote on Twitter, 'that it took this long [for a black British woman to top the non-fiction bestseller list] is a horrible indictment of the publishing industry.'[12]

The title of Eddo-Lodge's book is masterful, as too is its cover – so much so that another publisher was accused in 2019 of 'ripping off' its aesthetic.[13] Rendered in black ink on white paper, with the words 'white people' left blank, the title page captures both the invisibility of white privilege *and* Eddo-Lodge's counter-intuitive refusal to 'confess' her experience to white readers. In this gesture, *Why I'm No Longer Talking* epitomises a somewhat reticent politics that, broadly speaking, differentiates British from American anti-racist non-fiction. In the latter, the act of 'talking about race' is everywhere. From Beverly Daniel Tatum's *Can We Talk About Race?* (2008) and Ijeoma Oluo's *So You Want to Talk About Race* (2018) to Robin DiAngelo's *White Fragility: Why It's So Hard for White People to Talk About Racism* (2018), the soft power of 'conversation', 'communication' and even 'confession' is ceaselessly invoked. Of course, generating public discussion of structural racism is an admirable achievement; greater understanding of Black experience among white readers has precipitated a necessary shift in contemporary culture, both within and outside institutions. Nevertheless, an over-emphasis on 'talk' risks reducing tangible anti-racist actions to little more than white acknowledgement – and, at worst, commodification – of Black experience. As Oluo herself has remarked, her book was intended as 'a tool to help you discuss issues of racism in your workplace, your towns, you schools'; the question, 'how can I better talk about this?', 'isn't even step 1 – it's the beginning of your research on the way to step one'.[14]

I have learned from my own contributions to the advancement of racial equality in higher-education institutions that it is very possible to 'talk' about race without being anti-racist. From decolonising curricula seminars to day-to-day committee meetings, 'talk' too often means 'talking for' or 'talking over', and too rarely includes that other important component of any meaningful conversation: 'listening to'. The characteristic white impulse to find a quick, catch-all 'solution' to institutional racism – something I have witnessed on numerous occasions, including once in a group discussion of *Why I'm No Longer Talking* itself – unwittingly repeats what Eddo-Lodge describes as a 'glaring lack of empathy for those of us who have been visibly marked out as different for our entire lives, and live the consequences'.[15] This is not to dismiss the value of 'talk', but we should caution against the decoupling of such conversations from properly anti-racist policymaking, the latter of which has historically preceded and precipitated – rather than followed – progressive cultural shifts.[16] Eddo-Lodge herself is quite explicit about this, making clear that her book is no end in itself, but a means to further anti-racist action: 'It has been written to counter the lack of the historical knowledge and the political backdrop you need to anchor your opposition to racism. I hope you use it as a tool.'[17]

Nevertheless, in Britain's universities, where Eddo-Lodge's book increasingly circulates as a point of reference, gestures towards 'culture change' and 'having difficult conversations' are frequently prioritised over the commitment of meaningful resources. In support of this, decisionmakers cite anything from a narrowly neoliberal understanding of institutional 'reputation' to ever-deepening austerity measures.[18] In such institutions, the emphasis on 'talk' risks becoming a simultaneously visible and vacuous replacement for the creation and implementation of anti-racist policies.[19] Perhaps this explains Eddo-Lodge's decision to avoid giving too many interviews or talks in such spaces.[20] This is not to deny the tireless work undertaken by countless individuals and groups in higher-education institutions every day, nor to suggest that they are entirely ineffective. But it is to acknowledge that, as Gilroy has remarked, 'neoliberalism loves diversity. Corporate multiculturalism speaks to the needs of globalised capital hungry for new markets and investors. The decorative presence of black professors, like that of black cops, guarantees nothing at the level of institutional outcomes.'[21]

The radical edge of Eddo-Lodge's book lies precisely in its targeting of this pseudo-corporate diversity agenda, which it understands and refuses in a single gesture. Consider the first sentences of the original 2014 blogpost from which her book takes its name, and which is reprinted in full in its preface.

> I'm no longer engaging with white people on the topic of race. Not all white people, just the vast majority who refuse to accept the legitimacy of structural racism and its symptoms. I can no longer engage with the gulf of an emotional disconnect that white people display when a person of colour articulates their experience.[22]

This statement expresses exhaustion deriving from the author's overexposure to a white audience that, hypocritically, insists on access to – perhaps even commodification of – her experience as a person of colour, while refusing to recognise the institutionally racist conditions that have for so long defined it. As Eddo-Lodge explains, the 'gulf of emotional disconnect' that distances her from her white readers begins not in their failure to acknowledge Black experience *per se*, but in their inability to accept structural racism as an experiential reality. This incredibly important distinction is reflected in the book's title, which refuses and educates white readers all at once.

Eddo-Lodge carries this dual gesture, which refuses to fetishise individual experience without losing sight of its importance as a political resource, throughout the rest of her book. In a chapter entitled 'The System', for example, Eddo-Lodge recounts how the 1993 murder of Stephen Lawrence – a racist attack that led to the Macpherson Report and its subsequent revelations of institutional racism in the British police forces – initiated, autobiographically, the dawning of her political consciousness.[23] Throughout the book, she pegs important moments in her own autobiographical development to the historical and political contexts of her time, revealing how they fundamentally impinged upon her experience of Britain and the world. In these brief moments, a posture of autobiographical confession is made but never indulged, always paving the way for deeper institutional critique. 'Perhaps I am betraying my ignorance, but until I went actively digging for black British histories, I didn't know them', Eddo-Lodge concedes, before adding a crucial qualification: 'But I don't think my ignorance was an individual thing. That I had to go looking for significant moments in black British history suggests to me that I had been kept ignorant.'[24]

The book is full of such elegant manoeuvres, wherein individual experience of structural racism reveals the concrete manifestations of the latter without overly fetishising the former. She recounts interviews with real individuals to enrich her argument with experiential detail, while always pseudonymising her interlocutors with the dual effect of generalising their experiences and protecting their identities. These diversions into individual anecdote are always used to illuminate the historical conditions of empire and institutional racism that have given concrete shape to, though never wholly defined, Black experience of and in Britain. Eddo-Lodge's interleaving of auto/biography with structural critique allows for this strategic shifting of experience away from individuals to institutions, and from people to policies. It is precisely in this cross-genre movement that the anti-racism of Britain's new wave of non-fiction is most powerfully articulated.

Beyond experience: Anti-racist non-fiction in Britain

There can be no doubt that the thread of refusal that runs through *Why I'm No Longer Talking* has alienated some white readers – not so much the British National Party racists, but the well-meaning 'Nice White People' – who wanted not to be denied this 'access', but to be told in a kind of twelve-step programme 'how to recognise [their] privilege, combat racism, and change the world'.[25] I quote these ambitious words from the subtitle of *Me and White Supremacy* (2020) by Layla Saad, a British social-media influencer and author. Google lists Saad's book in the genre of 'self-help' and, indeed, it is a didactic introduction aimed specifically at white readers who want to tackle racism through behavioural change.

As Saad writes, it is 'a book that is designed for you [the reader] not just to read but to work through. The best way to do that is to purchase a journal to use for working through each day's journal prompts.'[26] Readers are advised to complete the book in twenty-eight days, taking daily notes that can be returned to 'again and again as you do the lifelong work of antiracism'.[27] Since November 2020, readers are able to purchase a companion book, *Me and White Supremacy: A Guided Journal*, to be used in tandem with the original release to 'continue your anti-racism journey'.[28]

As a diary not only encouraging, but actually requiring, readerly action, the genre of Saad's book resolves the tensions around 'talking', 'listening' and 'taking action' that Eddo-Lodge's book so productively exposes. The problem, of course, is that the action for which Saad advocates focuses wholly on individual behaviours, rather than a recognition and challenging of racist policies and institutions themselves. Saad is well aware of this, and my intention is in no way to demean her work, nor to downplay the very real violence of 'microaggressions' and everyday racism. *Me and White Supremacy* has made thousands of individual white readers acutely aware of their racial privileges and has been rightly commended for this work. However, the limitations of her book reveal some of the expectations that white readers especially have attached, with the careful encouragement of the publishing industry, to the new market of anti-racist non-fiction.

Saad speaks to the connections between personal experience and institutional racism in an illustratively titled concluding section of *Me and White Supremacy*, 'Moving from the Personal to the Systemic'.

> Systems do not change unless the people who uphold them change, and each person is responsible for upholding the system. So it is your responsibility within yourself, your communities, your educational institutions, your corporations, and your government institutions to do the work that you *can* do every day to create the change the world needs by creating change within yourself.[29]

Neoliberal ideology, almost by definition, reduces systemic forces to individual actors; under neoliberalism, 'problems have no source other than those that are held to embody them'.[30] Of course, Saad does not entirely reduce racism to individual actions. Nevertheless, her suggestion that individual improvement and 'personal transformation' is the only work we '*can* do to create the change the world needs' is a damning indictment of modern democracy, raising the more worrying question of what we *can't* yet do – vote for an anti-racist political party in Britain, for example, or legally enforce the diversity of university hiring committees. It evidences a serious lack of procedures capable of holding institutions to account on issues of racial inequality. We should value and encourage improved mutual care, greater sensitivity and critical self-awareness among individuals within an institution and in wider society, and proper resources should be committed to supporting those ends. But if those behavioural attributes are not historicised and politicised, and if they are not matched by meaningful and well-resourced policy initiatives that are embedded in communities, then it becomes difficult to describe such actions as anti-racist actions.

We have to take seriously the possibility that Britain's anti-racist non-fiction sells well not because 'Nice White People' want to improve racial equality, but because they want to improve *themselves*. Your guided journal on 'white privilege' certifies your 'anti-racist' credentials, becoming a trophy to leave leaning on the bookshelf behind you in online video calls. In the worst instances, purchasing, reading and even 'talking about' such books might assuage white people of the 'discomfort' they felt when confronted with the images of racist police violence in the spring and summer of 2020 – a discomfort to which their privilege had rendered them unaccustomed. Such work is important, but it cannot be called anti-racist until it is connected to the proactive making of anti-racist policies and other well-funded and legally binding commitments – everything from individual scholarships to access schemes to properly enforced diversity requirements. The fact that so many are in no position to implement such change is not the fault of individuals, whether authors or readers, but of a socioeconomic dispensation that hollows out public institutions until all but a few of their members are disempowered.[31] This is why the alienation induced in white readers by the title of Eddo-Lodge's book, rather than posing an end to the conversation ('no longer talking'), is exactly where anti-racist politics must *begin*. This is not about 'you', the individual white reader; it is about the institutions that have profited you, the colonial wealth from which they were built and the policies that have kept their implicit racial logics in place. In the end, it is about systemic forces that are, by definition, beyond individual experience, while also being formative of it.

Although *Why I'm No Longer Talking to White People about Race* has deservedly become the standard-bearer of Britain's anti-racist non-fiction, it has initiated a wave of many other titles that, while addressing broad issues of imperial history and institutional racism, focalise their narratives through the individual experiences of their authors. Some leading examples include Akala's *Natives*, to which I will shortly turn; journalist Afua Hirsch's *Brit(ish): On Race, Identity, and Belonging* (2018); author and music journalist Jeffrey Boakye's *Black, Listed* (2019); television presenter and travel writer Johny Pitts's *Afropean* (2019); counsellor Susan Cousins's *Overcoming Everyday Racism* (2019); academic and presenter Emma Dabiri's *Don't Touch My Hair* (2019) and her follow-up book *What White People Can Do Next* (2021); geneticist and broadcaster Adam Rutherford's

How to Argue with a Racist (2020); and TED speaker and activist Sophie Williams's *Anti-Racist Ally* (2020). These books all trouble the same genre boundaries that usually distinguish memoirs or autobiographies from 'self-help' and 'how to' books. Explicitly self-identifying memoirs have fared reasonably well in Britain – Stuart Hall's *Familiar Stranger* (2017), Benjamin Zephaniah's *Life and Rhymes* (2018), Stormzy's *Rise Up* (2019) – though the genre is not so popular as it is in the USA.[32] A number of highly readable non-fiction books on more specialist topics have had notable success, such as Kalwant Bhopal's *White Privilege* (2018) or Angela Saini's *Superior* (2019), each of which makes clear the author's personal relationship with their material. Even David Olusoga, in his landmark study *Black and British* (2016), begins his extensive recovery of Britain's forgotten Black history with reflections on his childhood experience of racist abuse: 'It is difficult to regard a word as benign when it has been scrawled onto a note, wrapped around a brick and thrown through one's living-room window in the dead of night, as happened to my family when I was a boy of fourteen.'[33]

In the UK marketplace, these titles have been accompanied by the rise of anti-racist essay collections, which marks a notable divergence from the counterpart market in the USA. This trend owes much to the novelist Nikesh Shukla's expert curation of twenty-one 'beautiful, powerful, unapologetic essays', gathered together in *The Good Immigrant* (2016).[34] This timely collection was published by Unbound, a crowdfunding publisher that allowed Shukla to bypass the usual gatekeepers of an industry that, in 2016, had not yet had its appetite whetted for the financial remunerations of anti-racist non-fiction in the UK. The book includes contributions from leading cultural figures of colour in Britain – including Eddo-Lodge – and each essay is written in the same generic blending of personal memoir with anti-racist critique that marks the anti-racist non-fiction texts listed above. *The Good Immigrant* was a huge success, receiving excellent reviews and being voted in one poll as the British public's favourite book of 2016 – a culturally and politically divisive year for the UK, it should be noted, and a time when anti-immigrant rhetoric was overt and explicit.

Along with *No Longer Talking*, *The Good Immigrant* was in many ways the first book to reignite the anti-racist possibilities of non-fiction in Britain. A quick survey of just some of the essay collections published since then demonstrates the astonishing popularity of the form: Sabrina Mahfouz's *The Things I Would Tell You* (2017); Beverly Bryan, Stella Dadzie and Suzanne Scafe's *The Heart of the Race* (2018); Derek Owusu's *Safe* (2019); Mariam Khan's *It's Not About the Burqa* (2019); *gal-dem*'s *'I Will Not Be Erased'* (2019); Chelsea Kwakye and Ore Ogunbiyi's *Taking Up Space* (2019); Charlie Brinkhurst-Cuff's *Mother Country* (2019); and Yomi Adegoke and Elizabeth Uviebinené's *Slay In Your Lane* (2019). I have taken the time to list these multiauthored titles because they push against the publishing industry's penchant for books that focus solely on individual experience, effort and success. Many of these collections bring together the experience of communities, refusing the divisively individualistic response to political issues that has become so pervasive in the broad terrain of neoliberal identity politics. The collections by women of colour in particular resemble the collaborative, Black feminist ethos of Black Lives Matter founders Alicia Garza, Patrisse Cullors and Opral Tometi, and, beyond them, the Combahee River Collective itself. They leave the reader with an impression of collective experience that is structurally defined, achieving in their form the same analytic connections between individual identities and social and historical conditions that has rendered Britain's anti-racist non-fiction so effective.

With this brief survey, I have tried to show how Britain's new anti-racist non-fiction is amorphous, multifaceted and diverse, both in terms of the authors who write it and the approaches and experiences on which they draw. Together, these titles mark an important cultural shift that responds – often directly – to the resurgent white nationalism and imperial nostalgia that was made unmistakably visible by the Brexit referendum, and which has been perpetrated through vile policy packages such as the 'Hostile Environment'.[35] It is true that the somewhat exponential explosion of such titles is partly a consequence of the faddy publishing industry, and Mishti Ali from *gal-dem* is right 'to question how far the publishing industry's anti-racism can go when it stands to benefit so much from people of colour's sustained suffering'.[36] She makes the important observation that many of these books started out as blogs, essays and other more accessible anti-racist resources, raising the question of whether their 'bookification' is really code for their commodification.[37] To this point, we might also note the extent to which this work treads in the groundbreaking footsteps of iconic twentieth-century anti-racist works in Britain, from historian Peter Fryer's *Staying Power* (1984, reissued in 2018) to Stuart Hall's many co-edited essay collections, such as *Resistance Through Rituals* (1975) or *Policing the Crisis* (1978) – collaborative projects that, though more strictly academic, have in their form and their emphasis on subcultural experience much in common with *The Good Immigrant*.

Keeping these qualifications firmly in view, the recent rise of anti-racist non-fiction in Britain nevertheless forms a rich and up-to-date repository of information for contemporary readers, including people of colour, long-committed anti-racists and those newly awakened to the country's imperial history by the events of both June 2016 and June 2020. It has proved that tackling institutional racism is not only an academic endeavour; to understand it, and to draw up properly anti-racist policies, personal experiences must be taken into account. In its most persuasive instances, it has broached this agenda while resisting the commodifying tendencies of the publishing industry and the narrow identity politics of neoliberal individualisation, claiming ground through the genre-blending of its form for an anti-racism that works not only in theory, but in practice as well.

Anti-racist non-fiction as anti-racist practice

Of all the anti-racist non-fiction I have mentioned so far, it is perhaps Akala's *Natives* that works alongside Eddo-Lodge's book to exemplify this point. Akala dropped out of college and did not attend university, but in 2018, just months after *Natives* was published, he was awarded two honorary doctorates – from Oxford Brookes University and the University of Brighton – for his work of anti-racist non-fiction. For David Olusoga, *Natives* is not 'an easy book to categorise': 'It has been described as a polemic, which in certain respects it is', he observes, 'but it is also a form of biography, a work more interestingly and experimentally structured than any out-and-out polemic.'[38] To explain this structure, Olusoga settles on *The Autobiography of Malcolm X* as an illuminating and well-chosen point of reference. For *Natives* is simultaneously an astonishingly detailed and often searing indictment of British racism *and* an autobiography of its author to date, suggesting in its compositional form that the two cannot be separated. In *Natives*, Akala does not advance a series of talking points that introduce readers to an abstract, anti-racist rhetoric. Instead, racial categories are 'denatured', to use Gilroy's term; Akala's experiences and examples reveal the tangible ways in which often reified concepts such as 'whiteness' or 'racism' are historically and politically 'assembled and brought to actual and virtual life'.[39]

Natives begins as any life story might: 'I was born in the 1980s and I grew up in the clichéd, single-parent working-class family.'[40] However, though ostensibly centring his personal autobiography with this sentence, Akala's emphasis on the 'typicality' of his upbringing allows him to pivot between the experiential and the structural, a dual movement best epitomised in the author's own self-naming. On the one hand, the author and narrator, 'Akala', guides us through meticulously historicised critiques of Britain's institutional racism; on the other, casually racist schoolteachers, instances of street violence and gang-related crime and repeated encounters with the police are experienced by the book's protagonist, Kingslee Daley, the author's off-stage name. Embodying this duality, Akala builds outwards from his experience of the world, showing how it rubs up against the racist policies that have historically impinged upon people of colour in Britain, and young Black boys in particular.

Akala's is therefore a purposefully genre-meshing book. From his extensive subaltern histories of slave rebellions to his in-depth social commentary on Black British youth culture, he regularly draws on existing academic writing, some of which he even cites directly in the body of his text. And yet, he remains sharply attuned to – and is sometimes quite scathing of – the limitations of academic discourse: 'PhDs and scriptwriters will come to the hood to drain your wisdom for their ethnographic research, as will journalists next time there is a riot. They will have careers, you will get a job. Wash, rinse, repeat.'[41] The implied 'you' in this comment is especially revealing, indicating that Akala intends his book for young Black men like himself. *Natives* holds a poise of refusal that resembles the political caution of *Why I'm No Longer Talking to White People about Race*. White readers are welcome if they are here to listen, but this is not 'about' them or their need to 'talk'. More powerfully still, the intellectual rigour of Akala's historical research and anti-racist arguments disrupts the crude divisions that are too often drawn between 'academia' and 'community', the university and the 'real' world and critical analysis and life writing; in his life and work, Akala bridges these divides, embedding the resources of the first in the practicalities, politics and policies that govern the second. It is this particular interleaving of an historically informed, anti-racist critique, on the one hand, and the frank autobiographical experiences of British racism, on the other, that allows *Natives* to epitomise in its generic composition the practical anti-racism of recent anti-racist non-fiction.

Throughout the book, Akala therefore implicitly raises the question of whether an overwhelmingly white academy is able to produce effective anti-racist writing. It is not that he devalues academic research; rather, he is aware how, from his particular identity position, something as simple as his 'experiences in school' can be used to explain a vast 'backdrop of history'.[42] Akala often cites statistics in *Natives*, but he is conscious of their limitations too. As he notes, only his 'individual experience' can breathe life into 'all those graphs and lines'.[43] By amalgamating his own individual autobiography with structural critique, Akala self-consciously builds a political worldview that extends outwards from both his own identity and that of his implied readers. The result is a grounded anti-racism that rejects both the mysticism of amorphous 'systems' *and* the neoliberal reduction of politics to individual behaviours. It is an anti-racism that is lived through clear directions and aims, not only highlighting to community members the value of education, but also emphasising to academic readers the relevance of their research and teaching to cultural life in Britain after empire.

Since *Natives* was released, Akala has toured venues across the UK to give talks and interviews promoting the book. Living in London, I attended one of the Hackney nights of Akala's tour, hosted at EartH (Evolutionary Arts

Hackney) on the Stoke Newington Road. After a characteristically articulate interview, Akala invited members of the audience to form long queues down the left- and right-hand-side aisles of the auditorium. When audience members reached the stage, they were given the opportunity to ask Akala a question. This was a radically democratic forum, allowing anyone who wanted to speak the time and space to do so, and this second half of the event went on for over an hour. There were a number of fascinating exchanges, but the most powerful contributions were made by a series of Black British mothers who had accompanied their sons to the event. Respectful of their individual experiences, and refusing quick or simplistic answers, Akala's anti-racist work that evening was to build social and political connections between the individuals gathered in the room. He transformed a book reading into something resembling the pan-African Saturday school that, before community centres were closed by funding cuts to local councils through the 2010s (and which provided a notable and much-needed alternative to state-led educational institutions), Akala himself had attended as a boy; it was a space where people were allowed to speak of their experiences and, as importantly, where other people listened.[44] Akala moved beyond mere 'writing' and 'talking', instead using his thorough and compelling research to bind together the lived experiences of a local community into a coherent anti-racist practice.

In his well-known 1979 article 'The Great Moving Right Show', Stuart Hall remarked on the rise of far-right populism that had grown in Britain in the wake of Enoch Powell's 'Rivers of Blood' speech. His observations resonate with disconcerting prescience in our own times, relevant as they still are to the lingering power of imperial nostalgia and the persistent obsession with immigration that has marked recent attempts to ignite a 'culture war' around race. Hall also describes the gap between talk and action, or 'thoughts' and 'class struggle' (as Hall would term them), that the endemic marketisation of higher education has deepened with such catastrophic effects. However, I also believe that Hall's words could be written of the anti-racist non-fiction that is rising in Britain today. Here they are, in abbreviated form.

> [Far right populism's] success and effectivity does not lie in its capacity to dupe unsuspecting folk but in the way it addresses real problems, real and lived experiences, real contradictions. It works on the ground of already constituted social practices and lived ideologies. ... What makes these representations popular is that they have a purchase on practice, they shape it, they are written into its materiality. ... This is exactly the terrain on which the forces of opposition must organise, if we are to transform it.[45]

I will not conclude this chapter by overemphasising the concrete impacts of today's anti-racist non-fiction; as Hall would have known, hopeful rhetoric is all too immaterial when Britain's contemporary political direction is taken into account. However, his description of the power of addressing 'real problems', 'lived experiences' and 'social practices' together begins, I think, to explain not only the popularity of anti-racist non-fiction in Britain, but also its continued importance for the work of anti-racism. For it is precisely by embedding imperial history and anti-racist ideology into the real lives of both those who confront and those who witness Britain after empire that books such as Akala's, Eddo-Lodge's and many others besides have heeded Hall's advice and seized the terrain – all the better for transforming it.

Notes

1. Alison Flood, 'Black British Authors Top UK Book Charts in Wake of BLM protests', *The Guardian*, 10 June 2020, www.theguardian.com/books/2020/jun/10/black-british-authors-uk-book-charts-blm-bernardine-evaristo-reni-eddo-lodge-waterstones [accessed 15 March 2021]. In the same week, Bernadine Evaristo became the first Black British woman to top the UK *fiction* bestseller lists with her novel *Girl, Woman, Other* (London: Penguin, 2020).
2. Good introductions into the historical origins and ongoing discussion of African American life writing include: Charles T. Davis and Henry Louis Gates Jr, eds, *The Slave's Narrative* (New York: Oxford University Press, 1985); Angelo Costanzo, *Surprizing Narrative: Olaudah Equiano and the Beginnings of Black Autobiography* (Westport, CT: Praeger, 1987); William L. Andrews, *To Tell a Free Story: The First Century of Afro-American Autobiography, 1760–1865* (Urbana: University of Illinois Press, 1988); and Eric D. Lamore, 'The Futures of African American Life Writing', *a/b: Auto/Biography Studies*, 27:1 (Summer 2012), pp. 1–18.
3. Combahee River Collective, 'Statement', in *How We Get Free: Black Feminism and the Combahee River Collective*, ed. by Keeanga-Yamahtta Taylor (Chicago, IL: Haymarket Books, 2017), p. 19.
4. 'What we were saying is that we have a right as people who are not just female, who are not solely Black, who are not just lesbians, who are not just working class, or workers – that we are people who embody all of these identities, and we have a right to build and define political theory and practice based upon that reality. ... We didn't mean that if you're not the same as us, you're nothing. We were not saying that we didn't care about anybody who wasn't exactly like us.' Barbara Smith, 'Interview with Keeanga Yamahtta-Taylor', in *How We Get Free: Black Feminism and the Combahee River Collective*, ed. by Keeanga-Yamahtta Taylor (Chicago, IL: Haymarket Books, 2017), pp. 61–62.
5. Scholars have emphasised the invisibility of white privilege ever since the sociologist Peggy McIntosh advanced her famous 'invisible knapsack' metaphor in 1989. But I mean this 'invisibility' in a deeper sense, too. As the postcolonial anthropologist Nicholas Thomas wrote some time ago, it is imperative to think

both 'about ways of analysing colonialism and about the positions and politics of such analyses in the present'. Such ideas have a long and sometimes ambivalent history in postcolonial studies, but they have rightly become mainstream in decolonial scholarship today. The movement to 'decolonise the university' in particular connects modes of academic analysis with a self-reflexive critique of the institutions – and their (lack of) diversity – in which those analyses are advanced. See Peggy McIntosh, 'White Privilege: Unpacking the Invisible Knapsack', in *Understanding Prejudice and Discrimination*, ed. by Scott Plous (New York: McGraw-Hill Education, 2002), pp. 191–196; Nicholas Thomas, *Colonialism's Culture* (Princeton, NJ: Princeton University Press, 1994), p. 2; Gurminder K. Bhambra, Dalia Gebrial and Kerem Nişancıoğlu, 'Introduction', in *Decolonising the University* (London: Pluto Books, 2018), pp. 1–15.

6 Paul Gilroy, 'The End of Anti-Racism', *Journal of Ethnic and Migration Studies*, 17:1 (1990), pp. 71–83, my emphasis. Gilroy has long considered the difficulties of being 'against race', not only for the white beneficiaries of institutional racism, but also for those who have used 'the concepts and categories of their rulers, owners, and persecutors to resist the destiny that "race" has allocated to them'. When 'ideas of racial particularity are inverted in this defensive manner', he acknowledges, 'they become difficult to relinquish'. See Paul Gilroy, *Against Race: Imagining Political Culture Beyond the Colour Line* (Cambridge, MA: The Belknap Press of Harvard University Press), p. 12.

7 For a history of the dovetailing of identity politics with neoliberalism, see Alana Lentin and Gavan Titley, *The Crises of Multiculturalism: Racism in a Neoliberal Age* (London and New York: Zed Books, 2011).

8 For a materialist critique of contemporary identity politics, see Asad Heider, *Mistaken Identity: Race and Class in the Age of Trump* (London and New York: Verso, 2018).

9 Micha Frazer-Carroll, 'Reading about Racism Won't Turn You into an Ally – But It's a Step Towards It', *The Independent*, 25 June 2020, www.independent.co.uk/arts-entertainment/books/features/reni-eddo-lodge-racism-why-im-no-longer-talking-white-people-about-race-a9585046.html [accessed 15 March 2021].

10 Mishti Ali, 'We Need to Talk about the Anti-Racism Genre', *gal-dem*, 23 December 2020, https://gal-dem.com/anti-racism-genre-black-lives-matter-race-literature/ [accessed 15 March 2021].

11 Alison Flood, 'Reni Eddo-Lodge Polemic Tops Poll of Most Influential Books by Women', *The Guardian*, 27 April 2018, www.theguardian.com/books/2018/apr/27/reni-eddo-lodge-poll-most-influential-women-why-im-no-longer-talking-to-white-people-about-race [accessed 15 March 2021].

12 Reni Eddo-Lodge, Twitter, 10 June 2020, https://bit.ly/2HSbFAw [accessed 11 March 2021]. On Monday, 15 June 2020, the Black Writers' Guild penned an open letter to the publishing industry accusing companies of 'raising awareness of racial inequality without significantly addressing their own'. See BBC, 'Reni Eddo-Lodge: Author Makes Book Chart History', 16 June 2020, www.bbc.co.uk/news/entertainment-arts-52993678.

13 Lanre Bakare, 'Publisher Accused of "Ripping Off" Best-Selling Book on Racism', *The Guardian*, 18 July 2019, www.theguardian.com/books/2019/jul/18/publisher-accused-of-ripping-off-best-selling-book-on-racism [accessed 11 March 2021]. The book was Ben Lindsay's *We Need to Talk About Race* (2019), and it used the same block black lettering on white background, although the similarities ended there – Lindsay's book is about the relationship between race, Christianity and the Church.
14 Ijeoma Oluo, Twitter, 1 June 2020, https://bit.ly/36zJAZf [accessed 9 March 2021].
15 Reni Eddo-Lodge, *Why I'm No Longer Talking to White People about Race* (London: Bloomsbury, 2018), pp. xi–xii.
16 This is a central argument, forcefully made, in Ibram X. Kendi's *How to Be an Antiracist* (London: Bodley Head, 2019), see especially chapter 1.
17 Eddo-Lodge, *Why I'm No Longer Talking*, p. xvii.
18 For a thorough analysis of the ways in which neoliberalism intensifies racism in the university, see John Holmwood, 'Race and the Neoliberal University: Lessons from the Public University', in *Decolonising the University*, ed. by Gurminder K. Bhambra, Dalia Gebrial and Kerem Nişancıoğlu (London: Pluto Books, 2018), pp. 37–52.
19 See Sara Ahmed's discussion of the gap between 'saying' and 'doing' as a way to understand institutional power. In Sara Ahmed, *On Being Included: Racism and Diversity in Institutional Life* (London: Duke University Press, 2012).
20 Eddo-Lodge does give talks about her work, but she chooses her platforms strategically, based on a careful consideration of their personal cost to her. She has refused countless requests to appear on television and radio programmes, and has said she might have published the book under a pseudonym had she anticipated the impact it would have. See Nosheen Iqbal, 'Reni Eddo-Lodge: "The Debate on Racism is a Game to Some and I Don't Want to Play"', *The Guardian*, 21 June 2020, www.theguardian.com/books/2020/jun/21/reni-eddo-lodge-uk-book-charts-debate-racism-game-some-dont-want-to-play [accessed 9 March 2021].
21 George Yancy and Paul Gilroy, 'What "Black Lives" Means in Britain', *The New York Times*, 1 October 2015, https://opinionator.blogs.nytimes.com/2015/10/01/paul-gilroy-what-black-means-in-britain [accessed 9 March 2021].
22 Eddo-Lodge, *Why I'm No Longer Talking*, p. ix.
23 Eddo-Lodge, *Why I'm No Longer Talking*, pp. 57–62.
24 Eddo-Lodge, *Why I'm No Longer Talking*, p. 54.
25 Layla Saad, *Me and White Supremacy: How to Recognise Your Privilege, Combat Racism and Change the World* (London: Quercus, 2020).
26 Saad, *Me and White Supremacy*, chapter 5.
27 Saad, *Me and White Supremacy*, chapter 5.
28 Saad, *Me and White Supremacy*.
29 Saad, *Me and White Supremacy*, chapter 11.
30 Lentin and Titley, *The Crisis of Multiculturalism*, p. 57.
31 As Eddo-Lodge remarks: 'If you're really interested in creating anti-racist change, you have to look around you and see where you hold the influence and that is very different from one person to the next.' Iqbal, 'Reni Eddo-Lodge', n.p.

32 Stormzy's memoir is explicitly billed as a '[p]art inspirational self-help manual, part business guide, part exploration of how its author ... transformed himself into the scene's biggest star'.
33 David Olusoga, *Black and British: A Forgotten History* (London: Pan Publishing, 2016), p. xvi.
34 Nikesh Shukla, ed., *The Good Immigrant* (London: Unbound, 2017), p. xvi. Off the back of the success of this first collection, Shukla has edited with Chimene Syleyman a North American edition, entitled *The Good Immigrant USA: 26 Writers Reflect on America* (London: Dialogue Books, 2019).
35 For another excellent non-fiction title that addresses this issue in detail, see Maya Goodfellow, *The Hostile Environment: How Immigrants Became Scapegoats* (London; New York: Verso, 2019).
36 Ali, 'We Need to Talk about the Anti-Racism Genre'.
37 In response to this and the events of June 2020, the Black Writers Guild launched a new initiative to 'give publishers the tools to collect data that will enable them to report on how they are performing where writers from different ethnic groups are concerned'. See Black Writers Guild, 'The Black Writer's Guild', 15 September 2020, www.alcs.co.uk/news/the-black-writers-guild [accessed 15 March 2021].
38 David Olusoga, 'Natives by Akala Review – the Hip-Hop Artist on Race and Class in the Ruins of Empire', *The Guardian*, 24 May 2018, www.theguardian.com/books/2018/may/24/natives-race-class-ruins-empire-akala-review [accessed 15 March 2021].
39 Yancy and Gilroy, 'What "Black Lives" Means in Britain', n.p.
40 Akala, *Natives: Race and Class in the Ruins of Empire* (London: Two Roads, 2018), p. 1.
41 Akala, *Natives*, p. 199.
42 Akala, *Natives*, p. 246.
43 Akala, *Natives*, p. 247.
44 Akala, *Natives*, p. 14.
45 Stuart Hall, 'The Great Moving Right Show', *Marxism Today* (January 1979), p. 20.

Bibliography

Akala, *Natives: Race and Class in the Ruins of Empire* (London: Two Roads, 2018).
Ali, Mishti, 'We Need to Talk about the Anti-Racism Genre', *gal-dem*, 23 December 2020, https://gal-dem.com/anti-racism-genre-black-lives-matter-race-literature [accessed 25 November 2021].
Andrews, William L., *To Tell a Free Story: The First Century of Afro-American Autobiography, 1760–1865* (Urbana: University of Illinois Press, 1988).
Bakare, Lanre, 'Publisher Accused of "Ripping Off" Best-Selling Book on Racism', *The Guardian*, 18 July 2019, www.theguardian.com/books/2019/jul/18/publisher-accused-of-ripping-off-best-selling-book-on-racism [accessed 25 November 2021].
BBC News, 'Reni Eddo-Lodge: Author Makes Book Chart History', 16 June 2020, www.bbc.co.uk/news/entertainment-arts-52993678 [accessed 25 November 2021].
Bhambra, Gurminder K., Dalia Gebrial and Kerem Nişancıoğlu, 'Introduction', in *Decolonising the University* (London: Pluto Books, 2018), pp. 1–15.

Combahee River Collective, 'Statement', in *How We Get Free: Black Feminism and the Combahee River Collective*, ed. by Keeanga-Yamahtta Taylor (Chicago, IL: Haymarket Books, 2017), pp. 15–27.

Costanzo, Angelo, *Surprizing Narrative: Olaudah Equiano and the Beginnings of Black Autobiography* (Westport, CT: Praeger, 1987).

Davis, Charles T. and Henry Louis Gates Jr, eds, *The Slave's Narrative* (New York: Oxford University Press, 1985).

Eddo-Lodge, Reni, *Why I'm No Longer Talking to White People about Race* (London: Bloomsbury, 2018).

Flood, Alison, 'Reni Eddo-Lodge Polemic Tops Poll of Most Influential Books by Women', *The Guardian*, 27 April 2018, www.theguardian.com/books/2018/apr/27/reni-eddo-lodge-poll-most-influential-women-why-im-no-longer-talking-to-white-people-about-race [accessed 25 November 2021].

Flood, Alison, 'Black British Authors Top UK Book Charts in Wake of BLM Protests', *The Guardian*, 10 June 2020, www.theguardian.com/books/2020/jun/10/black-british-authors-uk-book-charts-blm-bernardine-evaristo-reni-eddo-lodge-waterstones [accessed 25 November 2021].

Frazer-Carroll, Micha, 'Reading about Racism Won't Turn You into an Ally – But It's a Step Towards It", *The Independent*, 25 June 2020, www.independent.co.uk/arts-entertainment/books/features/reni-eddo-lodge-racism-why-im-no-longer-talking-white-people-about-race-a9585046.html [accessed 25 November 2021].

Gilroy, Paul, 'The End of Anti-Racism', *Journal of Ethnic and Migration Studies*, 17:1 (1990), pp. 71–83.

Gilroy, Paul, *Against Race: Imagining Political Culture Beyond the Colour Line* (Cambridge, MA: The Belknap Press of Harvard University Press).

Goodfellow, Maya, *The Hostile Environment: How Immigrants Became Scapegoats* (London and New York: Verso, 2019).

Hall, Stuart, 'The Great Moving Right Show', *Marxism Today* (January 1979), pp. 14–20.

Heider, Asad, *Mistaken Identity: Race and Class in the Age of Trump* (London; New York: Verso, 2018).

Holmwood, John, 'Race and the Neoliberal University: Lessons from the Public University', in *Decolonising the University*, ed. by Gurminder K. Bhambra, Dalia Gebrial and Kerem Nişancıoğlu (London: Pluto Books, 2018), pp. 37–52.

Iqbal, Nosheen, 'Reni Eddo-Lodge: "The Debate on Racism is a Game to Some and I Don't Want to Play"', *The Guardian*, 21 June 2020, www.theguardian.com/books/2020/jun/21/reni-eddo-lodge-uk-book-charts-debate-racism-game-some-dont-want-to-play [accessed 25 November 2021].

Kendi, Ibram X., *How to Be an Antiracist* (London: Bodley Head, 2019).

Lamore, Eric D., 'The Futures of African American Life Writing', *a/b: Auto/Biography Studies*, 27:1 (Summer 2012), pp. 1–18.

Lentin, Alana and Gavan Titley, *The Crises of Multiculturalism: Racism in a Neoliberal Age* (London; New York: Zed Books, 2011).

McIntosh, Peggy, 'White Privilege: Unpacking the Invisible Knapsack', in *Understanding Prejudice and Discrimination*, ed. by Scott Plous (New York: McGraw-Hill Education, 2002), pp. 191–196.

Olusoga, David, *Black and British: A Forgotten History* (London: Pan Publishing, 2016).

Olusoga, David, 'Natives by Akala Review – the Hip-Hop Artist on Race and Class in the Ruins of Empire', *The Guardian*, 24 May 2018, www.theguardian.com/books/2018/may/24/natives-race-class-ruins-empire-akala-review [accessed 25 November 2021].

Saad, Layla, *Me and White Supremacy: How to Recognise Your Privilege, Combat Racism and Change the World* (London: Quercus, 2020).

Saad, Layla, *Me and White Supremacy: A Guided Journal* (London: Quercus Books, 2020).

Shukla, Nikesh, ed., *The Good Immigrant* (London: Unbound, 2017).

Shukla, Nikesh and Chimene Syleyman, eds, *The Good Immigrant USA: 26 Writers Reflect on America* (London: Dialogue Books, 2019).

Smith, Barbara, 'Interview with Keeanga Yamahtta-Taylor', in *How We Get Free: Black Feminism and the Combahee River Collective*, ed. by Keeanga-Yamahtta Taylor (Chicago, IL: Haymarket Books, 2017), pp. 29–69.

Thomas, Nicholas, *Colonialism's Culture* (Princeton, NJ: Princeton University Press, 1994).

Yancy, George and Paul Gilroy, 'What "Black Lives" Means in Britain', *The New York Times*, 1 October 2015, https://opinionator.blogs.nytimes.com/2015/10/01/paul-gilroy-what-black-means-in-britain [accessed 25 November 2021].

5

Empire, war and class in Graham Swift's *Last Orders* (1996)

Ed Dodson

Hilary Mantel might be best known in the twenty-first century for her Booker Prize-winning depictions of Tudor England, yet certain of Mantel's earlier novels, including *A Change of Climate* (1994), track the exploits of English men and women who travel to former British colonial outposts. When the protagonists of *A Change of Climate* return from southern Africa to East Anglia, they find themselves unsettled, discovering 'it is hard to sit in the fitful English sunshine' and pondering whether it is possible to ever wholly 'return from Africa'.[1] Empire pervades contemporary English fiction and its impact is pronounced even in the work of white writers who, for the most part, are separated from postcolonial scrutiny on biographical or racial grounds.[2] While Mantel explores the haunting, violent legacies of colonialism in South Africa and Bechuanaland, J. G. Ballard's *Cocaine Nights* (1996) envisions expatriate life on the Costa del Sol as an intra-European form of neocolonialism. In *On Chesil Beach* (2007), Ian McEwan situates his narrative of sexual liberation within the context of postwar decolonisation, while David Mitchell's *Black Swan Green* (2006) narrates the disturbing internalisation of the rhetoric of the Falklands War by way of its jingoistic teenage protagonist.

Postcolonial literary analysis – that is, analysis directed towards the questions of race, empire and decolonisation that form the purview of this book – is applied typically to Black and Asian writers. Another way of putting this, within the context of postwar British literature at least, is that postcolonial reading methods have developed in response to the work of writers such as Salman Rushdie, Hanif Kureishi and Zadie Smith. Yet this means that general surveys of postwar and contemporary English or British literature frequently use 'postcolonial' as a euphemism for 'non-white', and this becomes a way of lumping all such writers under one heading.[3]

Such literary categorisations are often tied to authors' biographies. This is true for gender and sexuality as much as for race. Most of the writers classified as postcolonial in these surveys – who are sometimes called 'Black British' writers – were born in, or their parents were born in, (former) British colonies.⁴ As a result, they are perceived to have a particular investment in postcolonial questions of race and empire – a perception that is often, but by no means always, true.⁵ Several critics have resisted such racial categorisation by arguing that white writers from Scotland, Wales or Northern Ireland might also be considered postcolonial (or at least brought productively into postcolonial conversations) and a parallel is suggested between the 'peripheries' of the Empire and the 'peripheries' of the UK, especially in the era of devolution.⁶

One can resist racial categorisation further by making a distinction between postcolonial authors and postcolonial texts. As a white Englishman with no personal or familial connections to empire, Graham Swift would not usually be viewed as a postcolonial *author*; his biography is not postcolonial. In much postcolonial criticism there is an implicit link between postcolonial author and text. As the opening page of a foundational work in the field declares: 'this book is concerned with writing by those peoples formerly colonized by Britain'.⁷ The emphasis here is on *who* rather than *what*. Critics such as John McLeod, however, 'push against those expectations of experiential proprietorship'.⁸ McLeod and others argue that 'authorial ethnicity' ought not define what is or is not considered a postcolonial *text*, or what is or is not considered a text worthy of postcolonial analysis.⁹

The authors and texts introduced at the beginning of this chapter warrant further postcolonial analysis, and this line of inquiry could also be extended to works by other writers typically viewed outside of a postcolonial framework. Indeed, I have written elsewhere about the striking yet under-acknowledged roles of race, empire and decolonisation in texts by Alan Hollinghurst and Julian Barnes.¹⁰ This chapter draws upon the critical outlook outlined above to examine Graham Swift's *Last Orders* (1996), contributing to this book's wider examination of the historical, literary and cultural afterlives of empire in postwar Britain, while considering these specifically through the Swiftian lenses of war, class and demythologisation.¹¹

From his debut *The Sweet-Shop Owner* (1980) to his most recent novel *Here We Are* (2020), Swift's writing is both fascinated by and attests to what Marina MacKay calls 'the relentlessness of the [Second World] war in "ordinary life" in the United Kingdom'.¹² But by 'writing across the war … not writing directly about it', as Max Saunders states regarding the role of the First World War in Ford Madox Ford's *Parade's End* (1924–1928), Swift also introduces histories and memories of empire and decolonisation into his narratives of postwar Englishness.¹³ This is evident in the role of wartime colonial trade in Swift's breakthrough novel *Waterland* (1983), and to a greater extent through the ambitious drawing together of the Second World War, the 1982 Falklands War and the 'Troubles' in Northern Ireland in his 1988 novel *Out of this World*. While there is much more to be said in this vein about (the somewhat forgotten) *Out of this World*, it is Swift's Booker

Prize-winning 1996 novel *Last Orders* that will be the focus of this chapter, due to its striking and politically contentious figuration of the Second World War and its aftermath in global and imperial terms. Swift uses this historical framing to examine the effects of decolonisation – the Fall of Aden/Eden – on the dynamics of race and class in postwar England. In this way, Swift takes his readers inside the lived experience of what I shall call demythologisation, or the difficulties of 'working through' (in Paul Gilroy's well-known formulation) tenacious imperial mythologies.[14] By conveying the power of myth, alongside its painful contradictions and false promises, Swift's fiction does not offer postcolonial subversion or critique but examines the breaking from and clinging to imperial ideas and desires in postwar England.

The narrative confinement of *Last Orders*, which focuses on a single day's journey through southeast England, offers a stark contrast to the temporal and conceptual expansiveness of Swift's earlier, markedly postmodern novel *Waterland*. At the time of Swift's Booker nomination and victory in 1996, this sense of confinement came to be viewed as part of a broad aesthetic and political problem within English writing. Lisa Jardine, writing to some degree in accordance with contemporaneous comments by James Wood, claimed that by contrast with the 'wider and bigger contemporary issues' tackled by American writers, many English authors were 'smug and parochial' and wrote 'narrow-minded' books.[15] Alongside works by Martin Amis, Pat Barker and Julian Barnes, Jardine dismissed *Last Orders* as 'a book about four middle-aged men in a pub worrying about their friend's ashes. The subject is parochial. It is meaningless to a wider audience outside this country.'[16] 'Swift's narrow-minded parochialism' and 'nostalgia for a fading way of life' are also critiqued by critics Kate Flint and Nicholas Tredell, the latter arguing that 'feminists, gays and ethnic minorities are almost invisible' in Swift's fiction, and this novel in particular; furthermore, 'images of past, problematic glories (the British Empire, the industrial Revolution, the Second World War) cast a warm, nostalgic glow over an alien present'.[17] Swift is made to stand in contrast to postcolonial writers such as Hanif Kureishi and Caryl Phillips, who, for Flint, 'energize much of the best of current British writing [through their] forces of mobility and transculturation' and their transcending of 'national boundaries or identities'.[18]

Before addressing these issues of racial representation and national nostalgia, it is important to recognise that such critics are too quick to divide white and non-white contemporary English authors into sealed categories: parochial and nostalgic versus diverse and progressive. In doing so, they overlook both the range of literary imaginings of England and Englishness after empire and the fact that this range is not necessarily determined by race. Swift's non-fiction collection *Making an Elephant* (2009) outlines his literary and personal relationships with white writers like Patrick McGrath and

Ted Hughes, alongside Kazuo Ishiguro, Caryl Phillips and Salman Rushdie, who are typically categorised as postcolonial authors. More importantly, Swift has rejected repeatedly and persuasively critical assumptions about the irrelevance or limitations of 'the local'. 'The London suburbs', he suggests in a potential nod to Hanif Kureishi's *The Buddha of Suburbia* (1990), 'are as rich a field as anywhere, as rich a beginning to a novel as any beginning': 'localness is the key. If you are going to write about things which are in fact universal and timeless, then the way to do it is through the focus of the local ... that small world opens up to the big world.'[19]

Last Orders intersects 'small' and 'big' worlds in two ways, both of which draw histories of empire and decolonisation into the novel's depiction of postwar Englishness. First, memories of the North African desert contribute to a reconceptualisation of the Second World War in specifically global and imperial terms. Second, memories of Aden (in present-day Yemen) provide Swift with a potent symbol of the postimperial 'Fall'.[20] These two historical and geographical contexts allow us to see that Swift's *Last Orders*, as Raphael Samuel writes of Elizabeth Gaskell's *Cranford* (1851–1853), is both a 'provincial' novel *and* one that registers external, or rather imperial, 'pressure'.[21] After contesting dominant readings of the novel as parochial, we will turn to the aforementioned issues of race and nostalgia, and these analyses will help us to see how Swift foregrounds class as a determining factor in experiences of imperial and postimperial Englishness.

Last Orders is narrated in the first person by, for the most part, four men – Ray, Vince, Lenny and Vic – as they drive from their native Bermondsey to the seaside town of Margate. They are travelling, on 2 April 1990, in order to scatter the ashes of their recently deceased friend Jack Dodds. Their journey is interspersed with each character's memories, many of which return to their respective experiences of the Second World War. These wartime memories act as the glue which holds the protagonists together; Ray and Jack became best friends on the battlefield; 'somewhere in the same desert Lenny ["Gunner"] Tate was advancing and retreating, though we never knew him then';[22] Vic was in the Navy during the war; and Vince – 'a war baby' (p. 156) – was adopted by Jack and his wife Amy after his parents were killed in the Blitz. Lenny's dad was also killed in the war.

For Ingrid Gunby, Swift deploys these memories of the Second World War in order to revise progressively postwar Englishness and avoid the trap of regressive nostalgia. 'In *Last Orders*', she argues, 'Swift has created an elegy that seeks to move postwar Englishness from melancholia towards mourning'.[23] Gunby is keen to separate the Second World War from the British Empire and its decline, her overall thesis being that the latter tends to dominate discussions of postwar Englishness at the expense of the former.[24] There are, however, many important connections between the two, both historically and within Swift's text. As MacKay and Lyndsey Stonebridge outline, the Second World War 'ultimately hastened the end of the empire and the superpower status attendant on it. Financially bust by 1941 and unmistakeably a satellite of American power, Britain was losing the war while winning it.'[25] Consequently, for Gilroy, contemporary Britain's obsessive memorialisation of the Second World War is haunted incessantly by a repressed awareness of postimperial decline. In particular, the 'ugly chant' sung at England football matches – 'Two world wars and one World Cup' – gives voice not only to 'warped patriotism', but also 'supply[s] a wealth of valuable insights into the morbid culture of a once-imperial nation that has not been able to accept its inevitable loss of prestige in a determinedly postcolonial world'.[26] The Second World War acts as a melancholic cipher through which to at once disavow and covertly mourn the loss of empire.

Gunby's separation of the war from empire and decolonisation is not only drawn into question at a theoretical level, by critics such as Gilroy, but also at a narrative one, by novelists such as Evelyn Waugh and Olivia Manning, as well as contemporary writers including Swift and Michael Ondaatje.[27] The eponymous figure of Ondaatje's *The English Patient* (1992) – Ladislaus de Almasy – is described as a 'desert Englishman' and 'colonist'; he was also, as we come to learn, a smuggler of German spies across North Africa during the war (betraying the expertise he gained as a British cartographer/explorer in the region).[28] The ending of the war, described in *The English Patient* as 'a strange time ... a period of adjustment', provides cause for extended colonial nostalgia, expressed in the form of romantic yearnings for the North African desert: 'some of the English love Africa. A part of their brain reflects the desert precisely. So they're not foreigners there.'[29] Ondaatje's eponymous explorer, heavily invoking the mythology of 'Lawrence of Arabia', describes the desert as 'a place of faith', where one 'disappeared into landscape ... I wanted to erase my name and the place I had come from. By the time the war arrived, after ten years in the desert, it was easy for me to slip across borders, not belong to anyone, to any nation.'[30]

Nostalgia for the lost freedoms of the wartime desert is central to *Last Orders*. As Ray's and Jack's only military experiences were as part of the colonial North African campaign, war and empire are imbricated throughout the novel. The two first met in Egypt, as documented by 'a photo of Jack and me, taken that afternoon, sitting on a camel, with the Pyramids behind us. There must be a thousand bloody photos of old desert campaigners sitting on camels with the Pyramids behind them' (p. 90). The setting of the photograph and the reference to 'old desert campaigners' embeds Ray and Jack in a colonial lineage; the Second World War was by no means the first, or last, time that British troops would be stationed in Africa. Ray recalls how he 'advanced with Jack from Egypt into Libya and retreated with him to Egypt and advanced again into Libya. A small man at big history' (p. 90). That last sentence evokes Ray's sense of pride as he moves from colony to colony, from 'Belhamed' (Libya) to 'Matruh' (Egypt) (p. 90) to the 'battle of El Alamein' (Egypt) (p. 100).[31] As he happily proclaims: 'we're in Cairo, in Egypt, in Africa, in the middle of a war' (p. 92). The colonial theatre of war enabled Ray, as his father puts it, to 'see a bit of the world ... more than the back end of Bermondsey' (p. 279). This freedom to travel also allows Ray and Jack seek out local sex workers: 'I looked, and I thought, I want one of those. I want one like that' (p. 89). Here we sense the ease with which white British colonial soldiers feel entitled to take their 'pick' of sexual options (p. 91). As Jack, in fundamentally orientalist and exoticist language, says: 'different place, different rules, eh?' (p. 89).[32]

Vince is the only one of Swift's protagonists too young to have fought in the Second World War, whether in Africa or Europe. But it is through Vince that Swift introduces another military-imperial context into the novel. Vince refers to his time 'in the Middle East' (p. 44), 'the arsehole of Arabia' (p. 103), throughout the narrative. Although these phrases are geographically imprecise, his specific location is named several other times: when he refers to 'the hippie trail to Aden' (p. 104); when he asks rhetorically, 'you ever done a stretch in Aden?' (p. 159); and by 'the tattoo on his forearm, blue and red, made in Aden, a little scroll with his initials on with a fist holding a thunderbolt on top: "V.I.P."' (p. 249). All of these instances indicate the sense of pride – macho pride, as the 'fist' and 'thunderbolt' on his tattoo suggest – that Vince attaches to his memories of military service in Aden. The particular place that it holds in his personal memory and historical consciousness is most clearly expressed by the phrase 'the bleeding garden of Aden' (p. 157). His pun on Aden/Eden conjures up the former colony as an idyllic, heavenly location. It also invokes the myth of the Fall of Man – both the biblical loss of innocence and the historic loss ('last orders') of British power and prestige.

Aden becomes mythologically entangled with the Fall in this way because, as Peter Widdowson points out, in 1967 'Britain finally evacuated its armed forces from Aden ... thus indicating that it was abandoning any role east of Suez and was effectively no longer a world power.'[33] The phrase 'east of Suez' alludes to Kipling's famous poem 'Mandalay' (1892), which popularised this saying as a marker of Britain's colonial commitments.[34] Imperial historian John Darwin also associates the retraction of the 'east of Suez' commitment – 'the most far-reaching change in Britain's world position to occur since the withdrawal from India twenty years before' – with withdrawal from Aden.[35] In Graham MacPhee's terms,

British withdrawal from its colonial base at Aden on the Arabian Peninsula in 1967 in the wake of a bloody counter-insurgency war known as the Aden Emergency, quickly followed by withdrawal from its Gulf protectorates in 1971, signalled for many the effective end of the Empire.[36]

The postimperial significance of Aden was most clearly expressed in a speech by Labour Prime Minister Harold Wilson on 1 October 1968. Wilson's leader's address at the Blackpool Party Conference justified 'the evacuation of Aden' and the 'withdrawal of all our forces from our Far Eastern bases and from the Persian Gulf' as part of 'the emerging pattern of post-Imperial Britain, of the new Britain in a fast changing world'.[37] 'Our people', he argued, need

> to accept Britain's new role in the world for the later 1960s and the 1970s. This is not easy. It has not been easy for any of us to readjust to the new situation ... the rejection of unilateral, go-it-alone, do-it-yourself, military adventures, the rejection equally of Suez imperialism ...[38]

Aden was meant to be a post-Suez turning point and the beginning of 'postimperial Britain'. This was a beginning that Wilson encouraged people to 'accept', even tentatively welcome.[39]

Wilson's hope that Britain might 'adjust to the new situation' of a modernising and decolonising world stands in sharp contrast to a speech made by the Conservative prime minister fourteen years later. For Margaret Thatcher, 'those' – like Wilson, perhaps – who thought 'that Britain was no longer the nation that had built an Empire and ruled a quarter of the world ... were wrong'.[40] The Falklands victory of 1982 was the moment that Britain 'ceased to be a nation in retreat'.[41] Thatcher was strategically vague as to the specific date at which 'retreat' began, but India (1947), Suez (1956) and Aden (1967) would have been the most common reference points in her own and her audience's minds. As Edward Said writes, certain 'British intellectuals, political figures, and historians believe that giving up the empire – whose symbols were Suez, Aden, and India – was bad for Britain and bad for "the natives," who both have declined in all sorts of ways ever since'.[42]

How, then, does Swift's deployment of a highly symbolic (post)colonial location – Aden – relate to these competing visions of postimperial Britain: one of modernisation and one of nostalgia? It is important to remember that not only was Vince stationed in Aden, but he has 'the honour of being one of the last troops to clear out of Aden' (p. 69). This detail suggests that Vince acts as a nostalgic emblem of the postimperial Fall, of the generation who lived through (or was unable to prevent) Britain's loss of status as a world power. This epochal shift is stamped, in tattoo form, onto his body; Vince may have been 'made in Aden' but he's 'at the bottom end of Bermondsey Street' (p. 165) now. A number of critics consider *Last Orders* to offer a form of 'post-colonial critique', through its 'undoing', 'dissolving' and 'erasing' of Englishness.[43] These do not mention Aden, but one might follow their logic to argue that Vince's memories of Aden allow Swift to critique rather than condone the delusions of postimperial nostalgia. Yet Swift is not such a straightforwardly identitarian or postmodernist writer, and he is not as interested in the theoretical deconstruction of mythologies as the struggles of demythologisation at an individual level. What happens, Swift asks, when tenacious imperial mythologies outlast the material reality of empire and linger as afterlives?

Aden reappears in a key scene later in the novel, as Vince is negotiating a business deal with Hussein. Hussein is the only non-white character in *Last Orders* and, in Flint's terms, he is a 'stereotype, seen through the stereotype of a racist gaze'.[44] Hussein, as we shall see, is certainly reduced to stereotype by Vince's 'racist gaze'; Vince's 'gaze', however, is not *itself* stereotypical. In a significant if risky manoeuvre, *Last Orders* situates Vince's racism historically and socially, showing that it emerges from a specifically postimperial and working-class location. In this way, Swift's narrative challenges the one provided by imperial historians such as Bernard Porter, in which the British working-classes were largely unaffected by empire or its demise.[45]

Vince, a used-car dealer, associates Hussein's negotiating skills with 'haggle fever, call of the old bazaar' (p. 166). Vince then claims that 'where he [Hussein] comes from they dress 'em up like nuns' (p. 166). This comment is prompted by Vince's guilt at pimping out his daughter Kath in order to make a sale: 'there goes Vince Dodds who sold his daughter to an Ayrab' (p. 166). Vince's orientalism and racism, as his stream-of-consciousness narration goes on to reveal, is bound up with the Fall of empire. Vince's hatred of Hussein's 'brown bollocks' (p. 165) stems from his fear

> that he knows I've got to smile and lay it on thick and act like I'm his humble servant when what I'm thinking is, You towel-head toe-rag, we used to shoot your lot when we was in Aden. And your lot used to take off squaddies' heads ... there I was once, showing the flag, oiling the rag, in that stinking, flyblown heat-trap he'd be at home in, and now here he is at the bottom end of Bermondsey Street, slipping across from his City glass-house, getting me to find him fancy cars, getting me to say, 'Right you are, Mr Hussein, yes sir, Mr Hussein,' at a wave of his wallet.
>
> (pp. 165–166)

Vince hates having to 'act like I'm his humble servant' because he, or rather 'we', once had the upper hand. Where? 'In Aden', of course. Orientalist images of Hussein as a 'towel-head toe-rag ... tak[ing] off squaddies' heads' stem from memories, or rather memories turned into violent fantasies, of colonial military experience. The rhythm and rhyme of the phrase 'showing the flag, oiling the rag' conveys poetically Vince's romantic attachment to time spent fighting 'your lot' in the Middle East. The shift from the imperfect tense of 'used to' to the present of 'now' signals just how much that pride has dissipated. Central to this post-Aden/Eden sense of national diminishment is what Alison Light calls 'the treacherous instability of former models of masculine power';[46] Vince's macho tattoo, 'made in Aden', provides no salvation for him now. If anything, it probably diminishes his opportunities back home: 'it doesn't seem to help a man much', as Ray laments, 'having been at the battle of El Alamein' (p. 100).

As well as providing a highly mythologised historical grounding for Vince's racial prejudices, this passage also intersects racial and class conflict. This is despite Swift's claim, after the publication of *Last Orders*, that 'I don't think in terms of class. I write about human beings.'[47] Vince resents having to struggle to close a deal with the wealthy businessman Hussein. He feels like he has been reduced to a 'humble servant', attendant upon the 'wave of his wallet' (p. 166). Vince's expression of racism, then, is also an expression of working-class angst against a man with 'a bleeding Rolex' (p. 167) and a 'posh pad' (p. 168); as Brian Finney writes, Vince's 'racist attitude towards Hussein ... is itself partly the product of his resentment at Hussein's wealth and privileged status'.[48] Vince takes a swipe at the 'City' and the culture of deference – 'Right you are, Mr Hussein, yes sir' – to which he must conform in order to make a decent living.

Swift is in politically controversial territory here. It is clear from the extremely offensive and violent register of Vince's language that Swift is not endorsing his perspective. Moreover, Vince's moral character is undermined fundamentally by his exploitation of his young daughter's body for commercial purposes. For Emma Parker, Swift uses 'the marginalized history of post-colonial subjects like Hussein' to subvert 'the imperialism of official history'; the Thatcherite 'myth of English pre-eminence ... is undermined by Hussein'.[49] Parker's statements suggest that Swift gives voice to Hussein, when in fact he is only viewed through Vince's perspective (and for no longer than four pages). Hussein's 'marginalized history' is never articulated. By engaging so intimately with the mentality of racism, at the expense of Hussein's perspective or that of any other non-white characters, Swift might be considered to provide a justification for prejudice – or, at least, to fail to provide a counterpoint.

Swift also risks perpetuating another form of prejudice: demonising white working-class communities as parochial, nostalgic and ultimately racist. As Owen Jones argues in *Chavs* (2011), contemporary political discourse in Britain often presents the white working-class

> as a lost tribe on the wrong side of history, disorientated by multiculturalism and obsessed with defending their identity from the cultural ravages of mass

immigration. The rise of the idea of a 'white working class' fuelled a new bigotry. It was OK to hate the white working class, because they were themselves a bunch of racist bigots.[50]

These race- and class-based risks cannot be avoided in Swift's novel. However, as various postcolonial writers and critics argue, there can be something politically progressive in taking seriously, rather than instinctively rejecting, the postimperial anxieties experienced by certain parts of the white working class (anxieties that are by no means exclusive to, but perhaps felt in particular ways by, these communities). For Yasmin Alibhai-Brown, 'the easiest thing in the world would be to deride ... attempts at finding something to replace lost kingdoms and dreams'.[51] As she sees it, 'the more challenging task is that of deconstruction and reconstruction' in order that the English might 'develop this confident, post-imperial cultural identity, [instead of being] locked as they are somewhere between embarrassment and guilt'.[52] Likewise, for Kureishi,

> It is the British, the white British, who have to learn that being British isn't what it was. ... Much thought, discussion and self-examination must go into seeing the necessity for this, what this 'new way of being British' involves and how difficult it might be to attain.[53]

Stuart Hall specifies the class-basis of this project: 'if you're serious about a multicultural society, you would address the sense of alienation of white working-class people, who have to be won over to a new conception of themselves where Britain's not lording it from a gunboat'.[54] Alibhai-Brown impels us to 'reconstruct', Kureishi to 'think' and 'discuss', and Hall to 'address'. These verbs are all rather vague. How, then, might a work of fiction like Swift's relate to this otherwise rather imprecise theoretical and political project?

The issue of voice adoption – the problem of speaking *for* other groups – has dominated critical discussions of class in *Last Orders*.[55] Lawrence Driscoll has politicised this critique by accusing *Last Orders* – alongside great swathes of contemporary British literature, from Martin Amis to Zadie Smith – of adopting 'the view from above: a presentation of a working-class world by someone *outside* that class ... an extended look into that working-class milieu from a middle-class authorial perspective'.[56] In particular, Driscoll claims that *Last Orders* 'quite clearly illustrates that even in the act of "resisting" their duty, the ideological and economic boundaries in these characters [sic] lives ensures that there really is nowhere for them to go'.[57]

Swift's close attention to his characters' experiences of fixity and stasis – as opposed to freedom and movement – does not, however, have to be considered as an aesthetic or political problem. It is precisely these experiences which bring the thematics of class and postimperialism together in his novel. One of the first jokes in *Last Orders* is that, despite its name, their local pub the Coach and Horses 'aint ever gone nowhere, has it?' (p. 9). It is a joke that the protagonists return to because it doubles as a form of self-denigration. Ray tells himself several times throughout the novel that he 'could see the world', but, apart from his time in Africa during the war, it never comes to be (p. 128; p. 281). As Jack complained to him once: 'it's like the whole world's buggering off. 'Cept Amy [his wife] and me' (p. 191). Ray agreed: 'me and Carol [his wife, who had just left him] are just getting all cooped up, we aint seeing much of the world, are we? I'll get us a means of travel' (p. 191). Yet, by the time of Jack's death in 1990, he is still pretending that he 'could see the world. I could go to Bangkok' (p. 128); 'I could see the world. It can't all be sea and desert. I could see the other side of the world, Sydney Harbour, Bondi Beach, it must knock Margate into a cocked hat...' (p. 281).

Ray singles out Sydney because that is where his daughter Sue emigrated many years ago. Sue's experience reminds us that it is not the case that the postimperial English, working-class or otherwise, are unable to 'see the world'; the old 'White Dominions' continue to offer a space, both imagined and actual, of English retreat. Indeed, according to Vince, the most important shift for the postwar English is 'mobility ... Time was when the only way you got to travel was in the Army ... But watch 'em all on the move now, watch 'em all going places' (p. 105). This boom in 'mobility', however, is the exact opposite of the protagonists' own experiences, all of whom (including Vince) only travelled 'in the Army'. At one stage they believed themselves to be 'small m[e]n at big history', able to 'see a bit of the world', but now this illusion has disintegrated into what Light terms a 'strongly anti-heroic mood'.[58]

This sense of diminished freedom and entrenched parochialism is tied both to the end of the war and the Fall of Aden. Lenny's most significant revelation in the novel is that he once convinced his daughter Sally, who had become pregnant through 'Vincey's doing', to have an abortion: 'it was me who said, when she came right out with it and said she wanted to have the baby, "No you don't, my girl." ... And she aint ever forgiven me since' (p. 203). He recalls the event in disturbingly militaristic terms.

> And the fact is that when you can remember, just a few years before, loading and firing, loading and firing, whacking it home and knowing that that's a few more of 'em blown to bits, and not thinking twice about it, even being glad, because it's them not you, less of them to do it to you and it's only what's asked of you, any case, what you're trained for, then what's one little unborn sod who aint ever going to see the light of day?
>
> (p. 204)

Lenny claims that his experience of war has directly influenced his inability to empathise, to take into consideration either 'one little unborn sod' or his daughter's feelings on the matter. His military mindset outlasts the reality of conflict. Lenny justifies the forced abortion further by stating:

> And what they call a sin and a crime and against the law at one time aint at another, is it? Like if it'd been five years later, we could've solved that little problem, no fuss, all above board and legal. Different times, different rules. Like one moment we're fighting over a whole heap of desert, next we're pulling out of Aden snappy.
>
> (p. 204)

Lenny was not stationed in Aden. Aden is referenced here, it seems, because the Abortion Act – which legalised abortion by registered practitioners – was passed in the same year that Britain began its withdrawal from Aden: 1967. Swift thus highlights a parallel between these seismic shifts in Britain's legal and imperial histories, two aspects of Wilson's modernising, liberalising vision. But there is also a violent potency to Swift's choice of symbolic partners – abortion and decolonisation – that cannot be contained by such precise historical contextualisation. The conflation of imagery suggests that the end of empire might be considered as a form of abortion on a national or global scale, just as Sally's was on a personal one. Although Lenny enforced this abortion, he later recognises that 'that's when it really happened, that's when we parted company, though it wasn't till later, till she teamed up with that Tyson toe-rag, then started taking on all-comers, that I washed my hands altogether' (p. 204). If the abortion was the moment when Lenny and Sally's relationship began to collapse, 'pulling out of Aden snappy' suggests a hastily severed relationship between Britain and the Middle East: a catastrophic rupture that will be difficult to repair.

This is a highly visceral response to the postimperial 'Fall'. The characters in *Last Orders* seem to experience it as a kind of death, or aborted life. In this way, Swift's novel provides a particularly white working-class and male version of Englishness after empire: one in which memories of military service abroad intersect with and compound experiences of fixity in postwar life. This chapter's close textual analysis has sought to reveal Swift's contribution to the examination of imperial afterlives, foregrounding in particular his dissection of the difficulties of postimperial demythologisation, as well as his attention to the ways in which these processes interact with experiences of class and gender. In Swift's version of postwar Englishness, imperial legacies, particularly as they relate to war, are fundamentally constitutive of national life. 'There is', as Stuart Hall writes, 'no understanding Englishness without understanding its imperial and colonial dimensions'.[59] Consequently, and as I have begun to demonstrate, postcolonial questions of race, empire and decolonisation cannot be 'bracketed' by authorial ethnicity; these questions are at stake whenever we are reading, teaching and writing about contemporary English literature.[60]

Notes

1 Hilary Mantel, *A Change of Climate* (London: Penguin, 1995), p. 250.
2 Although the focus in this book is on the wider categories of Britain and Britishness, in this chapter I refer mostly to England and Englishness. This is primarily to align my analysis with Graham Swift's own specifically chosen points of reference, but also to demonstrate the significance of empire and imperial afterlives to English culture, as much as to the so-called 'peripheries' of the UK.
3 Andrzej Gasiorek, *Post-War British Fiction* (London: Edward Arnold, 1995); Peter Childs, *Contemporary British Novelists* (Basingstoke: Palgrave, 2005); Brian Finney, *English Fiction Since 1984* (Basingstoke: Palgrave, 2006); and Nick Bentley, *Contemporary British Fiction* (Edinburgh: Edinburgh University Press, 2008).
4 Mark Stein, *Black British Literature: Novels of Transformation* (Columbus: Ohio State University Press, 2004).
5 Numerous writers have complained about the 'ghettoisation' of Black and Asian literature, including: Bernardine Evaristo (Alastair Niven, 'Alastair Niven in Conversation with Bernardine Evaristo', *Wasafiri*, 16:34 (2001), pp. 15–20, p. 18); and Aminatta Forna (cited by: Deirdre Osborne, ed., 'Introduction', *The Cambridge Companion to British Black and Asian Literature* (Cambridge: Cambridge University Press, 2016), pp. 1–20, p. 9).
6 Richard J. Lane and Philip Tew, *Contemporary British Fiction*, ed. by Richard Lane, Rod Mengham and Philip Tew (Cambridge: Polity, 2003); Randall Stevenson, *A Reader's Guide to the Twentieth-Century Novel in Britain* (London: Harvester Wheatsheaf, 1993).
7 Bill Ashcroft, Gareth Griffiths and Helen Tiffin, *The Empire Writes Back* (London: Routledge, 2002), p. 1.
8 John McLeod, 'Comments at the *Thoughts on British Black and Asian Literature (1945–2010)* Symposium', Goldsmiths College, 27 January 2017 (unpublished).
9 Michael Perfect, *Contemporary Fictions of Multiculturalism* (Basingstoke: Palgrave Macmillan, 2014). See also Alberto F. Carbajal, *Compromise and Resistance in Postcolonial Writing* (Basingstoke: Palgrave Macmillan, 2014).
10 Ed Dodson, 'Sexuality, Race and Empire in Alan Hollinghurst's "A Thieving Boy" (1983)', *Journal of Postcolonial Writing*, 52:6 (2016), pp. 700–712; Ed Dodson, 'The Partial Postcoloniality of Julian Barnes's *Arthur & George*', *Journal of Modern Literature*, 41:2 (2018), pp. 112–128.
11 A film adaptation of *Last Orders* was released in 2001, directed by Fred Schepisi. The focus of this chapter is on Swift's original novel.
12 Marina MacKay, *Modernism and World War II* (Cambridge: Cambridge University Press, 2007), p. 17.
13 Max Saunders, 'Introduction', in *Parade's End* by Ford Madox Ford (London: Everyman's Library, 1992), pp. xiv–xv, p. xi. Saunders adapts the phrase 'writing across the war' from Malcolm Bradbury.
14 Paul Gilroy, *After Empire: Melancholia or Convivial Culture?* (London: Routledge, 2004), p. 70.

15 Quoted by: Nigel Reynolds, 'Book Prize Judge Attacks "Smug" English Novelists', *The Telegraph*, 7 May 1997, p. 5. In a chapter entitled 'England' in John Sturrock's *The Oxford Guide to Contemporary Writing* (Oxford: Oxford University Press, 1996), Wood argued that postwar English fiction, unlike American, had been dogged by 'a certain parochialism ... an inability to rise out of material contexts and up into some upper atmosphere of the soul' (p. 133).
16 Quoted by: Reynolds, 'Book Prize Judge Attacks "Smug" English Novelists'.
17 Kate Flint, 'Looking Backward? The Relevance of Britishness', in *Unity in Diversity Revisited?*, ed. by Barbara Korte and Peter Klaus Müller (Tübingen: Narr, 1998), pp. 35–50, p. 43, p. 40; cited by Raphaël Ingelbien, '"England and Nowhere"', *English*, 48 (1999), pp. 33–48, p. 33.
18 Flint, 'Looking Backward?', p. 37, p. 48.
19 Stef Craps, 'An Interview with Graham Swift', *Contemporary Literature*, 50:4 (2009), pp. 637–661, p. 652. See also: Graham Swift, 'Swift Response to a Slur', *The Guardian*, 22 May 1997, p. 18; and, 'I Do Like to Be Beside the Seaside: Nice, 1997' in Graham Swift's *Making an Elephant* (London: Picador, 2010).
20 Throughout this chapter, I use the term postimperial to refer to a former imperial nation after the demise or transformation of its imperial status. This is in contrast to use of the term postcolonial to refer to a colony after its liberation from colonial rule.
21 For Raphael Samuel, 'Mrs Gaskell's *Cranford* (1851) is as provincial a novel as it would be possible to imagine ... Yet India is quite an insistent pressure on the story' (*Theatres of Memory Vol. 2* (London: Verso, 1998), p. 74). James Procter, in his analysis of Pat Barker and David Peace, argues that 'the regional novel has played, and continues to play, a significant imaginative role during the period of empire's passing' ('The Return of the Native', in *End of Empire and the English Novel Since 1945*, ed. by Bill Schwarz and Rachael Gilmour (Manchester: Manchester University Press, 2011), pp. 203–217, p. 203).
22 Graham Swift, *Last Orders* (London: Picador, 1996), p. 90. All further references to *Last Orders* are incorporated into the text.
23 Ingrid Gunby, 'Postwar Englishness in the Fiction of Pat Barker, Graham Swift and Adam Thorpe' (unpublished PhD thesis, University of Leeds, 2002), p. 246.
24 Gunby, 'Postwar Englishness', p. 9.
25 Marina MacKay and Lyndsey Stonebridge, *British Fiction after Modernism* (Basingstoke: Palgrave, 2007), p. 6.
26 Gilroy, *After Empire*, p. 117.
27 Waugh's *Sword of Honour Trilogy* (1952–1961) follows Guy Crouchback's Second World War experiences in British Egypt and Dakar (French West Africa), among other places; Manning's *Levant Trilogy* (1977–1980) follows Harriet and Guy Pringle, as well as Simon Boulderstone, in wartime Egypt, Jerusalem and Syria. As McLeod argues, 'Manning's writing highlights the crucial relationship between the Second World War and decolonization' ('The Novel and the End of Empire', *British and Irish Fiction since 1940*, ed. by Peter Boxall and Bryan Cheyette (Oxford: Oxford University Press, 2016), pp. 80–93, p. 88).
28 Michael Ondaatje, *The English Patient* (London: Bloomsbury, 1992), p. 48, p. 141.

29 Ondaatje, *The English Patient*, p. 54, p. 33.
30 Ondaatje, *The English Patient*, p. 139. In *Seven Pillars of Wisdom* (1926), T. E. Lawrence's loosely autobiographical account of the Arab Revolt against the Ottoman Turks, he writes: 'for years we lived anyhow with one another in the naked desert, under the indifferent heaven. By day the hot sun fermented us; and we were dizzied by the beating wind … devoted to freedom' (*Seven Pillars of Wisdom* (Stroud: Nonsuch, 2006), p. 21).
31 'In Manning's vision', as Phyllis Lassner writes, 'El Alamein is a center of action that, even as it becomes the site of British victory, destabilizes the imperial presence' (*Colonial Strangers: Women Writing the End of the British Empire* (London: Rutgers University Press, 2004), p. 35). The Battle of El Alamein is also referred to in *The English Patient* (p. 164).
32 For a more detailed examination of 'erotic exoticism' in colonial and postcolonial Egypt, interweaved with the legacies of E. M. Forster, see my aforementioned article on Alan Hollinghurst's 1983 short story *A Thieving Boy* (Dodson, 'Sexuality, Race and Empire').
33 Peter Widdowson, *Graham Swift* (Tavistock: Northcote House, 2006), p. 80.
34 'Ship me somewheres east of Suez, where the best is like the worst' (Rudyard Kipling, 'Mandalay', in *Empire Writing*, ed. by Elleke Boehmer (Oxford: Oxford University Press, 2009), pp. 107–109, p. 109).
35 John Darwin, Britain and Decolonisation: *The Retreat from Empire in the Post-War World* (Basingstoke: Palgrave Macmillan, 1992), p. 291.
36 Graham MacPhee, *Postwar British Literature and Postcolonial Studies* (Edinburgh: Edinburgh University Press, 2011), p. 53. As MacPhee points out, and as *Out of this World* makes clear, this was not really the end of Britain's formal empire: 'a number of the troops who returned from Aden in 1967 were redeployed to Derry in the North of Ireland following the Battle of the Bogside' (pp. 68–69, fn. 29).
37 Harold Wilson, 'Leader's Speech, Blackpool 1968', British Political Speech, n.d., www.britishpoliticalspeech.org/speech-archive.htm?speech=166 [accessed 17 October 2020].
38 Wilson, 'Leader's Speech'.
39 Wilson, 'Leader's Speech'. There are notable parallels here to the so-called 'Winds of Change' speech delivered by Conservative Prime Minister Harold Macmillan on 3 February 1960: 'the wind of change is blowing through this continent [Africa] and whether we like it or not, this growth of national consciousness is a political fact', www.bbc.co.uk/archive/tour-of-south-africa--rt-hon-macmillan/zv6gt39 [accessed 11 December 2021].
40 Margaret Thatcher, 'Speech to Conservative Rally at Cheltenham', Margaret Thatcher Foundation, 3 July 1982, www.margaretthatcher.org/document/104989 [accessed 17 October 2020].
41 Thatcher, 'Speech to Conservative Rally'.
42 Edward Said, *Culture and Imperialism* (London: Chatto and Windus, 1993), p. 163.

43 Emma Parker, '"No Man's Land"', in *Posting the Male*, ed. by Daniel Lea and Berthold Schoene (Amsterdam: Rodopi, 2003), pp. 89–104; Hywel Dix, 'Devolution and Cultural Catch-Up', in *Literature of an Independent England*, ed. by Michael Gardiner and Claire Westall (Basingstoke: Palgrave Macmillan, 2013), pp. 188–199; and David Rogers, 'Postscript', in *The Revision of Englishness*, ed. by David Rogers and John McLeod (Manchester: Manchester University Press, 2004), pp. 169–184.
44 Flint, 'Looking Backward?', p. 4.
45 The British Empire, Bernard Porter claims, did not 'impact significantly on the culture (or cultures) of the non-elite majority' (*The Absent-Minded Imperialists* (Oxford: Oxford University Press, 2004), p. 194). For the opposing view, see James Epstein, 'Taking Class Notes on Empire', in *At Home with the Empire*, ed. by Catherine Hall and Sonya Rose (Cambridge: Cambridge University Press, 2006), pp. 251–274.
46 Alison Light, *Forever England* (London: Routledge, 1991), p. 8.
47 Cited by: 'Untitled', *Scotsman*, 31 October 1996.
48 Finney, *English Fiction Since 1984*, p. 197.
49 Parker, '"No Man's Land"', p. 100, p. 101.
50 Owen Jones, *Chavs* (London: Verso, 2012), pp. 8–9.
51 Yasmin Alibhai-Brown, 'Bring England in from the Cold', *New Statesman*, 11 July 1999, pp. 24–26.
52 Alibhai-Brown, 'Bring England in from the Cold'.
53 Hanif Kureishi, 'London and Karachi', in *Patriotism*, ed. by Raphael Samuel (London: Routledge, 1989), pp. 270–286, p. 286.
54 Cited by: Maya Jaggi, 'Prophet at the Margins', *The Guardian*, 8 July 2000, www.theguardian.com/books/2000/jul/08/society [accessed 11 December 2021].
55 For Gaby Wood, the characters' 'Cockney twang, can seem tricky, and the slang is sometimes forced' ('Involuntary Memories', *London Review of Books*, 8 February 1996), www.lrb.co.uk/the-paper/v18/n03/gaby-wood/involuntary-memories [accessed 11 December 2021]; for Sam Jordison, it 'all seem[s] a bit cor-blimey-guvnor' ('Booker Club', *The Guardian*, 24 July 2012).
56 Lawrence Driscoll, *Evading Class* (New York: Palgrave, 2009), p. 147. The class disjunct between the backgrounds of Swift and his characters is not as strict as Driscoll makes out. Swift's 'mother came from the more up-market end of Sydenham, while his father – a naval fighter pilot in the Second World War – was brought up in the lower-class area of Sydenham down the hill' (Widdowson, *Graham Swift*, p. 2). Swift attended the elite boarding school Dulwich College as 'a scholarship boy' (Swift, *Making an Elephant*, p. 203).
57 Driscoll, *Evading Class*, p. 148.
58 Light, *Forever England*, p. 8.
59 Stuart Hall, 'Keynote Lecture at *The Missing Chapter: Cultural Identity and the Photographic Archive* symposium', May 2008, Autograph ABP, Rivington Place (unpublished).
60 On the 'bracketing' of the postcolonial, see Susheila Nasta, 'End of Empire and the English Novel', *British Academy Review* 19 (January 2012), pp. 46–49, p. 47.

Bibliography

Alibhai-Brown, Yasmin, 'Bring England in from the Cold', *New Statesman*, 11 July 1999, pp. 24–26.

Ashcroft, Bill, Gareth Griffiths and Helen Tiffin, *The Empire Writes Back: Theory and Practice in Post-Colonial Literature* (London: Routledge, 2002).

Bentley, Nick, *Contemporary British Fiction* (Edinburgh: Edinburgh University Press, 2008).

Carbajal, Alberto F., *Compromise and Resistance in Postcolonial Writing: E.M. Forster's Legacy* (Basingstoke: Palgrave Macmillan, 2014).

Childs, Peter, *Contemporary British Novelists: British Fiction Since 1970* (Basingstoke: Palgrave, 2005).

Craps, Stef, 'An Interview with Graham Swift', *Contemporary Literature*, 50:4 (2009), pp. 637–661.

Darwin, John, *Britain and Decolonisation: The Retreat from Empire in the Post-War World* (Basingstoke: Palgrave Macmillan, 1992).

Dix, Hywel, 'Devolution and Cultural Catch-Up', *Literature of an Independent England: Revisions of England, Englishness and English Literature*, ed. by Michael Gardiner and Claire Westall (Basingstoke: Palgrave Macmillan, 2013), pp. 188–199.

Dodson, Ed, 'Sexuality, Race and Empire in Alan Hollinghurst's "A Thieving Boy" (1983)', *Journal of Postcolonial Writing*, 52:6 (2016), pp. 700–712.

Dodson, Ed, 'The Partial Postcoloniality of Julian Barnes's *Arthur & George*', *Journal of Modern Literature*, 41:2 (2018), pp. 112–128.

Driscoll, Lawrence, *Evading Class in Contemporary British Literature* (New York: Palgrave, 2009).

Epstein, James, 'Taking Class Notes on Empire', *At Home with the Empire: Metropolitan Culture and the Imperial World*, ed. by Catherine Hall and Sonya Rose (Cambridge: Cambridge University Press, 2006), pp. 251–274.

Finney, Brian, *English Fiction Since 1984: Narrating a Nation* (Basingstoke: Palgrave Macmillan, 2006).

Flint, Kate, 'Looking Backward? The Relevance of Britishness', in *Unity in Diversity Revisited?*, ed. by Barbara Korte and Peter Klaus Müller (Tübingen: Narr, 1998), pp. 35–50.

Gasiorek, Andrzej, *Post-War British Fiction: Realism and After* (London: Edward Arnold, 1995).

Gilroy, Paul, *After Empire: Melancholia or Convivial Culture?* (London: Routledge, 2004).

Gunby, Ingrid, 'Postwar Englishness in the Fiction of Pat Barker, Graham Swift and Adam Thorpe' (unpublished PhD thesis, University of Leeds, 2002).

Hall, Stuart, 'Keynote Lecture at *The Missing Chapter: Cultural Identity and the Photographic Archive* Symposium', May 2008, Autograph ABP, Rivington Place (unpublished).

Ingelbien, Raphaël, '"England and Nowhere": Contestations of Englishness in Philip Larkin and Graham Swift', *English*, 48 (1999), pp. 33–48.

Jaggi, Maya, 'Prophet at the Margins', *The Guardian*, 8 July 2000, www.theguardian.com/books/2000/jul/08/society [accessed 11 December 2021].

Jardine, Lisa, 'How Britain Wrote Off the English Novel', *The Telegraph*, 8 May 1997, p. 5.

Jardine, Lisa, 'Saxon Violence', *The Guardian*, 8 December 1992, p. 4.
Jones, Owen, *Chavs: The Demonization of the Working Class* (London: Verso, 2012).
Jordison, Sam, 'Booker Club: *Last Orders* by Graham Swift', *The Guardian*, 24 July 2012, www.theguardian.com/books/2012/jul/24/booker-club-graham-swift-last-orders [accessed 11 December 2021].
Kipling, Rudyard, 'Mandalay', in *Empire Writing*, ed. by Elleke Boehmer (Oxford: Oxford University Press, 2009), pp. 107–109.
Kureishi, Hanif, 'London and Karachi', in *Patriotism: The Making and Unmaking of British National Identity. Volume II: Minorities and Outsiders*, ed. by Raphael Samuel (London: Routledge, 1989), pp. 270–286.
Lane, Richard J. and Philip Tew, 'Introduction [to section on "Cultural Hybridity"]', in *Contemporary British Fiction*, ed. by Richard J. Lane, Rod Mengham and Philip Tew (Cambridge: Polity, 2003), pp. 143–144.
Lassner, Phyllis, *Colonial Strangers: Women Writing the End of the British Empire* (London: Rutgers University Press, 2004).
Lawrence, T. E., *Seven Pillars of Wisdom* (Stroud: Nonsuch, 2006).
Light, Alison, *Forever England: Femininity, Literature and Conservatism Between the Wars* (London: Routledge, 1991).
MacKay, Marina, *Modernism and World War II* (Cambridge: Cambridge University Press, 2007).
MacKay, Marina and Lyndsey Stonebridge, *British Fiction after Modernism: The Novel at Mid-Century* (Basingstoke: Palgrave, 2007).
McLeod, John, 'Comments at the *Thoughts on British Black and Asian Literature (1945–2010)* Symposium', Goldsmiths College, 27 January 2017 (unpublished).
McLeod, John, 'The Novel and the End of Empire', in *British and Irish Fiction since 1940*, ed. by Peter Boxall and Bryan Cheyette (Oxford: Oxford University Press, 2016), pp. 80–93.
Macmillan, Harold, 'The Wind of Change', https://web-archives.univ-pau.fr/english/TD2doc1.pdf [accessed 11 December 21].
MacPhee, Graham, *Postwar British Literature and Postcolonial Studies* (Edinburgh: Edinburgh University Press, 2011).
Mantel, Hilary, *A Change of Climate* (London: Penguin, 1995).
Nasta, Susheila, 'End of Empire and the English Novel', *British Academy Review*, 19 (January 2012), pp. 46–49.
Niven, Alastair, 'Alastair Niven in Conversation with Bernardine Evaristo', *Wasafiri*, 16:34 (2001), pp. 15–20.
Ondaatje, Michael, *The English Patient* (London: Bloomsbury, 1992).
Osborne, Deirdre, ed., 'Introduction', in *The Cambridge Companion to British Black and Asian Literature* (Cambridge: Cambridge University Press, 2016), pp. 1–20.
Parker, Emma, ' "No Man's Land": Masculinity and Englishness in Graham Swift's *Last Orders*', in *Posting the Male: Masculinities in Post-war and Contemporary British Literature*, ed. by Daniel Lea and Berthold Schoene (Amsterdam: Rodopi, 2003), pp. 89–104.
Perfect, Michael, *Contemporary Fictions of Multiculturalism: Diversity and the Millennial London Novel* (Basingstoke: Palgrave Macmillan, 2014).
Porter, Bernard, *The Absent-Minded Imperialists: Empire, Society, and Culture in Britain* (Oxford: Oxford University Press, 2004).
Procter, James, 'The Return of the Native: Pat Barker, David Peace and the Regional Novel after Empire', in *End of Empire and the English Novel Since 1945*, ed. by

Bill Schwarz and Rachael Gilmour (Manchester: Manchester University Press, 2011), pp. 203–217.

Reynolds, Nigel, 'Book Prize Judge Attacks "Smug" English Novelists', *The Telegraph*, 7 May 1997, p. 5.

Rogers, David, 'Postscript: Englishness in Transition: Swift, Faulkner and an Outsider's Staunch Belief', in *The Revision of Englishness*, ed. by David Rogers and John McLeod (Manchester: Manchester University Press, 2004), pp. 169–184.

Said, Edward, *Culture and Imperialism* (London: Chatto and Windus, 1993).

Samuel, Raphael, *Theatres of Memory Vol. 2* (London: Verso, 1998).

Saunders, Max, 'Introduction', in *Parade's End* by Ford Madox Ford (London: Everyman's Library, 1992), pp. xiv–xv.

Spencer, Richard, 'Britain Returns "East of Suez" with Permanent Royal Navy Base in Gulf', *The Telegraph*, 6 December 2014, www.telegraph.co.uk/news/uknews/defence/11277194/Britain-returns-East-of-Suez-with-permanent-Royal-Navy-base-in-Gulf.html [accessed 11 December 2021].

Stein, Mark, *Black British Literature* (Columbus: Ohio State University, 2004).

Stevenson, Randall, *A Reader's Guide to the Twentieth-Century Novel in Britain* (London: Harvester Wheatsheaf, 1993).

Swift, Graham, *Last Orders* (London: Picador, 1996).

Swift, Graham, *Making an Elephant* (London: Picador, 2010).

Swift, Graham, 'Swift Response to a Slur', *The Guardian*, 22 May 1997, p. 18.

Thatcher, Margaret, 'Speech to Conservative Rally at Cheltenham', 3 July 1982, www.margaretthatcher.org/document/104989 [accessed 11 December 2021].

'Untitled', *Scotsman*, 31 October 1996.

Widdowson, Peter, *Graham Swift* (Tavistock: Northcote House, 2006).

Wilson, Harold, 'Leader's Speech, Blackpool 1968', n.d., www.britishpoliticalspeech.org/speech-archive.htm?speech=166 [accessed 11 December 2021].

Wood, Gaby, 'Involuntary Memories', *London Review of Books*, 8 February 1996, www.lrb.co.uk/the-paper/v18/n03/gaby-wood/involuntary-memories [accessed 11 December 2021].

Wood, James, 'England', in *The Oxford Guide to Contemporary Writing*, ed. by John Sturrock (Oxford: Oxford University Press, 1996), pp. 113–141.

Young, Robert, *Colonial Desire: Hybridity in Theory, Culture, and Race* (London: Routledge, 1995).

Young, Robert, *Empire, Colony, Postcolony* (Somerset: Wiley, 2013).

Young, Robert, *The Idea of English Ethnicity* (Oxford: Blackwell, 2008).

Part III

Racial others, national memory

6

White against empire: Immigration, decolonisation and Britain's radical right, 1954–1967

Liam J. Liburd

Introduction

On 20 April 1968, Conservative MP and Shadow Defence Secretary Enoch Powell rose before a meeting at the Conservative Political Centre in Birmingham and delivered his now infamous 'Rivers of Blood' speech. In the speech, Powell expressed vociferous opposition to immigration from Britain's former colonies. Though it did not mention the Empire, the speech also represented the crystallisation of Powell's growing pessimism regarding British colonialism.[1] Once a loyal imperialist and aspiring viceroy of India, in a series of speeches and articles from 1964, Powell denounced the Empire as a 'myth' detrimental to Britain's future.[2] Deprived of imperial power, Powell called on Britain to reject its responsibilities to its former imperial subjects. He prophesied disastrous consequences if Britain continued accepting Commonwealth immigrants, warning that one day the 'black man will have the whip hand over the white man'.[3] Numerous scholars have interpreted the speech as the expression of a nightmare vision of the colonial order inverted.[4] This chapter draws inspiration from their efforts to analyse Powell's politics in light of the legacy of the British Empire. It looks through that same lens at those on Powell's right – the 'radical right' – who had been campaigning against immigration in strikingly similar terms since the late 1950s.

This chapter deals with several radical-right groups that merged in 1967 to form the National Front. These include the League of Empire Loyalists, the British National Party (itself a merger of the White Defence League and the National Labour Party) and the Greater Britain Movement. Examining their publications, the chapter argues that they too grew disillusioned with the Empire, leading them to conclusions very similar to those expressed by Powell in April 1968. The activists and ideologues of these groups experienced decolonisation and Commonwealth immigration as interlinked civilisational crises. Closely following events on the rapidly decolonising

African continent, the members of these radical-right groups came to see themselves as a 'species of white settler' and, using antisemitic conspiracy theory, portrayed Britain itself as akin to a besieged white-settler colony.[5] This culminated in calls for Britain to withdraw from or dissolve the 'coloured' Commonwealth and align itself with the 'white' Dominions and those nations, like South Africa and Rhodesia, which broke with the Empire in the name of white minority rule.

This chapter borrows the term 'radical right' from the work of Alan Sykes. Sykes defined the radical right as a political tendency whose adherents were fervently imperialist, elitist, authoritarian and obsessed with the preservation of racial 'purity' and national sovereignty.[6] Among the ranks of the British radical right were fascists as well as dissident Conservatives. Throughout the twentieth century, the radical right conceived of the British Empire in utopian terms; the Empire represented Britain's past greatness and the means of its salvation in future. Radical-right activists' utopian faith in the Empire was matched by their perpetual fear that Britain was on the brink of colonial collapse.[7]

In the study of right-wing extremism and fascism, there has been a tendency to treat fascist groups as a species apart, largely divorced from indigenous political traditions and national histories. Sykes's definition encourages us to consider fascists and right-wing extremists together as part of 'radical right' continuum, on the basis of the ideas they share rather than on whether they share forms of political organisation or aesthetics. In doing so, historians are able to paint a more complex and nuanced picture of the radical right, one that illuminates its very real connections to the main course of British history.

Though the groups examined in this chapter were prone to splits and were either largely electorally unsuccessful or did not contest elections at all, they nevertheless left their mark on the mainstream. Their activists were some of the first in Britain to protest in an organised form against Commonwealth immigration.[8] Their slogans – 'Keep Britain White', for instance – were taken up by parliamentary critics of immigration such as the Conservative MP Cyril Osborne.[9] Equally, they were initially at the forefront of the mostly unexamined '*pro*-apartheid' movement, supporting South Africa on the streets of Britain.[10] Echoes of their ideas appear still to be disfiguring the contemporary British political scene.

However, when it comes to studies of the metropolitan reverberations of the end of empire, the radical right have regularly been left out. Despite his interest in 'the political right outside (or largely outside) the bounds of the Conservative Party', Bill Schwarz's work on decolonisation and whiteness in modern Britain has so far dealt mainly with Powell and the Monday Club.[11] Camilla Schofield, author of a recent biography of Powell, argues that Powell represents something 'quite different' to the radical-right groups discussed herein.[12] However, much like Powell, those on the British radical right were deeply 'touched by the lessons of empire's end'.[13]

Both Schwarz and Schofield present Powellism as a manifestation of a racial or 'ethnic' populism.[14] Long before Powell, 'ethnic populism' was associated with the British Empire, fuelling ideals of trans-imperial white solidarity such as 'Greater Britain'. Powell worked the core of this idea – of white Britons united – into a narrative of victimhood, in which 'ordinary' Britons had been betrayed by treacherous politicians, who gave away their Empire and opened up their country to 'invading' immigrants. While there are important differences between Powell and the British radical right, both constitute manifestations of 'ethnic populism' and displayed a preoccupation with the anticipated cataclysmic consequences of the end of empire.

This chapter reconsiders this collection of radical-right groups as thwarted manifestations of 'ethnic populism' thus illuminating their connections to the broader history of modern Britain. Historians and cultural critics interested in racism and the legacy of empire in modern Britain have long been anxious about discussing right-wing extremism. They have been keen to avoid 'othering' British racism by portraying it as 'un-British' and unrelated to the nation's history, more akin to German Nazism than to any indigenous political tradition.[15] As a result, many have failed to appreciate that those on the British radical right 'are *British*' and that their ideas 'reflect British history and British political problematics'.[16] Nowhere is the clearer than in its adherents' obsession with the Empire and their fretful fears of decolonisation.

Defending 'white Africa'

The British radical right had long been obsessed with the Empire. Britain's first self-identifying fascist group, the British Fascisti, was founded in 1923 and consisted of many die-hard imperialist ex-military men who had served in the colonies.[17] This strain of fervent fascist imperialism continued into the 1930s with Sir Oswald Mosley's British Union of Fascists (BUF).[18] The imperial enthusiasms of those on the radical right remained undimmed and, if anything, intensified as the Second World War accelerated the rise of anti-colonial nationalism throughout the Empire. A. K. Chesterton made his return to politics in 1954 with the founding of the League of Empire Loyalists (LEL). Chesterton had been a key member of the BUF and was a biographer of Mosley and one of the few prominent BUF activists not to be interned under wartime regulations.[19]

From its inception, the LEL championed the cause of white settlers in Africa. Their concern for the survival of white minority rule reflected the background of the LEL's founder and leader. Chesterton was the child of British settlers and had been born in South Africa several months before the outbreak of the South African War. A childhood spent playing 'the "little master"' to a cast 'of coloured servants and black mine workers' left him accustomed to an authoritarian, racially stratified social order and convinced of the inferior nature of 'the African'.[20] He had returned to Africa during the Second World War as an officer in the British Army, and, as his personal recollections of this time document, the move reignited his white-supremacist passions.[21] He returned from military service and secured a position as assistant editor and leader-writer for the semi-respectable Conservative journal *Truth*.[22] From 1944 to 1953, he spent his time excoriating British colonial policy from columns and articles in *Truth*.

The colonial policies of the 1945–1951 Labour government and the 1951–1955 Conservative government represented an attempt to preserve the Empire while adjusting to new geopolitical realities.[23] As well as increasing nationalist opposition to colonial rule, Britain faced American pressure to decolonise or significantly reform imperial rule, serious economic problems and a heavy reliance on American loans.[24] Policymakers thus accelerated the progression of some of Britain's colonies towards Dominion status, attempting to keep former colonial possessions within the framework of empire – now recast as a 'multiracial Commonwealth of nations'.[25] This shift saw India, Pakistan, Ceylon and Burma achieve independence over the course of 1947 and 1948.

When it came to British Africa, however, colonial policymakers favoured a more 'gradual, smooth and efficiently controlled' process of 'political advancement' towards greater self-government 'within a Commonwealth framework'.[26] Especially after 1947, Britain relied even more intensely on the natural resources of its African colonies in the struggle to rebuild the war-torn metropole. The British government's approach was one of '[l]imited local concessions and the cultivation of amenable working relationships with "moderate" (pro-Western) Africans'.[27] Through this approach, they hoped to marginalise 'extremists', allow for 'measured political development along British-approved lines' and, fundamentally, preserve British rule.[28]

While British colonial policy during the late forties and early fifties represented neither 'whole "decolonization"' nor the '"dismantling [of] the empire"', Chesterton interpreted it as outright surrender.[29] He attributed the reforming tendency and quasi-liberal aspirations of postwar colonial policy to a Jewish plot to establish a 'World Government'.[30] Chesterton's views were heavily inspired by a 'materialist' reading of the infamous *Protocols of the Elders of Zion* and the work of antisemitic writers like Arthur Kitson, Nesta Webster and A. N. Field.[31] Wall Street-based Jewish financiers, he argued, were directing 'the great new world imperialisms' of the USA and the

USSR in a deliberate attempt to liquidate European colonial possessions.[32] Chesterton claimed that, to this end, they were sponsoring nationalist movements throughout the Empire, first in Asia and then in Africa.

After *Truth* changed owners in 1953, Chesterton's vociferous imperialist antisemitism resulted in the heavy editing of his articles. In protest at this and the magazine's change of political 'line', he noisily resigned.[33] Chesterton then worked briefly for the pro-white-settler lobbying organisation the London Committee of the United Central Africa Association, and then for a time as Lord Beaverbrook's 'literary adviser and personal assistant'.[34] In the same year, after securing the financial support of R. K. Jeffrey, an eccentric British expatriate living in Chile, Chesterton was able to found his own journal, *Candour*.

A year later, he founded the League of Empire Loyalists, envisioned as a pressure group that would work to influence public opinion in the direction of 'policies favourable to national and imperial survival'.[35] LEL activists attempted to do this through a mixture of publicity stunts at Conservative Party meetings and conferences, and by counter-demonstrations against anti-imperialist groups like the Movement for Colonial Freedom.[36] They also kept in touch with their 'kinsmen overseas' via a 'Commonwealth-wide network of sympathisers', particularly in southern Africa.[37]

'The coloured invasion'

The LEL's focus on the overseas situation meant that it came late to the issue of Commonwealth immigration. The late 1940s saw a new wave of migration to Britain from the Caribbean, India and Pakistan, prompted by the promise of employment and the extension of British citizenship under the 1948 Nationality Act. While its members had long opposed the so-called 'Black Invasion', the LEL did not begin organising an official campaign against 'coloured immigration' until 1958.[38] From early 1958, W. J. Harrison, the LEL's new director of organisation, recommended that the group's activists use 'the "Black Invasion" ... as our main line to introducing people to the wider issues of our Imperial betrayal'.[39]

However, this new campaign did not come fast enough for some of the LEL's younger, more radical activists. In 1957, Colin Jordan, Midlands organiser and a member of the LEL's National Committee, left to found the White Defence League (WDL).[40] In April 1958, prominent League members John Bean and John Tyndall also broke with the LEL in frustration over Chesterton's unwillingness to contest elections, founding the National Labour Party (NLP) on 24 May (Empire Day) 1958.[41] While these two groups were more openly interested in neo-Nazism than the LEL, the most significant divisions between the three of them were primarily the result of a clash of personalities and tactical differences. Ideologically, particularly where the Empire was concerned, they were more or less aligned. The NLP remained 'dedicated to the British and Imperial cause' while the White Defence League's *Black & White News* carried advertisements for both *Candour* and the League of Empire Loyalists.[42]

The NLP and the WDL came to the public's attention as a result of their activities during the summer of 1958. In a series of racist riots during late August and early September 1958, crowds of white residents in Nottingham and Notting Hill began attacking West Indians on the street and in their homes.[43] The activists of the NLP and the WDL had begun campaigning in Notting Hill shortly before the riots and afterwards became a regular presence. The NLP even petitioned on behalf of the nine white youths arrested for their part in instigating the London riots.[44] Contemporaneous accounts blamed the NLP, the WDL and Oswald Mosley's Union Movement (the postwar successor to the BUF) for exacerbating the racial tensions that fuelled the violence.[45]

For those on the radical right, what happened in the summer of 1958 in Nottingham and Notting Hill was refracted through the lens of increasing racial tensions in Britain's African colonies. During the late fifties, the priorities of the British government in terms of colonial policy and those of white settler communities increasingly diverged.[46] The former intended to preserve African loyalty to Britain by working with moderate nationalists, guiding their politically 'immature' subjects towards self-government within the Commonwealth. However, white settlers, particularly those in the Central African Federation and South Africa, were keen to preserve their privileges. They were beginning to bristle at the first gentle breezes of what was, several years later, memorably termed the 'wind of change'.

Radical-right activists thus formulated their anti-immigrant stance in an atmosphere of racialised violence at home and challenges to white rule abroad. They began to discuss Britain's so-called 'colour problem' with frequent and direct references to events in southern Africa. Activists from the NLP and LEL declared almost joyously that Britons were now directly embroiled in the same struggle as their 'white kinsmen' overseas. The first issue of the NLP's newspaper *Combat* appeared shortly after the riots and celebrated the newfound affinity between white Britons in the metropole and 'our white kinsmen in South Africa and the Southern States of America'.[47] Chesterton expressed similar sentiments in *Candour*. He saw the riots as a violent reaction against what he believed was a global push for racial integration. 'War', he wrote, was being waged 'on the Whiteman'.[48] In his view, white rioters in Britain were now united in common cause with Southern segregationists in the USA, white settlers opposed to racial ' "integration" in

East Africa and the Rhodesias', and the antipodean defenders of 'the "White Australia" policy'.[49] While the LEL abjured the 'street fighting' tactics of the NLP and the WDL, their activists were now out campaigning against immigration on the streets of London and beyond.[50]

Having collaborated extensively in their anti-immigration campaigns following the 1958 riots, the WDL and the NLP merged in 1960 to form the British National Party (BNP). The BNP pledged to 'stand against the Black invasion of Britain and the betrayal of our White kinsmen overseas'.[51] Brought together, its activists continued to conflate colony and metropole in their discussions of decolonisation and immigration. For instance, the BNP's *Combat* portrayed the Congo Crisis, following the Belgian withdrawal in 1960, as emblematic not only of the fate to which Britain was leaving its 'White kinsmen', but also as an illustration of the potential metropolitan consequences of Commonwealth immigration.

They drew comparisons between the rape and murder of white women by 'Black troops' in the Congo and the symbolic and demographic 'wounding and murder of White people' in Britain by the arrival of increasing numbers of 'coloured immigrants'.[52] The BNP wondered how long it would be before this colonial-style violence transitioned from the metaphorical to the physical, with 'Congo antics enacted' on the streets of the metropole.[53] They called for 'White solidarity' between Britons and whites in 'South Africa, Kenya ... Rhodesia [and] even the Southern States of the U.S.A.'.[54]

The LEL's journal *Candour* contained similarly fevered imaginings of the colony impinging upon the metropole. A 1961 article complained that 'the coloured invasion is increasingly bringing barbarism to Britain' with reports of ' "tribal war" ' on the streets of Brixton.[55] Another article one year later remarked on the resurgence of witchcraft in Nyasaland alongside tales of similar 'Black Magic' practices by West African immigrants in Birmingham and London.[56] Areas with particularly high immigrant populations, the article went on to claim, were allegedly the site of 'voodoo orgies and riots'. The collapse of colonialism, according to the journals of the LEL and the BNP, had resulted in a process of reverse colonisation and the transformation of Britons into the metropolitan equivalent of white settlers.

White against empire

Alongside their growing identification with white settlers, these radical-right groups gradually turned away from the existing Commonwealth and towards visions of an alternative alliance of white nations. The NLP was one of the first radical-right groups to turn its back on the Commonwealth. An article in an early issue of *Combat*, written by one of the NLP's founders, proposed a new alliance to preserve 'that which is best in the old British Empire' – in their view, the 'White Dominions'.[57] When the NLP and WDL merged to form the BNP, opposition to the 'multiracial' Commonwealth and the promotion of 'white solidarity' formed part of its programme.[58]

While Chesterton harboured a rather fanciful dream of a British 'return' to lost colonies into the 1960s, he quickly became similarly disillusioned.[59] Long sceptical of the ideal of a 'multiracial' Commonwealth, for him and his LEL colleagues, South Africa's departure from the organisation in 1961 proved the final straw.[60] Though critical of Afrikaner nationalism, Chesterton's loyalties lay with the white supremacy of his native South Africa over British imperial liberalism.[61] In an article written shortly after South Africa's withdrawal, Chesterton denounced the Commonwealth as an 'internationalist agency' under the sway of the anti-British rulers of newly independent nations such as India's Jawaharlal Nehru and Ghana's Kwame Nkrumah.[62] The time had come, he continued, for its dissolution. In place of the 'liquidated Commonwealth', wrote Chesterton, 'the White Dominions' needed to unite in defence of their national sovereignty and against 'the despotic power of Wall Street'.[63]

A new radical-right group advancing a similar line emerged in 1964. The Greater Britain Movement (GBM) had splintered from another splinter group. It was formed by John Tyndall after he left Colin Jordan's National Socialist Movement which, in turn, had originally broken away from the BNP in 1962. Pledging to resist the spread of 'the rule of the jungle from Africa to Britain and America', the GBM also promoted a union of 'White kinsmen'.[64] This union was to comprise of the 'Anglo-Saxon' Dominions and South Africa.[65] Such was the GBM's racially charged opposition to the Commonwealth that one GBM activist, Martin Webster, was imprisoned in August 1964 for assaulting Kenyan prime minister Jomo Kenyatta during a diplomatic visit to London.[66]

Behind the LEL, BNP and GBM's shared visions of an alternative white alliance lay a growing dissatisfaction with the Commonwealth remnants of the Empire. They felt that the world had turned against the white-supremacist principles that had historically driven and legitimised British imperialism. Indeed, the world and the position of the British Commonwealth within it was changing. In Africa, 'white rule had been obliterated north of the Zambezi' between 1959 and 1964, with the rapid creation of nearly thirty independent African states.[67] By 1964, little remained of the Empire besides 'a range of small scattered islands, Hong Kong, and Southern Rhodesia'.[68] Beyond the Commonwealth, the end of European colonialism was also transforming the United Nations. By 1961, with the addition of newly independent ex-colonial states, African and Asian countries had gained a majority on its General Assembly.[69] Anti-colonial critics now possessed an international forum.

Radical-right groups threw their weight behind those who had clung to their white-supremacist convictions and seceded from the Commonwealth. Rhodesia, in particular, became the new great white hope of the British radical right. After the dissolution of the Central African Federation (CAF) in 1963 and the subsequent granting of independence to the former CAF territories of Nyasaland (as Malawi) and Northern Rhodesia (as Zambia), Southern Rhodesia came under pressure to extend voting rights beyond its white population.[70] On 11 November 1965, Ian Smith, prime minister of the Rhodesian Front government, issued a Unilateral Declaration of Independence (UDI) from the British Commonwealth in protest and the independent state of Rhodesia was born.

The LEL's support for Smith predated the UDI. Its activists cheered him on when he came to Britain for negotiations with Harold Wilson's government in 1964. LEL demonstrators met him at the airport, broadcasting slogans from a loud hailer and saluting Smith as 'a champion of civilisation in Africa'.[71] A 'cavalcade' of cars bearing LEL activists then followed Smith to his hotel, where he was greeted by yet more activists bearing banners 'emphasising the League's support for its Rhodesian kinsmen'. Despite his support for the Rhodesians and their cause, from the pages of *Candour*, Chesterton desperately urged them to refrain from withdrawing from the Commonwealth.[72] However, after the UDI, he nonetheless continued in his passionate support, praising Rhodesia for daring 'to stand fast, declare unswerving allegiance to the Crown and defy, not only a British Government but the entire finance-regimented world'.[73]

The BNP had none of Chesterton's reticence and urged Southern Rhodesia to withdraw from the Commonwealth back in 1963.[74] *Combat* encouraged its readers to join the Anglo-Rhodesian Society and BNP members also attended meetings of the similarly pro-white-settler Conservative Monday Club.[75] *Combat* reported that the BNP held pro-Rhodesia marches in Sheffield, Birmingham, Coventry and Manchester 'among other areas' in the wake of the UDI.[76] Bean wrote of Ian Smith in messianic terms, referring to him as the saviour of 'Western man everywhere' and the man who could arrest 'the self-inflicted decline of Western power'.[77] The GBM's Martin Webster was similarly effusive, dubbing South Africa and Rhodesia 'the only sparks of sanity ... in the whole world'.[78]

Alongside these expressions of solidarity for 'Right, Royal, Heroic Rhodesia', the LEL, BNP and GBM frequently made comparisons between Britain's world position and that of separatist settler nations like Rhodesia.[79] And they reinforced their delusions with antisemitic conspiracy theory. Chesterton elaborated on his belief that decolonisation was a sinister,

Jewish-directed scheme in a book entitled *The New Unhappy Lords* (1965). The book, and Chesterton's worldview more generally, proved highly influential in radical-right circles.[80] The BNP's *Combat* reviewed it positively and, throughout this time, Chesterton continued to act as an unofficial political adviser to the GBM's leader John Tyndall.[81]

Seen through the warped looking glass of Chesterton's antisemitic conspiracies, as laid out in *The New Unhappy Lords*, Britain appeared to radical-right activists as a victim of a decolonising world. Chesterton portrayed Britain similarly to South Africa and Rhodesia, as a white nation whose national sovereignty and racial integrity was menaced by international interference. Chesterton and the BNP's John Bean even speculated that Britain itself might be 'abandoned' to 'black rule', as they argued 'White Africa' had been betrayed.[82] In the fevered imaginations of these white supremacists, Britain faced a Commonwealth run by anti-British 'coloured leaders' and a United Nations dominated by newly independent former colonies, both of which they believed were mere puppets of a near-omnipotent Jewish enclave.[83] In addition to this, they also believed that the Jews were importing Commonwealth immigrants and that these would soon form a Black majority in Britain comparable to the 'native hordes' of Africa.[84] Viewed in this way, the radical right recast Britain as the metropolitan equivalent of a beleaguered settler colony.

The LEL, BNP and GBM were by no means alone in resorting to conspiracy theory in their attempts to explain the seemingly inexplicable and rapid collapse of British colonial rule. The aforementioned Conservative Monday Club – founded by pro-Empire, pro-white-settler Conservatives in 1961 – perceived a similar plot (directed by Soviet communists rather than Jews) dedicated to 'the elimination of the white man in Africa'.[85] The conspiracy theories of Chesterton and his acolytes also found an echo in the paranoid regimes of separatist settler states in southern Africa. In 1964, the Rhodesian government employed South African journalist Ivor Benson as an adviser and charged him with reorganising the state-run broadcasting network into a government propaganda arm.[86] Benson was an antisemitic conspiracy theorist and a prominent activist in the Candour League, one of a series of LEL-affiliated groups throughout the Commonwealth.[87] Through his work in Rhodesia, he heavily influenced the worldview of the Rhodesian Front government and even the rhetoric of its prime minister.[88] Chesterton was also engaged in a longrunning correspondence with Hendrik van den Burgh, the head of the South African Republic's Intelligence Department and later founder of the country's secret police force. Van den Burgh was a subscriber to *Candour* and a fan of *The New Unhappy Lords*.[89] Their relationship went beyond ideological influence, however, as he and Chesterton passed each other information regarding anti-colonial and anti-apartheid activists throughout the sixties.

However, back in Britain, beyond the circle of his devotees in the LEL, BNP and GBM, Chesterton's ideas proved far less influential. Throughout their existence, these groups remained small and largely unsuccessful organisations. At its height in 1958 as a repository for die-hard Tory imperialists, the LEL had 3,000 members and many more supporters.[90] By 1961, however, this had dropped to an estimated 300. After the death of Chesterton's wealthy benefactor, R. K. Jeffrey, in the same year and the subsequent legal wrangling over his estate, the LEL also struggled to find funding. The BNP had an estimated membership of around 500, while estimates for the GBM range from between 100 and 150 members.[91] Their attempts to electorally exploit opposition to immigration also met with failure. The LEL's 'Independent Loyalist' candidates performed dismally in 1957 and 1964.[92] John Bean stood in Southall during the 1964 election, achieving only 9 per cent of the vote.[93] Outside of their own efforts, the BNP also sent members to help the Conservative candidate Peter Griffiths's notoriously racist campaign during the 1964 Smethwick by-election.[94]

Given their small size and largely similar ideas, the leading figures in these organisations began to consider merging during 1966. Later that year, the BNP and the LEL agreed on the terms of a merger and, in February 1967, formed the National Front (NF). Tyndall and his followers were initially excluded from the NF on account of their overt neo-Nazism but were later admitted after further negotiations and the dissolution of the GBM in September 1967.[95]

The NF's programme reflected the ideas of its constituent organisations. It contained promises to terminate 'non-white immigration', and to repatriate all 'non-white immigrants' and their dependents that had entered Britain since the passing of the 1948 Nationality Act.[96] Alongside this went plans for the replacement of the Commonwealth with 'a modern British world system' composed of sovereign but co-operating nations, including Australia, New Zealand, Canada, Rhodesia, and, if they desired it, South Africa and Ireland.[97] Their manifesto also contained audacious proposals to admit 'Afro-Asian countries' if they wished to join and would agree to do so on subordinate terms.

Conclusion

By the time of Powell's speech, the NF was a little over a year old. In the wake of the speech, *The Times* reported that the radical right were 'rejoicing'.[98] They interviewed Chesterton, now chairman of the NF, who boasted that '[w]hat Mr. Powell has said does not vary at all from our views'.[99] The article also noted that the NF claimed to be attracting new members of all ages and classes in branches throughout the country. In the end, though Powell's anti-immigrant intervention 'supplied ... the National Front ... with the oxygen it needed', they failed to take advantage of the post-Powell furore.[100] In the subsequent 1970 general election, the NF fielded ten candidates, all of whom failed even to achieve the minimum number of votes necessary to secure the return of their election deposit. NF activists continued to popularise and proselytise Powellite racism into the 1970s and 1980s. Though they remained electorally unsuccessful, they remained a political and (sometimes deadly) physical threat to Britons of African Caribbean and South Asian descent.

NF activists had reached largely similar conclusions as those of Powell in his 'Rivers of Blood' speech, only via a different route. While Powell responded to his loss of imperial faith by retreating into visions of a pastoral and white 'old England', the NF moved in the direction of visions of an unapologetically white supremacist neocolonial world order.[101] With the rise of pro-Brexit English nationalism after 2016, some commentators have begun to reassess the legacy and influence of Powell, an anti-European Economic Community and anti-immigration spokesman.[102] However, there are also unsettling affinities between the NF's visions of a neoimperial 'modern British world system' and post-Brexit ideas of a renewed and intensified relationship between Britain and its former imperial subjects and Commonwealth allies.[103] This is not to mention the ease with which the modern successors of the NF, activists from groups like the other British National Party (founded in 1982), Britain First and the followers of Stephen Yaxley-Lennon (Tommy Robinson) infiltrated the pro-Brexit movement.[104] As this chapter has sought to demonstrate, and as recent events reflect, the British radical right were never far from the mainstream. Their history is bound up in important, unsettling and hitherto underappreciated ways with decolonisation and the legacy of empire in modern Britain. In dark political times, we ignore these entanglements at our peril.

Notes

1 A Conservative [anonymously authored by Powell], 'Patriotism Based on Reality Not on Dreams', *The Times*, 2 April 1964, p. 13; 'Speech to the Royal Society of St. George, 22 April 1964', in *A Nation Not Afraid: The Thinking of Enoch Powell*, ed. by John Wood (London: B. T. Batsford Ltd., 1965), pp. 143–146; 'Speech at Trinity College, Dublin, 13 November 1964', in *A Nation Not Afraid: The Thinking of Enoch Powell*, ed. by John Wood (London: B. T. Batsford Ltd., 1965), pp. 136–143.
2 Camilla Schofield, *Enoch Powell and the Making of Postcolonial Britain* (Cambridge: Cambridge University Press, 2013), p. 67.
3 'Text of Speech by Enoch Powell, 20th April 1968', in *Enoch Powell: The Man and his Thinking*, ed. by T. E. Utley (London: William Kimber, 1968), pp. 179–180.

4 Paul Gilroy, *Postcolonial Melancholia* (New York: Columbia University Press, 2004), p. 101; Wendy Webster, *Englishness and Empire 1939–1965* (Oxford: Oxford University Press, 2005), pp. 180–181; Daniel McNeil, '"The Rivers of Zimbabwe Will Run Red with Blood": Enoch Powell and the Post-Imperial Nostalgia of the Monday Club', *Journal of Southern African Studies*, 37:4 (2011), pp. 736–738; Schofield, *Enoch Powell*, pp. 7–8; Bill Schwarz, *Memories of Empire: The White Man's World* (Oxford: Oxford University Press, 2013), pp. 19, 29.
5 Schwarz, *Memories of Empire*, p. 12.
6 Alan Sykes, *The Radical Right in Britain: Social Imperialism to the BNP* (Basingstoke: Palgrave Macmillan, 2005), pp. 1–2, 9.
7 Sykes, *The Radical Right in Britain*, p. 3.
8 Richard Thurlow, 'The Guardian of the "Sacred Flame": The Failed Political Resurrection of Sir Oswald Mosley after 1945', *Journal of Contemporary History*, 33:2 (1998), p. 250.
9 Cyril Osborne, 'The Colour Problem in Britain – Right', *The Spectator*, 4 December 1964, pp. 7, 9.
10 Saul Dubow, 'New Approaches to High Apartheid and Anti-Apartheid', *South African Historical Journal*, 69:2 (2017), p. 313.
11 Bill Schwarz, 'Forgetfulness: England's Discontinuous Histories', in *Embers of Empire in Brexit Britain*, ed. by Stuart Ward and Astrid Rasch (London: Bloomsbury, 2019), p. 56.
12 Schofield, *Enoch Powell*, p. 3.
13 Schofield, *Enoch Powell*, p. 3.
14 Schwarz, *Memories of Empire*, pp. 53–106; Schofield, *Enoch Powell*, p. 20.
15 Tony Kushner, 'The Fascist as "Other"? Racism and Neo-Nazism in Contemporary Britain', *Patterns of Prejudice*, 28:1 (1994), pp. 29–30; Paul Gilroy, *There Ain't No Black in the Union Jack: The Cultural Politics of Race and Nation* (London: Routledge, [1987] 2002), pp. 153–154; Paul Gilroy, *Against Race: Imagining Political Culture Beyond the Colour Line* (Cambridge, MA: The Belknap Press of Harvard University Press, 2001).
16 John E. Richardson, 'British Fascism, Fascist Culture, British Culture', *Patterns of Prejudice*, 53:3 (2019), p. 245.
17 Liam J. Liburd, 'Thinking Imperially: The British Fascisti and the Politics of Empire, 1923–1935', *Twentieth Century British History*, 32:1 (2021), pp. 46–67.
18 Liam J. Liburd, 'Beyond the Pale: Whiteness, Masculinity and Empire in the British Union of Fascists, 1932–1940', *Fascism: Journal of Comparative Fascist Studies*, 7:2 (2018), pp. 275–296.
19 David Baker, *Ideology of Obsession: A. K. Chesterton and British Fascism* (London: I.B.Tauris, 1996), p. 193.
20 David Baker, 'A. K. Chesterton, the Strasser Brothers and the Politics of the National Front', *Patterns of Prejudice*, 19:3 (1985), pp. 26–27.
21 University of Bath Archives [hereafter UOBA]: A. K. Chesterton Papers, B.8, *All Aboard for Addis: A Personal Record of the Campaign in Abyssinia and Somaliland* [incomplete typescript], (n.d.).

22 Claire Hirshfield, 'The Tenacity of Tradition: *Truth* and the Jews 1877–1957', *Patterns of Prejudice*, 28:3–4 (1994), pp. 67–85.
23 David Goldsworthy, 'Keeping Change Within Bounds: Aspects of Colonial Policy during the Churchill and Eden Governments, 1951–57', *The Journal of Imperial and Commonwealth History*, 18:1 (1990), p. 81.
24 Elizabeth Buettner, *Europe after Empire: Decolonization, Society, and Culture* (Cambridge: Cambridge University Press, 2016), p. 41.
25 Buettner, *Europe after Empire*, p. 38.
26 Ronald Hyam, 'Africa and the Labour Government, 1945–1951', *The Journal of Imperial and Commonwealth History*, 16:3 (1988), p. 153.
27 Buettner, *Europe after Empire*, p. 43.
28 Buettner, *Europe after Empire*, p. 43.
29 Hyam, 'Africa and the Labour Government', p. 169.
30 A. K. Chesterton, 'The Mystery of Palestine', *Truth*, 145:3776 (4 February 1949), p. 116; A. K. Chesterton, 'Atomic Politics and World Power', *Truth*, 147:3832 (3 March 1950), pp. 208–209.
31 Richard C. Thurlow, 'The Powers of Darkness: Conspiracy Theory and Political Strategy', *Patterns of Prejudice*, 12:6 (1978), p. 4; Marinus F. La Rooij, 'From Colonial Conservative to International Antisemite: The Life and Work of Arthur Nelson Field', *Journal of Contemporary History*, 37:2 (2002), pp. 223–239.
32 A. K. Chesterton, 'Liquidation of the European Empires', *Truth*, 145:3772 (7 January 1949), p. 8.
33 'Entre Nous', *Truth*, 153:3988 (27 February 1953), p. 202; A. K. Chesterton, *"Truth" Has Been Murdered: Open Letter to Mr. Ronald Staples* (London: Britons Publishing Society, 1953).
34 The National Archives [hereafter TNA]: KV2/1350/422A, 'A Change of Command', *World Press News*, 27 February 1953; George Thayer, *The British Political Fringe* (London: Anthony Blond, 1965), p. 54; UOBA: Chesterton Papers, B.3, *Blame Not My Lute* [unpublished draft typescript of Chesterton's autobiography] (1966–1973), chapter 1, p. 1.
35 A. K. Chesterton, 'Now For The League of Loyalists', *Candour*, 1:22 (26 March 1954), p. 1.
36 'White Settlers Championed', *Candour*, 3:106 (2 December 1955), p. 8; Mark Pitchford, *The Conservative Party and the Extreme Right, 1945–75* (Manchester: Manchester University Press, 2011), pp. 58–59.
37 A. K. Chesterton, 'A Council of War', *Candour*, 6:188 (31 May 1957), pp. 169–171; TNA: FCO 141/6622, 'Visits to Kenya by the League of Empire Loyalists'; 'Loyalist Leaders Overseas', *Candour*, 7:207 and 208 (11 and 18 October 1957), p. 120; Graham Macklin, 'The British Far Right's South African Connection: A. K. Chesterton, Hendrik van den Bergh, and the South African Intelligence Services', *Intelligence and National Security*, 25:6 (2010), p. 824.
38 'League Demands – "Protect the Queen"', *Candour*, 7:207 and 208 (11 and 18 October 1957), p. 116.

39 'Views at a Glance', *Candour*, 1:12 (15 January 1954), p. 4; W. J. Harrison, 'Counter-Attack!', *Candour*, 8:225 (14 February 1958), p. 56.
40 Nigel Copsey, *Contemporary British Fascism: The British National Party and the Quest for Legitimacy* (Basingstoke: Palgrave Macmillan, 2004), p. 8.
41 John Bean and John Tyndall, '"We Were Not Furtive"', *Candour*, 8:238 (16 May 1958), p. 159; 'Pass the Ammunition!', *Combat*, 1 (Autumn 1958), n.p.; Copsey, *Contemporary British Fascism*, pp. 7–8.
42 Bean and Tyndall, '"We Were Not Furtive"', p. 159; *Black & White News* (n.d., c. 1958), p. 4.
43 Robert Miles, 'The Riots of 1958: Notes on the Ideological Construction of "Race Relations" as a Political Issue in Britain', *Immigrants & Minorities*, 3:3 (1984), pp. 254–255; Edward Pilkington, 'The West Indian Community and the Notting Hill riots of 1958', in *Racial Violence in Britain in the Nineteenth and Twentieth Centuries*, ed. by Panikos Panayi (London; New York: Leicester University Press, 2nd ed., 1996), pp. 176–180.
44 'Petition For Nine Youths', *The Kensington News and West London Times*, 24 October 1958, p. 1.
45 Ruth Glass, *Newcomers: The West Indians in London* (London, 1960), p. 172.
46 Schwarz, *Memories of Empire*, p. 347.
47 'Martyrs of Notting Hill', *Combat*, 1 (Autumn 1958), p. 1.
48 A. K. Chesterton, 'War on the Whiteman', *Candour*, 9:268 (12 December 1958), pp. 185–186.
49 A. K. Chesterton, 'Britain – or Bastardy?', *Candour*, 9:254 (5 September 1958), pp. 73–75.
50 'Stop Coloured Immigration', *Candour*, 9:254 (5 September 1958), p. 80; 'League Active in North and South', *Candour*, 9:256 (19 September 1958), p. 96.
51 'The British National Party', *Combat*, 6 (May–June 1960), pp. 4–5.
52 'Whites Under Attack', *Combat*, 7 (July–August 1960), p. 1.
53 Whites Under Attack', *Combat*, 7 (July–August 1960), p. 1.
54 Whites Under Attack', *Combat*, 7 (July–August 1960), p. 2.
55 '"Tribal War" in Brixton', *Candour*, 15:406 and 407 (4 and 11 August 1961), pp. 39–40.
56 Austen Brooks, Aidan Mackey and Leslie Greene, 'Witchcraft in Nyasaland', *Candour*, 16:435 (23 February 1962), p. 62; Austen Brooks, Aidan Mackey and Leslie Greene, '– And in Britain', *Candour*, 16:435 (23 February 1962), pp. 62–63.
57 John Bean, 'Political Coelacanths', *Combat*, 3 (April–June 1959), n.p.
58 'The British National Party', *Combat*, 6 (May–June 1960), pp. 4–5.
59 A. K. Chesterton, 'We British Must Return', *Candour Interim Report* (September 1963), p. 6.
60 A. K. Chesterton, 'Retreat to Barbarism', *Candour*, 1:17 (19 February 1954), p. 1.
61 'Gold Deal?', *Candour*, 25 and 26 (16 and 23 April 1954), p. 3; 'Malanite Victory', *Candour*, 44 (27 August 1954), p. 3; 'Raid on the Witwatersrand', *Candour*, 7:205 (27 September 1957), pp. 93–94.

62 A. K. Chesterton, 'Tomorrow – A Plan for British Society', *Candour*, 14:390 (14 April 1961), pp. 114.
63 Chesterton, 'Tomorrow – A Plan for British Society', p. 114.
64 'Global Race War Looms Nearer', *Spearhead*, 1 (August–September 1964), p. 1.
65 John Tyndall, 'The Meaning of Greater Britain', *Spearhead*, 8 (July 1965), p. 6.
66 'Two Months for Assault on Mr. Kenyatta', *The Times*, 7 August 1964, p. 6; 'Stop Press', *Spearhead*, 1 (August–September 1964), p. 6.
67 John Darwin, *Britain and Decolonisation: The Retreat from Empire in the Post-War World* (Basingstoke: Palgrave Macmillan, 1988), p. 245.
68 Buettner, *Europe after Empire*, p. 58.
69 Marilyn Lake and Henry Reynolds, *Drawing the Global Colour Line: White Men's Countries and the International Challenge of Racial Equality* (Cambridge: Cambridge University Press, 2008), p. 349.
70 Alice Ritscherle, 'Disturbing the People's Peace: Patriotism and "Respectable" Racism in the British Responses to Rhodesian Independence', in *Gender, Labour and Empire: Essays on Modern Britain*, ed. by Philippa Levine and Susan R. Grayzel (Basingstoke: Palgrave Macmillan, 2009), p. 198.
71 A. K. Chesterton, 'Loyalists Welcome Ian Smith', *Candour Interim Report*, 15 (September 1964), p. 8.
72 A. K. Chesterton, 'Not That Way, Rhodesians!', *Candour*, 17:445 (September 1965), pp. 41–42.
73 A. K. Chesterton, 'Right, Royal, Heroic Rhodesia', *Candour*, 17:447 (November 1965), pp. 57–58.
74 'African States Declare War on South Africa', *Combat*, 23 (July–August 1963), p. 3.
75 'A Victory for Patriotic Unity', *Combat*, 36 (November–December 1965), p. 2; 'Support Rhodesia', *Combat*, 36 (November–December 1965), p. 3.
76 'BNP Spearheads Support for Rhodesia', *Combat* 36 (November–December 1965), p. 7.
77 John Bean, 'Rhodesia: White World Survival at Stake', *Combat*, 36 (November–December 1965), pp. 1–2.
78 Martin Webster, 'Black Death?', *Spearhead*, 1 (August–September 1964), p. 2.
79 Chesterton, 'Right, Royal, Heroic Rhodesia', pp. 57–58.
80 Graham Macklin, 'Transatlantic Connections and Conspiracies: A.K. Chesterton and "The New Unhappy Lords"', *Journal of Contemporary History*, 47:2 (2012), pp. 270–290.
81 John Bean, 'Money Power Unveiled', *Combat*, 35 (September–October 1965), p. 4; Martin Walker, *The National Front* (London: Fontana, 2nd ed., 1978), pp. 48, 58.
82 'Rhodesia: Whites Betrayed', *Combat*, 26 (January–March 1964), p. 1; A. K. Chesterton, 'Survival of the White Races', *Candour Interim Report*, 13 (April/May 1964), pp. 1–3.
83 A. K. Chesterton, *The New Unhappy Lords: An Exposure of Power Politics* (Hampshire: Candour Publishing Company [1965] 1975), p. 143.

84 Chesterton, *The New Unhappy Lords*, pp. 170–171.
85 Harold Soref and Ian Greig, *The Puppeteers* (London: Tandem Books, 1965).
86 Elaine Windrich, *The Mass Media in the Struggle for Zimbabwe: Censorship and Propaganda under Rhodesia Front Rule* (Gweio: Mambo Press, 1981), pp. 10–13.
87 Ivor Benson, *Know Your Enemy* (Oxon, MA: Raymond Bamford, 1964); Brian Bunting, *The Rise of the South African Reich* (Harmondsworth: Penguin [1964] 1969), p. 71; John Parker, *Rhodesia: Little White Island* (London: Pitman, 1972), pp. 120, 122–123; Macklin, 'The British Far Right's South African Connection', p. 830.
88 Michael Evans, 'The Wretched of the Empire: Politics, Ideology and Counterinsurgency in Rhodesia, 1965–80', *Small Wars and Insurgencies*, 18:2 (2002), pp. 180–182; Windrich, *The Mass Media*, p. 11.
89 Macklin, 'The British Far Right's South African Connection', p. 838.
90 Walker, *The National Front*, p. 133.
91 Copsey, *Contemporary British Fascism*, p. 12; Walker, *The National Front*, p. 47.
92 F. W. S. Craig, ed., *Minor Parties at British Parliamentary Elections, 1885–1974* (Basingstoke: Macmillan, 1975), p. 49.
93 Walker, *The National Front*, p. 53.
94 Walker, *The National Front*, p. 55.
95 Copsey, *Contemporary British Fascism*, p. 15.
96 'Towards a National Front', *Candour*, 18:459 (December 1966), p. 176.
97 'Towards a National Front', p. 176.
98 'The Jordans and Mosleyites are Rejoicing', *The Times*, 24 April 1968, p. 10.
99 Chesterton's own feelings about Powell were ambivalent. He later accused Powell of having sinister links to the Bilderberg Group. His criticism of Powell eventually provoked a revolt against his chairmanship of the NF; see A. K. Chesterton, 'The Mystery of Enoch Powell', *Candour*, 19:476 (May 1968), pp. 49–50; Working Class Movement Library: Fascism, Box 5, Letter from the Action Committee to A. K. Chesterton (6 October 1970).
100 Harry Taylor, '"Rivers of Blood" and Britain's Far Right', *The Political Quarterly*, 89:3 (2018), p. 386.
101 Powell, 'Speech to the Royal Society of St. George', p. 144.
102 Colin Kidd, 'The Provocations of Enoch Powell', *New Statesman*, 28 August 2019, www.newstatesman.com/culture/books/2019/08/provocations-enoch-powell [accessed 10 December 2021].
103 David Thackeray and Richard Toye, 'Debating Empire 2.0', in *Embers of Empire in Brexit Britain*, ed. by Stuart Ward and Astrid Rasch (London: Bloomsbury, 2019), pp. 15–35.
104 David Lawrence, 'Far Right Flock to the Brexit Party', Hope Not Hate, 18 October 2019, www.hopenothate.org.uk/2019/10/18/far-right-flock-to-the-brexit-party [accessed 10 December 2021].

Bibliography

Baker, David, 'A. K. Chesterton, the Strasser Brothers and the Politics of the National Front', *Patterns of Prejudice*, 19:3 (1985), pp. 23–33.

Baker, David, *Ideology of Obsession: A. K. Chesterton and British Fascism* (London: I.B.Tauris, 1996).

Benson, Ivor, *Know Your Enemy* (Oxon, MA: Raymond Bamford, 1964).

Buettner, Elizabeth, *Europe after Empire: Decolonization, Society, and Culture* (Cambridge: Cambridge University Press, 2016).

Bunting, Brian, *The Rise of the South African Reich* (Harmondsworth: Penguin [1964] 1969).

Chesterton, A. K., *"Truth" Has Been Murdered: Open Letter to Mr. Ronald Staples* (London: Britons Publishing Society, 1953).

Chesterton, A. K., *The New Unhappy Lords: An Exposure of Power Politics* (Hampshire: Candour Publishing Company [1965] 1975).

Copsey, Nigel, *Contemporary British Fascism: The British National Party and the Quest for Legitimacy* (Basingstoke: Palgrave Macmillan, 2004).

Craig, Frederick W. S., ed., *Minor Parties at British Parliamentary Elections, 1885–1974* (Basingstoke: Macmillan, 1975).

Darwin, John, *Britain and Decolonisation: The Retreat from Empire in the Post-War World* (Basingstoke: Palgrave Macmillan, 1988).

Dubow, Saul, 'New Approaches to High Apartheid and Anti-Apartheid', *South African Historical Journal*, 69:2 (2017), pp. 304–329.

Evans, Michael, 'The Wretched of the Empire: Politics, Ideology and Counterinsurgency in Rhodesia, 1965–80', *Small Wars and Insurgencies*, 18:2 (2002), pp. 175–195.

Gilroy, Paul, *Against Race: Imagining Political Culture Beyond the Colour Line* (Cambridge, MA: The Belknap Press of Harvard University Press, 2001).

Gilroy, Paul, *Postcolonial Melancholia* (New York: Colombia University Press, 2004).

Gilroy, Paul, *There Ain't No Black in the Union Jack: The Cultural Politics of Race and Nation* (London: Routledge, [1987] 2002).

Glass, Ruth, *Newcomers: The West Indians in London* (London: George Allen & Unwin, 1960).

Goldsworthy, David, 'Keeping Change Within Bounds: Aspects of Colonial Policy during the Churchill and Eden Governments, 1951–57', *The Journal of Imperial and Commonwealth History*, 18:1 (1990), pp. 81–108.

Hirshfield, Claire, 'The Tenacity of Tradition: *Truth* and the Jews 1877–1957', *Patterns of Prejudice*, 28:3–4 (1994), pp. 67–85.

Hyam, Ronald, 'Africa and the Labour Government, 1945–1951', *The Journal of Imperial and Commonwealth History*, 16:3 (1988), pp. 148–172.

Kidd, Colin, 'The Provocations of Enoch Powell', *New Statesman*, 28 August 2019, www.newstatesman.com/culture/books/2019/08/provocations-enoch-powell [accessed 10 December 2021].

Kushner, Tony, 'Forgetfulness: England's Discontinuous Histories', in *Embers of Empire in Brexit Britain*, ed. by Stuart Ward and Astrid Rasch (London; New York: Bloomsbury, 2019), pp. 49–58.

La Rooij, Marinus F., 'From Colonial Conservative to International Antisemite: The Life and Work of Arthur Nelson Field', *Journal of Contemporary History*, 37:2 (2002), pp. 223–239.

Lake, Marilyn and Henry Reynolds, *Drawing the Global Colour Line: White Men's Countries and the International Challenge of Racial Equality* (Cambridge: Cambridge University Press, 2008).
Lawrence, David, 'Far Right Flock to the Brexit Party', *Hope Not Hate*, 18 October 2019, www.hopenothate.org.uk/2019/10/18/far-right-flock-to-the-brexit-party [accessed 10 December 2021].
Liburd, Liam J., 'Beyond the Pale: Whiteness, Masculinity and Empire in the British Union of Fascists, 1932–1940', *Fascism: Journal of Comparative Fascist Studies*, 7:2 (2018), pp. 275–296.
Liburd, Liam J., 'Thinking Imperially: The British Fascisti and the Politics of Empire, 1923–1935', *Twentieth Century British History*, 32:1 (2021), pp. 46–67.
Macklin, Graham, 'The British Far Right's South African Connection: A. K. Chesterton, Hendrik van den Bergh, and the South African Intelligence Services', *Intelligence and National Security*, 25:6 (2010), pp. 823–842.
Macklin, Graham, 'Transatlantic Connections and Conspiracies: A.K. Chesterton and "The New Unhappy Lords"', *Journal of Contemporary History*, 47:2 (2012), pp. 270–290.
McNeil, Daniel, '"The Rivers of Zimbabwe Will Run Red with Blood": Enoch Powell and the Post-Imperial Nostalgia of the Monday Club', *Journal of Southern African Studies*, 37:4 (2011), pp. 731–745.
Miles, Robert, 'The Riots of 1958: Notes on the Ideological Construction of "Race Relations" as a Political Issue in Britain', *Immigrants & Minorities*, 3:3 (1984), pp. 252–275.
Parker, John, *Rhodesia: Little White Island* (London: Pitman, 1972).
Pilkington, Edward, 'The West Indian Community and the Notting Hill riots of 1958', in *Racial Violence in Britain in the Nineteenth and Twentieth Centuries*, ed. by Panikos Panayi (London; New York: Leicester University Press, 2nd ed., 1996), pp. 171–184.
Pitchford, Mark, *The Conservative Party and the Extreme Right, 1945–75* (Manchester: Manchester University Press, 2011).
Rasch, Astrid and Stuart Ward, eds, *Embers of Empire in Brexit Britain* (London: Bloomsbury, 2019).
Richardson, John E., 'British Fascism, Fascist Culture, British Culture', *Patterns of Prejudice*, 53:3 (2019), pp. 236–252.
Ritscherle, Alice, 'Disturbing the People's Peace: Patriotism and "Respectable" Racism in the British Responses to Rhodesian Independence', in *Gender, Labour and Empire: Essays on Modern Britain*, ed. by Philippa Levine and Susan R. Grayzel (Basingstoke: Palgrave Macmillan, 2009), pp. 197–218.
Schofield, Camilla, *Enoch Powell and the Making of Postcolonial Britain* (Cambridge: Cambridge University Press, 2013).
Schwarz, Bill, 'Forgetfulness: England's Discontinuous Histories', in *Embers of Empire in Brexit Britain*, ed. by Stuart Ward and Astrid Rasch (London: Bloomsbury, 2019), pp. 49–58.
Schwarz, Bill, *Memories of Empire: The White Man's World* (Oxford: Oxford University Press, 2013).
Soref, Harold and Ian Greig, *The Puppeteers* (London: Tandem Books, 1965).
Sykes, Alan, *The Radical Right in Britain: Social Imperialism to the BNP* (Basingstoke: Palgrave Macmillan, 2005).

Taylor, Harry, '"Rivers of Blood" and Britain's Far Right', *The Political Quarterly*, 89:3 (2018), pp. 385–391.

Thackeray, David and Richard Toye, 'Debating Empire 2.0', in *Embers of Empire in Brexit Britain*, ed. by Stuart Ward and Astrid Rasch (London: Bloomsbury, 2019), pp. 15–35.

Thayer, George, *The British Political Fringe* (London: Anthony Blond, 1965).

Thurlow, Richard C., 'The Powers of Darkness: Conspiracy Theory and Political Strategy', *Patterns of Prejudice*, 12:6 (1978), pp. 1–12, 23.

Thurlow, Richard, 'The Guardian of the "Sacred Flame": The Failed Political Resurrection of Sir Oswald Mosley after 1945', *Journal of Contemporary History*, 33:2 (1998), pp. 241–254.

Utley, T. E., ed., *Enoch Powell: The Man and his Thinking* (London: William Kimber, 1968).

Walker, Martin, *The National Front* (London: Fontana, 2nd ed., 1978).

Webster, Wendy, *Englishness and Empire 1939–1965* (Oxford: Oxford University Press, 2005).

Windrich, Elaine, *The Mass Media in the Struggle for Zimbabwe: Censorship and Propaganda under Rhodesia Front Rule* (Gweio: Mambo Press, 1981).

Wood, John, ed., *A Nation Not Afraid: The Thinking of Enoch Powell* (London: B. T. Batsford Ltd., 1965).

7

Racism, redistribution, redress: The Royal Historical Society and *Race, Ethnicity & Equality in UK History: A Report and Resource for Change*

Shahmima Akhtar

> Racism is always historically specific. Though it may draw on the cultural traces deposited by previous historical phases, it always takes on specific forms. It arises out of present not past conditions. Its effects are specific to the present organisation of society, to the present unfolding of its dynamic potential and cultural processes not simply to its repressed past.[1]

Stuart Hall, writing almost four decades ago, pinpointed the historical specificity of racism, its ingenuity and constant reformulation, its idiosyncrasies and contextual application. Accepting that racism is innovated across successive decades, generations and governments is a necessary truth. There is no one bad form of racism, whether in words or actions, but it is pervasive and prevalent in all of our bodies and institutions in the United Kingdom. To be racialised as non-white is to be subject to these racisms in varied micro or macro forms. To be racialised as white is to perhaps have to learn about such racism and begin to see it in all walks of life, forms of knowledge and structures of being. Taking the omnipresence of racism as a starting point, in spring 2018 the Royal Historical Society (RHS) undertook a survey of the field of history in the United Kingdom to expose and redress racism in the historical academy. This chapter considers the intellectual and practical development of the RHS's equalities work as it ties to the anti-racist work we can see in Britain more broadly. It maps the trajectory of the RHS's race equalities work; *Race, Ethnicity & Equality in UK History: A Report and Resource for Change* (hereafter the Race Report) was published in 2018, 'Roadmap for Change', which summarised how the report had been used by different universities and history departments in the UK, came out in 2019, and 'Race Update' was regularly published on the RHS's Historical Transactions blog in 2020. The chapter ends with a reflection on the society's future goals regarding race equalities within complementary initiatives in the heritage and museum sector, learned societies and secondary school education.

Origins and findings of the RHS Race Report

Recognition that Britain is multicultural and yet the teaching and studying of history in the higher-education sector is ignominiously white was underscored in the RHS Race Report. The 2011 Census showed that just under 20 per cent of the UK's population self-identified as other than 'White British', while the UK's 'Black and Minority Ethnic' (BME) population doubled in size from 1991 to 8 million people (14 per cent) in 2011.[2] Legally, the Equality Act 2010 brought together all previous anti-discrimination laws on equal pay, sex discrimination and the Race Relations Act. It became the basic framework against direct and indirect discrimination and rested on protected characteristics of age, disability, gender reassignment, race, religion or belief, sex, sexual orientation, marriage and civil partnership as well as pregnancy and maternity.[3] By using the Equality Act to frame the RHS Race Report, its authors emphasised the need for systemic and long-term change for BME individuals in higher education, including students, making clear that their wellbeing, progression and attainment was a legal, moral and human right.[4]

The RHS Race, Ethnicity and Equality Working Group (REEWG) established in 2017 produced the Race Report and its members continue to work systematically on these issues. The report found that history is the fifth-least-diverse subject in UK universities in terms of race and ethnicity. RHS received around 730 surveys, completed by staff and students in history varying from undergraduates and early-career researchers to permanent salaried and professorial level. Responses contained rich qualitative material in the free-text boxes (amounting to over 100 pages of commentary). While some of the latter was overtly racist, most respondents engaged thoughtfully with the survey. The embedded nature of racism within history at a higher-education level was revealed, coupled with a widespread desire – at all levels within the discipline – for change.

The report found that undergraduate-level history had an overwhelmingly white student population, that the numbers of BME students were even lower when it came to postgraduate-level history, and specifically that 'History academic staff are less diverse than Historical & Philosophical Studies student cohorts, with 93.7 per cent of History staff drawn from White backgrounds, and only 0.5 per cent Black, 2.2 per cent Asian and 1.6 per cent Mixed'.[5] The report identified that curriculum content from secondary-school level to university history diminished interest in history among BME students. History (not) taught at school relating to the presence of people of colour, whether through early settlement, colonialism or slavery, creates a false idea that Black and minority ethnic people have no history in Britain prior to late-twentieth-century migration. Thereby, if university is about discovery – discovery of the self and the world in which we live – then the low number of BME students who decide to study a history that seems not to include them is hardly surprising. Of course, there are many factors that influence a student's choice of degree, specifically future employment, financial prospects and career development, but interest in a subject is also significant. Consequently, if BME students have been unable to see and study *their* histories, *their* ancestors and cultures, it creates a false idea that history is not of any relevance to them, being outsiders and external to any shared histories of Britain's past.[6] For those that do pursue history in higher education, the report offered statistical data on the endemic experience of discrimination, bias and harassment suffered by BME staff and students, typically by their colleagues and peers. The report ended with recommending changes that addressed the 'leaky pipeline' issue in the form of dedicated funding under the scope of positive action, the need to expand the history curriculum and specific anti-racist and unconscious bias training.

The report detailed that at undergraduate level, 11 per cent of history and philosophy students are BME, despite BME students making up 23 per cent of the overall UK undergraduate population. At postgraduate level, 17 per cent of all UK postgraduates are of a BME background but within historical and philosophical studies department it drops to 9 per cent. When we begin to break down the data on staff in history departments, who are 94 per cent white, we can see that while 6 per cent come from a BME background, only 0.5 per cent are black.[7] By disaggregating the data, it is clear that the experiences of Black staff and students demands its own targeted response, and conflation with 'BME' often overshadows the specific inequalities experienced by those racialised as Black in the UK. 'Leading Routes' and 'Black in Academia' are exemplary examples of initiatives that recognise this fact and work to allay the specific marginalisation felt by Black staff and students in history higher education. Moreover, on the attainment gap, now more accurately referred to as the 'awarding gap' to recognise the role of academics in sustaining this inequality, BME students and white students are equally likely to get a 2:1 but BME students are 9 per cent less likely to get a First than a white student.[8] Furthermore, the report specifically found that the limited BME staff and students in history higher education experience a discriminatory and exclusionary working environment. For instance, 44 per cent of BME respondents faced problems with unconscious or implicit bias around race and ethnicity; 33 per cent of respondents reported witnessing discrimination or abuse of staff and students based on race and ethnicity. Further, 30 per cent of respondents reported having experienced such discrimination or abuse themselves. Finally, most discrimination or abuse was at the hands of the staff within their own department, and the rest was by students or the public.[9]

Aftermath and impact of the RHS Race Report

Within a few weeks of the report being issued, several history departments had held meetings or workshops to discuss it. The Race Report built on previous studies that have extensively documented the sustained racial and ethnic inequalities built into UK universities. The Black and Asian studies association, the History Matters group, the efforts of the Institute of Commonwealth Studies, the teaching resources of the Arts and Humanities Research Council-funded Runnymede Trust project 'Our Migration Story: The Making of Modern Britain' and the Institute of Historical Research's 'Teaching British Histories of Race, Migration and Empire', as well as the Museum Detox network, framed and continue to frame the RHS's and REEWG's work. Overall, the report evidenced widespread structural racial and ethnic biases that persistently harm BME staff and students within the majority-white historical discipline in UK universities.

To support the RHS's race equality agenda, the Past and Present Society funded a postdoctoral fellowship to further the work of the REEWG. In this position, which the author held for just over a year, various equality initiatives were reinforced, for instance, at least one working group member (as well as the postdoc) attended workshops held by universities to examine the Race Report, so as to gather more information and disseminate its findings and good practice. Instead of issuing a second Race Report, the REEWG will produce a series of bespoke handbooks on good practice related to key issues such as appointment panels; postgraduate supervision (including pipeline work, recruiting and funding); conference and seminar organisation; public engagement as well as outreach and impact; and the recruitment of authors and editors. These will be circulated to engaged departments in draft form, to be workshopped, refined and then issued as a series of PDFs for internal use.

In this role, I observed the actioning of the Race Report by various institutions to positive effect, whether engendering conversation on race equality, reformulating hiring practices, undertaking curriculum reviews, dedicating funding to tailored equality, diversity and inclusivity (EDI) training and countless other initiatives. However, amid this genuine engagement by the vast majority of higher-education institutions, I encountered a problematic trend, whereby some felt that there were quick solutions to the endemic racism in our universities. Specifically, certain individuals conceived of increased representation of BME staff whether in recent hires, the creation of EDI committees, or even staff members' willingness to talk on these topics to the rest of their department as being sufficient, as being good enough anti-racist work. Action that fundamentally overburdens the few existing BME staff to take responsibility to rectify and resolve their own oppression is simply not sufficient. It is not enough to increase representation. It is not enough to have an EDI committee. It is not enough to simply talk about racism in our profession. All of these initiatives are a starting point for greater recognition and resourcing of race equalities work through consultation and collaboration if they are to have any meaningful change.

It is worth pausing to focus on a particularly popular initiative at universities that can undermine actual anti-racist work – widening participation schemes. They are often worthwhile, necessary and largely positive. However, sometimes these schemes are in danger of merely focusing on attracting and recruiting BME students without adapting or modifying the university's offer. The prioritisation of increasing BME student numbers gestures towards a problematic belief by some that increasing diversity can take the place of genuine reform. While BME students should be recognised, welcomed and invited to participate in higher education, their diverse needs, whether related to the curriculum, leisure activities or job prospects, have to be accounted for. BME students may have specific needs around accommodation, commuting or else dietary requirements and places of worship, and making university education more accessible should complement widening participation schemes. Otherwise, we risk recruiting students who feel out of place in a majority-white environment and, more seriously, knowingly placing these students in harm's way.[10] Ultimately, we need to push back against the trend in our universities of increasing representation without change.

Further, the author launched 'Race Update' on the RHS Historical Transactions blog in January 2020. It offers short pieces on subjects related to race, ethnicity and equality in UK history higher education (from reviewing publications to events and initiatives) on a bi-monthly basis for those actively engaged in race equality work, whether professional services staff, postgraduate students, academics or otherwise. The updates include appraisals of reports, identifying core strategies, key examples and case studies for future use. It provides summaries on new developments in the field, ranging from recent to more established literature. The blog posts offer both a synopsis of each output and an analysis which is designed to assist staff and students to assess the relevance of any item for their own work. It keeps a regularly updated bibliography to get insights on, and to stay abreast of, anti-racist activity in university-based history. It contains collective resources for BME staff and students as well as white allies in the history sector working for change.

The Royal Historical Society has welcomed the creativity of responses and varied discussion sparked by the Race Report. In order to maximise on a pivotal moment in UK history, the RHS is keen to ensure that conversations around race, ethnicity and equality continue to flourish. In the words of Margot Finn, former president of the Royal Historical Society, these changes will 'make our discipline a safer, less hostile and positive space to exist in for BME staff, students and allies alike'.[11] One of the co-chairs of the REEWG, Jonathan Saha, described the Race Report as 'validating, challenging, shocking and affirming' in its exposure of underrepresentation and experience of bias, discrimination and workplace racism, and believes the counter is sustained, organised, consistent anti-racist action.[12]

There are many great projects within the historical academy in the 2020s, from stipended fellowships to train secondary school teachers on teaching diverse histories, to the Runnymede Trust's campaign for a Centre on Race, Migration and Empire, to developing BME fellowships for master's and PhD study, organising decolonial networks, history education action groups, collaborations with STEM and bespoke Black British history degrees, to name a few.[13] Moreover, the fact that UK grime artist Stormzy recently offered two scholarships to Black British students to study at the University of Cambridge in autumn 2020 reveals how wide the discourse on equality, diversity and inclusivity has spread in Britain. Clearly, there is a significant desire to increase access to university, reform the content of university courses and generally to reduce racism in history higher education. Yet, whether any of these actions will produce a less racist society is unclear. For instance, Stormzy's scholarship is an admirable endeavour, but such one-off financing will not change the overwhelming whiteness of Oxbridge. Further, stories of the stigma attached to Black and minority ethnic students who end up at these elite institutions are unfortunately common and there is a harmful assumption by some that these students were given preferential treatment. This inevitably betrays a misunderstanding of these schemes, which offers financial assistance to help overcome barriers BME students may face in accessing these spaces, whether through lack of external support or mentoring.

The overlaps and similarities between the Runnymede Trust's 2000 report on *The Future of Multi-Ethnic Britain* and its 2019 report on *Ethnicity, Race and Inequality in the UK: State of the Nation* indicate that there is still much to be done.[14] Both reports evidence in detail racial and ethnic inequality in various aspects of social and cultural life in Britain. For example, the latter includes fourteen academics who have authored chapters on racial discrimination in the labour market, in housing, as well as in arts and the media that is research-based and rooted in lived experience. It ends with recommendations 'to imagine a different or better future'.[15] Evidently, inequality has been continually reproduced in the intervening two decades in all realms of society. Yet, the report's authors reveal that change is gradual, and positive change has been achieved, even if some progress has been undone by successive governments, budgetary cuts and a hostile media. The recent 2019 *State of the Nation* report attests to the fact that the path to racial equality is not straightforward but invariably has successes and losses as an ongoing struggle.

Additionally, the RHS is increasingly working on its race equalities agenda in dialogue with other societies, including the British Sociological Association, the Royal Geographic Society and the Royal Chemistry Society. Specifically, the Race Report is a standing item on RHS Council agendas and features at regular RHS history heads of department meetings and most RHS symposia and events. Moreover, the Institute of Historical Research is investing significantly in equality, diversity and inclusion in history, with particular attention to early-career issues. It is through such collaborative efforts that meaningful change can be sustained, not just in the historical academy but in higher education more broadly.

In order to map the impact of the Race Report, the RHS published a 'Roadmap for Change' in 2019 which summarises how universities, learned societies and a variety of institutions have responded to the report and its findings. While the Race Report built on existing work by groups such as the Young Historians Project, the 'Roadmap for Change' surveyed the cumulative responses to exhaustive qualitative and quantitative data, proving conclusively that history in higher education needs to be made more equal and inclusive on racial and ethnic lines. The 'Roadmap for Change' includes specific events, workshops and working groups that have been formed to discuss subjects related to race and ethnicity in history. It covers particular literature, and also includes a survey of heads of departments detailing the range of activities that have been undertaken, covering hiring practices, curriculum audits and dedicated funding. It ends with a bibliography of new reports that can be added to the 2018 Race Report. Overall, the 'Roadmap for Change' only includes engagement that the RHS has been informed of, and there are of course many instances of good practice that may not have been reported. As a state-of-the-field report, a year on from the publication of the Race Report, it maps change and highlights areas where more action, particularly in the form of funding, is needed.

Specifically, the 'Roadmap for Change' includes twenty-six examples of post-Race Report responses and engagements by academics, universities and broader cultural institutions in the form of seminars, discussions, roundtables and pedagogical and written engagement with the 2018 Race Report. It contains ten examples of learned societies (such as the English Association and Political Studies Association) using the Race Report to begin collecting data on race and ethnicity among their respective memberships, as well as including twenty-three UK heads of department faculty, school or history subject area statements on how they used the Race Report in the year after its publication.[16] 'Roadmap for Change' demonstrates the actualisation of the RHS Race Report's 'Recommendations and Advice' section, which broadly involves positive action, being reflexive and aware of one's own positionality and the power of enabling student-led change.

The RHS as an institution is also committed to introspection via a race, ethnicity and equality lens. The society is working towards 'adding to its membership as needed and continuing to [support the Race Report's] operation'; it is further engaged in a continual review of previous years of speakers with an eye to amending the future programme as necessary. It is currently involved in an ongoing process to discuss and devise specific strategies for attracting more BME Members and Fellows and proactively encouraging BME nominations to the Council; it will systematically review the content of the Historical Transactions blog, the Society's Transactions, Camden series and monographs, as well as its website with a critical eye for diversity and inclusion. The RHS will continue working proactively with other UK-based history organisations to establish agreed practices and policies that promote BME equality in the form of bespoke handbooks. The RHS will advocate for new funding streams to conduct research on best practice for race and ethnic equality in the humanities and social sciences; it will work more proactively with schools and teachers to address the obstacles at this level identified in the Race Report to BME students' study of history; it will work with history departments as well as other bodies to improve the scope of the quantitative data on history as a discipline available to the profession.[17] The multiple strategies above demonstrate the RHS's genuine commitment to reform which exemplifies the level of short- as well as longer-term planning that is required to undertake sustainable change that relies on several steps, overlapping processes and continual reworking and redefining in order to transform the actual running and makeup of an organisation.

Other reports on race, ethnicity and equality in UK history higher education

Other high-calibre reports evidencing BME inequalities in higher education have been published in recent years. They have approached the subject from different angles, such as discussing the specific experiences of Black female professors in the UK, of which only one is a historian,[18] or reports that include data focusing on the awarding gap specifically.[19] Furthermore, there is rich qualitative and quantitative evidence on BME staff working in university libraries,[20] as well as informed debate on how we teach diverse histories in secondary schools.[21] Granulated data is available on the 'leaky pipeline' to postgraduate study and therein the academic profession.[22] Detailed evidence on the specific experiences of Black students in higher education has been published,[23] as well as debates on decolonising the curriculum that have reached broader audiences.[24] There has been larger consideration on how the relatively new open-access landscape in higher education has potential negative equality, diversity and inclusivity implications.[25] Inescapably, data on racial inequalities are extensive and damning, and the general feeling among those engaged in anti-racist work is that we have proven and evidenced sufficiently and now is the time for action and change.

Many universities throughout the UK are invariably engaging in race, ethnicity and equality work in history at different registers. Some believe that applying for the Race Equality Charter (REC) is key to anti-racist work in higher education.[26] The arguments in favour of the REC rest on it having reduced transaction costs as it uses existing university and departmental or else school- and college-level equality, diversity and inclusivity structures. Specifically, work through this charter can focus on examining the curriculum as well as reading lists in order to diversify content. Through the REC, departments may also be encouraged to support the transition of BME students from school to university as well as looking at the attainment gap and progression to postgraduate study. Those in favour of the scheme argue that the charter mark relies on multiple (institutional) avenues and systems of power which can help achieve similar goals. However, achieving the charter mark is not the same as achieving equality. And universities need to remain spaces where dissent and critical conversation (of the REC specifically) can take place. Importantly, the REC has the potential to be undermined if it reductively serves to allow universities to get a charter mark as an ostensible display of their commitment to racial and ethnic equality without any real effort to institute actual change to help BME staff and students.[27] An REC stamp risks becoming disingenuous in the context of a neoliberal higher-education market that is constantly in competition, and sees it merely as a way to improve the university's standing in league tables. Yet, on the other hand, it offers institutional support to anti-racist action in higher education. Overall, the decision to undertake the REC process or not therefore lies within the concerns and commitments of specific history departments across the UK.

The effort to transform history in universities has seen significant debate related to structural, intellectual, cultural and intersectional anti-racism action. If we believe that history's narrativisation of the past is tied to one's sense of self-hood, belonging and rootedness, the need to have a broader, more equitable and inclusive higher-education system is urgent and fundamental.[28] It is unjust to have a curriculum where one may not see another person of colour reflected in stories, texts or images. It is to deny individuals of their past, of their history, of their ancestry. We cannot countenance such silence and erasure in the teaching of our past, and it is by broadening our curriculum early on, supporting teachers financially and intellectually to do this, encouraging BME students into PGR study, as the types of questions we ask or else the assumptions we make can be rooted in our positionality, and ensuring promotion of BME colleagues at senior levels so that those making the strategic decisions may have lived experience of varied circumstances – and crucially be able to empathise with new student cohorts and our ever-changing society – that we might embed and sustain change.

David Olusoga has notably argued that we risk losing our past and our sense of identity if we continually read, write and experience a whitewashed version of history.[29] Olusoga explains that since what is taught and who does teaching is determined by access and power, a more diverse body of staff and students in history higher education is central to creating and sustaining a truly national history. He insists that an intersectional approach to the study of history will foster robust research and analysis – which is a carefully considered and rich methodological approach to studying our past. Moreover, Radhika Natarajan argues that decolonial work must go beyond diversifying reading lists and intersect with curriculum and module choice – historical, historiographical and political. She argues that the 'Imperial past is in dialogue with our present moment' and that colonial subjects, experiences and political demands are all interrelated.[30] Understanding, researching and analysing our shared history is a live political debate in Britain, and by directly tackling the political nature of all knowledge creation we can equip our students with the critical skills necessary to interrogate the ways in which history is made relevant to our contemporary lives. In this approach, the relationship between the forms of knowledge we discuss in the classroom and the inequities and violence that exist in global politics can be examined productively. Crucially, anti-racist work in higher education does not exist in isolation and the RHS is engaged in similar conversations on the purpose of history with the museum and heritage sector, which is also tackling debates on repatriation, commemoration and digital sustainability.[31]

Meleisa Ono-George points to the limits of diversity work, conceptually and practically. She holds the Race Report as a 'starting point', particularly to a sector which has seen race and racism as a marginal concern.[32] Specifically, Ono-George proposes an anti-racist pedagogy, which is an understanding of racism as historically and socially constructed, embedded and normalised within modern society. This theoretical approach (like Natarajan's) centres an anti-racist action that is an interrelated result of individuals and institutions. It challenges objectivity and refuses to promote the continual creation of dominant knowledge rooted in oppression, which historical study has been particularly guilty of perpetuating. Ono-George recognises that since universities are sites of knowledge production, they are partially responsible for unequal dynamics of power in society given that 'all education is political'. By adopting an anti-racist pedagogy, students will be encouraged to be reflexive, active participants, and engaged in collaborative learning, which can be applied to wider life. In this argument, Ono-George recognises the value of decolonising the curriculum. For instance, some academics have suggested offering grant schemes to identify diverse histories and embed them within a new curriculum.[33] There has been a recent proliferation in the number of research fellowships designed to investigate the colonial legacies of specific universities as part of decolonial practice. In order to effectively utilise this research, universities may choose to disseminate the findings of specific projects within the academy or hold open discussions on ways to move forward with the future organisation of the university. These cumulative approaches to the teaching, writing and researching of history offer varied avenues to pursue for a sector engaged in anti-racism.

This chapter has shown that there are multiple ways forward for the Royal Historical Society's race, ethnicity and equality agenda and those engaged in responding to and building on it. Arguably, the discourse of discrimination, inequality and privilege has become part of public consciousness in our wider world, as has the right-wing backlash to it.[34] The calls for decolonisation can be heard far and wide, from schools to universities, to the museum and heritage sector, to media makers, musicians and journalists. Focused action to make history higher education fairer has been taken up by exam boards, Members of Parliament and the Department of Education. Initiatives more established or else newer have flourished in a positive sign of growing commitment to racial and ethnic equality. It is with a holistic campaign that the fundamental work of anti-racism activism in UK history will affect desperately needed change. We know there is still a long road to travel and the RHS is committed to providing informed interventions in the historical discipline. While there is still significant work to do to displace history from its current place in UK universities as the fifth-least-diverse discipline in terms of BME inclusion, it is heartening to see that there is real commitment to change by specific universities, led by BME staff, students and white allies alike.

We know that the existence of evidence in and of itself will not lead to change – and relies on us using our power individually and collectively. For instance, you may have a large Twitter following, which means you can draw attention to certain policies. You may help edit a journal, so keep an eye out for who you tend to publish or reject. You may mark undergraduate or master's essays and exams, so read up on the awarding gap. You may be in charge of some departmental-level budget, so be cognisant as to who gets the funding and what types of events they are organising. You may host a reading group, so be selective in whose readings are picked. If organising a conference, avoid privileging any one demographic. There are multiple insertion points of change depending on your position in higher education, so be reflexive and introspective and see where your power lies, and therein lies the potential for action.

While literature on racism and higher education has proliferated in the public domain, we cannot allow the crucial work of anti-racism to be derailed or divested from.[35] Universities, in the wake of the ongoing Black Lives Matters movement, campaigns of 'Why is My Curriculum So White', 'Rhodes Must Fall' and countless others, face highly publicised and viral critiques of their racist history and we must avoid merely superficial changes being imposed. While it is important to have Black British history master's degrees, these must be supported with ongoing teacher support, funding and resources. We cannot have a decolonised university if all the work falls on the shoulders of the few BME colleagues that exist. It has become enviable for universities to be seen to have a Black History Month every October and a South Asian Heritage month every July to August, but we cannot let anti-racist action be reduced to these siloes and must continue to work to bring equalities to the fore of all activities and provisioning in higher education. It should not be monopolised by university managers interested in posturing, and must be embedded, integrated and resourced in order to effect sustained long-term change. It is difficult to resist external pressures to be reactive to ongoing inequalities but true allyship comes from deliberate thought and measured action. For instance, a conversation with a second-year BME student about the possibilities of PGR study may be entirely transformative in overcoming a lack of cultural capital (regarding possibilities for further study), possessed only by some of our students at university. However small, we can all use our power to make history higher education less racist and more decolonial and inclusive.

Notes

1 Cited in Paul Gilroy, *One Nation under a Groove: The Cultural Politics of "Race" and Racism in Britain* (Minnesota: University of Minnesota Press, 1990), p. 265. See also, Stuart Hall, 'Ethnicity, Identity and Difference', in *Becoming National: A Reader*, ed. by Geoff Ely and Ronald Grigor Suny (Oxford: Oxford University Press, 1996), pp. 339–349; and Stuart Hall, ed., 'Racism and Moral Panics in Post-War Britain', in *Five Views of Multi-Racial Britain; Talks on race Relations Broadcast by BBC TV. Second Edition* (London: Commission for Racial Equality, 1978).

2 Bridget Byrne, Claire Alexander, Omar Khan, James Nazroo and William Shankley, eds, *Ethnicity, Race and Inequality in the UK: State of the Nation* (Bristol: Bristol University Press, 2020), p. 9. I use 'BME' as a term to ensure

consistency with the statistical data on race in higher education while being aware of its conceptual limitations.
3 Kalwant Bhopal, *White Privilege: The Myth of a Post-Racial Society* (Bristol: Bristol University Press, 2018), pp. 55–56.
4 In 'Tackling Racial Harassment: Universities Challenged', the Equality and Human Rights Commission (EHRC) (2019) found that around a quarter of students from an ethnic minority background (24 per cent) and 9 per cent of white students said they had experienced racial harassment since starting their course. This equates to 13 per cent of all students. Further, 20 per cent of students had been physically attacked and 56 per cent of students who had been racially harassed had experienced racist name-calling, insults and jokes. In most cases, students said their harasser was another student, but a large number said it was their tutor or another academic. However, the report was widely criticised in its definition of racial harassment and its sample choice; Nicola Rollock noted that the EHRC's inclusion of anti-white harassment 'will only serve to confuse universities who already struggle to understand and address racism against black and Asian groups'; cited in David Batty, 'Universities Failing to Address Thousands of Racist Incidents', *The Guardian*, 23 October 2019, www.theguardian.com/world/2019/oct/23/universities-failing-to-address-thousands-of-racist-incidents [accessed 23 October 2019].
5 Hannah Atkinson, Suzanne Bardgett, Adam Budd, Margot Finn, Christopher Kissane, Sadiah Qureshi, Jonathan Saha, John Siblon and Sujit Sivasundaram, *Race, Ethnicity & Equality in UK History: A Report and Resource for Change* (London: Royal Historical Society, 2018), p. 8 (hereafter 'Race Report').
6 Notably, the Black Curriculum is a social enterprise founded in 2019 to address the lack of Black British history in the UK curriculum. Their aims are: to provide a sense of belonging and identity to young people across the UK; to teach an accessible Black British history curriculum that raises attainment for young people; and to improve social cohesion between young people in the UK. They deliver arts-focused Black history programmes, provide teacher training and campaign with young people aged eight to sixteen with a long-term aim to change the national curriculum.
7 Race Report, p. 8.
8 Race Report, p. 40. Debra Cureton, 'Bridging the BME Gap', University of Wolverhampton, 28 April 2016, www.wlv.ac.uk/news-and-events/wlv-blog/2016/april-2016/bridging-the-bme-gap [accessed 21 February 2021].
9 Race Report, pp. 54–55.
10 University drop-out rates vary significantly by ethnicity, with Black students almost one and a half times more likely to drop out than white or Asian students. Cited in Universities UK/National Union of Students, 'Black, Asian and Minority Ethnic Student Attainment at UK Universities: #CLOSINGTHEGAP', May 2019, p. 7, www.universitiesuk.ac.uk/sites/default/files/field/downloads/2021-07/bame-student-attainment.pdf [accessed 1 November 2019].
11 Margot Finn, 'Decolonising History? Reflections on the Royal Historical Society's 2018 Report', in *The White Elephant in the Room: Ideas for*

Reducing Racial Inequalities in Higher Education, ed. by Hugo Dale-Rivas (Location: HEPI, 2019).

12 Jonathan Saha, 'The RHS Race, Ethnicity & Equality Report: A Response to Critics', History Workshop Online, 30 October 2018, www.historyworkshop.org.uk/the-rhs-race-ethnicity-equality-report-a-response-to-critics [accessed 15 September 2022].

13 See, for instance, 'Times Letters: Need to Teach Colonial History in Schools', *The Times*, 13 June 2020, www.thetimes.co.uk/article/times-letters-need-to-teach-colonial-history-in-schools-hm5rb90w0 [accessed 15 September 2022].

14 Commission on the Future of Multi-Ethnic Britain, *The Future of Multi-Ethnic Britain* (London: The Runnymede Trust, 2000), also known as 'The Parekh Report'; Bridget Byrne, Claire Alexander, Omar Khan, James Nazroo and William Shankley, eds, *Ethnicity, Race and Equality in the UK: State of the Nation* (Bristol: Bristol University Press, 2020).

15 Byrne et al., *Ethnicity, Race and Equality in the UK*, pp. 237–242.

16 Royal Historical Society, 'Race, Ethnicity and Equality in UK History: RHS Roadmap for Change Update', December 2019, https://files.royalhistsoc.org/wp-content/uploads/2020/11/24094341/RHS-REEWG-Roadmap-Update-Dec-2019-FINAL2.pdf [accessed 1 December 2019]. A further 'Roadmap for Change Update' was published in November 2020, https://files.royalhistsoc.org/wp-content/uploads/2020/11/25110548/RHS_Roadmap_2_25_November_2020_WEB.pdf [accessed 1 December 2020].

17 Race Report, pp. 96–97.

18 Nicola Rollock, *Staying Power: The Career Experiences and Strategies of UK Black Female Professors* (London: University and College Union, 2019), prominently featured in *The Guardian*, *The Times Higher Educational Supplement*, *The Voice* and *Vogue*. The report was commissioned by the University and College Union (UCU) to investigate the smallest group of professors in terms of both race and gender – there are just twenty-five Black British female professors in UK universities. It revealed a sustained culture of bullying and stereotyping to the detriment of Black academics in these roles.

19 Universities UK and National Union of Students, 'Black, Asian and Minority Ethnic Student Attainment at UK Universities: #CLOSINGTHEGAP', May 2019, www.universitiesuk.ac.uk/sites/default/files/field/downloads/2021-07/bame-student-attainment.pdf [accessed 1 November 2019] found that the most significant contributing factor to the BME attainment gap, according to 87 per cent of respondents, was a lack of role models from different ethnic minority backgrounds. This was closely followed by curriculum delivery (82 per cent), a lack of diversity in the ethnicity of senior staff (79 per cent) and curriculum design (77 per cent). Lower socioeconomic background (75 per cent) and university culture and leadership (72 per cent) were more commonly perceived as contributory factors to the BME attainment gap among student representatives.

20 Mohammed Ishaq and Asifa Maaria Hussain, 'BAME Staff Experiences of Academic and Research Libraries', SCONUL, June 2019, www.sconul.ac.uk/sites/default/files/documents/BAME%20staff%20experiences%20of%20academic%20and%20research%20libraries_0.pdf [1 November 2019]

found that 44 per cent of BME staff experienced racial abuse in academic and research libraries, and 80 per cent were unhappy with how their reports were dealt with and felt it was insufficient. Significantly, librarians prioritised career progression and mentoring as the most important form of anti-racism action.

21 Kimberley McIntosh, Jason Todd and Nandini Das, *Teaching Migration, Belonging, and Empire in Secondary Schools* (London: TIDE and the Runnymede Trust, 2019) explains why a new approach to teaching migration, belonging and empire is required to reflect changing classroom demographics. For instance, nearly 17 per cent (one in six) of children from birth to age fifteen in England and Wales are from Black and minority ethnic backgrounds, and BME young people make up around 27 per cent (more than one in four) of state-funded primary and secondary school pupils. It stresses that teaching migration, belonging and empire is not only relevant to BME students but offers 'all young people a fuller understanding of the varied and wide-ranging cultural inputs that have contributed to the making of Britain' in an inclusive and representative curriculum.

22 Leading Routes, 'The Broken Pipeline: Barriers to Black PhD Students Accessing Research Council Funding', September 2019, https://leadingroutes.org/the-broken-pipeline [accessed 1 November 2019]. FOI data collected from UK Research and Innovation revealed that from 2016 to 2019, of the total 19,868 PhD funded studentships awarded by UK Research and Innovation research councils collectively, 245 (1.2 per cent) were awarded to Black or Black Mixed students, with just thirty of those being from Black Caribbean backgrounds, see Advance HE, 'Equality in Higher Education: Statistical Report 2018', September 2018, www.advance-he.ac.uk/knowledge-hub/equality-higher-education-statistical-report-2018 [accessed 1 November 2019]. This is compounded by the fact that of 16.8 per cent of all postgraduate research students who were from BME backgrounds (Advance HE, 2018), just 4 per cent identified as Black, see HESA, 'Higher Education Student Statistics: UK, 2019/20', September 2019, www.hesa.ac.uk [accessed 1 November 2019].

23 Sofia Akel, *Insider-Outsider: The Role of Race in Shaping the Experiences of Black and Minority Ethnic Students* (London: Goldsmiths, 2019) examined the role of race in shaping the experiences of BME students at Goldsmiths Students' Union and how racism permeates the academic lifecycle. The report found that while almost half (45 per cent) of students at Goldsmiths are from minority backgrounds, some have frequently experienced both overt and indirect racism from their white peers and white staff, and did not trust the South London University to handle complaints. It further found that 26 per cent of those surveyed reported experiencing racism from students and staff, including the use of racist slurs such as the n-word and the p-word in lectures. Almost half (49 per cent) of respondents felt that Goldsmiths' curriculum did not represent the lives and achievements of BME people. Additionally, more than three-quarters (79 per cent) of those surveyed said they did not know where to report a hate crime at Goldsmiths.

24 Mia Liyanage, 'Miseducation: Decolonising Curricula, Culture and Pedagogy in UK Universities', HEPI number Debate Paper 23, July 2020, www.hepi.ac.uk/2020/07/23/miseducation-decolonising-curricula-culture-and-pedagogy-in-uk-universities/ [accessed 1 August 2020] addresses the common misconceptions about decolonisation and recommends a series of practical steps towards its implementation using testimony from sixteen interview respondents across academia, activism and policy. It argues that decolonisation is both a vital and a beneficial next step for our universities. Over five chapters, Liyanage maps 'What decolonisation looks like' as a student-led initiative. The report takes at its starting point a definition of decolonisation that 'entails a fundamental re-evaluation of the existing forms of teaching, learning and pastoral support in Higher Education'. In this way, decolonisation becomes about facing the ways in which our institutions materialise an unequal society which requires sustained commitment to 'reassessing curricula, attainment and representation concurrently'.

25 Margot Finn, *Plan S and the History Journal Landscape: Royal Historical Society Guidance Paper* (London: Royal Historical Society, 2019) brought EDI concerns to current open-access discussions. The report surveyed UK and international history journals with reference to their planning for Plan S-aligned open-access (OA) mandates. Plan S was first announced by cOAlition S in September 2018 and is supported by UK Research and Innovation and the Wellcome Trust. The report notes that Plan S makes no reference to equality, diversity and inclusion (EDI). Finn notes that 'UK research organisations should be proactive in testing and articulating any aspects of proposed policies that may prove deleterious to researchers with "protected characteristics" under the 2010 Act'. Finn references specific EDI concerns relevant to the development of Plan S-aligned OA policies on pp. 7–8, 23, 26–27, 53, 55, 60, and 70–72, and notes funding bodies and universities legal requirements with respect to EDI.

26 Kalwant Bhopal and Clare Pitkin, *Investigating Higher Education Institutions and Their Views on the Race Equality Charter* (London: University and College Union, 2018).

27 See, for instance, Sara Ahmed, 'Equality Credentials', feministkilljoys, 10 June 2016, https://feministkilljoys.com/2016/06/10/equality-credentials [accessed 1 November 2019] for similar criticisms of Athena SWAN.

28 See Suhaiymah Manzoor-Khan, *Postcolonial Banter* (Birmingham: Verve, 2019) for the conditional nature of 'citizenship' conferred to BME Britons.

29 David Olusoga, 'We Risk Losing Slices of Our Past if We Don't Root Out Racism in Our Universities', *The Guardian*, 21 October 2018, www.theguardian.com/commentisfree/2018/oct/21/we-risk-losing-slices-of-our-history-if-we-dont-root-out-racism-in-our-unversities [accessed 1 November 2019]; and 'Britain Can No Longer Ignore Its Darkest Chapters – We Must Teach Black History', *The Guardian*, 15 June 2020, www.theguardian.com/books/2020/jun/15/britain-can-no-longer-ignore-its-darkest-chapters-we-must-teach-black-history [accessed 1 November 2019].

30 Radhika Natarajan, 'Imperial History Now', History Workshop, 17 March 2019, www.historyworkshop.org.uk/imperial-history-now [accessed 1 November 2019].

31 See Robert R. Janes and Richard Sandell, ed., *Museum Activism* (London: Routledge, 2019).
32 Meleisa Ono-George, ' "Power in the Telling": Community-Engaged Histories of Black Britain', History Workshop, 18 November 2019, www.historyworkshop.org.uk/imperial-history-now [accessed 1 November 2019].
33 ManchesterHistory1, 'UoM Modern British Historians Respond to the RHS Race Report', History@Manchester, 27 February 2019, https://uomhistory.com/2019/02/27/uom-modern-british-historians-respond-to-the-rhs-race-report/ [accessed 1 November 2019].
34 The Conservative think-tank Policy Exchange launched a monitoring project called 'History Matters' in June 2020, which 'confirms that history is the most active front in a new culture war' and tracks institutions who have taken steps to remove statues, rename buildings or update university curricula. Available at https://policyexchange.org.uk/history-matters-project [accessed 25 August 2022].
35 Notable works in the last two years include: Katy Sian, *Navigating Institutional Racism in British Universities* (Leeds: Palgrave Macmillan, 2019); Lola Olufemi, Odelia Younge, Waithera Sebatindira and Suhaiymah Manzoor-Khan, *A FLY Girl's Guide To University: Being a Woman of Colour at Cambridge and Other Institutions of Elitism and Power* (Birmingham: Verve, 2019); Jason Arday and Heidi Safia Mirza, ed., *Dismantling Race in Higher Education: Racism, Whiteness and Decolonising the Academy* (London: Palgrave Macmillan, 2018).

Bibliography

Ahmed, Sara, 'Equality Credentials', *feministkilljoys*, 10 June 2016, https://feministkilljoys.com/2016/06/10/equality-credentials [accessed 1 November 2019].
Akel, Sofia, *Insider-Outsider: The Role of Race in Shaping the Experiences of Black and Minority Ethnic Students* (London: Goldsmiths, 2019).
Arday, Jason and Heidi Safia Mirza, eds, *Dismantling Race in Higher Education: Racism, Whiteness and Decolonising the Academy* (London: Palgrave Macmillan, 2018).
Atkinson, Hannah, Suzanne Bardgett, Adam Budd, Margot Finn, Christopher Kissane, Sadiah Qureshi, Jonathan Saha, John Siblon and Sujit Sivasundaram, *Race, Ethnicity & Equality in UK History: A Report and Resource for Change* (London: Royal Historical Society, 2018).
Batty, David, 'Universities Failing to Address Thousands of Racist Incidents', *The Guardian*, 23 October 2019, www.theguardian.com/world/2019/oct/23/universities-failing-to-address-thousands-of-racist-incidents [accessed 23 October 2019].
Bhopal, Kalwant, *White Privilege: The Myth of a Post-Racial Society* (Bristol: Bristol University Press, 2018).
Bhopal, Kalwant and Clare Pitkin, *Investigating Higher Education Institutions and Their Views on the Race Equality Charter* (London: University and College Union, 2018).

Byrne, Bridget, Claire Alexander, Omar Khan, James Nazroo and William Shankley, eds, *Ethnicity, Race and Inequality in the UK: State of the Nation* (Bristol: Bristol University Press, 2020).

Commission on the Future of Multi-Ethnic Britain, *The Future of Multi-Ethnic Britain* (London: The Runnymede Trust, 2000).

Cureton, Debra, 'Bridging the BME Gap', University of Wolverhampton, 28 April 2016, www.wlv.ac.uk/news-and-events/wlv-blog/2016/april-2016/bridging-the-bme-gap [accessed 21 February 2021].

Equality and Human Rights Commission, *Tackling Racial Harassment: Universities Challenged* (London: Equality and Human Rights Commission, 2019).

Finn, Margot, 'Decolonising History? Reflections on the Royal Historical Society's 2018 Report', in *The White Elephant in the Room: Ideas for Reducing Racial Inequalities in Higher Education*, ed. by Hugo Dale-Rivas (Location: Higher Education Policy Institute, 2019).

Finn, Margot, *Plan S and the History Journal Landscape: Royal Historical Society Guidance Paper* (London: Royal Historical Society, 2019).

Gilroy, Paul, *One Nation under a Groove: The Cultural Politics of "Race" and Racism in Britain* (Minnesota: University of Minnesota Press, 1990).

Hall, Stuart, 'Ethnicity, Identity and Difference', in *Becoming National: A Reader*, ed. by Geoff Ely and Ronald Grigor Suny (Oxford: Oxford University Press, 1996), pp. 339–349.

Hall, Stuart, ed. 'Racism and Moral Panics in Post-war Britain', in *Five Views of Multi-Racial Britain; Talks on race Relations Broadcast by BBC TV. Second Edition* (London: Commission for Racial Equality, 1978).

Ishaq, Mohammed and Maaria Asifa Hussain, 'BAME Staff Experiences of Academic and Research Libraries', SCONUL, June 2019, www.sconul.ac.uk/sites/default/files/documents/BAME%20staff%20experiences%20of%20academic%20and%20research%20libraries_0.pdf [1 November 2019].

Janes, R. Robert and Richard Sandell, eds, *Museum Activism* (London: Routledge, 2019).

Leading Routes, 'The Broken Pipeline: Barriers to Black PhD Students Accessing Research Council Funding', September 2019, https://leadingroutes.org/the-broken-pipeline [accessed 1 November 2019].

Liyanage, Mia, 'Miseducation: Decolonising Curricula, Culture and Pedagogy in UK Universities', HEPI number Debate Paper 23, July 2020, www.hepi.ac.uk/2020/07/23/miseducation-decolonising-curricula-culture-and-pedagogy-in-uk-universities [accessed 1 August 2020].

ManchesterHistory1, 'UoM Modern British Historians Respond to the RHS Race Report', History@Manchester, 27 February 2019, https://uomhistory.com/2019/02/27/uom-modern-british-historians-respond-to-the-rhs-race-report [accessed 1 November 2019].

Manzoor-Khan, Suhaiymah, *Postcolonial Banter* (Birmingham: Verve, 2019).

McIntosh, Kimberley, Jason Todd and Nandini Das, *Teaching Migration, Belonging and Empire in Secondary Schools* (London: TIDE and the Runnymede Trust, 2019).

Natarajan, Radhika, 'Imperial History Now', History Workshop, 17 March 2019, www.historyworkshop.org.uk/imperial-history-now [accessed 1 November 2019].

Olufemi, Lola, Odelia Younge, Waithera Sebatindira and Suhaiymah Manzoor-Khan, *A FLY Girl's Guide to University: Being a Woman of Colour at Cambridge and Other Institutions of Elitism and Power* (Birmingham: Verve, 2019).

Olusoga, David, 'Britain Can No Longer Ignore Its Darkest Chapters – We Must Teach Black History', *The Guardian*, 15 June 2020, www.theguardian.com/books/2020/jun/15/britain-can-no-longer-ignore-its-darkest-chapters-we-must-teach-black-history [accessed 1 December 2020].

Olusoga, David, 'We Risk Losing Slices of Our Past if We Don't Root Out Racism in Our Universities', *The Guardian*, 21 October 2018, www.theguardian.com/commentisfree/2018/oct/21/we-risk-losing-slices-of-our-history-if-we-dont-root-out-racism-in-our-unversities [accessed 1 November 2019].

Ono-George, Meleisa, '"Power in the Telling": Community- Engaged Histories of Black Britain', History Workshop Online, 18 November 2019, www.historyworkshop.org.uk/imperial-history-now/ [accessed 1 November 2019].

Rollock, Nicola, *Staying Power: The Career Experiences and Strategies of UK Black Female Professors* (London: University and College Union, 2019).

The Royal Historical Society, 'Race, Ethnicity & Equality in UK History: RHS Roadmap for Change Update', December 2019, https://files.royalhistsoc.org/wp-content/uploads/2020/11/24094341/RHS-REEWG-Roadmap-Update-Dec-2019-FINAL2.pdf [accessed 1 December 2019].

Saha, Jonathan, 'The RHS Race, Ethnicity & Equality Report: A Response to Critics', History Workshop Online, 30 October 2018, www.historyworkshop.org.uk/the-rhs-race-ethnicity-equality-report-a-response-to-critics [accessed 15 September 2022].

Sian, Katy, *Navigating Institutional Racism in British Universities* (Leeds: Palgrave Macmillan, 2019).

The Times, 'Times Letters: Need to Teach Colonial History in Schools', 13 June 2020, www.thetimes.co.uk/article/times-letters-need-to-teach-colonial-history-in-schools-hm5rb90w0 [accessed 15 September 2022].

Universities UK and National Union of Students, 'Black, Asian and Minority Ethnic Student Attainment at UK Universities: #CLOSINGTHEGAP', May 2019, www.universitiesuk.ac.uk/sites/default/files/field/downloads/2021-07/bame-student-attainment.pdf [accessed 1 December 2019].

8

Exemplar empires: Battles over imperial memory in contemporary Britain

Astrid Rasch

Decades after decolonisation, the meaning of the imperial past remains hotly contested in modern Britain, with both public and scholarly debates centring upon two opposing poles of celebration or lamentation. Both sides draw on traditions of legitimating and critiquing empire that have their roots in the colonial era.[1] Yet their interventions also speak to a contemporary moment of British culture wars in which colonial memory enters debates about Brexit, Rhodes Must Fall, the Windrush scandal, the National Trust, curriculum development or the Black Lives Matter protests.[2] Frequently tied to questions about national self-image and actions, including the appropriateness of everything from apologies and reparations to overseas interventions, the imperial past is used to justify contemporary political views.

It is well established that collective memory is often contentious because of its ability to supply a 'usable past' for the present.[3] As Britain struggles to find its place in the world after the upheavals of decolonisation and Brexit, it is no surprise that colonial histories are called upon to do explanatory work.[4] But in order to understand the heated nature of the debate about Britain's imperial past, we must first pay attention to its texture.[5] When we do, we will notice something odd about this debate. While clearly disagreeing strongly, scholars of empire seemingly agree on several matters of content and style. First, they often invoke the same historical events: from transatlantic slavery and the Amritsar massacre to the spread of global trade and Indian railways. It seems the debate is not only, and perhaps not mainly, one about facts. Second, on either side of what looks like an intractable divide, scholars insist that the issue they are debating is complex – and that their opponents fail to grasp that complexity.[6] Apparently, these scholars agree that the British Empire cannot be reduced to a simple question of for or against. To begin to understand why the debate is nevertheless so fierce, in this chapter, I will study it as a case of disagreement over what I call 'exemplar empires'.

Given the differences between, say, settler colonialism in Australia, plantation colonialism in the Caribbean, the British Raj in India and the informal empire in Argentina, it is more apt to talk not of *the* British Empire, but of a number of British Empire*s*. However, this chapter argues that contemporary British memory culture is marked by a singularisation of the imperial past. Here, the Empire is summed up in a few emblematic images and episodes that are seen as representative of the whole. This is a useful strategy for managing complexity. It is communicatively impractical to have to refer to the imperial past in all its variegated forms whenever one wants to invoke it. We think in symbols, and it makes sense for us to use shorthands to stand in metonymically for the whole. The disagreement at the level of description is about what shorthands – exemplar empires – are most suitable to sum up half a millennium of imperial activities.

In this chapter, I will attempt to account for the vehemence of this debate by examining how people draw on, and give weight to, differing exemplar empires. While the rhetorical patterns I study are widespread in arguments about empire, my interest here is in public interventions by scholars, that is, the intersection between academic and popular discussion. I will focus on two moments of particularly fierce debate, the reception of Niall Ferguson's 2003 bestseller *Empire: How Britain Made the Modern World* and the accompanying TV series, and the controversy surrounding the 2017 opening of a research centre dedicated to studying 'Ethics and Empire' at the University of Oxford, headed by theologian Nigel Biggar. The conflicts can be partly explained by these scholars' involvement in contested contemporary political questions, drawing lessons from the past. In the context of the wars in Iraq and Afghanistan, Ferguson commended the USA on taking up the mantle of the British Empire, while Biggar, facing the twin challenges of Brexit and Scottish nationalism, listed the habit of 'deploying hard power' as part of 'what the United Kingdom is good for'. His conclusion that such interventionism 'is the legacy of empire' suggests the way the colonial past is put to contemporary – and controversial – use.[7] Ferguson's book is included in this chapter's discussions because it was clearly aimed at a general audience. Indeed, Elizabeth Buettner notes the influence of the book and TV series, with university students of imperial history often claiming 'that their initial interest had been sparked by Ferguson's multimedia contributions'.[8] In the following, I will look at how these two publicly vocal scholars and their critics have discussed the British Empire often using similar rhetorical flourishes: accusing their opponents of reducing past complexities, disagreeing over how best to sum up empire, questioning each other's moral evaluation of it and worrying that their version of the past is forgotten. While interested in their similarities, I am not arguing that all researchers necessarily have a reductive view of empire, nor that they are equally misguided in their assessments of the past and how it is remembered in contemporary Britain. While empire remains only one of several interests for Ferguson and Biggar, many of their critics have devoted entire careers to the study of colonialism, and their challenges to overly positive representations of the imperial past are based on solid research.

In his essay (and subsequent book) 'The Imperial History Wars', Dane Kennedy explores the renewed interest in the imperial past among US and UK historians in recent decades. He suggests that this upsurge in scholarly interest has been fuelled by racial anxieties at home as well as by the wars in the Falklands, Iraq and Afghanistan, and that more attention ought to be paid to 'the role that social and ideological forces play in shaping the questions we pose and the answers we offer about the imperial past'.[9] While Kennedy's focus is on the strictly professional work of these scholars, imperial historians have not restricted themselves to debating the past in monographs and journal articles. Instead, the conversation – sustained by historians, postcolonial critics and even theologians – has moved into the public sphere of newspaper commentary, television appearances and online fora. As it enters the public sphere, the debate becomes about more than historiography; it develops into arguments over memory, identity and politics, and these in turn have the potential to shape British cultural memory of the imperial past. In order to understand the emotional force of these charged discussions, then, it may be helpful to turn to memory studies. Like Iwona Irwin-Zarecka, I am interested in understanding what it is 'that makes people care so much about "their" past'.[10] Inspired by her approach of asking 'questions about the texture of conflict itself',[11] I will dissect the dynamics of how scholars debate the memory of empire in the British public sphere and in turn draw a wider conclusion about how public memory of empire is formed.

Scholars of memory have long debated whether and how to distinguish between history and memory.[12] Describing the difference between the two, historian Peter Novick suggests the following:

> To understand something historically is to be aware of its complexity, to have sufficient detachment to see it from multiple perspectives, to accept the ambiguities, including moral ambiguities, of protagonists' motives and behavior. Collective memory simplifies; sees events from a single, committed perspective; is impatient with ambiguities of any kind; reduces events to mythic archetypes.[13]

This, of course, is a somewhat optimistic view of the historical practice. The reliance of history on narrative and the selective, interpretive process involved have been familiar since Hayden White's intervention fifty years ago.[14] However, the ideal of history as at least striving for a detachment from its object of interrogation persists. Likewise, while collective memory is often contentious (as the present cases demonstrate), Novick's point about the tendency to reduction is well made. Proponents of any given account of the past will tend to simplify their story in ways that might raise eyebrows in academic research. Yet as we will see, this clear line between complexity and simplicity is continuously muddied.

As academics, the scholars I examine are committed to the idea of complexity. Yet when appearing in the public sphere, they are faced with the pressure for simplicity in communication. As I will demonstrate, the awareness of complexity as well as the pressure for simplicity are integral to their topic of discussion as the richness of the imperial past makes it at once necessary and problematic to reduce. Once reduced to exemplar empires, the battle over how to judge them and which exemplars to remember can begin.

Committed to complexity

On either side of the divide, we find the insistence that the imperial past is more complex than one's opponents will admit. Ferguson opens *Empire* with the claim that '[i]t is nowadays quite conventional to think that, on balance, [Empire] was bad'.[15] He finds evidence of this in calls for reparations and apologies, in the tone of BBC coverage and in the attitude of his fellow students during his Oxford days.[16] Placing himself as providing a more complex narrative, Ferguson states: 'The question is not whether British imperialism was without blemish. It was not. The question is whether there could have been a less bloodless path to modernity.'[17] His professed hope is to 'enable the reader to decide'.[18] Yet critics have rejected his claim to evenhanded attention to the nuances of the imperial past. In his scholarly review of Ferguson's television series, historian Jon Wilson concludes that the reality of empire was much more complex than what Ferguson would allow. Indeed, '"empire" meant many different things in many different places'.[19] In *The Guardian*, Wilson says Ferguson's 'fable' is inspired by nineteenth-century imperialists: 'based on a version of British history last taught well over half a century ago, these kinds of arguments [of benign imperialism] are not taken seriously by historians today'.[20] Professor Priyamvada Gopal also dismisses Ferguson's 'fairytale' as not only 'simplistic' but an 'aggressive rewriting of history'.[21] To his detractors, Ferguson's supposed attention to the complexities of empire is rejected as a rhetorical ploy, serving only, in Pankaj Mishra's words, to 'absolve himself from admitting to the role of imperialism's structural violence in the making of the modern world'.[22]

A similar dynamic of an empire-celebrant's professed complexity dismissed by his critics was evident in the controversy surrounding the launch of Biggar's 'Ethics and Empire' centre. The homepage of the centre set the scene for its intervention: 'In most reaches of contemporary academic discourse ...

the topic of ethics and empire raises no questions to which widely accepted answers are not immediately to hand. By definition, "empire" is imperialist; imperialism is wicked; and empire is therefore unethical. Nothing of interest remains to be explored.'[23] Against this perceived lack of academic curiosity, Biggar's centre said it 'begs to differ', aiming instead to point out the diversity of historical experience covered by the term 'empire'. Biggar was already well known for coupling a pro-empire stance to a right-wing agenda and for defending Cecil Rhodes as well as political scientist Bruce Gilley's 2017 call for 'recolonisation'. Consequently, the launch of the centre caused a stir among scholars of empire. In December 2017, an open letter by Biggar's Oxford colleagues complained about what they saw as the project's reductive take on the past: 'far from offering greater nuance and complexity, Biggar's approach is too polemical and simplistic to be taken seriously'.[24] A second letter, signed by scholars from numerous universities, also maintained that 'the crude cost/benefit analysis proposed by the Ethics and Empire project wilfully obscures the complexities which scholars of empire have carefully unpicked in recent decades'.[25] What is striking here is how Biggar and his detractors seem to agree that empire is complex, while seeing it as misrepresented and simplified in the hands of their opponent.

The rhetorical starting point for Biggar and Ferguson as well as their detractors is a commitment to the idea of scholarly curiosity, of openness to nuance and the absence of pre-existing moral and political assumptions that might steer the researcher. If all agree that these are the standards with which to pursue research, and on the complexity of the imperial past, it may be hard to grasp the emotional intensity of their debate. Studying the texture of the conflict, however, we will see that it is as much about memory and politics as about historiography. This is a descriptive disagreement about how best to sum up empire and a normative dispute about whether and how to judge it morally. These disagreements are intensified by the fear of forgetting.

A descriptive disagreement: Exemplar empires

To understand this disagreement, it is instructive to consider it first at the level of description. If forced to sum up the centuries of imperial experience, how would each side characterise Britain's former empire? Imperial historians have long maintained that their object of study is too complex to be referred to in the singular; John Gallagher and Ronald Robinson propose that imperial historians are 'very much at the mercy of [their] own particular concept of empire' as they are 'writing about different empires … generalizing from eccentric or isolated aspects of them'.[26] It is significant that they use the plural to refer not to *the* British Empire, but to a number of British Empire*s*. In subsequent decades, their colleagues have followed suit by showing the diversity of the intentions and means by which the various parts of the Empire were acquired and run.[27] 'Empire' names so much that it makes the concept groan at the seams.

This complexity makes imperial history particularly open, or vulnerable, to individual interpretation, as it cannot be captured in a single frame. Yet we try to. As Ann Rigney explains, 'memories are always "scarce" in relation to everything that theoretically might have been remembered' and so a process of selection is always in play.[28] In order to be able to refer to the imperial past at all, people have to summarise it, using a metonymic concept of 'the British Empire'. In metonymy, a smaller part stands for the whole, so that, say, slavery might come to stand for the Empire. Drawing on Pierre Nora, Rigney describes the 'convergence' that happens as a complex historical period becomes distilled into a few 'sites of memory' which, in Nora's words, 'provide "a maximum amount of meaning in a minimum number of signs"'.[29] This distillation may be inconsequential if there is agreement upon both what the part and the whole are, but in the case of the memory of empire, that is far from the case. Rather, there is both disagreement on which signs or 'sites' are the most appropriate and on what meaning they are imbued with, that is, what totality they represent.

On the level of description, then, different people have in mind different core ideas about what the Empire was. For some, the most suitable exemplars of British colonialism are slavery, the Amritsar massacre, the genocide of Aboriginal peoples, the concentration camps of the Mau Mau and Boer Wars or the dispossession of Indigenous lands. For others, drawing on a longstanding tradition of defending empire through its 'civilising' mission,[30] empire is better summed up as the spread of Western medicine, democracy and the rule of law, the fight against fascism during the Second World War, the abolition of the slave trade, railways in India or global trade. These differences in exemplar empires signal larger disagreements about the nature of British colonialism in its entirety. Because the imperial past encompasses such complexity, it is possible for one person to associate it with slavery and for another to link it to railway construction, for one person to think of it at its most basic as the spread of liberal ideas and for another to see it primarily as an institution of physical and epistemic violence. Importantly, I am not arguing that these reductions are equally accurate. Nor are they equally appropriate. But they are all reductions of a complex system into a series of emblematic features.

Let us compare some examples of the kinds of characteristics invoked by scholars who debate the memory of empire in the public. Ferguson says his book seeks to show that the legacy of Empire is not just 'racism, racial discrimination, xenophobia and related intolerance' – which in any case existed long before colonialism – but

- the triumph of capitalism as the optimal system of economic organization;
- the Anglicization of North America and Australasia;
- the internationalization of the English language;
- the enduring influence of the Protestant version of Christianity; and, above all
- the survival of parliamentary institutions, which far worse empires were poised to extinguish in the 1940s.[31]

In pedagogical fashion, Ferguson has listed what he sees as the most significant legacies of empire. The choice of these is not innocent, nor is it likely that readers of this book will agree that all of these are positive legacies. Ferguson's political observations, that is, his judgement of what is good for society today, influence what he chooses to highlight as positive aspects in the past. Indeed, in the television series that accompanied *Empire*, he summarises the same list and boldly states: 'These are the pillars of the modern world, and if you like the modern world, you can't deny its debt to the British Empire.'[32] In Ferguson's writing as well as in the public mind, modernity is equated with progress, and as a result appears as a positive legacy of colonialism. While we cannot give Ferguson credit for inventing this liberal justification of empire, his work serves to legitimise the idea that the Empire brought progress. At the same time, by dismissing the link between racism and empire (quoted from the 2001 Durban Declaration of the World Conference against Racism, Racial Discrimination, Xenophobia and Related Intolerance), Ferguson belittles what research has established as central legacies of colonialism. Thus, he not only highlights what he sees as the most emblematic features of the imperial past, but also rejects those that others have put forward.

Responding to Ferguson's 'elevation … to chief imperial historian on the BBC and now Channel 4', Gopal provides a counter-narrative that emphasises different exemplars. In Ferguson's representation, she says, '[c]olonialism – a tale of slavery, plunder, war, corruption, land-grabbing, famines, exploitation, indentured labour, impoverishment, massacres, genocide and forced resettlement – is rewritten into a benign developmental mission marred by a few unfortunate accidents and excesses'.[33] Ferguson and Gopal both reduce the past in order to construct radically opposing narratives. Like Ferguson, Gopal dismisses the narrative of her opponent to highlight an abbreviated list of imperial atrocities. In Ferguson's volume, slavery and Amritsar are discussed, but they are not what he chooses to emphasise when boiling down the past to its essentials. Indeed, as Elizabeth

Buettner notes, '"[b]lemishes" are briefly invoked to clear the decks for Ferguson's unabashed emphasis on the positive side of Britain's imperial "balance sheet"'.[34] Conversely, while Gopal agrees with Ferguson that colonialism is linked to the entrenchment of capitalism, her discussion in *Insurgent Empire* (2019) of the 'intertwining of racial, capitalist and colonial ideologies' indicates that this is hardly an occasion for celebration.[35] On the level of description, then, Ferguson and Gopal would agree on many of the events of the past but disagree on which of these best sum up the Empire. They have in mind different exemplar empires. This descriptive disagreement is intertwined with a prescriptive disagreement about how Britain should act in the present and future, with different exemplars emphasised to argue for, say, interventionism or racial justice.

Faced with other people's exemplar empires, those who debate the past gain new ammunition. These reductions can serve precisely to prove that one's opponent oversimplifies the past. Biggar may have in mind arguments like Gopal's when he suggests one should be careful not to 'believe what strident anti-colonialists tell us – namely, that our imperial past was one long, unbroken litany of oppression, exploitation and self-deception'. Rather, he insists that the British Empire was 'morally mixed': 'Pride at the Royal Navy's century-long suppression of the Atlantic slave trade ... will not be entirely obscured by shame at the slaughter of innocents at Amritsar in 1919.'[36] While exemplar empires can be useful shorthands to refer to a complex past, they allow for accusations of reductive generalisations.

Biggar's reference to the Amritsar massacre demonstrates how it is possible to acknowledge alternative visions of the imperial past while insisting that this image does not warrant as much attention as one's own favoured exemplar empire. Indeed, participants in debates surrounding British colonialism will often recognise the historical factuality of the exemplar put forth by their opponents; only the truly fact-resistant will try to deny the existence of slavery. But these scholars tend to suggest that some exemplars are more emblematic or important than others. Diagnosing disagreements over the imperial past on the descriptive level, then, I argue that they are heated because scholars lack consensus on which shorthands most suitably sum up the past. However, deciding what element should weigh heavier on the scale of historical judgement is not only a question of description but of evaluation, which is deeply normative.

A normative disagreement: Moral balance sheets

When scholars debate empire in the public sphere, they argue not only over how one might best describe the imperial past, but also about how one ought to judge it. Obviously, how one evaluates empire as a whole is closely related to what aspects of the imperial past one finds most emblematic. If one believes, like Ferguson, that the most significant legacy of the Empire was that it 'enhanced global welfare',[37] it is not odd that one values it more positively than if one believes, as Gopal does, that it was characterised rather by 'massacres, genocide and forced resettlement'.[38] The disagreement over how best to describe empire is thus entangled with the disagreement over how to judge it. As Irwin-Zarecka observes, it is not always clear whether a person disagrees with the descriptive or the normative aspect of historical narratives.

> Even debates that appear as purely intellectual exercises can – and often do – acquire moral dimension; being 'right' and 'wrong' about the meaning of history is both a cognitive and an ethical category. People on the opposing sides of a dispute judge each other in those terms; as the words used are so frequently the same, it is important for analysts to appreciate their separate realms of reference.[39]

Thus, when Wilson describes Ferguson's history as 'simply wrong',[40] his implied meaning is in both a factual and a moral sense. While Wilson argues that 'good television doesn't have to preach simplistic morality',[41] his own attack on Ferguson as a 'glossy glorification of imperial violence' comes with a moral evaluation (made urgent by the context of the Iraq War) of both Ferguson's history writing as 'misleading and dangerous' and of empire as 'always counter-productive'.[42] The contested debates over empire thus operate also on a normative level, where scholars publicly evaluate it in moral terms. This debate tends to develop into a discussion about whether such evaluation is even appropriate. Because moral evaluation assesses some aspects of the past as more morally salient than others, scholars often accuse one another of doing reductive 'balance sheet history'. Again, the consequence of having to refer to exemplar empires is that one's moral evaluation can also be accused of simplification.

Many of those involved in the debate will insist that the idea of passing moral judgement over the imperial past is mistaken. At such moments, moral evaluations are interpreted as compromising academic rigour. Taking issue with the claim on the Ethics and Empire homepage that conventional scholars see imperialism as wicked, the critical Oxford academics write in their statement: 'No historian (or, as far as we know, any cultural critic or postcolonial theorist) argues simply that imperialism was "wicked". Good and evil may be meaningful terms of analysis for theologians. They are useless to historians.'[43] Their worries are echoed in the second petition, which states that it is not 'possible to clearly demarcate "empire" as a fixed and stable subject which can be imputed with moral characteristics through time'.⁴⁴ Both these groups of scholars, then, problematise the feasibility or soundness of making generalising moral value judgements over the imperial past as a whole. In this, they dismiss as insincere the stated intention 'to develop a nuanced and historically intelligent Christian ethic of empire', that is, according to the centre, not to replace 'wicked' with 'good'.⁴⁵ The attack on moralism in the petitions jars with the impression that it is at least partly moral indignation that is driving the criticism of Biggar's centre. Indeed, it is a tenet of much work in critical theory and decolonial studies that ethics and epistemology cannot and should not be separated – that scholars of decolonisation must themselves work to further decolonisation within and outside the academy. One might say that it is not the notion that one can write in morally laden terms that is at issue for writers on both sides, but rather it is when they disagree with the tenor of an argument that it becomes viewed as moralising. As researchers speak in normative terms, they become vulnerable to accusations of doing propaganda.

Ferguson and Biggar are less reluctant than their critics about making explicit moral evaluations. Ferguson counters what he claims is the prevailing view of empire as 'one of history's Bad Things' with the 'plausible case that [it] … was a Good Thing'.⁴⁶ Given the ambitions of Biggar's centre, he, too, is hardly afraid of speaking in terms of morality. However, like his opponents, and like Ferguson, he seems to be driven by a sense that what he takes to be the prevailing normative assessment of empire is wrong, or at least simplistic, and stands in the way of scholarly curiosity. Exactly what is meant by the 'historically intelligent' ethic he wants to develop is unclear, but he pits it against the moral evaluations of historians, which he claims 'are typically covert, unreflective, and unaccountable'.⁴⁷

A particular version of the criticism of moral judgement of the past is the accusation that one's opponent is doing 'balance sheet history', considering various parts of the past against one another and concluding whether the total adds up to a positive or negative track record. A pertinent example is Ferguson's rhetorical question about the Second World War: 'the British sacrificed her Empire to stop the Germans, Japanese, and Italians from keeping theirs. Did not that sacrifice alone expunge all the Empire's other sins?'⁴⁸ This assessment, however, is predicated on the kind of reduction with which we have seen historians take issue. In order to measure different parts of history on the moral scales of the present, one needs to reduce them to simple blocks of 'faults' and 'benefits' that will fit on those scales.

Precisely for that reason, such 'balance sheet history' will often meet with criticism from colleagues, in particular if they disagree with one's normative evaluation overall. When criticising Biggar's Ethics and Empire project, the Oxford signatories insist that the centre could not pretend to offer serious history when it proposes such arguments as that the British empire's abolition of the slave trade stands simply as a positive entry in a balance-book against (for example) the Amritsar massacre or the Tasmanian genocide. Abolition does not somehow erase the British empire's own practice of slavery and the benefits it continued to reap from the slave trade long after it ended – such as railway investments in the UK or cotton imports from the US South.[49]

The premise here is a rejection of the notion that history can be measured on a balance sheet. However, the authors risk continuing the balancing logic when their riposte is to re-emphasise the significance of slavery by reminding us of its enduring legacies. Rather than abandoning the balance book altogether, the signatories increase the size of the negative entries. Biggar, in return, insists that the accusation is a 'strawman'.

> Nowhere have I argued that the sins of empire are outweighed by its benefits; I have merely made the point that empire is morally complex and ambiguous. On the whole I don't believe in crude, utilitarian analyses: the goods and evils involved are far too various in kind to be 'weighed' or 'balanced' in any truly rational way. Most cost-benefit analysis is merely prejudice masquerading as mathematics.

Biggar turns the accusation back on his opponents and implies that he would not himself be prone to balance sheeting. This despite the fact that he is not averse to statements that clearly use a similar logic, as we saw above in his argument that pride in the Navy's fight against the slave trade cannot be outweighed by shame at the Amritsar massacre.[50] Not only do terms like 'pride' and 'shame' imply a moral evaluation of the past; Biggar is clearly putting the sources of these emotions on a scale when insisting that one will not crowd out the other – and when he suggests that the source of pride is only one of any number of examples, he reveals which side of the scales he thinks is heavier.

Biggar's reference to 'pride' and 'shame' and Ferguson's 'Good Thing/ Bad Thing' dichotomy reveal a tendency to binary thinking that also influences wider public discourse about empire, including a much-cited 2014 YouGov poll that asked Britons whether they felt 'proud' or 'ashamed' of the British Empire.[51] This dichotomous understanding of the available emotional responses to the colonial past may itself go some way towards explaining the heated nature of the debate. However, importantly, Biggar and Ferguson's critics are not asking for contrition, but for recognition. But in the binary scheme of pride and shame, questioning the appropriateness of pride and demanding an engagement with the fullness of imperial history is interpreted as enforced shame.[52]

The scholarly commitment to complexity means that it is more appealing to dismiss the balance sheet of another than to embrace one's own use of the method. The insistence that one cannot simply pass judgement on the entire history of empire is associated with the truism found on both sides of the debate that history in general, and imperial history in particular, is complex. But despite many claims to the contrary, scholars who debate empire publicly do seem to pass judgement, settling on exemplar empires while insisting that the imperial experience was quite diverse. As they debate the meaning of the imperial past, both sides tend to offer their own position as the necessary nuancing of an otherwise simplified debate. However, those interventions are themselves premised on the carving up of the past in piles of 'good' and 'bad'. In that process, empire is repeatedly established as an entity whose moral meaning may be assessed in the singular. The implicit or explicit moral component of disputes over empire helps to explain their emotional vehemence. How the past is remembered is not merely about historical accuracy but about good and evil and everything in between. Finally, as we will see below, the debate over empire becomes heated when people fear that certain aspects of it might be forgotten.

The fear of forgetting

In his conclusion to *Empire*, Ferguson cites Rudyard Kipling's poem 'The White Man's Burden' and claims that '[n]o one would dare use such politically incorrect language today'.[53] And yet, use it is precisely what he does. As Gopal puts it in her critical review of Ferguson's public appearances, '[b]ehind such talk and the embrace of the broadcasters is the insistence that we are being offered gutsy truths that the "politically correct" establishment would love to suppress. This is the neo-conservative as spunky rebel against liberal tyranny.'[54] Ferguson relies on what Sara Ahmed would call an 'inflationary logic' that magnifies the power of those perceived to prohibit his point of view.[55] In the opening sequence of the television series, he suggests that '[t]he empire's sins tend to be better remembered than its achievements.'[56] In the same vein, we have seen Biggar's centre attacking the 'conventional' view which, it is claimed, permeates 'most reaches of contemporary academic discourse'.[57] In Biggar's case, the narrative of a repressed version of the past is often told as a personal story of victimisation at the hands of those who wish to silence his unpopular views, drawing on the idea of speaking for a silent majority who are afraid to speak up in defence of empire because of the 'intimidation' of a 'small minority'.[58] This perception of a silenced story is used to provide rhetorical leverage to Ferguson and Biggar's arguments as the necessary adjustment of a debate that has swung too far to one side. I have explored this dynamic in more detail elsewhere,[59] but what interests me here is how the notion of societal forgetting constitutes an imagined threat which adds to the urgency of those who debate empire and how this dynamic is related to the use of exemplar empires.

The trope of a conventional story crowding out an alternative account can also be found among Biggar and Ferguson's critics. Backed by polling that demonstrates the overwhelmingly positive view of empire in the British public,[60] scholars have pointed out that it is in fact the celebratory account that has been dominant. As Wilson remarks of Ferguson's TV series,

> 'Empire' reflects the belief amongst Channel 4 executives in the dominance of a liberal-left conception of empire that emphasizes its vices over its virtues. But the well-meaning burghers of Hampstead do not have quite the same hold over the popular imagination as the series producers presume. The views expressed in the *Daily Mail* and *Daily Telegraph*, it might be suggested, have a far stronger hold. [61]

He goes on to list what is remembered and forgotten in the British press, pitting the forgotten 'deeds of Indian or Caribbean troops on the Western front' against the celebrated 'white Australian and New Zealand soldiers at Gallipoli', the focus on the 'black hole of Calcutta' against neglected Indian famine deaths, and so on.[62] In setting up these contrasts, Wilson draws on a number of exemplars to suggest that in the public sphere, if not among scholars of colonialism, the dominant narrative of empire is a positive one. Connecting Ferguson to past 'self-aggrandising myths of empire' and 'contemporary US imperial propaganda', Gopal accuses 'the British media [of] colluding in a dangerous denial of the past' and argues that '[f]orgetting history is tempting but undermines a society's capacity for change'.[63] In other words, it is possible for discussants on either side to perceive their interpretation of the past as forgotten or pushed aside by a master narrative.

This concern that a part of the past is being 'forgotten' or 'obscured' may help to explain the vehemence of the debate, with various participants concerned that their opponents not only overrepresent one aspect of the past, but that that omission represents a broader amnesia, or even what Dietmar Rothermund calls a 'conspiracy of silence'.[64] Correspondingly, the idea that one is bringing back into public memory a forgotten past lies at the centre of many arguments. Geoffrey Cubitt speaks of the 'moral imperative' underlying memorialisation, summarised in the phrase 'Lest we forget'.[65] The moral imperative is related to the moral evaluation described above, but also to the popular understanding of how memory works as a field of competition. Even the terms used to analyse memory debates like 'master narrative' and 'counter-memory' seem to imply that there is one governing account against which others may hope to subversively assert themselves. In reality, there will often be a tug-of-war between different accounts, and these may hold primacy among variant groups.[66] The spectre of forgetting informs both sides of this debate. The notion of imperial amnesia *tout court* tends to be code for the perceived underrepresentation of a particular version of the imperial past. Indeed, the lament that Britons fail to engage with the past is often followed by observations about how they engage *wrongly* with the past.

In *Multidirectional Memory* (2009), Michael Rothberg suggests that collective memories of the Holocaust and of colonialism need not be read as competitive. Instead, Rothberg insists that memory is not 'a zero-sum game', and he demonstrates how these memory cultures have actually drawn sustenance from one another.[67] However, despite Rothberg's astute observation, actors who argue over the past in the public sphere clearly act as though they were indeed engaged in a game where there can be only one winning account. I believe the logic of singularisation of the imperial past plays a role in this. The tendency to reduce imperial complexity to a few exemplar empires means that people can feel threatened that their version of the past will be drowned out if other accounts are allowed to stand unopposed. In popular imagination, the inverse of remembering is forgetting, not more remembering. The politicised nature of the past makes it all the more important that one's account is not pushed to the margins.

Conclusion

I have argued here that the necessary reduction to 'exemplar empires' and the resultant accusations of simplifying, balance sheeting and forgetting may help to account for the continuing, heated and public debates over Britain's imperial past.

Of course, the disagreement over exemplar empires and how to evaluate them is only the tip of the iceberg. Imperialism is closely linked to British society and identity, and debates surrounding colonial histories often become even fiercer when those associations are made explicit. Thus, the Empire has been used to argue over contemporary racism, Brexit and the wars in Iraq and Afghanistan. On several occasions, the argument has turned very personal indeed. When he felt Mishra accused him of racism, Ferguson threatened with a libel suit.[68] When she referred to an article by Biggar as 'outright racist imperial apologetics', Gopal became the target of venomous attacks by online trolls, the *Daily Mail* and Biggar himself.[69] While it has been outside the scope of this chapter to address it, the way in which the imperial past gets linked to emotionally charged discussions about identity, race and Britain's role in the world constitutes a crucial venue for future research. History debated in the public sphere is about more than getting one's facts straight. It is about how the past is remembered by the population more widely, about how it is morally assessed in the present, about who we are by virtue of how we read our past and about how we can feel and act now and in the future, given a past in which we take pride or shame.

Through their public interventions, scholars of empire legitimise certain representations of the past and provide the rest of society with a vocabulary through which to understand and discuss that past. When they simplify the issues at hand, they invite others to follow suit. The reduction of historical complexity to exemplar empires thus affects the memory of colonialism that circulates in British society beyond the discussions between academics. In a polarised debating climate, there is little appetite for recognising nuances in the opponent's viewpoint or admitting one's own simplifications. Attention to the much-vaunted complexity of the colonial past is jeopardised when remembering empire becomes less about historical understanding and more about defending a political position.

Notes

1 Priyamvada Gopal, *Insurgent Empire: Anticolonial Resistance and British Dissent* (London; New York: Verso Books, 2019); Kenneth Pomeranz, 'Empire & "Civilizing" Missions, Past & Present', *Daedalus*, 134:2 (2005), pp. 34–45.
2 Katie Donington, 'Relics of Empire? Colonialism and the Culture Wars', in *Embers of Empire in Brexit Britain*, ed. by Stuart Ward and Astrid Rasch (London: Bloomsbury, 2019).
3 James V. Wertsch, 'Collective Memory', in *Memory in Mind and Culture*, ed. by Pascal Boyer and James V. Wertsch (Cambridge: Cambridge University Press, 2009), p. 122.
4 Stuart Ward and Astrid Rasch, eds, *Embers of Empire in Brexit Britain* (London: Bloomsbury, 2019).
5 Iwona Irwin-Zarecka, *Frames of Remembrance: The Dynamics of Collective Memory* (New Brunswick, NJ: Transaction Publishers, 1994), p. 67.
6 Ironically, I will myself have to simplify this debate into one where participants see empire either as 'a good or bad thing' (Niall Ferguson, *Empire: How Britain Made the Modern World* (London: Allen Lane, 2003), p. xi) in order to study the patterns of argumentation.
7 Ferguson, *Empire*, pp. 377–381; Nigel Biggar, 'What the United Kingdom is Good For', These Islands, 24 October 2017 www.these-islands.co.uk/publications/i260/what_the_united_kingdom_is_good_for.aspx [accessed 11 August 2020].
8 Elizabeth Buettner, *Europe after Empire: Decolonization, Society, and Culture* (Cambridge: Cambridge University Press, 2016), p. 442.
9 Dane Kennedy, 'The Imperial History Wars', *Journal of British Studies*, 54:1 (2015), p. 6; Dane Kennedy, *The Imperial History Wars: Debating the British Empire* (London: Bloomsbury, 2018).

10 Irwin-Zarecka, *Frames of Remembrance*, p. 71.
11 Irwin-Zarecka, *Frames of Remembrance*, p. 67.
12 For introductions to this debate, see, e.g., Geoffrey Cubitt, *History and Memory* (Manchester: Manchester University Press, 2007); James V. Wertsch, *Voices of Collective Remembering* (Cambridge: Cambridge University Press, 2002), pp. 19–20; Astrid Erll, *Memory in Culture* (Basingstoke: Palgrave Macmillan, 2011), pp. 39–45.
13 Peter Novick, *The Holocaust in American Life* (Boston, MA: Houghton Mifflin Harcourt, 2000), pp. 3–4.
14 Hayden White, *Metahistory: The Historical Imagination in Nineteenth-Century Europe* (Baltimore, MA: Johns Hopkins University Press, 1973).
15 Ferguson, *Empire*, p. xi.
16 Ferguson, *Empire*, pp. xii–xiii, xvii.
17 Ferguson, *Empire*, p. xxviii.
18 Ferguson, *Empire*, p. xxviii.
19 Jon Wilson, 'Niall Ferguson's Imperial Passion', *History Workshop Journal*, 56 (2003), pp. 175–183, p. 182.
20 Jon Wilson, 'False and Dangerous', *The Guardian*, 8 February 2003, www.theguardian.com/education/2003/feb/08/highereducation.britishidentity [accessed 13 August 2020].
21 Priyamvada Gopal, 'The Story Peddled by Imperial Apologists Is a Poisonous Fairytale', *The Guardian*, 27 June 2006, www.theguardian.com/commentisfree/2006/jun/28/comment.britishidentity [accessed 9 August 2019].
22 Pankaj Mishra, 'Watch This Man', *London Review of Books*, 3 November 2011, pp. 10–12.
23 'Ethics and Empire – McDonald Centre', www.mcdonaldcentre.org.uk/ethics-and-empire [accessed 30 May 2019].
24 James McDougall, Erin O'Halloran, Hussein Ahmed Hussein Omar and Peter Hill, 'Ethics and Empire: An Open Letter from Oxford Scholars', The Conversation, 19 December 2017, http://theconversation.com/ethics-and-empire-an-open-letter-from-oxford-scholars-89333 [accessed 8 January 2019].
25 Jon Wilson, 'A Collective Statement on "Ethics and Empire"', Scholarsofempire, 21 December 2017, https://medium.com/oxfordempireletter/a-collective-statement-on-ethics-and-empire-19c2477871a0 [accessed 4 September 2018].
26 Jon Gallagher and Ronald Robinson, 'The Imperialism of Free Trade', *The Economic History Review*, 6:1 (1953), pp. 1–15, p. 1.
27 David Fieldhouse, 'Can Humpty-Dumpty Be Put Together Again? Imperial History in the 1980s', *The Journal of Imperial and Commonwealth History*, 12:2 (1984), pp. 9–23; Alan Lester, 'Imperial Circuits and Networks: Geographies of the British Empire', *History Compass*, 4:1 (2006), pp. 124–141; Ann Laura Stoler and Frederick Cooper, 'Between Metropole and Colony', in *Tensions of Empire: Colonial Cultures in a Bourgeois World* (Berkeley: University of California Press, 1997), pp. 1–56.
28 Ann Rigney, 'Plenitude, Scarcity and the Circulation of Cultural Memory', *Journal of European Studies*, 35:1 (2005), pp. 11–28, p. 17.

29 Pierre Nora, *Les Lieux de mémoire*, 1997 [1984–1992], Vol. I, p. 38, cited in Rigney, 'Plenitude, Scarcity and the Circulation of Cultural Memory', p. 18.
30 Kenneth Pomeranz, 'Empire and "Civilizing" Missions'.
31 Ferguson, *Empire*, p. xxvii.
32 David Wilson, *Empire: How Britain Made the Modern World* (Channel 4).
33 Gopal, 'A Poisonous Fairytale'.
34 Buettner, *Europe after Empire*, p. 442.
35 Gopal, *Insurgent Empire*, p. 359.
36 Nigel Biggar, 'Don't Feel Guilty about Our Colonial History', *The Times*, 30 November 2017, www.thetimes.co.uk/article/don-t-feel-guilty-about-our-colonial-history-ghvstdhmj [accessed 30 May 2019].
37 Ferguson, *Empire*, p. xx.
38 Gopal, 'A Poisonous Fairytale'.
39 Irwin-Zarecka, *Frames of Remembrance*, p. 83.
40 Wilson, 'False and Dangerous'.
41 Wilson, 'Niall Ferguson's Imperial Passion', p. 182.
42 Wilson, 'False and Dangerous'.
43 McDougall et al., 'An Open Letter'.
44 Wilson, 'A Collective Statement on "Ethics and Empire"'.
45 'Ethics and Empire – McDonald Centre'.
46 Ferguson, *Empire*, pp. xvii, xxi.
47 Nigel Biggar, 'Here's My Reply to Those Who Condemn My Project on Ethics and Empire', *The Times*, 23 December 2017, www.thetimes.co.uk/article/heres-my-reply-to-those-who-condemn-my-project-on-ethics-and-empire-cw5f2z80x [accessed 8 January 2019].
48 Ferguson, *Empire*, p. 363. See also Lawrence James, 'Yes, Mistakes Were Made, but We Must Never Stop Being Proud of the Empire', 18 April 2012, www.dailymail.co.uk/debate/article-2131801/Yes-mistakes-stop-proud-Empire.html [accessed 7 June 2019].
49 McDougall et al., 'An Open Letter'.
50 Biggar, 'Don't Feel Guilty about Our Colonial History'.
51 Will Dahlgreen, 'The British Empire Is "Something to Be Proud Of"', YouGov, 26 July 2014, https://yougov.co.uk/topics/politics/articles-reports/2014/07/26/britain-proud-its-empire [accessed 22 September 2017].
52 I thank the anonymous reviewer for this point.
53 Ferguson, *Empire*, p. 380.
54 Gopal, 'A Poisonous Fairytale'.
55 Sara Ahmed, 'Open Forum Imaginary Prohibitions: Some Preliminary Remarks on the Founding Gestures of the "New Materialism"', *European Journal of Women's Studies*, 15:1 (2008), pp. 23–39, p. 31. I explore this in more detail in Astrid Rasch, '"Keep the Balance": The Politics of Remembering Empire in Postcolonial Britain', *Journal of Commonwealth and Postcolonial Studies*, 7:1 (2019), pp. 218–219.
56 Wilson, *Empire*, episode 1, 'Why Britain?'.
57 Ferguson, *Empire*, p. xx; 'Ethics and Empire – McDonald Centre'.

58 Currently unavailable online, the original essay 'Outing Yourself as a Rightist Isn't Easy' was published in *The Conservative*, 3 (April 2017). A copy can be found at michaelroberts4004, 'Oxford Theologian Outs Himself – as Being on the Right', Peddling and Scaling God and Darwin, 2017, https://michaelroberts4004.wordpress.com/2017/06/22/oxford-theologian-outs-himself-as-being-on-the-right [accessed 17 August 2020].
59 Rasch, '"Keep the Balance"'.
60 Dahlgreen, 'The British Empire Is "Something to Be Proud Of"'.
61 Wilson, 'Niall Ferguson's Imperial Passion'.
62 Wilson, 'Niall Ferguson's Imperial Passion'.
63 Gopal, 'A Poisonous Fairytale'.
64 Dietmar Rothermund, 'Introduction: Memories of Post-Imperial Nations', in *Memories of Post-Imperial Nations: The Aftermath of Decolonization, 1945–2013*, ed. by Dietmar Rothermund (New Delhi: Cambridge University Press, 2015), p. 5.
65 Geoffrey Cubitt, *History and Memory* (Manchester: Manchester University Press, 2007), p. 144.
66 See Astrid Rasch, 'Subversion or Identity Work: Tracing the Reception of Zimbabwean Counter-Narrative Memoirs', *Journal of Southern African Studies*, 47:5 (2021), pp. 817–834.
67 Michael Rothberg, *Multidirectional Memory: Remembering the Holocaust in the Age of Decolonization* (Palo Alto, CA: Stanford University Press, 2009).
68 Niall Ferguson, 'Letters', *London Review of Books*, 17 November 2011, www.lrb.co.uk/the-paper/v33/n22/letters [accessed 30 August 2022]; Alexander Abad-Santos, 'A Harvard Professor's Fight Over a Bad Book Review Goes Legal', *The Atlantic*, 29 November 2011, www.theatlantic.com/business/archive/2011/11/harvard-professors-fight-over-bad-book-review-goes-legal/334958 [accessed 18 August 2020].
69 See Richard Drayton, 'Biggar vs Little Britain', in Ward and Rasch, eds, *Embers of Empire in Brexit Britain*, p. 145; Devarshi Lodhia, 'Cambridge Lecturer Condemns Daily Mail over "Racist and Sexist Hatchet Job"', Varsity Online, 12 April 2018, www.varsity.co.uk/news/15297 [accessed 14 August 2020].

Bibliography

Abad-Santos, Alexander, 'A Harvard Professor's Fight Over a Bad Book Review Goes Legal', *The Atlantic*, 29 November 2011, www.theatlantic.com/business/archive/2011/11/harvard-professors-fight-over-bad-book-review-goes-legal/334958 [accessed 18 August 2020].

Ahmed, Sara, 'Open Forum Imaginary Prohibitions: Some Preliminary Remarks on the Founding Gestures of the "New Materialism"', *European Journal of Women's Studies*, 15:1 (2008), pp. 23–39.

Biggar, Nigel, 'Don't Feel Guilty about Our Colonial History', *The Times*, 30 November 2017, www.thetimes.co.uk/article/don-t-feel-guilty-about-our-colonial-history-ghvstdhmj [accessed 30 May 2019]

Biggar, Nigel, 'Here's My Reply to Those Who Condemn My Project on Ethics and Empire', *The Times*, 23 December 2017, www.thetimes.co.uk/article/heres-my-reply-to-those-who-condemn-my-project-on-ethics-and-empire-cw5f2z80x [accessed 8 January 2019].

Biggar, Nigel, 'What the United Kingdom is Good For', These Islands, 24 October 2017 www.these-islands.co.uk/publications/i260/what_the_united_kingdom_is_good_for.aspx [accessed 11 August 2020].

Buettner, Elizabeth, *Europe after Empire: Decolonization, Society, and Culture* (Cambridge: Cambridge University Press, 2016).

Cubitt, Geoffrey, *History and Memory* (Manchester: Manchester University Press, 2007).

Dahlgreen, Will, 'The British Empire Is "Something to Be Proud Of"', YouGov, 26 July 2014, https://yougov.co.uk/topics/politics/articles-reports/2014/07/26/britain-proud-its-empire/ [accessed 22 September 2017].

Donington, Katie, 'Relics of Empire? Colonialism and the Culture Wars', in *Embers of Empire in Brexit Britain*, ed. by Stuart Ward and Astrid Rasch (London: Bloomsbury, 2019).

Drayton, Richard, 'Biggar vs Little Britain', in *Embers of Empire in Brexit Britain*, ed. by Stuart Ward and Astrid Rasch (London: Bloomsbury, 2019).

Erll, Astrid, *Memory in Culture* (Basingstoke: Palgrave Macmillan, 2011).

'Ethics and Empire – McDonald Centre', www.mcdonaldcentre.org.uk/ethics-and-empire [accessed 30 May 2019].

Ferguson, Niall, *Empire: How Britain Made the Modern World* (London: Allen Lane, 2003).

Ferguson, Niall, 'Letters', *London Review of Books*, 17 November 2011, www.lrb.co.uk/the-paper/v33/n22/letters [accessed 30 August 2022].

Fieldhouse, David, 'Can Humpty-Dumpty Be Put Together Again? Imperial History in the 1980s', *The Journal of Imperial and Commonwealth History*, 12:2 (1984), pp. 9–23.

Gallagher, Jon and Ronald Robinson, 'The Imperialism of Free Trade', *The Economic History Review*, 6:1 (1953), pp. 1–15.

Gopal, Priyamvada, *Insurgent Empire: Anticolonial Resistance and British Dissent* (London; New York: Verso Books, 2019).

Gopal, Priyamvada, 'The Story Peddled by Imperial Apologists Is a Poisonous Fairytale', *The Guardian*, 27 June 2006, www.theguardian.com/commentisfree/2006/jun/28/comment.britishidentity [accessed 9 August 2019].

Irwin-Zarecka, Iwona, *Frames of Remembrance: The Dynamics of Collective Memory* (New Brunswick, NJ: Transaction Publishers, 1994).

James, Lawrence, 'Yes, Mistakes Were Made, but We Must Never Stop Being Proud of the Empire', 18 April 2012, www.dailymail.co.uk/debate/article-2131801/Yes-mistakes-stop-proud-Empire.html [accessed 7 June 2019].

Kennedy, Dane, 'The Imperial History Wars', *Journal of British Studies*, 54:1 (2015), pp. 5–22.

Kennedy, Dane, *The Imperial History Wars: Debating the British Empire* (London: Bloomsbury, 2018).

Lester, Alan, 'Imperial Circuits and Networks: Geographies of the British Empire', *History Compass*, 4:1 (2006), pp. 124–141.

Lodhia, Devarshi, 'Cambridge Lecturer Condemns Daily Mail over "Racist and Sexist Hatchet Job"', Varsity Online, 12 April 2018, www.varsity.co.uk/news/15297 [accessed 14 August 2020].

McDougall, James, Erin O'Halloran, Hussein Ahmed Hussein Omar and Peter Hill, 'Ethics and Empire: An Open Letter from Oxford Scholars', The Conversation, 19 December 2017, http://theconversation.com/ethics-and-empire-an-open-letter-from-oxford-scholars-89333 [accessed 8 January 2019].

michaelroberts4004, 'Oxford Theologian Outs Himself–as Being on the Right', Peddling and Scaling God and Darwin, 2017, https://michaelroberts4004.wordpress.com/2017/06/22/oxford-theologian-outs-himself-as-being-on-the-right [accessed 17 August 2020].

Mishra, Pankaj, 'Watch This Man', *London Review of Books*, 3 November 2011, pp. 10–12.

Novick, Peter, *The Holocaust in American Life* (Boston, MA: Houghton Mifflin Harcourt, 2000).

Pomeranz, Kenneth, 'Empire & "Civilizing" Missions, Past & Present', *Daedalus* 134:2 (2005), pp. 34–45.

Rasch, Astrid, '"Keep the Balance": The Politics of Remembering Empire in Postcolonial Britain', *Journal of Commonwealth and Postcolonial Studies*, 7:1 (2019), pp. 212–230.

Rasch, Astrid, 'Subversion or Identity Work? Tracing the Reception of Zimbabwean Counter-Narrative Memoirs', *Journal of Southern African Studies*, 47:5 (2021), pp. 817–834.

Rigney, Ann, 'Plenitude, Scarcity and the Circulation of Cultural Memory', *Journal of European Studies*, 35:1 (2005), pp. 11–28.

Rothberg, Michael, *Multidirectional Memory: Remembering the Holocaust in the Age of Decolonization* (Palo Alto, CA: Stanford University Press, 2009).

Rothermund, Dietmar, 'Introduction: Memories of Post-Imperial Nations', in *Memories of Post-Imperial Nations: The Aftermath of Decolonization, 1945–2013*, ed. by Dietmar Rothermund (New Delhi: Cambridge University Press, 2015).

Stoler, Ann Laura and Frederick Cooper, 'Between Metropole and Colony', in *Tensions of Empire: Colonial Cultures in a Bourgeois World* (Berkeley: University of California Press, 1997), pp. 1–56.

Ward, Stuart and Astrid Rasch, eds, *Embers of Empire in Brexit Britain* (London: Bloomsbury, 2019).

Wertsch, James V., 'Collective Memory', in *Memory in Mind and Culture*, ed. by Pascal Boyer and James V. Wertsch (Cambridge: Cambridge University Press, 2009).

Wertsch, James V., *Voices of Collective Remembering* (Cambridge: Cambridge University Press, 2002).

White, Hayden, *Metahistory: The Historical Imagination in Nineteenth-Century Europe* (Baltimore, MA: Johns Hopkins University Press, 1973).

Wilson, David, *Empire: How Britain Made the Modern World* (Channel 4).

Wilson, Jon, 'A Collective Statement on "Ethics and Empire"', Scholarsofempire, 21 December 2017, https://medium.com/oxfordempireletter/a-collective-statement-on-ethics-and-empire-19c2477871a0 [accessed 4 September 2018].

Wilson, Jon, 'False and Dangerous', *The Guardian*, 8 February 2003, www.theguardian.com/education/2003/feb/08/highereducation.britishidentity [accessed 13 August 2020].

Wilson, Jon, 'Niall Ferguson's Imperial Passion', *History Workshop Journal*, 56 (2003), pp. 175–183.

Part IV

At home in postcolonial Britain

9

Empire, security and citizenship in Arab British fiction

Tasnim Qutait

Speaking at a security conference in Munich in 2011, David Cameron argued that state multiculturalism had failed, having pursued a misguided policy of 'hands-off tolerance' where 'not enough is shared'.[1] His speech set out the need for a cohesive civic vision, elsewhere termed British values, the absence of which has left 'young Muslims feeling rootless'.[2] Cameron's suggestion was that a project of ethical re-education would serve to better inoculate against radicalisation. Much of the conference's subsequent press coverage focused on the phrase 'hands-off tolerance', encapsulating as it does the perceived abdication of government responsibility in confronting extremism. However, this rhetoric calling for a change in policy disguised continuities in political discourse around immigration in postimperial Britain, encapsulated ironically in the double logic of the statement that 'not enough is shared'. Though the terminology of managing difference has shifted, the emphasis remains on a future-oriented vision, placing the onus for social cohesion on immigrant communities, while tending to disregard both historical forms of injustice and ongoing discrimination. The War on Terror did not alter this logic, but rather intensified the focus on mitigating future risks under expanded systems of surveillance and security.

While 'security' tends to be seen as an uncomplicated good for everyone in society, scholars such as Gand Chowdhry, Sheila Nair, Pinar Bilgin, Tarak Barkawi and Mark Laffey have questioned its apparent apoliticism, arguing for the need to interrogate the historical conditions which determine who is protected and who is policed. Over the past two decades, security studies have focused on threats impacting Western liberal democracies, even as global phenomena such as climate crises and the rise of violent non-state actors disproportionately impact less economically developed countries. Zoë Marriage states that 'the security agenda globally has been driven by Northern concern over disorder, migration and terrorism'.[3] According to Pinar Bilgin, rather than constituting a blind spot in the field, 'the historical absence of non-Western insecurities has been constitutive both of the discipline [security studies] and of subjects and objects of security in different parts of the world', an absence which calls on us to find ways to contest the norms of how security is defined and for whom.[4] This chapter makes the case that focusing on literature as an object of analysis offers a textured approach towards interrogating how we construct security and risk, which, as Louise Amoore describes, are '[i]ndifferent to the contingent biographies that actually make up the underlying data ... not centered on who we are, nor even on what our data say about us, but on what can be imagined and inferred about who we might be – on our very proclivities and potentialities'.[5] In what follows, I examine four novels by Arab British writers, tracing how writers who identify as both Arab and British negotiate dual affiliations and reflect on the narratives of belonging which make the paradigms of security and risk management comprehensible.

Arab British/British Muslim

Camillia Fawzia El Solh notes that 'the presence of Arabs in Britain has tended to receive an almost incidental mention in published research on ethnic minorities'.[6] The first wave of Arabs immigrating to Britain began in the 1860s, when Yemeni sailors who were recruited to serve on British merchant vessels arrived to form the first settled Muslim communities in South Shields and Cardiff.[7] However, the majority of the Arab British community immigrated after the 1990s, which has contributed to this community being subsumed within the larger category of British Muslims. Accordingly, the category of 'Arab British literature', a small but growing body of works, is more often discussed under the broader categories of either Muslim writing or Anglophone Arab writing. As acknowledged by those working within the field, these labels involve a form of reduction, making either a region or religion the primary marker of identity.

Although the term 'Muslim writing' is now often used as though it is self-explanatory, its reliance on religion can be ambiguous. Claire Chambers describes how difficult it is to offer an 'established and transparent definition' for this label in her book *British Muslim Fictions* (2011).[8] Clearly, the emergence of Muslim writing as a literary genre cannot be disentangled from the historical construction of immigrant communities from Muslim-majority countries. According to Fred Halliday, it was only after the campaign against Salman Rushdie's *The Satanic Verses* in 1989 and then the first Gulf War that 'it became more common to talk of a "Muslim community" in Britain, of "Islam in Britain" and of "British Muslims" rather than referring to communities in ethnic or geographic terms'.[9] This mobilising of religion rather than class or ethnicity to define a British Muslim community was in other words framed by security concerns, and the past two decades have further consolidated the logic subsuming people from Muslim-majority countries into a single 'Muslim community'.

In the aftermath of 9/11 and especially following the 7/7 attacks in London, the homogenisation of Muslims has gone hand-in-hand with pre-emptive securitisation, with media representations of the 'Muslim community' both impacting and impacted by securitisation policies and programmes such as the UK Government's Prevent Strategy, instituted in 2011. Since mainstream stories about Muslims remain circumscribed within a risk management paradigm, the focus is often on how far representations replicate or complicate stereotypes rather than questioning the security lens applied (for example, a representation of a female suicide bomber can be described as empowering). What is needed is greater attention to the fact that current security discourses are inextricable from protracted conflicts in the Middle East, and therefore we need more scholarship on how the themes of security have been represented in fiction by writers from the region. This discussion is currently lacking in part due to a lack of familiarity; literature from the Middle East remains peripheral in comparative and world literature paradigms, including works written in English.

In what follows, I seek to investigate how Arab British writers represent the frameworks of security, both exploring how security functions under autocratic Arab states which cannot guarantee the security of their citizens, and how it functions for immigrants in Britain identified as Arab and/or Muslim. I first discuss novels by Leila Aboulela and Jamal Mahjoub which represent the formative experience of the Gulf War to explore the processes of identity formation for Sudanese immigrants in Britain. I then turn to novels by Robin Yassin-Kassab and Selma Dabbagh, where the protagonists negotiate the ever-present frameworks of security in Syria and Palestine, respectively, before confronting forms of securitisation based on racial or religious categories in Britain. My discussion of these four texts is far from comprehensive; instead, I draw connections between them, reflecting on the potential of literary texts to raise questions about how security is constructed and for whom the dominant understandings of security work. Through examining representations of how security is defined in the context of the enduring afterlives of empire, we can, as Anthony Burke describes, 'interrogate the images of self and other that animate (in)secure identities' and 'expose the violence and repression that is so often relied on to police them'.[10]

Insecurity, indifference and the stranger

Jamal Mahjoub's *Travelling with Djinns* (2003) follows the protagonist Yasin's road trip across Europe with his young son Leo, seeking to establish a connection with his child before an impending divorce. Yasin, the son of a Sudanese nationalist father and an English mother, works as a journalist in Britain, and is preoccupied, if not obsessed, with questions of identity and history. Thinking about his motivations for this journey, Yasin reflects that since he does not 'have an Africa to run away to … Europe is [his] dark continent and [he is] searching for the heart of it'.[11] Yasin's invocation of colonial adventure in reverse provides a backdrop to the novel's intertwining of past and present in order to pass on to his son some form of narrative about his heritage.

The journey functions as a frame narrative, allowing Mahjoub to weave Yasin's narration around flashbacks beginning with his childhood in Sudan. In a passage which reflects the novel's concern with the construction of history, Yasin recalls that as a child he learned that '[h]istory, the hard stuff, the earth-shattering events' was all about 'other people, other places'.

> In class we learned that history consisted of foreign words like Verdun and the Treaty of Versailles, Auschwitz, Pearl Harbor, Hiroshima, Dien Bien Phu. Those distant lawns and pavilions, those men in wide hats and breeches. We memorised words like Realpolitik and Von Bismarck, the scramble for Africa, without really understanding how they had affected us.[12]

The passage above, in its rapid listing of events, captures the fragmentary, impersonal version of colonial history Yasin is offered in his education, where what constitutes globally significant history is limited to the dominant actors of Europe and the USA. Yasin's sense of alienation from this Eurocentric history is further captured in his fascination with a photograph of colonial figures 'sitting on the deck of a Nile streamer at dusk, deciding our future', as he thinks how 'curiously absurd' it is that 'these strangers wearing rows of medals and huge mustaches had something to do with our present situation'.[13] Later, Mahjoub uses precisely the same word, absurd, when Yasin considers his father's dreams of independent Sudan and his 'absurd conviction that the curious collection of ethnicities, races and creeds fenced in together by colonial rule could be turned into a cohesive nation'.[14] In this echo across pages, 'absurd' codifies the extent to which the dream of national independence has failed under the contradictions of upholding *uti possidetis juris*, the borders of colonial rule, as the principle upon which to found an independent state. For the adult Yasin, to speak of 'the absurd conviction' that independent Sudan could hold together is a conscious repudiation of the postcolonial nationalist narrative, a recognition that '[t]he great age of national independence had proved to be nothing more than a neocolonial mirage'.[15] Mahjoub's exploration of the tragedies enforced by colonial borders anticipates a future collapse of national coherence, a collapse which proved true in 2011, seven years after this novel was published, when the founding of South Sudan finally proved the failure of the Sudanese national unity effort following colonisation.

One of the main strands of the narrative involves the protagonist's realisation of the discrepancies between his Western education and his contingent belonging as an immigrant during the Gulf War, a formative experience altering Yasin's perception of himself as a journalist and of the British media. Though the protagonist's parents are Sudanese and English, he finds himself confusingly being aligned with both Iraqis and Kuwaitis on either side of the war. At a time when '[i]t was open season on Arabs', his name and his identity locate him as the other; as his editor tells him, 'with a name like yours, nobody can be sure which side you're on'.[16] At the same time, Yasin is expected 'to be grateful that Britain had put its troops' lives at risk to save the likes of me and mine'.[17] Through these contradictions, Yasin seems to occupy the position not of friend or enemy but of the 'stranger', the figure Zygmunt Bauman identifies as one who 'disturbs the resonance between physical and psychical distance: he is physically close while remaining spiritually remote ... an incongruous and hence resented synthesis of nearness and remoteness'.[18] Over the course of the war, Yasin is interpolated into an ambiguous category through association with faraway others ('the likes of me and mine'), rather than a secured British subject.

Throughout the novel, Mahjoub explores how the assurance of security for some at the cost of others requires psychical distance. Watching coverage of the war, Yasin feels that 'morbid fascination' is combined with detachment, as though '[i]t wasn't really happening'.[19] Mahjoub's reflections on the unreality of the televised war echo responses such as Jean Baudrillard's *The Gulf War Did Not Take Place* (1991) by juxtaposing the visual, unreal spectacle of war with its visceral reality.

> The war began on television ... at a late hour which coincided with prime time in the Eastern seaboard of the United States ... It was like a fireworks display ... Years later I met an Iraqi painter who had been there that night. During the bombing, he said, it was like being in a dream from which you could never wake. Light travels faster than sound. You saw the explosion before you heard or felt it. Buildings, cars, walls, people would vanish in front of your eyes in a flash of light and smoke and then the shock would hit you.[20]

Mahjoub turns to the second person here to place the reader within this double image of the display of firepower and its impact on the ground, reflecting on the asymmetries of (in)security and their implications. Indifference to the security of the other is built into the assurance of security, not only in the construction of friend and foe but in the fragmentation of the political community into hierarchies of citizenship, which demands that we overlook how security acts on different bodies.

In a later passage, Mahjoub again uses the second person to convey the impact of divisive security rhetoric during the Gulf War. For Yasin, as the product of a postcolonial education system, the discrimination he faces cannot be separated from negotiating his own belonging in the postimperial British context. As he realises, though 'you grow up learning about the England of *David Copperfield*', idealised images of England will not protect you from a reality where 'you might well be subject to insults, nasty looks and random searches. There are firebombs and stabbings, people have petrol and dog excrement pushed through their letterboxes, and even if it doesn't happen to you personally, you know it could.'[21] Yasin's idealisation of England is contrasted with a multiculturalism experienced as threat, requiring the restoration of boundaries. While Yasin has inherited his father's 'high ideas about western civilization', he experiences rising xenophobia during the war as a challenge to the promise of full inclusion offered to those who embrace British norms, and begins to reconsider his views: '[f]or the first time in my life I began to wonder about the integrity of the British press, which I had always been led to believe was second to none (my father of course)'.[22] Mahjoub here reflects on the familiar theme of a romanticised relationship with the colonial power which is belied by reality. These passages carry an echo of similarly jarring realisations in the autobiographical works of writers such as Stuart Hall[23] and Jamaica Kincaid,[24] reflecting on the discrepancy between their education in Britain's former colonies and the realities of their experience as immigrants in the postimperial nation.

Mahjoub explores the ramifications of this disillusionment through the character of Yasmina, Yasin's sister, who blames her parents and her education for indoctrinating her into '[c]ultural slavery … [t]he big postcolonial trap'.[25] Feeling under siege, she becomes conscious of the need to create an alternative identity and seeks to reconstruct her identity through religion, taking on 'the drab greys of a Muslim feminist … emancipated and devout in one breath'.[26] Mahjoub represents Yasmina as the foil to the protagonist. Yasin's empathetic condemnation of her turn to Islam is rooted in an understanding of what it means to be subject to 'the fate of banal indifference offered by secular postmodern Britain'.[27] If *Travelling with Djinns* is a story about a quest, the object is to replace indifference to the other's insecurity with an indifference to origin; Yasin expresses his aspiration to be part of the 'vast, nameless body of mongrel humanity', and to feel that 'there is nothing odd about us really in that chaotic tumble … Nothing odd about us at all'.[28] Finally, however, as the repetitions here suggest, this surety in rootlessness remains an aspiration, as the novel traces how Yasin repeatedly encounters the tensions between the ideals of cosmopolitanism and a reality dominated by systemic and trenchant inequalities.

Towards the end of the novel, there are several metafictional passages reflecting on what it means to write about Sudan from the diaspora and for a primarily Western audience. Yasin, watching as '[t]he place [he] came from' becomes 'a metaphor for human suffering on an unimaginable scale', feels a sense of responsibility to bear witness to this suffering, which is reported in Britain as '[t]he internecine complexities of distant backwaters'.[29] However, attempting to break through this indifference leaves him with limited options; on the one hand, his family chastise him for writing about Sudan too lyrically, the beautiful images of 'pomegranate and hibiscus' covering over 'the obscenity of what we allowed the world to do to our country'.[30] On the other hand, he is faulted for fuelling prejudices 'about us being backwards … [a]t each other's throats'.[31] Mahjoub's writer-protagonist registers an awareness of a security context for reading literature from the Global South, reflecting on the role of cultural representation in providing the imagery through which we determine whose security matters.

Mahjoub's fiction, exploring as it does the historical and contemporary implications of British Sudanese identity, intersects in several crucial ways with the writings of Leila Aboulela; both writers are concerned with the strategies through which Sudanese immigrants attempt to negotiate belonging in postimperial Britain. Aboulela has also written about the impact of the Gulf War in her fiction as well as on her personal life. In an article reflecting on moving from Sudan, Aboulela states that she 'arrived in Scotland in time for the war. In time to watch the Gulf War on TV.'[32] Elsewhere, Aboulela has described how she began writing in part as a response to the narratives she encountered about Muslims and Islam during the war.[33]

Aboulela's second, semi-autobiographical novel *Minaret* (2005) follows the protagonist Najwa from Khartoum to London, with the war beginning shortly after her arrival. As in Mahjoub's novel, the protagonist watches coverage of the war in Britain, and this proves a formative experience, underscoring the shift in Najwa's circumstances from growing up as a Westernised teen in Sudan to working as a nanny and maid in London. Early on, Najwa describes how the people she meets in exile become meaningful to her because they have 'bonded watching the Gulf War on TV', and reflects on how the coverage subsumes her attention to the extent that when the media's attention shifts to other subjects she feels 'a sense of anticlimax now that the war was over', the news leaving her 'unfulfilled'.[34] Najwa describes that during this period she 'for the first time in [her] life' felt that she 'disliked London and envied the English, so unperturbed and grounded, never displaced, never confused. For the first time, [she] was conscious of [her] shitty-colored skin next to their placid paleness.'[35] Aboulela's visceral language here contrasts Najwa's internalised colorism, her sense of her 'shitty-coloured skin' which marks her as other, with the white viewers who she believes to be unmoved by the violence of this televised war. As Sara Ahmed describes, 'the subject is not … simply differentiated from the (its) other but comes into being by learning how to differentiate between others'.³⁶ In this case, differentiation is based on assumptions about security; the disturbing self-hatred in Najwa's description of her own skin demonstrates a process of internalisation not just of colourism but of the colour line between those who are secured, full citizens and those whose insecurity can be tolerated.

Class, too, plays a role in who deserves to feel secure. Najwa realises that she herself has been protected from the forms of insecurity she is currently experiencing through class privilege, recalling herself as a child 'coming to London every summer – walking into an ice-skating rink in Queensway as if [she] had every right to be there. Money did that. Money gave [her] rights.'³⁷ Najwa is a member of the postcolonial elite who later becomes a political refugee in the same metropolis she once experienced as a holiday destination. Based on this experience, she understands stability to mean fully belonging to a state which would protect her from the vicissitudes of life: '[a] place where we could make future plans and it wouldn't matter who the government was – they wouldn't mess up our day-to-day lives. A country that was a familiar, reassuring background, a static landscape on which to paint dreams.'³⁸ Najwa's assumption that the citizens of stable countries are 'never displaced, never confused' conveys her belief that some people are able to take risks without completely forfeiting their security.³⁹ As an immigrant whose imagined return to Sudan hinges on political reform, she understands indifference, this not needing to care about politics, as emerging from a placid sense of stability.

Like Mahjoub, Aboulela explores two diverging ways of dealing with xenophobia and witnessing violence from afar. One course of action is represented by Najwa's friend Anwar who initially puts his life on hold, awaiting return to Sudan, but gradually comes to see himself as part of the melting pot of the metropolis.

> He used English words more and more, was less sharp in his criticism of the West. And this was the same Anwar who had led student demonstrations against the IMF and burnt the American flag. I did not dare ask him if he felt his anti-imperialist convictions contradicted seeking political asylum in London.⁴⁰

Having once attributed responsibility for the wrongs of the world to the global forces of imperialism and capitalism, Anwar comes instead to enjoy the anonymity of life in London, telling Najwa: 'here no one knows our background, no one knows whose daughter you are, no one knows my politics. We are both niggers, equals.'⁴¹ While there is an obvious irony to this juxtaposition, it represents Anwar's movement away from identifying as an exile from Sudan to a broader understanding of marginality in the metropolitan centre, which he finds potentially empowering.

This mode of Third World cosmopolitanism proves insufficient for Najwa. Instead, she begins to define herself in religious terms, asserting that from now on she will 'just think of [herself] as a Muslim'.[42] Here the narrative takes on the tone of a spiritual autobiography, as her experience of insecurity prompts a search for answers: 'Explain to me why I came down in the world. Was it natural, was it curable?'[43] The narrative begins to take on a confessional tone, as Aboulela explores the interrelationship between Najwa's sense of alienation and the coherent answers provided by religious ideology, tracing the shift away from national to religious frameworks. After Najwa decides to wear the hijab, she is verbally abused on the street for being Muslim, confirming her sense of herself as the stranger, recognisable as someone who does not belong. As Ahmed suggests, the stranger is not somebody we do not know but rather 'some-body whom we have already recognised in the very moment in which they are "seen" or "faced" as a stranger'.[44] In giving herself new visibility as Muslim and taking on the identity of the recognisable other, Najwa seeks to own her place within the security regime, reacting to rising anti-Muslim sentiment by narrowing her identity to this allegiance she feels is under attack.

The Gulf War had a particularly marked impact on Arab immigrants in Britain partly due to unprecedented live media coverage. According to Paul Tabar, '[a]lthough political tensions have always brought the question of loyalties and identities to the fore, very few world historical events have been as immediate and intense as the Gulf War was for Arab communities in the diaspora'.[45] While different from Mahjoub's novel in style and tone, Aboulela's *Minaret* dramatises a similar discordant sense of dislocation and grievance resulting from viewing the Gulf War on television. Both writers explore how rising xenophobia drives their protagonists to alter their sense of belonging in and to contemporary Britain, renegotiating how they relate to both a former colonial power and the postimperial metropolis.

Comfort zones and conflicted worlds

Many Arab British writers explore the shift from being securitised subjects of Arab regimes to being immigrants, or the children of immigrants, in a British security environment. Robin Yassin-Kassab, describing the motivation for his novel *The Road from Damascus* (2008), writes that '[a] large proportion of Arabs in London are refugees from war, foreign occupation, or oppressive regimes'.[46] Yassin-Kassab's novel was an effort to represent 'how … religious and political questions are transplanted from countries like Iraq and Syria … and how an often traumatic past in Muslim countries weighs upon the present in multicultural London'.[47] The novel thus seeks to trace how the insecurity of life under dictatorship continues to impact the characters' lives in Britain. However, in contrast to the author's professed interest in how immigrants negotiate past trauma as they relocate, the novel's reception has tended to focus on fears of *future* insecurity within the national framework, that is, the danger such immigrants could potentially pose to Britain. For example, one reviewer describes the novel as 'a fascinating guide into the ghetto of superficially harmonious multicultural communities that make up Britain's simmering laboratory of fundamentalism'.[48] This framing positions the novel as a window onto segregated and dangerously 'simmering' communities, justifying fears about the political failures of multiculturalism. Yassin-Kassab's interest in how past experiences of war and violence continue to play out in immigrants' lives after they relocate are relevant only insofar as those experiences dramatise the potential risk immigrants pose to wider British society. This shifts attention from the insecurity that immigrants live through to the insecurity they could potentially represent beyond their 'multicultural communities'.

The Road from Damascus is set in the summer of 2001, with the narrative leading to the climactic point of the events of 9/11. Yassin-Kassab writes that the novel 'describes or explains the wider context the events of that day arose from, although it does not directly address the specific contexts in the Gulf, Palestine, and south Asia'.[49] Characters also reflect on the Gulf War, the end of the Israeli occupation of Lebanon and the second Palestinian *Intifada*. The longer sweep of historical context supports the novel's exploration of the failures of Arab secular states, the backlash of Islamist movements and the impacts of these competing ideologies on the diaspora. These threads are held together through the narrative's main plot, which follows the ideological transformations of the protagonist, Sami. As the novel opens, Sami is rethinking his secular Baathist ideology, inherited from his father, which justifies the Syrian state's brutal crackdowns on dissidents as necessary to prevent disorder. The novel then turns into a narrative of disenchantment as the protagonist begins to see the flaws in these ideas, negotiating his identity as a Syrian living in London.

The narrative is for the most part set in London; however, the novel opens when Sami is in Damascus, visiting his parents' homeland, where he experiences tensions that lead him to imagine 'roadblocks, men with armbands and guns' where '[t]he wrong identity would end you at the intersection'.[50] Sami's recognition of the exclusionary practices that are constitutive of national identity is woven into his sense of disconnection from his Syrian roots. In Syria, policing the boundaries is based on religious affiliation ('[d]ead for wearing a cross. Dead for wearing a hijab. Dead for Ali's sword swinging from your car mirror').[51] Only a few pages later, the protagonist returns to London and, upon visiting a pub, finds '[a]n expressionless black man just inside. Security, measuring him. After that, the clientele was blanket white. There were probably Poles and Albanians, certainly Irish. But it was undifferentiated to Sami ... The multicoloured neighbourhood hadn't made it across the threshold.'[52] This scene introduces Sami's return to London through his encounter with the racialised hierarchies of immigrants in the communal space of the pub. The parallel is implicit; in both instances, Sami is vigilant to the potential for violence when the trespassing stranger crosses a boundary and is seen to represent a threat to social order. That Sami is 'measured' by security (a Black man, symbolically standing on the threshold) involves an act of reading bodies which enables, to use Ahmed's words, the 'legitimation of certain forms of mobility or movement within the public, and the delegitimation of others'.[53] The novel represents exclusion in London as based on colour and class, with mounting inequalities fueling 'the new forms of religion, the fundamentalisms, the blood and soil movements, the BNP'.[54] The parallel between these scenes in the early pages highlight the fact that Sami does not escape the securitising gaze by returning from Damascus to London, but instead transitions into a new form of security logic.

The novel also addresses the characters' own maintaining and policing of religious and ethnic boundaries in order to define themselves. Sami is resentful of the idea that '[i]n Britain Muslims meant Pakis',[55] and reacts against this racist trope by paradoxically participating in it, aligning himself against religion and with his father's pan-Arabism. Meanwhile, his wife Muntaha decides to wear a hijab as an alternative to Sami's Ba'athist rhetoric, which she considers outdated in global politics. Instead, Muntaha states, categorically, 'I'm British anyway. I'm a British Muslim.'[56] In yoking faith to nation in this way, Muntaha connects herself to the sanctioned discourse of a British Islam, even at the cost of a stigmatised, visible Muslim identity. Religion becomes a tool to redefine her politics, an altered sense of community which she turns to in order to distance herself from her previously strong relationship to Iraq, her country of origin.

Elsewhere in the novel, Muntaha reflects that 'to imagine the country she had come from was to weep. It made her private grief irrelevant and so it was comforting to imagine it as often as she could.'[57] As in Aboulela's novel, where the protagonist finds community in exile through watching the Gulf War on television, this paradoxical description of comfort in imagining suffering translates shared insecurity into community. An extreme version of this attitude is exemplified by Muntaha's brother Ammar, who undergoes his own transformation from an obsession with hip-hop to jihadism, understanding the world through Muslim suffering and Western imperialism. After the attacks of 9/11, he revels in the collapse of his own framework, since it means that 'the heart of America' now 'looks like Gaza ... like Baghdad'.[58]

The shock of the attacks on the US homeland, entirely different from the expected violence in Arabic-speaking countries, becomes an instructive moment in the novel, registering the different attitudes among Sami, Muntaha and Ammar, while underscoring their shared sense that what they are witnessing is 'melting the frame of everything, making history collapse'.[59]

Reflecting on the role of 'Islam in the writing process' in a post-9/11 context, Yassin-Kassab discusses his character Ammar as representing 'Islam as Western identity politics, a somewhat panicked response to dislocation and racism' in which identifying as Muslim is a 'statement of individuality and defiance of convention'.[60] Yassin-Kassab is interested in thinking through how Islam functions as an identity, including his protagonist's transformation from Ba'athist secular nationalism to a 'trembling, contingent faith'.[61] The novel's exploration of religion and security attempts to represent the difficulty of such contingency, which cannot be factored into a single framework for what security means or how risk is calculated. This difficulty becomes clear, as Sami discovers when he is arrested, because his experimentation with a more spiritual outlook is deemed suspicious. Encapsulating the double logic of Cameron's '[n]ot enough is shared' speech, Sami's interrogation is 'a two-pronged attack of, on the one hand, co-optation and Working Together rhetoric – nice cop – and on the other, some heavy security work by those ... unable to distinguish Wahhabi nihilists from the plain dull religious and the vaguely, perhaps, spiritual'.[62] In this passage, the rhetoric of working together is juxtaposed with what cannot be shared or understood if the singular and limited framework that constructs security in Britain is not interrogated. After he is arrested, the protagonist is accused of stealing his own identity, since the Sami the police are familiar with from previous encounters 'doesn't have a beard ... takes drugs, drinks alcohol ... He's the kind you kill'.[63] Here, Sami is misrecognised as an extremist based on a security logic where only certain forms of extremism register; it is ironically at the point when Sami abandons his father's strident, secular Ba'athist politics to become vaguely spiritual that he is perceived as most threatening.

The final text I discuss here, Selma Dabbagh's *Out of It* (2012), opens with one of the protagonists, Rashid, receiving a visa to study in London, which he sees as his escape from a besieged Gaza. In the opening pages, he imagines zooming out of Gaza to see

> how the earth would look from up there: like dried out coral, ridged, chambered and sandy ... he traced his finger over the satellite pictures of it when dreaming of escape ... [a]t that height, the line that fenced them in would barely be made out, nor would the checkpoints, not from up there, but even from that stratospheric distance, the contrast with the other side would be stark ... That side glinted. Solar panels and swimming pools twinkled in the sun.[64]

The gulf between the dual worlds in this passage drives Rashid's notions of leaving, in order to be 'out of it', no longer contained by the securitised environment of Gaza. However, once in London, he finds himself repeatedly drawn back to what it means to be Palestinian. He reflects on 'the otherness of the passengers' in the underground, asking 'what of their national duties? What of his? Pulling him out of any comfort zone presented to him, pushing him out into a conflicted world.'[65] This description of the dual geographies of security echoes the separateness of what Bauman has described as a 'synthetic image of self-inflicted brutality' in public consciousness, 'an image of mean streets, no-go areas writ large, a magnified rendition of a gangland, an alien, subhuman world beyond ethics and beyond salvation', dissociated from the comfort zones.[66] Such a separation between zones of conflict and comfort, as though they are self-evident and unchanging, disconnects the present situation from both its historical roots and present-day realities, including the sales of weapons and the impact of self-interested foreign policies.

Dabbagh's novel works to place these realities back into the narrative, especially in the sections of the narrative set in London. As Palestinians living in a former colonial metropolis, both Rashid and his twin sister Iman find it difficult to rest easy in the comfort zones presented to them. In a scene which in part supplies context to the reader unfamiliar with Palestinian history, Rashid's professor speaks to him about how the British Mandate government's Defense Regulations are 'the same laws that are now being used for closures, house-sealings, curfews, demolitions'.[67] The present situation in Palestine, the ongoing occupation using the same laws that were enforced by colonial rule, speaks to a reality which Derek Gregory theorises as a 'colonial present', where exemplary violence continues to be legitimised through marking 'other people as irredeemably Other'.[68] Dabbagh here connects the traumas of the colonial past to its repercussions on the present. Iman, for example, is questioned on the neutrality of international law in the context of Gaza: 'you say "international," but is that right? These are the justifying laws of conflict and empire.'[69] As the past intrudes on the division of the world into conflict and comfort zones, we witness the problems the protagonists face in their attempts to escape, to be 'out of it', realising that there is no outside to this global order.

Like *The Road from Damascus*, Dabbagh's novel reaches its climactic point in a scene of mistaken identity. In this case, the protagonist Rashid is arrested having been mistaken for a wanted Palestinian activist following a demonstration in London. The irony of this situation is that Rashid is viewed as that which he, and in particular his friends, feels he should be, a committed Palestinian activist. When his friends mobilise to help him (using the arrest as propaganda for their cause), the scene ends comically with their disappointment when he is only charged with drug possession, to which Rashid responds: 'What is it that you wanted me to do, exactly? ... Strap myself to some explosives?'[70] Rather than simply revealing the ineptitude of British security forces, the confusion about Rashid's identity and the dissonance regarding his lack of political commitment reveals that in leaving Gaza for London, he has simply exchanged one security context for another, rather than achieving his dream of being 'out of it'. There is no point at which he escapes the logic of security; though ideologically he attempts to avoid Palestinian politics, he is always fully imbricated within a framework where he typifies 'the Palestinian'.

In an interview with Dabbagh, Lindsey Moore asks whether the author agrees with Edward Said's description of the state of exile, the idea that not being at home can be 'a creatively, intellectually and politically enabling state'. Dabbagh supports this sentiment, but adds a crucial caveat: 'I have a British passport ... I doubt that the joys of a "counterpoint" identity are felt by those Palestinians stuck in refugee camps in Lebanon, Egypt or Syria, for example, where the lack of "oneness" or deficit of a recognized political identity is structurally and legally stacked against them in everything that they do.'[71] In a critical context which has tended to celebrate vulnerability and insecurity as potentially liberating and as forms of resistance, Dabbagh's comments emphasise that it is metaphorical homelessness which is considered to be subversive, and reflects on what the reality of not being at home means for those without the cushioning effect of money, class or cultural capital. Empowering homelessness in this case is enabled by the security of having a legal guarantee of belonging, at least in the sense of citizenship.

In recent years, following the Windrush scandal and with increasing numbers of British citizens being stripped of their passports in ISIS-related cases, that guarantee has been revealed as contingent. Writing about the story of one such citizen who has been 'made un-British', Kamila Shamsie asks: '[w]hy has it been possible for the British government to start exiling its citizens, without a criminal trial, without the right to defence, without open examination of the evidence? Why has it been so possible to create a two or three tier system of citizenship?'[72] These questions not only undermine the concept of equal citizenship, but also the notion that it is possible to ascend into a 'protected' category within the prevailing security framework which is driven by the concerns of the Global North. The rhetoric of security where 'not enough is shared' in terms of values emphasises a future vision of social cohesion, and so avoids confronting colonial legacies and ongoing stratifications of citizenship where 'not enough is shared' because belonging is contingent.

Literary texts reflect on the asymmetries of security in modern Britain and their impact on the formation of identity, as well as what it means to move between the security systems of the 'conflicted world' and its barricaded comfort zones.[73] The writers discussed here began writing in a post-9/11 context where, as Dabbagh puts it, 'the mention of anything to do with the Arab world and Muslims threw up a host of negative associations'.[74] This comment reveals the impact of securitisation on writers, including how an awareness of the mainstream reader's concerns and questions shapes the writing process. Yet literature does more than respond to or simply reflect what already exists in the world. Asked about the value of literature, Dabbagh provides a list which I abbreviate as follows: 'to bear witness/reclaim history; to provide solace … to recognise heroism that is generally unsung … to create beauty; to interrogate societal values; and to positively visualise the future'.[75] The verbs that Dabbagh uses, 'provide', 'create' and 'visualise', speak to how literature produces meaning. This generative quality does not mean that literary texts are able to take us 'outside' the logic of security, but they do allow us to expand our collective imaginations to think about what it means to be secure, and whose security matters, as necessary steps to creating a more equitable world.

Notes

1. David Cameron, 'PM's Speech at Munich Security Conference', GOV.UK, 5 February 2011, www.gov.uk/government/speeches/pms-speech-at-munich-security-conference [accessed 10 March 2020].
2. Cameron, 'PM's Speech'.
3. Zoë Marriage, *Cultural Resistance and Security from Below: Power and Escape through Capoeira* (Abingdon: Routledge, 2019), p. 3.
4. Pinar Bilgin, 'The "Western-Centrism" of Security Studies: "Blind Spot" or Constitutive Practice?', *Security Dialogue*, 41:6 (2010), pp. 615–622, p. 616.
5. Louise Amoore, *The Politics of Possibility: Risk and Security Beyond Probability* (Durham, NC: Duke University Press, 2013), p. 61.
6. Camillia Fawzi El-Solh, 'Arab Communities in Britain: Cleavages and Commonalities', *Islam and Christian–Muslim Relations*, 3:2 (1992), pp. 236–258, p. 236.
7. Mohammed Siddique Seddon, *The Last of the Lascars: Yemeni Muslims in Britain 1836–2012* (Markfield: Kube Publishing Ltd, 2014).
8. Anastasia Valassopoulos, 'Britain Through Muslim Eyes: An Interview with Claire Chambers', *Journal of Postcolonial Writing*, 55:1 (2019), pp. 121–129, p. 125.
9. Fred Halliday, *Britain's First Muslims: Portrait of an Arab Community* (London: I.B.Tauris, 2010), p. ix.
10. Anthony Burke, 'Aporias of Security', *Alternatives: Global, Local, Political*, 27:1 (2002), pp. 1–27, p. 7.
11. Jamal Mahjoub, *Travelling with Djinns* (London: Vintage, 2004), p. 59..
12. Mahjoub, *Travelling with Djinns*, p. 62.

13 Mahjoub, *Travelling with Djinns*, p. 62.
14 Mahjoub, *Travelling with Djinns*, p. 90.
15 Mahjoub, *Travelling with Djinns*, p. 140.
16 Mahjoub, *Travelling with Djinns*, p. 96.
17 Mahjoub, *Travelling with Djinns*, p. 95.
18 Zygmunt Bauman, *Modernity and Ambivalence* (Cambridge: Polity Press, 1991), p. 60.
19 Mahjoub, *Travelling with Djinns*, p. 96.
20 Mahjoub, *Travelling with Djinns*, p. 94.
21 Mahjoub, *Travelling with Djinns*, p. 288.
22 Mahjoub, *Travelling with Djinns*, p. 95.
23 Stuart Hall, *Familiar Stranger: A Life between Two Islands* (London: Penguin, 2017).
24 Jamaica Kincaid, 'On Seeing England for the First Time', *Transition*, 51 (1991), pp. 32–40.
25 Mahjoub, *Travelling with Djinns*, p. 166.
26 Mahjoub, *Travelling with Djinns*, p. 138.
27 Mahjoub, *Travelling with Djinns*, p. 288.
28 Mahjoub, *Travelling with Djinns*, p. 173.
29 Mahjoub, *Travelling with Djinns*, p. 134.
30 Mahjoub, *Travelling with Djinns*, p. 293.
31 Mahjoub, *Travelling with Djinns*, p. 290.
32 Leila Aboulela, 'Travel Is Part of Faith', *Wasafiri*, 15:31 (2000), pp. 41–42, p. 41.
33 Anita Sethi, 'Interview: Leila Aboulela', *The Observer*, 5 June 2005, www.theguardian.com/books/2005/jun/05/fiction.features2 [accessed 10 March 2020].
34 Leila Aboulela, *Minaret: A Novel* (London: Bloomsbury, 2015), p. 229..
35 Aboulela, *Minaret*, p. 174.
36 Sara Ahmed, *Strange Encounters: Embodied Others in Post-Coloniality* (Abingdon: Routledge, 2013), p. 24.
37 Aboulela, *Minaret*, p. 94.
38 Aboulela, *Minaret*, p. 165.
39 Aboulela, *Minaret*, p. 74.
40 Aboulela, *Minaret*, p. 156.
41 Aboulela, *Minaret*, p. 157.
42 Aboulela, *Minaret*, p. 110.
43 Aboulela, *Minaret*, p. 240.
44 Ahmed, *Strange Encounters*, p. 21.
45 Paul Tabar, *Lebanese Diaspora: History, Racism and Belonging* (Beirut: Lebanese American University, 2005), p. 271.
46 Robin Yassin-Kassab, 'Islam in the Writing Process', *Religion & Literature*, 43:1 (2011), pp. 139–144, p. 141.
47 Yassin-Kassab, 'Islam in the Writing Process', pp. 139–144, p. 141.
48 Iason Athanasiadis, 'Book Review: "The Road from Damascus"', *The Washington Times*, 26 February 2010, www.washingtontimes.com/news/2010/feb/26/book-review-the-road-from-damascus [accessed 3 March 2020].

49 Yassin-Kassab, 'Islam in the Writing Process', p. 142.
50 Robin Yassin-Kassab, *The Road to Damascus* (London: Penguin, 2008), p. 7.
51 Yassin-Kassab, *The Road from Damascus*, p. 7.
52 Yassin-Kassab, *The Road from Damascus*, p. 29.
53 Ahmed, *Strange Encounters*, p. 32.
54 Yassin-Kassab, *The Road from Damascus*, p. 105.
55 Yassin-Kassab, *The Road from Damascus*, p. 61.
56 Yassin-Kassab, *The Road from Damascus*, p. 98.
57 Yassin-Kassab, *The Road from Damascus*, p. 234.
58 Yassin-Kassab, *The Road from Damascus*, p. 316.
59 Yassin-Kassab, *The Road from Damascus*, p. 315.
60 Yassin-Kassab, *The Road from Damascus*, p. 142.
61 Yassin-Kassab, *The Road from Damascus*, p. 348.
62 Yassin-Kassab, *The Road from Damascus*, p. 335.
63 Yassin-Kassab, *The Road from Damascus*, p. 335.
64 Selma Dabbagh, *Out Of It* (London: A&C Black, 2011), p. 5.
65 Dabbagh, *Out Of It*, p. 120.
66 Zygmunt Bauman, *Work, Consumerism And The New Poor* (Maidenhead: McGraw-Hill Education, 2004), p. 85.
67 Dabbagh, *Out Of It*, p. 129.
68 Derek Gregory, *The Colonial Present: Afghanistan, Palestine, Iraq* (Oxford: Wiley-Blackwell, 2004), p. 16.
69 Dabbagh, *Out Of It*, p. 65.
70 Dabbagh, *Out Of It*, p. 247.
71 Lindsey Moore, 'A Conversation with Selma Dabbagh', *Journal of Postcolonial Writing*, 51:3 (2015), pp. 324–339, p. 331.
72 Kamila Shamsie, 'Exiled: The Disturbing Story of a Citizen Made UnBritish', *The Guardian*, 17 November 2018, www.theguardian.com/books/2018/nov/17/unbecoming-british-kamila-shamsie-citizens-exile [accessed 12 March 2020].
73 Dabbagh, *Out Of It*, p. 120.
74 Moore, 'A Conversation with Selma Dabbagh', p. 331.
75 Moore, 'A Conversation with Selma Dabbagh', p. 330.

Bibliography

Aboulela, Leila, *Minaret: A Novel* (London: Bloomsbury, 2015), p. 229.
Aboulela, Leila, 'Travel Is Part of Faith', *Wasafiri*, 15:31 (2000), pp. 41–42, p. 41.
Ahmed, Sara, *Strange Encounters: Embodied Others in Post-Coloniality* (Abingdon: Routledge, 2013).
Amoore, Louise, *The Politics of Possibility: Risk and Security Beyond Probability* (Durham, NC: Duke University Press, 2013).
Athanasiadis, Iason, 'Book Review: "The Road from Damascus"', *The Washington Times*, 26 February 2010, www.washingtontimes.com/news/2010/feb/26/book-review-the-road-from-damascus [accessed 3 March 2020].
Bauman, Zygmunt, *Modernity and Ambivalence* (Cambridge: Polity Press, 1991).

Bauman, Zygmunt, *Work, Consumerism and the New Poor* (Maidenhead: McGraw-Hill Education, 2004).
Bilgin, Pinar, 'The "Western-Centrism" of Security Studies: "Blind Spot" or Constitutive Practice?', *Security Dialogue*, 41:6 (2010), pp. 615–622, p. 616.
Burke, Anthony, 'Aporias of Security', *Alternatives: Global, Local, Political*, 27:1 (2002), pp. 1–27.
Cameron, David, 'PM's Speech at Munich Security Conference', GOV.UK, 5 February 2011, www.gov.uk/government/speeches/pms-speech-at-munich-security-conference [accessed 10 March 2020].
Dabbagh, Selma, *Out Of It* (London: A&C Black, 2011).
El-Solh, Camillia Fawzi, 'Arab Communities in Britain: Cleavages and Commonalities', *Islam and Christian–Muslim Relations*, 3:2 (1992), pp. 236–258.
Gregory, Derek, *The Colonial Present: Afghanistan, Palestine, Iraq* (Oxford: Wiley-Blackwell, 2004).
Hall, Stuart, *Familiar Stranger: A Life between Two Islands* (London: Penguin, 2017).
Halliday, Fred, *Britain's First Muslims: Portrait of an Arab Community* (London: I.B.Tauris, 2010).
Kincaid, Jamaica, 'On Seeing England for the First Time', *Transition*, 51 (1991), pp. 32–40.
Mahjoub, Jamal, *Travelling with Djinns* (London: Vintage, 2004).
Marriage, Zoë, *Cultural Resistance and Security from Below: Power and Escape through Capoeira* (Abingdon: Routledge, 2019).
Moore, Lindsey, 'A Conversation with Selma Dabbagh', *Journal of Postcolonial Writing*, 51:3 (2015), pp. 324–339.
Seddon, Mohammed Siddique, *The Last of the Lascars: Yemeni Muslims in Britain 1836–2012* (Markfield: Kube Publishing Ltd, 2014).
Sethi, Anita, 'Interview: Leila Aboulela', *The Observer*, 5 June 2005, www.theguardian.com/books/2005/jun/05/fiction.features2 [accessed 10 March 2020].
Shamsie, Kamila, 'Exiled: The Disturbing Story of a Citizen Made UnBritish', *The Guardian*, 17 November 2018, www.theguardian.com/books/2018/nov/17/unbecoming-british-kamila-shamsie-citizens-exile [accessed 12 March 2020].
Tabar, Paul, *Lebanese Diaspora: History, Racism and Belonging* (Beirut: Lebanese American University, 2005).
Valassopoulos, Anastasia, 'Britain Through Muslim Eyes: An Interview with Claire Chambers', *Journal of Postcolonial Writing*, 55:1 (2019), pp. 121–129, p. 125.
Yassin-Kassab, Robin, 'Islam in the Writing Process', *Religion & Literature*, 43:1 (2011), pp. 139–144.
Yassin-Kassab, Robin, The Road to Damascus (London: Penguin, 2008).

10

Black, beautiful and essentially British: African Caribbean women, belonging and the creation of Black British beauty spaces in Britain (c. 1948–1990)

Mobeen Hussain

Introduction

Andrea Levy (1956–2019), in a 2014 essay, described being Black in Britain as realising that her experience of growing up in this country was part of what it meant to 'be black' with all its 'agonies of skin shade'.[1] Levy's comments reveal how such agonies of skin shade, informed by colonial hierarchies, manifested in the everyday experiences of African Caribbean women and their conceptions of beauty. Being beautiful functions by giving value to certain attributes and devaluing or stigmatising others in opposition to that idealised beauty. Contemporary Eurocentric beauty ideals are not only the dominant global beauty paradigm but remain the most prevalent, informed by imperial pasts and racial hierarchies, while being imbricated within notions of nationhood and belonging. By developing Bourdieu's conception of 'social capital', Margaret Hunter proposes that beauty work generates forms of social capital which can be transformed into other forms of capital in the African American context.[2] Beauty is, by Hunter's estimation, an investment that can bestow privileges including 'learning, earning and marrying more'.[3] However, Levy also wrote that 'America's story will not do' for Black experiences in Britain.[4] Taking this assertion as a crucial node of analysis in postwar Britain, this chapter maps a specifically Black British beauty story.

The chapter explores the creation of Black British beauty spaces for African Caribbean women in postwar Britain between 1948 and 1990, scrutinising both these physical spaces and the literary narratives which represent them as previously overlooked in discussions about postwar migration and multiculturalism.[5] In doing so, it considers how phenomenological negotiations of beauty, often multilayered and divisive, became resources for fashioning Black British identities. I suggest that African Caribbean women mediated Eurocentric beauty ideals, using elements of both conformity and subversion, to create innovative beauty spaces. In particular, this chapter launches an interdiscursive reading of visual and textual outputs in two pioneering Black-owned newspapers, *The West Indian Gazette and Afro-Asian Caribbean News* (1958–1964) (henceforth *Gazette*) and *The Voice* (1982–present). Both publications, founded in London, reported on cultural and sociopolitical issues and provide some insights into the opinions of Black readers by presenting a range of contributors and voices. Both newspapers consistently featured 'Letters to the Editor' which document public exchanges on contemporary issues such as who counted as 'Black' and how Black communities' fashion themselves.[6]

I read such exchanges in the *Gazette* and *The Voice* alongside Andrea Levy's fiction. Levy, born in London in 1956 to Jamaican migrant parents, was determined to record a previously undocumented contemporary Black British experience having realised that Black British narratives were largely absent from British public knowledge.[7] Levy's storytelling was informed by her personal and familial experiences – she interviewed her mother about her family's history for *The Fruit of the Lemon* (1999).[8] Her earlier novels – including *Every Light In the House Burnin'* (1994), *Never Far From Nowhere* (1996) and *The Fruit of the Lemon* – are imbued with strong autobiographical undercurrents, mapping second-generation African Caribbean experiences in Britain and establishing 'Black British' as an emerging identity. Beauty narratives are not the primary focus of these texts, yet all three situate beauty ideals and practices as part of wider social struggles that African Caribbean women faced in Britain. Limited postwar first-generation testimony makes newspaper material and fictional accounts particularly valuable, underpinning this chapter's readings of both historical and literary sources. This interdisciplinary approach, supplemented by anecdotal evidence and testimonies from the seminal Black feminist study *The Heart of the Race* (1985), accentuate the importance of Black beauty discourse in identity formation.[9]

Postwar communities, haircare and salons: The heart of the community

The politics of postwar integration of migrant communities in Britain and negotiations of 'postcoloniality' have received considerable attention within academic scholarship following Paul Gilroy's assertion that modern British society exhibits a remarkable amnesia about its own imperial history.[10] This strategic forgetting obscures how and why the 1948 British Nationality Act granted United Kingdom citizenship to the Empire's colonial and former colonised peoples. As Peter Fryer, who interviewed Jamaicans arriving on the *Empire Windrush*, stated, the 'British economy, short of labour, needed these willing hands'.[11] Between 1955 and 1960, Caribbean women represented 40 per cent of the total number of immigrants to Britain, and by the mid-1970s, approximately 40 per cent of the total Black population was born in Britain.[12] Many African Caribbean people faced structural discrimination in housing and employment, and, against the backdrop of increasingly racist rhetoric across the political spectrum (a context addressed elsewhere in this collection by Liam J. Liburd), Black women began forming their own organisations, expanding on the collective action against systemic racism by the British Black Panthers and the Black Unity and Freedom Party.[13] Female students of African descent came together with other Black women living in Britain in 1978 to launch the Organisation of Women of African and Asian Descent (OWAAD), a national network made up of anti-capitalist and anti-imperialist activists that inspired women to set up local groups including Brixton Black Women's Group.[14] As part of anti-racist community building, the formation of identities through quotidian beauty consumption played a formative role in nurturing spaces of belonging for African Caribbean women in Britain. A generational shift also occurred as second- and third-generation migrants began to identify as 'Black British'. Within these shifting identifications, configurations of hair and skin colour were navigated in salons, Black businesses and beauty contests across Britain.

African Caribbean women in Britain and African American women were engaged in broader networks of transatlantic exchanges whereby imported ideals from the USA were combined with images of beauty and messages of resistance in the colonial Caribbean. In 1920s Jamaica, Marcus Garvey, leader of the Universal Negro Improvement Association, promoted Black pride to reclaim African-based 'natural' aesthetics as part of colonial resistance.[15] Visits from activists like Frantz Fanon, Malcolm X and Aimé Césaire, who reflected on Black negative self-image, were also part of these transatlantic networks of 'Blackness' in Britain.[16] Narratives and expectations surrounding African Caribbean hair in Britain, within public consumption and representation, played out in the pages of the *Gazette*. The newspaper was born as a defiant, unifying response to the racial violence of the 1958 Notting Hill and Nottingham 'riots'. Claudia Jones, a Trinidadian-born communist exile from America, founded the paper for West Indians and other non-white migrants. It was produced with limited resources but received support from famous Black patrons including Paul Robeson and Corinne Skinner-Carter.[17] The *Gazette* published on Black oppression in Britain and across the world.[18] News about discrimination was often accompanied by advertisements and stories about beauty culture.

However, advertisements for beauty products often conflicted with features about belonging and pride in Britain. One advert for a popular hair relaxer *Perma STRATE* used the slogan 'for really STRAIGHT hair' (Figure 10.1), perpetuating a clear set of European beauty ideals. The advertisement advocated the message that to be accepted within and outside the Black community, and to be the best one can be (like the desired celebrities

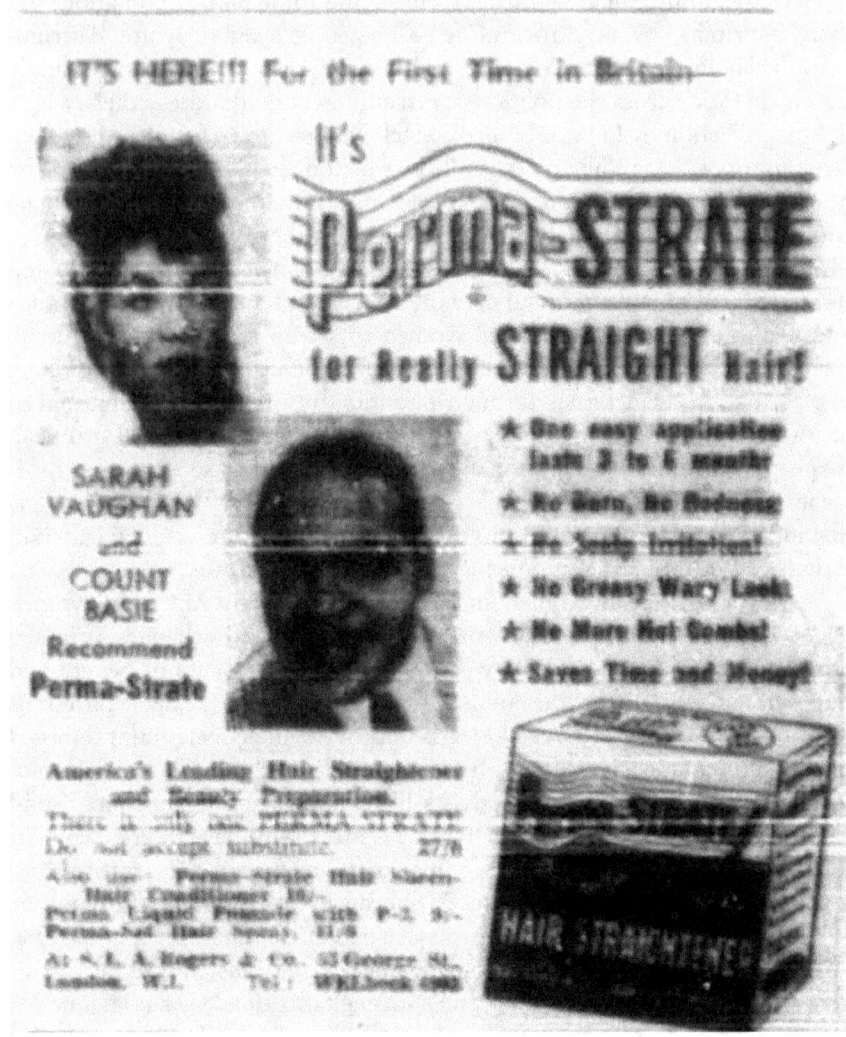

Figure 10.1 'Perma STRATE', *The West Indian Gazette*, December 1959 p. 4 © British Library Board, Mic.B.967.

recommending the product), both men and women needed to change a visible barrier to acceptance: the texture of their hair.

Combining celebrity endorsements, photographs and an unambiguous slogan, this advertisement suggested that chemically relaxing one's hair was the route to happier relationships and success. This reflects a wider uncomfortable balance between progressive editorial content and advertising within Black publications, who compromised content to augment revenue.[19] Marcus

Garvey's *Negro World* paper lambasted beauty products that targeted changing aesthetically 'Black' features but advertised skin-lightening products in the late 1920s.[20] Advertisements helped to create demand for specific kinds of products but they also reflected a demand that already existed – for products that enabled Black women to conform to Eurocentric beauty ideals.

An interviewee in *The Heart of the Race* recalled that 'magazines told us that to have straightened hair and fair skin was to be beautiful and feminine, that to be Black and female was to be poor and ugly'.[21] Yet, the use of beauty advertisements for both hair and skin products in the *Gazette*, and later in *The Voice*, point to navigations within beauty work by African Caribbean women – female readers were confronted with messages that conformed to racialised, desired beauty ideals but they also chose to rework or reject them. In the case of the *Gazette*, Rochelle Rowe has argued that Jones's interest in racially conscious grooming was grounded in a culture of resistance.[22] Such complex modes of grooming played out in numerous ways. The *Gazette* addressed the palpable need for suitable haircare for Black women. 'Beauty Tropical', a popular beauty column published in the *Gazette*, described the problem of haircare for African Caribbean migrants as environmental. The column stated that many complaints had been made by 'ladies' who had arrived from tropical countries, concluding that the 'harsh, cold, wet climate of Britain was never designed for we "Children of the Sun"'.[23] Advertisements in the *Gazette* for shops and chemists catering to African haircare also vastly grew between 1959 and 1963, proffering products fresh from the States which established American hegemony in Britain. In this way, the *Gazette* was an important vehicle for promoting the growing use of African American hair products in Britain and cultivating self-care.

The growth of Black haircare products continued throughout the late 1960s, reflecting trends in globalised social movements including the 'Black is Beautiful' discourse taken up by the Black Panther movement in America and later in Britain. This mantra inspired the natural hair movement of the late 1960s and early 1970s and contributed to the popularity of the Afro as an expression of 'authentic' Blackness and pride. An interviewee in *The Heart of the Race* noted that the 1960s symbolised conscious self-fashioning to align with principles of Black power: 'we stopped straightening our hair … resisting the social, cultural and commercial pressures to strive to imitate the white ideal of womanhood. We learnt to reject those products which merely embodied the potential to rub away some of our Blackness.'[24] The texture of one's hair became a cultural signifier of identity in which the Afro served as a performative political statement. However, the Afro itself also exemplified artifice in its sustained cultivation. Researcher Debbie Weekes argues that the Afro also invoked a 'dualistic logic of binary oppositionality' between that which appears natural and authentic and that which is cultivated.[25] Thus, the Afro was also a beauty choice even as its performativity offered a politicised Black identity. This cultivation was just one example of a temporally specific beauty reconfiguration. Brands like World of Curls, Lustrasilk and TBC used full-page spreads in newspapers and magazines to showcase a variety of haircare products catering to changing trends.[26]

Simultaneously, women were also expected to change their hairstyles to conform to notions of femininity and professionalism well into the 1980s and 1990s. In a feature entitled 'So you want to be a model?', fashion model Della Finch gave advice about modelling as a Black woman. She stated that 'plaits and dreadlock are out – they make the clothes look too ethnic' yet maintained that 'light skin is no automatic advantage!'[27] Here, both relaxed and natural hair were accepted, but more African-looking or politically perceived hairstyles are deemed undesirable and 'too ethnic', suggesting that cultivating hairstyles interpreted as 'respectable' could offset the value of 'light skin'. However, the emphasis on 'no automatic advantage' indicates that the latter was still desirable. Ayana Byrd and Lori Tharps, in the African American context, note a proliferation of discrimination cases in the late 1980s against employers who questioned the professionalism of cornrows and braids in the workplace and point to persistent associations between hair choices and political affiliations.[28] In professionalised settings, historically derogatory descriptions of natural African hair texture were rebranded with contemporary linguistic changes such as smart, clean, sharp and respectable. Many news stories in *The Voice* also highlight multiple cases of discrimination against those who choose to maintain their natural, 'un-European' hairstyles in British spaces of work. In one story, 'Rastas Rejoice', Rastafarians were recognised as an ethnic group and men with dreadlocks could not be ordered to cut their hair by bosses.[29]

Alongside the growth in haircare products, many Black hairdressing salons emerged, reflecting a transition from self-haircare at home to salon culture across Britain from the late 1950s. Actress Isabelle Lucas has described how she approached the Trinidadian-born pianist Winifred Atwell for advice when she arrived in London in 1954 because there were no beauty salons for Black women.[30] Atwell styled hair at home and gave Lucas hair-straightening irons.[31] Atwell later opened one of the first Black hairdressing salons in Brixton.[32] The hairdressing salon signifies an important means of financial and emotional support for Black women. Paula Black has stressed the historic role of salons as centres of communities and political impulses for African American women.[33] For African Caribbean women in Britain, the salon also became intrinsically linked to community building and establishing better economic opportunities. Black women tended to have the lowest-paid, least-skilled jobs with appalling work conditions due to long-term economic decline, sexual divisions of labour and public-sector cuts which disproportionately affected Black communities.[34]

While present from the publication's inception, advertisements for hairdressing salons in the *Gazette* increased in frequency from 1963. References to hair salons in *The Voice* also mushroomed, emboldening specific advertising pages for Hair and Beauty. It was reported that there were 'over 90 black hair salons in London' by 1982.[35] Many also functioned as training academies, including the *Madame Rose Academy*, inspired by the famous African American haircare entrepreneur Madam C. J. Walker.[36] The complexities of hair technologies and their synthesis with community formations are addressed throughout Andrea Levy's first novel, *Every Light In the House Burnin'*. It follows the reminiscences of Angela, a second-generation African Caribbean girl, as she remembers her childhood in 1950s and 1960s Britain.[37] Through her characters, Levy, in her own words, explores 'aspects of [her] life, although in fiction'.[38] Angela's migrant mother relaxed hair with a gas ring and hot metal comb: 'I heard a sizzling sound and smelt burning', which created 'normal hair' with all 'frizz gone'.[39] Ideals of fashioning straight, 'frizz'-free hair became widely attainable aspirations by the mid-twentieth century and were normalised through self-haircare.

For Angela, going to the hair salon is portrayed as a rite of passage: 'I looked forward to the day when I'd go with the women in my family to the hairdressers to have my frizz tamed permanently. I was twelve when my mum agreed that it was time.'[40] The salon becomes a site of cultural, social and gendered belonging which connects her to 'the women in my family' and the wider African Caribbean community in London. Angela's entry into this space signals her maturity, but also her desire to escape her hair's natural texture. The salon space functions, in *Every Light in the House Burnin'*, as a vital Black community space in Britain.

> The salon was quite smart from the outside ... There were pictures on the walls of women, white women with hair in different styles. But once you got through the beaded curtain into the back, it was a different matter ... Everyone in the salon was black and female ... People from the Caribbean like my mum and dad, only 'real' black people with dark brown skin.[41]

The salon is a subterranean construction functioning under the veneer of a white ideal; it functions beneath an external display of 'white women with hair in different styles'. A dual performativity is at work in the salon through the pictures of the women. This space becomes a metaphor for the role of minorities in Britain as marked by 'in the back', depicting a private Black *and* female space. Yet, it still evokes white beauty ideals through pictures of white women. Once inside, Angela also describes how the women 'began talking quietly in thick Caribbean accents and I couldn't understand what they were saying', making her feel 'out of place'.[42] Her discomfort, as a lighter-skinned girl, partly stems from being surrounded by those she identifies as ' "real" black people with dark brown skin', bringing tensions between race and colour to the fore.[43] Here, the salon is capable of accommodating conflicting subjectivities, ascribing moments of authenticity and artifice to the minority Black consumer. This scene speaks to the ways in which Black women experienced the salon – even while salons were sites for engendering Black female solidarity, they were also entangled within the contradictory demands of white beauty ideals. Therefore, hair salons functioned as fractured spaces, accommodating both European and Black beauty ideals, and as intergenerational transnational spaces of shared experience, education and agency in fashioning femininity and the groomed self. Haircare products and salons, thus, were mutually dependent resources for women as part of communities-in-the-making.

Exhibiting beauty

Pigmentocracy (a system in which wealth and social status are determined by the shade of one's skin colour) and colourism (prejudice based on skin shade) also pervaded the quotidian experiences of African Caribbean women in Britain.[44] Both are crucial to understanding the emotive subjectivities surrounding skincare commodities. Colourism is a system rooted in the histories of the Caribbean and the USA, as slave-owning colonial societies, operating through principles such as the one-drop rule in the USA, which maintained myths of white racial purity. These intertwined and violent imperial histories, including the systematic rape of enslaved African women by white masters (a tool of labour reproduction), preferential treatment of lighter-skinned slaves and the creolisation of Caribbean societies, led to the production of racial hierarchies and, in turn, shade hierarchies.[45] These shade hierarchies were reproduced to create classifications such as 'mulatto' and 'quadroon' with (unattainable) whiteness at the top.[46]

Skin shade was not only a physical indicator of race but one of cultural and social respectability.[47] Cultural theorist Stuart Hall describes his father as a 'lower-middle-class Jamaican' and his mother as of a 'light-skinned, English-orientated, plantation-oriented faction' who 'thought she was practically "English"'.[48] A brown shade, as opposed to a darker one, was preferred – this process of 'browning', as Shirley Tate describes, signified a middle-class respectability in the Caribbean.[49] Henrice Altink has recently shown how, even after Jamaican independence, attempts were made by people of African descent to 'raise the colour' of their offspring by 'marrying light'.[50] These ideals of lighter skin were transported to Britain at the intracommunity level (within Black communities) and worked in parallel with intercommunity racial discrimination faced by minorities. The interplay of racism, colourism and the relational value of skin colour is also depicted in Levy's *Never Far From Nowhere*, which follows the diverging paths of two sisters born to first-generation Jamaican migrant parents, Olive and Vivien. Vivien narrates that 'the Caribbean legacy left me with fair skin and black wavy hair. And Olive with black skin [and] a head of tight frizzy hair.'[51] Olive faces continuous structural racism in 1970s Britain – including at the hands of the police, who plant drugs on her – whereas Vivien's physiognomy allows her to take on a 'Mediterranean' persona, effectively passing as white.[52] These differences produce tensions between the sisters, Olive states: 'I didn't have a choice, I never had any choices, you had all the choices.'[53] As choice and capital are linked to skin shade, it is no surprise that skin-lightening products became vital resources for migrants in postwar Britain.

Hunter describes how the merging of new technologies with colonial ideologies created a context in which consumers could purchase 'racial capital' through skin-bleaching creams (and later cosmetic surgeries).[54] Tate has argued that many African Caribbean women do not buy into 'wanting to be white' but a light-brown complexion is preferred, and that such products offer Black women a wider range of choices.[55] Yet, in the immediate post-Windrush period, aspirations to whiteness in shade/hair/consumer behaviours – through intrinsic links to privilege and mobility and due to experiences of racial discrimination – became very real ideals for many African Caribbean women. As one of the interviewees stated in *The Heart of the Race*: 'if Black women have been guilty of wearing straightening wigs or applying bleaching creams to our skins, it was because … of the message that fair skin can be a passport out of poverty and exploitation'.[56]

The *Gazette* explicitly advertised skin-'bleaching' creams. Carole Boyce Davies, Claudia Jones's biographer, maintains that 'black female identity was always the primary position' in Jones's activism and resistance.[57] Jones had spent her childhood in Harlem and was influenced by the long history of beauty culture and the use of bleaching creams as resources for respectable and cultivated beauty.[58] She hoped to foster self-pride among Black women in Britain in a similar way by selectively buying into hegemonic consumption practices and white beauty ideals to achieve the racialised respectability of middle-class 'browning'. Essentially, this seemingly contradictory position was one beauty strategy utilised by women to improve social and material conditions. Yet, the creams had always been controversial, even before the anti-racist campaigning of the 1960s. Madam C. J. Walker, who also saw her products as a way of negating oppressive attitudes towards African American womanhood, refused to sell skin lighteners.[59] One brand advertised in the *Gazette* between 1962 and 1965 was Skinlite (Figure 10.2). It was promoted with the slogan 'for a LIGHTIER, LIVELIER, LOVELIER COMPLEXION' and first appeared above an article about a

Figure 10.2 'Carmen Skinlite Bleach Cream', *The West Indian Gazette*, February 1962, p. 12 © British Library Board, Mic.B.967.

British immigration bill.[60] The editorial choice to advertise products which endorsed messages that 'lighter' was indeed 'lovelier' diluted attempts at cultivating Black pride across the publication.

Here, Caribbean racial hierarchies and the dominance of European beauty ideals, and lighter skin shade, were still prescribed to Black women. Dark skin became a veil that hid one's natural luminescence, which skin lighteners would uncover.[61] The use of such slogans and messages to advertise skin-lightening products is reminiscent of products sold throughout England in the nineteenth century and early twentieth century. Both Pears and Lux soap used racialised images of Black people to represent darker skin tones with uncivility and dirt. Such companies employed a type of commodity racism which symbolised the power of soap in, as Hall notes, 'wash[ing] black skin white' and the capacity to purify dark colonial subjects as part of a civilising mission.[62] Pears advertisements, initially targeting metropole consumers, and other brands took a subtler direction when targeting non-Europeans but still indulged in images portraying the inferiority of African, and thereby Black, aesthetics. In the Skinlite advertisement, the message of previous advertising methods has been reconfigured to appeal to Black consumers, focusing on beauty and opportunity instead of cleanliness but continuing to espouse ideas of civility and respectability.

Although there are no official sale statistics available for bleaching creams, partly due to the controversies surrounding such products and desires to appear *naturally* lighter, various sources suggest their widespread use in twentieth-century Britain. As part of transatlantic circulation of ideas, many African Caribbean migrants brought colonially informed and culturally specific beauty ideals (of shade) and products to Britain. A letter addressing the inadequacies of British cosmetic regulation, published in the *British Medical Journal* in May 1984, indicates the popularity of skin-bleaching creams. Dermatologists C. M. Ridley and S. J. Adams noted having recently seen a patient with 'patchy depigmentation' after using a 'cosmetic cream' which promised a 'healthy bright and lovely appearance'.[63] The letter stated that 'a survey of shops in an area with a large population of West Indian women has shown that many creams similar to the one used by our patient are available' and that many consumers recognised 'bright' to mean 'light'.[64] Skin bleaching was also explicitly advertised and referenced in the beauty columns of 1950s and 1960s Black media outlets, suggesting that companies often followed shifting values of consumers as well as engendering demand. Many sociologists have exposited that the negative stigma attached to 'bleaching' meant that such products were gradually marketed as skin brighteners and skin toners by the end of the twentieth century.[65] Advertisements in the *Gazette* and *The Voice* emphasised the 'medicat[ing]' effect of such commodities, equating whiteness with modern living by using scientific jargon in marketing.[66] By the 1990s, the language of lightness, as Tate notes, was to focus on a 'browning' that looked natural, yet this artifice still upheld Caribbean middle-class preferences for brown, light-skinned beauty.

The development of cosmetics for darker skin tones, such as foundation and lipstick, however, differed from the contentions surrounding bleaching creams, although both shared the language of beauty as a commodity. The use of mainstream 'white' makeup in the 1950s and 1960s was not necessarily an attempt to emulate white beauty ideals but based on the practical constraints of limited choices. Actress Cleo Sylvestre remembers, 'there would be a range of white make-up and you'd start frantically mixing around trying to get some deeper colours' in the 1960s television industry.[67] The 1980s saw a growth in cosmetics suited to darker shades, allowing for a Black British beauty ideal to emerge. In the USA, Johnson Publishing Company, publisher of *Ebony* magazine, launched Fashion Fair cosmetics in 1973, which aimed to broaden Black beauty options and complement an array of complexions. In Britain, options remained limited, although there was a clear market for darker shades of cosmetics. In some cases, these limitations prompted women to represent and cater for their own beauty needs. Activist and writer Barbara Jackson, for instance, collaborated with Hugh Charlton on a project to import Black cosmetics to the UK.[68] A 1982 advert in *The Voice* for the 'Paradise House of Beauty', which imported beauty products from America, declared that 'gone are the days when the black woman had to use the darkest tints designed for white burnt skin'.[69] From the 1980s, there was a steady growth in Black ranges by other multinational companies such as Unilever and Palmer's, often appropriating Black faces onto white companies and products.

A feature in *The Voice* entitled 'Black, Beautiful and Essentially British', which presented Christine Dinham – a sportswoman with dark skin and permed hair – as the 'new image' of beauty, represented a shift in cultural ownership.[70] The article described how her image was 'fast becoming identified with the black British woman' rather than an African American or Eurocentric ideal, asserting that we can 'promote our own black British image' to market British-made brands. Black British magazines like *Chic* and *Black Beauty* advertised brands like Dark and Lovely which were not advertised, even implicitly, as skin-lightening products. The use of alternative beauty products demonstrated a renegotiation of mainstream beauty consumption whereby some Black women catered to their *own* beauty needs.

Tate has contended that the challenge for African Caribbean people in Britain lay in how to claim both Blackness and Britishness without assimilating to whiteness as a 'necessary part of our future'.[71] Her observations are pertinent to the establishment of Black businesses in the 1970s and 1980s. Just as the Notting Hill Carnival was a major cultural event for the Black community in the 1950s, I contend that the 'Afro-Hair & Beauty' exhibitions, established by Dyke and Dryden in 1982, were also major cultural spaces for Black people in Britain.[72] The directors of Dyke and Dryden built one of the first Black British cosmetic companies catering to non-white consumers. The exhibitions, initially held in London, were spaces that redefined Black beauty in Britain – marking the progression in activism which carved out opportunities alongside salon culture. Co-director Tony Wade, in his 2001 memoir, reflects on the 'lack of social capital', the 'absence of opportunity for managerial experience by the failure of employers to promote Black people' and the 'weak political leverage' of the Black community in the late 1960s and 1970s.[73] He describes the exhibitions as organisations 'dedicated to the education, development and promotion of ethnic hair care in Britain'.[74] Indeed, thousands of Black-owned businesses across the country – including salons, hairdressing schools and manufacturing and distribution outlets – exhibited skills and sold their products at the exhibitions.[75] American companies who had focused on the Caribbean market in Britain since the 1950s also used the exhibitions as a 'shop window' and 'the ideal platform for expanding their businesses' in Europe.[76] However, the exhibition disrupted their hegemony of beauty products, encouraging Black British commercial spaces instead.

Beauty contests: A contested space

The development of Black British beauty spaces was further complicated by beauty contests as events and arenas in which, as Carolyn Cooper notes, 'emotionally charged identity politics is played out in ways that are far more serious than mere entertainment'.[77] Unsurprisingly, pageants' ideal winners in the Caribbean were middle-class, lighter-skinned or 'mixed-race' women, presented as well travelled and cosmopolitan.[78] Early Miss Jamaica competitions marked the racial supremacy of the 'white creole planter-merchant class' in response to emerging anti-colonial resistance movements.[79] However, from the 1950s, many contests saw pushes for brown 'visions of beauty' with marginalised Black contestants voicing their discontent with judges.[80] The Jamaica 300, a national festival organised in 1955 to celebrate 300 years of Jamaica as a British colony, included 'Ten Types–One People' beauty contests that crowned ten different types of Jamaican beauty based on different identifiers and ancestral histories such as Miss Sandalwood and Miss Mahogany.[81] The most striking element of the contest was the 'novelty of a category for dark-skinned Afro-Jamaican women' and the rebranding of the 'Miss Ebony' contest for 'coal black and cool-black girls' in 1959.[82] Yet, only one category was reserved for the darker majority population of Jamaican society and was received as a tokenistic gesture intended to assuage anti-colonial feeling. A lighter-skinned brown winner continued to represent the modern, respectable and feminine standard of Jamaican beauty.

The first Black beauty contest in Britain was organised by Claudia Jones in 1959 as part of the Notting Hill Carnival. Over the preceding decade, Jones had protested the stereotypical representation of Black women in mass media as systemically objectifying and dehumanising. She railed against the acceptance of white ruling-class standards of 'desirability' (such as light skin) as forms of chauvinism.[83] While Jones protested and identified the power structures that afforded privilege to lighter-skinned women, her choice of beauty contests – traditionally seen as an archetypal space for objectification – appears to contradict her protests to objectification. However, for Jones, the choice to work within embedded beauty hierarchies was a strategy for gaining parity in a racist society. Jones used the *Gazette* to facilitate and fashion visual representations of respectable Black womanhood and femininity. The *Gazette* encouraged women to participate in the Carnival Queen contest, advocating greater inclusivity of heterogeneous forms of Black femininity and beauty. As a result, many darker-skinned women with a variety of features and hairstyles were contestants. However, winners were still predominantly lighter-skinned women. The Carnival Queen contest did attempt to extend, rather than restrict, beauty ideals. Yet, shade prejudices within diasporic communities, compounded by the kind of beauty products the *Gazette* advertised, meant darker shades and natural or unrelaxed hairstyles continued to operate at the margins of Black beauty. Such beauty practices were still othered as unrespectable in the late 1950s and early 1960s. Indeed, Rowe concedes that inclusivity of the contest did not necessarily have the power to 'erase ingrained shade prejudice'.[84] Therefore, early Black beauty contests in Britain bought into existing beauty hierarchies even if they sought to change them.

Later, coordinated responses to Black beauty ideals in Britain moved to explicitly dismantle the beauty schemas of the mid-twentieth century. In the 1970s, the London-based Black women's group Black Women's Action Committee (BWAC) rejected beauty contests as legitimate spaces in which to combat negative images of Black women. BWAC published various pamphlets as part of the Marxist Black Unity and Freedom Party output, including 'Black Women Judged as Cattle at Shows' (October 1970), 'The Oppressed of the Oppressed' (March 1971) and 'Black Women Speak Out' (May 1979).[85] The 'Black Women Judged as Cattle at Shows' pamphlets were distributed in 'places where "beauty contests" are held'.[86] Rather than reorienting beauty ideals within hierarchical structures like the *Gazette* and Dyke and Dryden, who viewed beauty businesses as points of agency for Black women, this group critiqued the continued 'exploitation and cheapening' of women by such ideals. The group foregrounded the degradation of women within mutually reinforcing patriarchal and capitalist structures by categorising beauty culture as exploitative rather than empowering. In doing so, the group problematised Jones's notion of cultivated respectability and took an intersectional approach in critiquing beauty contests.[87]

BWAC addressed both participants of beauty contests as well as those who enabled and promoted a racialised, exploitative beauty culture. First the committee aligned competitions with emotive images of slavery, abuse and unfreedom in attempts to 'decolonise the minds' of Black people in line with transatlantic pride movements. 'White beauty' was characterised as 'false beauty' and its emulation was rejected as a legitimate choice. They argued that 'out of this [beauty culture] can only emerge a mere caricature of European woman'. The discursive use of 'caricature' suggests that women who imitated this beauty ideal will also be ridiculed for emulating it – becoming absurd, artificial imitations of white women. The plurality of BWAC's approach can be situated within other collective organising in Britain, including the Black Panthers, whose discussions on the intersecting oppressions of race, class and gender constructed an empowering vision of Black womanhood.[88]

Second, the pamphlet marked the commodification and commercialisation of 'Black women's bod[ies]' by 'Greedy Capitalist Black businessmen' within an economy that capitalised on vulnerable consumerism and Black labour. The group looked beyond participation in contests to radically disrupt the racialised capitalist structures that encouraged the consumption of particular images, advocating that they be dismantled. BWAC argued that Black businessmen were the agents of 'official aids to white beauty' like skin lighteners and hair-straightening creams, effectively colluding in the oppression of Black women. By situating the work of contest winners in 'strip-tease clubs', BWAC provocatively delineated the limits to, and conflicting notions of, social capital. Their solution was to empower women through education.

As this chapter has demonstrated, between 1956 and 1980 women negotiated the messages advocated within beauty contests in a plurality of ways, ranging from advocating alternative competitions, like those organised by Claudia Jones, to unequivocal rejection by groups like BWAC. However, despite these divergent responses, such contests continued to be integral cultural events in Black British communities during the 1980s. Many contest winners, including Miss Attractive UK and Miss Black and Beautiful, were darker than their Caribbean counterparts. The intercommunity discrimination that Black communities faced in Britain helped to erode aspects of colourism within certain beauty spaces. Changing beauty standards and a greater variety of grooming products became self-fashioning resources in the forging of Black British identities. Therefore, despite resistance and protests from some Black women's collectives, pageants continued to be an important part of Black British life and offered a platform for exploring and celebrating divergent forms of beauty.

Conclusion

The American story, as Levy reminds us, cannot be transplanted to speak for Black British experiences. In this chapter, I have suggested the Black British beauty story can be reconstructed through the histories of postwar migration to Britain, the development of publications such as the *Gazette* and *The Voice* and the establishment of cultural events such as the Notting Hill Carnival and 'Afro-Hair & Beauty' competitions. These histories outline a wider process of actively decolonising previously white spaces in Britain. By mapping beauty ideals and practices over time, I argue here that these changes were a result of various transatlantic social exchanges and movements to establish Black communities and identities in Britain. Black beauty spaces, which responded to messages and representations of European beauty ideals in modern Britain, were irrevocably entangled with a racialised set of ideals. There were contradictions, including unwitting collusions by Black publications, as well as opportunities within publications and spaces (like the salon) to construct new identities and communities which pushed back against normative whiteness in Britain.

In the 1950s and early 1960s, the colonial experience of African Caribbean women meant lighter skin was seen as respectable. Skin shade was a significant social and class signifier. According to Tate, 'browning' does not have the same meaning today as it did twenty-five years ago; skin bleaching has been decolonised for African Caribbean women (and men) and is more relevant to the present international landscape.[89] In this reading, 'browning' of the skin and hair choices came to be another aspect of Blackness or any other performative beauty action. Yet, this understanding of 'browning' remains a product of colonially imbued hierarchies. Culturally ingrained colourism was transported to postwar Britain and many women attempted to achieve lighter skin through skin-bleaching creams. For many second- and third-generation Black British people, whiteness itself was not aspired to; rather, beauty practices were utilised to obtain the social acceptance and privilege attached to dominant white ideals.

My analysis has shown that, from the late 1960s, self-fashioning through discursive beauty practices evolved to subvert European beauty ideals within burgeoning Black consciousness movements such as Black is Beautiful. Specifically, the creation of various Black beauty spaces, including Black hair salons, beauty businesses, exhibitions and contests, became distinct spaces in which to negotiate notions of home and belonging. Woven into the social and spatial fabric of British society, these spaces were vital settings for communities to reclaim their image, to cultivate pride in their appearance and to resist white cultural hegemony. Within the multiplicity of self-fashioning beauty practices, Black businesses also developed away from predominant African American ideals and trends of Black beauty culture. Contests and pageants, in particular, demonstrate the plurality of responses to beauty as methods in the making of Black British identities. The Black Women's Action Committee chose to reject beauty contests as spaces that reinforced dominant beauty ideals, commodified women and capitalised on their exploitation as spectacles. Despite reclamations of 'Black, Beautiful and Essentially British', white-dominant and respectable 'browning' beauty ideals still operated as the norm in the 1980s. These were repeatedly reconstituted and embodied in various forms. Thus, personal and political beauty choices enabled the formation of distinctly Black British identities even as these identities inspired new spaces in which to articulate expressions of Blackness.

Notes

1 Andrea Levy, 'Back To Your Own Country', *Six Stories and an Essay* (London: Tinder Press, 2014), p. 11.
2 Margaret Hunter, *Race, Gender, and the Politics of Skin Tone* (New York: Routledge, 2005), p. 27.

3 Hunter, *Race, Gender and the Politics of Skin Tone*, p. 37.
4 Levy, 'Back To Your Own Country', p. 15.
5 The politics of hair and skin colour have been a prominent area of study in the USA. Some sociological scholarship has examined identity formations in late-twentieth-century Britain; however, postwar Black communities in Britain have not been discussed as extensively.
6 Silven Worrel, 'Black is Black', *The Voice*, 2 May 1989, p. 6; Wayne Pinnock, 'Why We Need More Self-Respect', *The Voice*, 5 December 1989, p. 6.
7 Andrea Levy and Charles Henry Rowell, 'An Interview with Andrea Levy', *Callaloo*, 38:2 (2015), p. 261.
8 Levy and Rowell, 'An Interview with Andrea Levy', p. 362.
9 Beverley Bryan, Stella Dadzie and Suzanne Scafe, *The Heart of the Race: Black Women's Lives in Britain* (London: Verso, 2018).
10 Paul Gilroy, *Postcolonial Melancholia* (New York: Columbia University Press, 2005), p. 13.
11 Peter Fryer, *Staying Power: The History of Black People in Britain* (London: Pluto Press, 1984), p. 372.
12 Ceri Peach, 'Trends in Levels of Caribbean Segregation', in *Caribbean Migration: Globalised Identities*, ed. by Mary Chamberlain (Abingdon: Routledge, 1998), pp. 210–225.
13 Ambalavaner Sivanandan, 'From Resistance to Rebellion: Asian and Afro-Caribbean Struggles in Britain', *Race & Class*, 23:2–3 (1981), p. 117.
14 Bryan et al., *The Heart of the Race*, p. 163.
15 Ayana Byrd and Lori Tharps, *Hair Story: Untangling the Roots of Black Hair in America* (New York: St Martin's Griffin, 2014), p. 38.
16 Winston James, 'Migration, Racism and Identity Formation: The Experience in Britain', in *Inside Babylon: The Caribbean Diaspora in Britain*, ed. by Winston James and Clive Harris (London: Verso, 1993), pp. 231–288, p. 236.
17 Bryan et al., *The Heart of the Race*, p. 137.
18 Bill Schwarz, ' "Claudia Jones and the West Indian Gazette": Reflections on the Emergence of Post-Colonial Britain', *Twentieth Century British History*, 14:3 (2003), pp. 264–285.
19 This juxtaposition of content versus beauty adverts can also be found in many mainstream white women's magazines.
20 Rochelle Rowe, *Imagining Caribbean Womanhood: Race, Nation and Beauty Contests, 1929–70* (Manchester: Manchester University Press, 2013), p. 157.
21 Bryan et al., *The Heart of the Race*, p. 223.
22 Rowe, *Imagining Caribbean Womanhood*, p. 158.
23 Carmen England, 'Beauty Tropical', *The West Indian Gazette*, May 1962, p. 12.
24 Bryan et al., *The Heart of the Race*, p. 224.
25 Debbie Weekes, 'Shades of Blackness: Young Female Constructions of Beauty', in *Black British Feminism: A Reader*, ed. by Heidi Safia Mirza (New York: Routledge, 1997), p. 116.
26 'The Best Thing Since…TCB', *The Voice*, 10 August 1985, p. 285.
27 Della Finch, 'So You Want To Be a Model?' *The Voice*, 7 June 1988, p. 32.
28 Byrd and Tharps, *Hair Story*, pp. 105–108.

29 'Rastas Rejoice', *The Voice*, 4 April 1989, p. 3.
30 Stephen Bourne, *Black in the British Frame: Black People in British Film and Television, 1896–1996* (London: Cassell & Co, 1998), p. 120.
31 Bourne, *Black in the British Frame*, p. 120.
32 Bourne, *Black in the British Frame*, p. 120.
33 Paula Black, *The Beauty Industry: Gender, Culture, Pleasure* (London: Routledge, 2004), p. 28.
34 Gail Lewis, 'Black Women's Employment and the British Economy', in *Inside Babylon: The Caribbean Diaspora in Britain*, ed. by Winston James and Clive Harris (London: Verso, 1993), pp. 73–75.
35 Isabel Appio, 'Hairboom', *The Voice*, 2 October 1982, pp. 14–15.
36 Rowe, *Imagining Caribbean Womanhood*, p. 167.
37 Andrea Levy, *Every Light in the House Burnin'* (London: Headline Publishing Group, 1994).
38 Andrea Levy and Susan Alice Fischer, 'Andrea Levy in Conversation with Susan Alice Fischer', *Changing English: Studies in Culture and Education*, 12:3 (2005), p. 362.
39 Andrea Levy, *Every Light in the House Burnin'*, p. 165.
40 Andrea Levy, *Every Light in the House Burnin'*, p. 165.
41 Andrea Levy, *Every Light in the House Burnin'*, p. 166.
42 Andrea Levy, *Every Light in the House Burnin'*, p. 166.
43 Lighter-skinned women had more opportunities in certain sectors but often faced highly charged questions about 'authentic blackness' within Black communities.
44 Margaret Hunter, ' "If You're Light You're Alright": Light Skin Color as Social Capital for Women of Color', *Gender and Society*, 16:2 (2002), pp. 176–178.
45 Gad Heuman, 'The Historiography of Slavery and Abolition in the Anglophone Caribbean', in *Beyond Fragmentation: Perspectives on Caribbean History*, ed. by Juanita De Barros, Audra Diptee and David V. Trotman (Princeton, NJ: Marcus Wiener, 2006), p. 94.
46 The eighteenth-century planter-historian Edward Long described how 'coloured' people with 'the pride of amended blood' aspired to 'mend their complexion' further by mixing with whites; see James, 'Migration, Racism and Identity Formation', p. 236.
47 James and Lewis use the term 'multi-layered pigmentocracy' to define connections between colour, class and privilege; see Winston James and Clive Harris, eds, *Inside Babylon: The Caribbean Diaspora in Britain* (London: Verso, 1993).
48 Stuart Hall, 'The Formation of a Diasporic Intellectual I', in *Empire Windrush: Fifty Years of Writing about Black Britain*, ed. by Onyekachi Wambu (London: Phoenix, 1999), p. 35.
49 Shirley Ann Tate, *Black Beauty: Aesthetics, Stylization, Politics* (Farnham: Ashgate, 2009), p. 92.
50 Henrice Altink, ' "Marrying Light": Skin Colour, Gender and Marriage in JAMAICA, c. 1918–1980', *The History of the Family*, 24:3 (2019), p. 608.
51 Andrea Levy, *Never Far From Nowhere* (London: Review, 1996), p. 2.

52 Levy, *Never Far From Nowhere*, p. 88.
53 Levy, *Never Far From Nowhere*, p. 278.
54 Margaret Hunter, 'Buying Racial Capital: Skin-Bleaching and Cosmetic Surgery in a Globalized World', *The Journal of Pan African Studies*, 4:4 (2011), p. 142.
55 Tate, *Black Beauty*, p. 92.
56 Bryan et al., *The Heart of the Race*, p. 226.
57 Carole Boyce Davies, *Left of Karl Marx: The Political Life of Black Communist Claudia Jones* (London: Duke University Press, 2008), p. 33.
58 Rowe, *Imagining Caribbean Womanhood*, p. 156.
59 Carla Rice, *Becoming Women: The Embodied Self in Image Culture* (London: University of Toronto Press, 2014), p. 236.
60 'Carmen Skinlite Bleach Cream', *The West Indian Gazette*, May 1962, n.p.
61 Evelyn Nakano Glenn, 'Yearning for Lightness: Transnational Circuits in the Marketing and Consumption of Skin Lighteners', *Gender & Society*, 22:3 (2008), pp. 281–302.
62 Stuart Hall, 'The Spectacle of the "Other"', in *Representation: Cultural Representations and Signifying Practices*, ed. by Stuart Hall (London: SAGE Publications, 1997), p. 241.
63 C. M. Ridley and S. J. Adams, 'British Cosmetic Regulations Inadequate', *British Medical Journal*, 288 (1984), p. 1537.
64 Ridley and Adams, 'British Cosmetic Regulations Inadequate'.
65 Evelyn Nakano Glenn, 'Consuming Lightness: Segmented Markets and Global Capital in the Skin Whitening Trade', in *Shades of Difference: Why Skin Color Matters*, ed. by Evelyn Nakano Glenn (Stanford, CA: Stanford University Press, 2009), pp. 166–187.
66 'Sulfur 8 Products', *The West Indian Gazette*, May 1962, p. 10.
67 Bourne, *Black in the British Frame*, p. 103.
68 Oumou Gueye, 'Interview of Barbara Jackson', *Oral Histories of the Black Women's Movement: The Heart of the Race* (London: Black Cultural Archives, 2009), ORAL/1/19, p. 7.
69 'Paradise House of Beauty', *The Voice*, 2 October 1982, p. 24.
70 'Black, Beautiful and Essentially British', *The Voice*, 7 July 1984, p. 27.
71 Shirley Anne Tate, 'Colour Matters, "Race" Matters: African Caribbean Identity in the 20th Century', in *Black Identity in the 20th Century: Expressions of the US and UK African Diaspora*, ed. by Mark Christian (London: Hansib Publications Limited, 2002), p. 209.
72 Tony Wade, *How They Made A Million: The Dyke and Dryden Story* (London: Hansib Publications Limited, 2001), p. 71.
73 Wade, *How They Made A Million*, p. 94.
74 Wade, *How They Made A Million*, p. 71.
75 Wade, *How They Made A Million*, p. 72.
76 Wade, *How They Made A Million*, p. 74.
77 Carolyn Cooper, 'Caribbean Fashion Week: Remodeling Beauty in "Out of Many One" Jamaica', *Fashion Theory*, 14:3 (2010), p. 388.
78 Rowe, *Imagining Caribbean Womanhood*, p. 1.

79 Cooper, 'Caribbean Fashion Week', p. 388.
80 Cooper, 'Caribbean Fashion Week', p. 388.
81 Rowe, *Imagining Caribbean Womanhood*, p. 122.
82 Rowe, *Imagining Caribbean Womanhood*, p. 123.
83 Claudia Jones, 'An End to the Neglect of the Problems of the Negro Woman!' (1949), *PRISM: Political & Rights Issues & Social Movement*, 467, https://stars.library.ucf.edu/prism/467 [accessed 29 May 2016].
84 Rowe, *Imagining Caribbean Womanhood*, p. 230.
85 Black Women's Action Committee, *Black Women Speak Out* (London: Black Women's Action Committee of the Black Unity and Freedom Party, 1970), Black Cultural Archives, WONG/6/39; Black Women's Action Committee, *The Oppressed of the Oppressed* (London: Black Women's Action Committee of the Black Unity and Freedom Party, 1971), Black Cultural Archives, WONG/6/39.
86 Black Women's Action Committee, *Black Women Judged as Cattle at Shows* (London: Black Women's Action Committee of the Black Unity and Freedom Party, 1970), Black Cultural Archives, WONG/6/39.
87 Intersectionality was coined by Kimberlé Crenshaw in 1989; however, Black feminists had long been discussing overlapping oppressions in their lives. Writing in 1983, Jenny Bourne asked for 'the values, ideas and images imposed on women and black people and the relationship these have to the overall exploitative system' to be questioned: Jenny Bourne, 'Towards an Anti-Racist Feminism', *Race and Class*, 25:1 (1983), p. 2.
88 Linda Lumsden, 'Good Mothers with Guns: Framing Black Womanhood in the Black Panther, 1968–1980', *Journalism and Mass Communication Quarterly*, 86:4 (2009), p. 920.
89 Shirley Anne Tate, 'Lightness, Skin Bleaching and Modern Blackness in Jamaica', 'Shade Matters' lecture, University of York, 13 October 2015.

Bibliography

Altink, Henrice, '"Marrying Light": Skin Colour, Gender and Marriage in Jamaica, c. 1918–1980', *The History of the Family*, 24:3 (2019), pp. 608–628.
Appio, Isabel, 'Hairboom', *The Voice*, 2 October 1982, pp. 14–15.
Baldwin, Davarian L., 'From the Washtub to the World: Madame C J Walker and the "Re-Creation" of Race Womanhood, 1900–1935', *The Modern Girl around the World*, ed. by The Modern Girl around the World Research Group (Durham, NC: Duke University Press, 2008), pp. 44–76.
'The Best Thing Since…TCB', *The Voice*, 10 August 1985, p. 285.
Black, Paula, *The Beauty Industry: Gender, Culture, Pleasure* (London: Routledge, 2004).
'Black, Beautiful and Essentially British', *The Voice*, 7 July 1984, p. 27.
Black Women's Action Committee, *Black Women Judged as Cattle at Shows* (London: BWAC, 1970). Black Cultural Archives, WONG/6/39.
Black Women's Action Committee, *Black Women Speak Out* (London: Black Women's Action Committee of the Black Unity and Freedom Party, 1970), Black Cultural Archives, WONG/6/39.

Black Women's Action Committee, *The Oppressed of the Oppressed* (London: Black Women's Action Committee of the Black Unity and Freedom Party, 1971), Black Cultural Archives, WONG/6/39.

Bourne, Jenny, 'Towards and Anti-Racist Feminism', *Race and Class*, 25:1 (1983), pp. 11–22.

Bourne, Stephen, *Black in the British Frame: Black People in British Film and Television, 1896–1996* (London: Cassell & Co, 1998).

Bryan, Beverley, Stella Dadzie and Suzanne Scafe, *The Heart of the Race: Black Women's Lives in Britain* (London: Verso Books, 2018).

Byrd, Ayana and Lori Tharps, *Hair Story: Untangling the Roots of Black Hair in America* (New York: St Martin's Griffin, 2014).

'Carmen Skinlite Bleach Cream', *The West Indian Gazette*, May 1962, n.p.

Cooper, Carolyn, 'Caribbean Fashion Week: Remodeling Beauty in "Out of Many One" Jamaica', *Fashion Theory*, 14:3 (2010), pp. 387–404.

Davis, Carole Boyce, *Left of Karl Marx: The Political Life of Black Communist Claudia Jones* (London: Duke University Press, 2008).

England, Carmen, 'Beauty Tropical', *The West Indian Gazette*, May 1962, p. 12.

Finch, Della, 'So You Want To Be a Model?' *The Voice*, 7 June 1988, p. 32.

Fryer, Peter, *Staying Power: The History of Black People in Britain* (London: Pluto Press, 1984).

Gilroy, Paul, *Postcolonial Melancholia* (New York: Columbia University Press, 2005).

Glenn, Evelyn Nakano, 'Consuming Lightness: Segmented Markets and Global Capital in the Skin Whitening Trade', in *Shades of Difference: Why Skin Color Matters*, ed. by Evelyn Nakano Glenn (Stanford, CA: Stanford University Press, 2009), pp. 166–187.

Glenn, Evelyn Nakano, 'Yearning for Lightness: Transnational Circuits in the Marketing and Consumption of Skin Lighteners', *Gender & Society*, 22:3 (2008), pp. 281–302.

Gueye Oumou, 'Interview of Barbara Jackson', in *Oral Histories of the Black Women's Movement: The Heart of the Race* (London: Black Cultural Archives, 2009), ORAL/1/19.

Hall, Stuart, 'The Formation of a Diasporic Intellectual I', *Empire Windrush: Fifty Years of Writing and Black Britain*, ed. by Onyekachi Wambu (London: Phoenix, 1999), pp. 34–38.

Hall, Stuart, 'The Spectacle of the "Other"', in *Representation: Cultural Representations and Signifying Practices*, ed. by Stuart Hall (London: SAGE Publications, 1997), pp. 223–291.

Heurman, Gad, 'The Historiography of Slavery and Abolition in the Anglophone Caribbean', in *Beyond Fragmentation: Perspectives on Caribbean History*, ed. by Juanita De Barros, Audra Diptee and David V. Trotman (Princeton, NJ: Marcus Wiener, 2006), pp. 93–112.

Hunter, Margaret, 'Buying Racial Capital: Skin-Bleaching and Cosmetic Surgery in a Globalized World', *The Journal of Pan African Studies*, 4:4 (2011), pp. 142–164.

Hunter, Margaret, '"If You're Light You're Alright": Light Skin Color as Social Capital for Women of Color', *Gender and Society*, 16:2 (2002), pp. 175–193.

Hunter, Margaret, *Race, Gender, and the Politics of Skin Tone* (New York: Routledge, 2005).

James, Winston, 'Migration, Racism and Identity Formation: The Experience in Britain', in *Inside Babylon: The Caribbean Diaspora in Britain*, ed. by Winston James and Clive Harris (London: Verso Books, 1993), pp. 231–287.

Jones, Claudia, 'An End to the Neglect of the Problems of the Negro Woman!' (1949), *PRISM: Political & Rights Issues & Social Movement*, 467, https://stars.library.ucf.edu/prism/467 [accessed 29 May 2016].

Levy, Andrea, 'Back To Your Own Country', in *Six Stories and an Essay* (London: Tinder Press, 2014), pp. 3–22.

Levy, Andrea, *Every Light in the House Burnin'* (London: Headline Publishing Group, 1994).

Levy, Andrea, *Fruit of the Lemon* (London: Headline Publishing Group, 1999).

Levy, Andrea, *Never Far From Nowhere* (London: Review, 1996).

Levy, Andrea and Susan Alice Fischer, 'Andrea Levy in Conversation with Susan Alice Fischer', *Changing English: Studies in Culture and Education*, 12:3 (2006), pp. 361–371.

Levy, Andrea and Rowell, Charles Henry, 'An Interview with Andrea Levy', *Callaloo*, 38:2 (2015), pp. 258–281.

Lewis, Gail, 'Black Women's Employment and the British Economy', in *Inside Babylon: The Caribbean Diaspora in Britain*, ed. by Winston James and Clive Harris (London: Verso Books, 1993), pp. 73–96.

Lumsden, Linda, 'Good Mothers with Guns: Framing Black Womanhood in the Black Panther, 1968–1980', *Journalism and Mass Communication Quarterly*, 86:4 (2009), pp. 900–922.

'Paradise House of Beauty', *The Voice*, 2 October 1982, p. 24.

Peach, Ceri, 'Trends in levels of Caribbean Segregation', in *Caribbean Migration: Globalised Identities*, ed. by Mary Chamberlain (Abingdon: Routledge, 1998), pp. 210–225.

Pinnock, Wayne, 'Why We Need More Self-Respect', *The Voice*, 5 December 1989, p. 6.

'Rastas Rejoice', *The Voice*, 4 April 1989, p. 3.

Rice, Carla, *Becoming Women: The Embodied Self in Image Culture* (London: University of Toronto Press, 2014).

Ridley, C. M. and S. J. Adams, 'British Cosmetic Regulations Inadequate', *British Medical Journal*, 288 (1984), p. 1537.

Rowe, Rochelle, *Imagining Caribbean Womanhood: Race, Nation and Beauty Competitions, 1929–70* (Manchester: Manchester University Press, 2013).

Schwarz, Bill, '"Claudia Jones and the West Indian Gazette": Reflections on the Emergence of Post-colonial Britain', *Twentieth Century British History*, 14:3 (2003), pp. 264–285.

Sivanandan, Ambalavaner, 'From Resistance to Rebellion: Asian and Afro-Caribbean Struggles in Britain', *Race & Class*, 23:2–3 (1981), pp. 111–152.

'Sulfur 8 Products', *The West Indian Gazette*, May 1962, p. 10.

Tate, Shirley Anne, *Black Beauty: Aesthetics, Stylization, Politics* (Farnham: Ashgate, 2009).

Tate, Shirley Anne, 'Colour Matters, "Race" Matters: African Caribbean Identity in the 20th Century', in *Black Identity in the 20th Century: Expression of the US and UK African Diaspora*, ed. by Mark Christian (London: Hansib Publications Limited, 2002), pp. 167–195.

Tate, Shirley Anne, 'Lightness, Skin Bleaching and Modern Blackness in Jamaica', 'Shade Matters' lecture, University of York, 13 October 2015.

Tate, Shirley Anne, *Skin Bleaching in Black Atlantic Zones: Shade Shifters* (London: Palgrave Macmillan, 2016).

The Voice (London: The Gleaner Company Limited and GV Media Group Limited, 1982–).

Wade, Tony, *How They Made A Million: The Dyke and Dryden Story* (London: Hansib Publications Limited, 2001).

Weekes, Debbie, 'Shades of Blackness: Young Female Constructions of Beauty', *Black British Feminism: A Reader*, ed. by Heidi Safia Mirza (New York: Routledge, 1997), pp. 113–126.

West Indian Gazette and Afro-Asian Caribbean News (London: Coloured Peoples Publishing House, 1958–1964).

Worrel, Silven, 'Black is Black', *The Voice*, 2 May 1989, p. 6.

11

Convivial cultures and the commodification of otherness in London nightlife in the 1970s and 1980s

Steve Bentel

I'm the all night drug-prowling wolf
Who looks so sick in the sun
I'm the white man in the Palais
Just lookin' for fun

Joe Strummer, 1978

In the summer of 1977, Don Letts, a London DJ born to Afro-Caribbean migrant parents, invited a white friend to attend a show at the Hammersmith Palais in West London. That night, the venue had presented a soul showcase, featuring top Jamaican artists, in an attempt to cater to the growing Black population in West London. Letts's friend, Joe Strummer, of the punk rock group The Clash, was excited. He knew that this was a show where he would experience life as a racial minority in a crowd. He assumed it would be deeply political and energise him for future political solidarity. This is not what Strummer experienced. He wrote about his experience and released it as the 1977 single 'White Man (in Hammersmith Palais)'. In it, he relayed both his disappointment at how apolitical the event was and, as the title suggests, the isolating feeling of being the white man 'only looking for fun'.[1] Strummer seems to imply that he was the only white man at the Palais that night. While this was not, in all likelihood, an accurate retelling of the story, Strummer does describe an increasingly common phenomenon among white Londoners in the 1970s, who were venturing into primarily Black spaces to experience nighttime entertainment and bolster political and social bona fides.

This chapter explores how elements of convivial culture were forged in London's musical and nightlife settings. Paul Gilroy defines 'convivial culture' as 'the processes of cohabitation and interaction that have made multiculture an ordinary feature of social life in Britain's urban areas and in postcolonial cities elsewhere'.[2] This builds upon the work of Bill Schwarz, who has shown that, during the same postwar period, white Britons 're-racialised' themselves as Britain transitioned into a postcolonial society.

Schwarz has argued that the political activities of people of African descent within Britain emphasised to white Britons that the old political order and the Empire were over.³ This chapter follows Schwarz in foregrounding white Britons' behaviours as responses to the presence of Black peoples within what Schwarz labelled their 'internal decolonisation'.⁴ However, instead of grappling with reactionary political responses, this chapter explores how white Londoners coopted elements from the cultures of racial newcomers to produce a new cultural sphere that celebrated differences but maintained certain racial hierarchies.

This chapter will show that the young white people who spent their nights sharing music and organising around musical activism built a shared culture that struck an often-tenuous balance between culturally appropriating Black spaces and music and building friendships and solidarities within them. These spaces had the power to make such interactions banal, but, particularly in the case of the Brixton Academy, they also foreground the possibility of interracial encounters. The spaces created atmospheres where those on the political left could benefit from what Kennetta Hammond Perry has called the 'mystique of British anti-racism' through trading in what one club owner called 'rebel chic'.⁵ The character of these interactions varied according to the nature of the contact zone. With the exception of several record stores, every privately owned venue discussed in this chapter was owned by white Londoners. These people managed and curated cross-racial interactions. They held positions of power in society and thus were able to determine how the elements derived from Black culture were incorporated.

These venues acted as 'contact zones' for Black and white Londoners. Mary Louise Pratt coined the term 'contact zone' to mean 'social spaces where cultures meet, clash, and grapple with each other, often in contexts of highly asymmetrical relations of power, such as colonialism, slavery, or their aftermaths as they are lived out'.⁶ The interactions in contact zones look quite different depending upon which side of the power dynamic is under investigation. For the purposes of this chapter, I focus on white actors in spaces associated with Blackness.

The musical spaces discussed in this chapter played an important role in forging a Black British identity, particularly for the first generation of British-born children of parents who were West Indian migrants. Eddie Chambers has demonstrated that reggae and dub music, along with their associated fashions, forged a uniquely Black British identity drawing not only on diaspora communities in the Caribbean and USA but, crucially, from an image of Africa as well.⁷ Barbara Bush makes a similar argument but emphasises an additional dimension: 'racial exclusions and confinement of Caribbean culture to the racial slum generated a greater sense of identification (both within and of these communities) with African Diaspora culture'.[8] Bush then continues, 'the liberation of culture, expressed through music, language, and religion, was thus essential to the creation of the African-Caribbean minority in Britain'.[9] In Gilroy's *The Black Atlantic* (1993), he identifies musical culture as important in shaping Black identities globally, pointing to Soul II Soul and Jazzie B's emergence in 1980s London as an assertive moment in Black British identity.[10] Soul II Soul's live debut with Jazzie B was, however, at the Fridge, a Brixton club run by white veterans of the punk scene that regularly catered to Brixton's gay community.

As this Black identity was developing, though, Dick Hebdige has shown that these Black cultures were fundamental in shaping white identities, presenting Black presence as the 'phantom histories' of various white subcultures.[11] Hebdige's seminal study *Subculture: The Meaning of Style* (1979) argued that youth culture was 'a succession of differential responses to the Black immigrant presence in Britain from the 1950s onwards', part of the wider phenomenon that Wendy Webster has described as the empire 'coming home'.[12] This took different forms in different contexts. This chapter bolsters that understanding by focusing on white Londoners who emphasised and incorporated their links to Black cultures through music and nightlife. In doing so, the phantom was no longer invisible or in the background, but was instead made known. However, the power structures shaping this process were still overwhelmingly white.

This chapter demonstrates, through an exploration of interracial contact zones, that Black people, either on a stage or in the community, created environments in which white Londoners asserted their membership in a culturally engaged or aware subset of the population. It begins on the mod circuit of the 1960s, where young Londoners let loose and grooved to African American music. The chapter then turns to the 1980s, when club owners and promoters like Simon Parkes, the heir to Britain's largest fish fortune, built a club in Brixton that traded on the image linked to Black British culture as 'rebel chic'.[13] Parkes's 'rebel chic' was built on outsiders' desires to prove their 'coolness' by visiting Brixton, a place defined to outsiders largely by violent depictions of the district in the national media. The violent atmosphere in Brixton could be commodified into a package of 'rebel chic' through secret agreements between Parkes and his fellow club owners and the gang leaders who exercised control over Brixton's streets. This allowed the area to maintain an 'affective ecology' with slight levels of danger for outsiders, while their lived experiences were, for the most part, safe.

Stephen Brooke argues the importance of reading affective ecologies – the interactions between human emotion and space, both public and private – into the history of everyday life in London.[14] Conviviality in musical environments was forged partly by tapping into this ecology, often through the consumption of the space in which it was produced. In Brixton, young people consumed an environment shaped by fear of and interest in racial difference and the radical politics associated with the neighbourhood. bell hooks adds the analytical frame of 'eating the other' in which ethnic difference became 'spice, seasoning that can liven up the dull dish that is mainstream white culture(s)'.[15] By consuming cultural practices and spaces, white Londoners forged their own new identities, while placing economic pressure on the same spaces they consumed to conform to their tastes.

The cultural practices described in this chapter have deep roots in London. Seth Koven provides an important framework for understanding the motivations of attendees of the Brixton Academy and similar venues through his study of wealthy Londoners crossing psychological boundaries during the late Victorian era. He described the desire of these temporary visitors who travelled into the slums of London to fulfil a combination of altruism and eros, generosity and sexual desire.[16] Koven describes the importance of mobility to 'slumming', outlining how wealthy Londoners travelled across the city – often towards East London – and entered neighbourhoods where they lacked roots to either visit for the night, or to resettle themselves as part of a grand project.[17] Through this chapter, we see the willingness of those living nearly a century after Koven's subjects to make similar journeys to their postcolonial analogues, racially diverse inner-city spaces. The mobile white side of cross-racial interactions in the late twentieth century relied on a combination of solidaristic, hedonistic and voyeuristic boundary crossing in order to expand the boundaries of daily interaction. Stuart Hall argued has argued that multiethnic 'city centres (were) increasingly trendified and colonised for urban nightlife and clubbing'.[18] In the process of doing so, a unique multiculture found spaces to flourish but also fell victim to commercial pressures through which white participants sanitised their experiences.

Brixton and the Academy

Brixton, more than anywhere else in London, was at the epicentre of a 'trendification' based on commodifying the area's racialised image. Brixton was constructed in the popular imagination of both Black and white Britons as the beating heart of Black Britain, despite consistent white majorities in the district. During the interwar period, Brixton was a well-to-do suburb with spacious homes and a thriving local shopping district. The bombings from the Second World War caused significant damage to the area and the population declined. When in 1948 the *Empire Windrush* brought hundreds of West Indian men to Britain, the job centre where many found work happened to be in Brixton. Because of this, in the years that followed, Brixton developed a sizeable local Black community built through more postcolonial migrants settling the district.[19] As the community grew, national differences between different island communities declined in importance and a shared Black diasporic identity emerged, with Brixton as an important focal point.[20]

As the years went by the dual burdens of racism and poverty afflicted Brixton and led to a stigma appearing around the district in the popular press. The area's 'front line' along Coldharbour Lane was at the centre of controversies surrounding overly aggressive police tactics in response to the street-crime 'crisis' of the late 1970s.[21] This crisis climaxed in the spring of 1981 when young Black and white Brixton residents took to the streets and engaged in a days-long battle against the police force accompanied by widespread property destruction and theft. This violence caused some commentators in the national press and the government to re-examine Brixton's struggles. It also left the area ripe for investment by individuals hoping to profit from polishing the area's rough edges.[22]

Outsiders began the process that Hall dubbed 'trendifying' Brixton in the 1960s. During this era, entertainment entrepreneurs Rik and Johnny Gunnell entered this community to open a new nightlife venue. They named their venue Ram Jam Club after African American jazz singer Geno Washington's Ramjam Band. The Gunnell Brothers cut their teeth in the cosmopolitan nightlife scene of Jazz Age and wartime Soho.[23] Their clubs included the Mapleton and the Flamingo, where they were introduced to Black American musicians and their styles of music. Gunnell clubs earned reputations for welcoming all types of people from marginalised communities, including African Americans and Caribbean Londoners.[24] As swinging Soho flourished in the 1960s, the Gunnell Brothers looked to London's periphery and sought a new venue to showcase soul and R&B music.

The Ram Jam Club opened its doors in 1966, providing a stage for artists of various musical backgrounds, from The Who to Otis Redding and Jimi Hendrix. Soul and R&B performances at Ram Jam and similar clubs brought together Black and white Londoners to listen to African American music.[25] Young white men in the mod subculture were particularly important to the development of the mystique of R&B clubs as they crisscrossed the city looking for new places to party each night. The Ram Jam was an important stop on their circuit.[26] In their regular London nightlife rotation, mods visited clubs across the capital, travelling north and south of the Thames to experience different Black DJs, bands and sound systems. At these parties, mods would encounter and partake in music produced by and (originally) for Black communities.[27]

Occasionally, the spectre of violence would accompany the mods. The rivalries between clubs, including the Ram Jam, and the competing underground operations behind them further encouraged adventure-seeking mods to sample venues in more unfamiliar, and often more racially diverse,

Convivial cultures in London nightlife 235

London locations.[28] The mod subculture died out in the 1970s but experienced a nostalgic revival in the 1980s. The revived mod movement would play an important role once again in bringing punters to Brixton in the mid-1980s.[29]

As London's economy waned in the 1970s, Brixton fell on hard times. In the media, it became a symbol of blight, symptomatic of an 'urban crisis' not unlike the one being experienced across the Atlantic. One key element of this was the media creation of a moral panic around muggings and the association in the white imagination between people of colour and crime.[30] In many ways, the narratives around race and crime in urban areas like Brixton were shaped by problems experienced across the Atlantic in the preceding decades. Otto Saumarez Smith has argued that America served as a 'forewarning' of what Britain's urban future *could* be.[31] America's 'inner-cities', an American nomenclature, experienced the combined struggles of deindustrialisation and cutthroat renewal projects that streamlined racially exclusive suburbanisation for white Americans.[32]

Because of its residents' struggles with both racism and poverty, Brixton was at the heart of this perceived transatlantic crisis, even if the British public and press felt the need to uphold a narrative of exceptionalism.[33] The area became shorthand for urban problems, especially for Black youth, so much so that even in cases of crime outside of Brixton it was dragged into the discussion by journalists attempting to contextualise crime.[34] Brixton was a ground zero of the tension between young Black men and the Metropolitan Police.[35]

This all came to a head in April 1981. The second weekend of the month saw large-scale, street-level uprisings, featuring widespread property destruction, violent clashes between young people and police officers and a strong backlash against the rioters from the press. The media portrayed the riots in racial terms and further stigmatised Brixton as a dangerous space filled with angry Black youth. This despite the fact that arrest records from that evening show that more young white people were arrested than Black.[36] However, the uprisings in Brixton and elsewhere in Britain spurred a national movement to increase funding for businesses in neglected urban districts.[37] It was during this fraught period in Brixton's history that the Brixton Academy emerged as a major venue for rock and roll.

The building that would house the Academy sat empty in early 1983. It was at this point that a young, cocky public-school graduate named Simon Parkes made the ludicrous offer to pay a pound and offer an exclusive beer contract for a decade to purchase the building. He desired a space in which he could live out his dreams of running a rock music venue and the large, former cinema just a short walk from Brixton station presented the perfect opportunity. Parkes was the grandson of a fish magnate and a former classmate of Prince Andrew. His only first-hand experience with Brixton was driving through the area during his childhood as his family made their annual trip to the Epsom Derby.[38] He was simultaneously a part of the economic elite but also saw himself as a self-described 'scrapper' and a feisty underdog – qualities heightened by a birth defect, the result of Thalidomide complications, that meant he was born missing part of his arm.[39] Identity duality seemed to have followed Parkes throughout his life, which makes it all the more fitting that he should open a venue for playing rock music in the neighbourhood that served as the heart of British reggae.

In the memoir of his time at the Academy, Parkes discussed trying to find the perfect name for his venue. His explanation for, 'The Apollo', his first choice, seemed to embody the mix of paternalism and self-interest demonstrated by Koven's Victorian slummers. 'The Apollo was the (name) for me. That was always the model for what I wanted to do with my venue in Brixton. A historic theatre, helping to restore a run-down Black neighbourhood through legendary gigs: it made sense.'[40] Parkes explained to me in an interview that he had grand plans for his Apollo. He sought a transatlantic expansion for the US TV series 'Live at the Apollo', a public broadcast programme that showcased musicians at the famed New York City jazz venue. The series would have linked the music scenes of Brixton and Harlem and emphasised the hope that a music venue could deliver both communities.[41] While the Apollo was locally owned and operated by influential African Americans, Parkes aimed to bring this hope from outside the local area as an altruistic act.

Parkes's linkage of Brixton and Harlem's cultural status fits within a broader understanding of both neighbourhoods and the 'urban crisis' moment. Scholars have noted the links between postcolonial British racism and the racial tensions of urban America.[42] In Robin D. G. Kelley and Stephen Tuck's collection *The Other Special Relationship: Race, Rights, and Riots in Britain and the United States*, scholars chronicle the cultural politics of these connections and highlight the importance for those involved in the struggle.[43] Parkes was clearly somewhat aware of the connections, but presumably perceived them more on the surface level.

Ultimately, though, Parkes found difficulty negotiating with his New York counterparts and, without their cooperation, found the Apollo name too presumptive. He settled on the Brixton Academy, a name with less meaning, but that he liked the sound of.[44] Parkes's immediate association of Brixton with Harlem is telling. It displays just how ingrained, even in upper-class white circles, Brixton's transition was from one of many working-class, inner-London neighbourhoods to the beating heart of Black London. The association also conflated the diasporic communities and urban struggles on both sides of the Atlantic into a singular narrative into which he could emerge as a healer and a curator of how that shared culture was presented in Britain.

Moving beyond those connections, though, we must examine the implications of attempting to bring rock music, a form of art that despite its African American roots had transformed into a predominantly white genre, into Brixton. It turned out initially to be a challenge for Parkes. His memoir outlines how the major obstacle for getting white artists to play the Academy was dealing with bookers who were much keener to see their artists perform at established venues like the Hammersmith Odeon. He remembers booker after booker saying the same thing to him: 'You'll never get a rock band to play in Brixton.'[45]

A critical reading of Parkes's memoir leaves me sceptical as to exactly how these conversations were conducted. Large bands like Deep Purple and The Clash had played Brixton before. Deep Purple played the very building which now housed the Academy, during its brief run in 1972 as the Sundown Club.[46] In fact, there was already a relatively well-established music venue in Brixton, in the aforementioned Ram Jam Club. It is quite possible that Brixton's image passed a cultural tipping point after the 1981 riots, but it does warrant some scepticism. It is impossible to determine if this upstart venue would have been more successful in booking bands to play an impoverished, racially diverse neighbourhood had the area not made headlines for being a flashpoint for the summer of 1981's national string of rioting. This was compounded by the subsequent investigation into the riots which kept Brixton in the press.[47]

With rock bookers not cooperating, and Parkes left strapped for cash, he began to look for different ways to make money. He began to book gigs targeting the local Afro-Caribbean community. The first gig he successfully booked was a show on 7 October 1983 by a relatively obscure Jamaican reggae artist, Eek-A-Mouse, as part of his UK tour.[48] Next, he brought an African dance troupe to perform.[49] The show after that then featured several smaller reggae acts catering to the local community.[50]

While Parkes's turn to the local community was not what he had envisioned in his initial bid to purchase the Academy, he quickly adapted. Entrepreneurs had long found creative ways of courting alternative market segments. In London, from the late nineteenth century, this included a growing queer community.[51] The proliferation of 'Pink pound' market strategies set an example for Parkes to adapt his venue to cater to the 'Black pound'.[52] After sustaining the venue for a few months on this strategy, Parkes worked to build an environment that could fuse his initial rock dreams and Brixton's consumer base.

The venue's first major show to draw black and white youth together occurred in early 1984 after a local unemployed young Black man convinced UB40 to play the Academy and secured himself long-term employment at the venue.[53] UB40 was an image of what the Academy could become: a racially diverse group playing reggae music for a popular, wide-scale audience. After booking UB40, the Academy achieved success in booking several well-known acts appealing to audiences from beyond Brixton.

In December 1984, the Academy hosted punk-rock reggae fusion group The Clash in a two-day set known at the time as 'Arthur Scargill's Christmas Party', a charity fundraiser for striking coal miners. The Academy secured the Scargill event largely because it offered the venue up for free at a time when many London venues had grown weary of hosting frequently destructive punk shows.[54] The radicals hosting and attending the show would only have accepted the venue's generous offer because it lived up to their standard of radicalism.

Around the same time, mainstream white acts continued booking the venue as its reputation grew. In 1985, two A-list rock stars, Pete Townshend of The Who and David Gilmour of Pink Floyd, graced the stage and, by the end of 1986, The Smiths, a far cry musically and demographically from Eek-A-Mouse, played their final show ever at an anti-apartheid gig in Brixton.

To many of these acts, playing Brixton may well have been a political act, like playing Rock Against Racism (RAR) gigs would have been a few years earlier.[55] Brixton was a symbolic heart of anti-Thatcher resistance, with the rate capping rebellions and the 1981 and 1985 uprisings boosting its profile as a site of resistance. Townshend, for example, was a supporter of RAR and provided technical support for its 1978 Carnival Against the Nazis. The Smiths brought themselves to Brixton during an era when they acted as a strong left-wing voice for the industrial Northwest amid deindustrialisation and social disintegration.

The choice to view and use Brixton this way did not necessarily require playing shows primarily to Brixton residents. Instead, the district acted as a stage on which white radicals could demonstrate their anti-racist bona fides. They could show that they didn't fear going to a neighbourhood so closely associated with Black Britons, even if audiences at most of the shows did not reflect this.

Around the same time that Parkes's Academy's prominence rose, other venues in the district also grew increasingly popular. The old Ram Jam Club was purchased in 1981 by Andy Czezowski and his partner Susan Carrington. Czezowski and Carrington were also district outsiders who had made their name in the music industry for operating the famous West End punk and reggae club the Roxy. At the Roxy, the duo shaped the early punk scene and employed Don Letts as a DJ. Among other things, Letts famously brought Joe Strummer to the Hammersmith Palais.[56] The Roxy hosted many famous bands during the peak of British punk in the late 1970s, including The Clash, The Damned, The Jam, Siouxsie and the Banshees and The Police. Thanks to the musical influence of people like Letts and the support of management, including Czezowski, the punk-reggae fusion sound flourished at the Roxy. Czezowski and Carrington reopened the Ram Jam under the name 'The Fridge'. The Fridge was a favourite for local and more distant Londoners, so much so that it moved into a larger venue, closer to the Academy in central Brixton, in 1985.[57]

The Fridge was slightly different from the Academy, catering to the 'New Romantic' movement popular in the mid-1980s. The New Romantic movement revolved around challenging social norms around the expression of gender and sexuality, a different type of 'rebel chic'. Alongside the New Romantic crowd, The Fridge catered to closely associated queer communities. This was more easily done in spaces like Brixton where privileged Londoners benefitted from mobility and anonymity. Parkes recalled how white, middle-class punters would arrive at Brixton's queer fetish nights from across London, casually toting duffel bags containing the clothing into which they would later change.[58]

This parallels Koven's observations about the importance of the privilege of changing clothing when engaging in a 'slum experience'.[59] In many ways, the participants in Brixton's queer club scene were not privileged. Anti-gay sentiment was high in Thatcher's Britain and the AIDS crisis defined the 1980s for many. Still, the ability to conceal this identity in transit emphasised the mobility that whiteness offered Brixton's nighttime incomers. It also demonstrated the importance of Brixton, a place defined for many by one element of its 'other-ness' and as a safe place to reveal other-ness of a different variety.

Despite Parkes's success at the Academy and the rise in other popular venues such as The Fridge, the level of everyday violence and gang activity for those living in Brixton should not be forgotten. The Academy had multiple incidents involving armed robbery, and management feared for the safety of people coming from the railway station. Parkes's memoir describes, without going into detail, how arrangements were made with local gang leaders to protect customers going to and from shows at the venue.[60] This arrangement allowed Londoners from outside the area to visit Brixton while safe from the violence of everyday life in the community. Simultaneously, though, the secret nature of the agreement allowed the customers to remain unaware of the protection they were under. They were therefore free to trade on the radical chic of their own experiences on Brixton's streets. In an interview, Parkes described how local gangs and businesses understood the commercial value of concertgoers to Brixton's economy. It also did not hurt the Academy's guests that it was right across the street from the Brixton Metropolitan Police station, where Parkes, through his public-school connections, knew how to get in contact with powerful people in management if necessary.[61]

Parkes maintained his connections with the circles he grew up in. In an interview, he described a particular event he attended in the late 1980s or early 1990s where the Prince and Princess of Wales and the Attenborough brothers were mingling with his old public-school connections. According to Parkes, men at the event found his ownership of a Brixton nightclub strange, but many of the women, particularly the younger ones, expressed interest. To them, Brixton was the cool place to go for weekend entertainment. While these particular women preferred gay nights at The Fridge because the men there would leave them alone, word of Brixton's perceived rough edges and intense party scene carried weight beyond the early eclectic gatherings of reggae fans and punks all the way up to royal soirees.[62] There were the postcolonial parallels to the Jazz Age tales of dukes and dustmen sharing the dance floor at places like the Hammersmith Palais, but taking place instead in a racialised district of a multicultural city. This only added to the manufactured mystique.[63]

The disconnect between the manufactured experience created by Brixton's entertainment venues and Brixton's daily reality began drawing more and more whites to the neighbourhood. These people brought with them their own expectations of what their visits should be like. This could be seen in reports of a white woman who became upset with a security guard who called her 'love' while checking her for admission to a Gil Scott-Heron reading in November 1984.[64] This particular punter was not the only audience member unimpressed with her night at the Academy. *New Musical Express* (*NME*) reviewed the show and the venue at the time, and offered the following scathing description: 'a venue for music less conducive and more forlorn and wretched than this superannuated Brixton corridor called The Academy is not lightly imaginable … just because Gil Scott Heron sends his messages to the sufferer doesn't mean we've got to suffer to see him does it?'[65] It seems possible that this suffering was part of the draw to the Academy, though. We certainly can see this in Parkes's descriptions. He saw himself as an underdog, going into a harsh environment and trying to use music to heal a community and chart a course for himself in life that broke free from the aristocratic world he never fit into. This healing mission was at least as much a personal project to live out his rock-star fantasies and build an identity independent of his family as it was about uplifting a struggling Black community.[66]

While Brixton's social conditions improved slightly in the mid-80s, they again hit a flashpoint in September of 1985 when the police shot Dorothy 'Cherry' Groce, the mother of a young man for whom they were searching. Because of its location near the police station, an uprising occurred right outside of Parkes's Academy. When the violence broke out, Parkes was at a wedding of an 'old money' friend and went down into Brixton dressed in formal regalia to keep an eye on the venue. It was at this point when he claims to have realised that his sympathies in the uprising lay with the young, diverse Brixtonites: his customers, his staff, and most importantly people he saw as his friends.[67] Because of his business, Parkes claimed that he was a part of Brixton, the community once again pushed to the point of taking to the streets, and he and his club were not going to desert them. From a financial standpoint, Parkes also noted that the uprisings helped further consolidate the Academy's 'rebel chic' credentials.[68] Despite his sympathies, Parkes was still only in a position to make a choice like this because he was an outsider. He was only able to go into business in Brixton because of his wealth and privilege. He commodified the environment while himself choosing to live elsewhere.[69]

By 1989, the Academy had outpaced Parkes's self-designated rival, the Hammersmith Odeon, in booking major rock-and-roll gigs. The Academy even made headlines in the stodgy *Sunday Times* when Parkes was profiled as the 'King of Gigs'.[70] Recording artists from seemingly all genres, including top hard-rock acts, George Michael and even the queen of pop music Diana Ross, were now playing at a rock venue located in the home of British reggae.

As the 1990s progressed, the Brixton Academy and Brixton more broadly became the original home in London for American rap and hip-hop. By showcasing acts like N.W.A. and Snoop Dogg, the Academy took up the mantle of promoting transatlantic Black music, while still hosting new romantics and post-punk bands. The racial makeup at various types of shows fluctuated, but the customer base was regularly diverse. Hip-hop's base market was primarily young and Black but, like many other forms of music with that target market, there was cultural cachet with young white people, particularly men, as well.

By the mid-1990s, Brixton's nightlife, whether that be rave, rap or post-punk and guitar rock, was a major feature of the 'Cool Britannia' moment. The Academy won 'Venue of the Year' at every *NME* Awards between 1995 and 2000.[71] It presented a diverse multicultural entertainment scene that thrived on massive, commercial success. It was undoubtedly also fundamental to the demographic change that would be central to all discussions of Brixton in the decades to come.

Conclusion

Brixton and its trendy nightclubs acted as sites for white and middle-class Londoners to showcase their openness to difference and shape their identities and engage with the nuances of the postcolonial cityscape. Mods paved the pathway for this with their nightly trips across London on a circuit, encountering new music, using various drugs and engaging in the occasional fight. Mods pushed the locus of nightlife in London from the urban 'centre' into various 'peripheral' neighbourhoods, settled by members of the postcolonial diaspora, including Brixton.

Through the 1970s and into the 1980s, Brixton solidified itself in popular imaginations as both the symbolic heart of Black Britain and also became shorthand for the British iteration of a racialised 'inner-city' crisis. In the 1980s, Brixton became a space into which white Londoners could traverse from the suburbs and the increasingly gentrified neighbourhoods in the urban core for nighttime entertainment. This was done under protections of which they were unaware, put into place through arrangements between club owners, local businesses and gang leaders. The spaces created atmospheres where white Londoners on the political left could benefit from Perry's 'mystique of British anti-racism' and those operating the clubs could work that 'mystique' into 'rebel chic'.[72]

In Brixton's clubs, Londoners of different races encountered one another. But often these spaces reinforced versions of the racial status quo, with white tastemakers profiting from the spaces they curated. Revellers and concert-goers often went with some sort of agenda for a political self-styling, but just as many engaged with Black spaces, to bring us back to Strummer, 'just looking for fun'. The range of these encounters shaped how white Londoners came to experience convivial multiculture, as Gilroy put it, as 'an ordinary feature of social life in Britain's (postcolonial) urban areas'.[73]

Notes

1 The Clash, 'White Man (In Hammersmith Palais)', single, CBS Records, 1978, vinyl.
2 Paul Gilroy, *After Empire: Melancholia or Convivial Culture* (London: Routledge, 2004), p. xi.
3 Bill Schwarz, 'Claudia Jones and the *West Indian Gazette*: Reflections on the Emergence of Post-Colonial Britain', *Twentieth Century British History*, 14:3 (Autumn 2003), pp. 264–285 and 'The Only White Man in There: The Re-Racialision of England 1956–1968', *Race and Class*, 38:1 (July 1996), pp. 65–78.
4 Schwarz, 'Claudia Jones and the *West Indian Gazette*', p. 285.
5 Kennetta Hammond Perry, *London is the Place for Me: Black Britons, Citizenship, and the Politics of Race* (Oxford: Oxford University Press, 2015), pp. 100–104; Simon Parkes with J. S. Rafaeli, *Live at the Brixton Academy: A Riotous Life in the Music Business* (London: Serpent's Tail, 2014), p. 130.
6 Mary Louise Pratt, 'Arts of the Contact Zone', *Profession* (1991), p. 34.
7 Eddie Chambers, *Roots & Culture: Cultural Politics in the Making of Black Britain* (London: I.B.Tauris, 2017).

8 Barbara Bush, 'The Dark Side of the City: Racialized Barriers, Culture, and Citizenship in Britain c. 1950–1990s', in *Rastafari: A Universal Philosophy for the Third Millennium*, ed. by Werner Zips (Kingston: Ian Randle, 2000), p. 170.
9 Bush, 'The Dark Side of the City', pp. 170–171.
10 Paul Gilroy, *The Black Atlantic: Modernity and Double Consciousness* (London: Verso, 1993), p. 86.
11 Dick Hebdige, *Subculture: The Meaning of Style* (New York: Routledge, 1979), p. 45.
12 Hebdige, *Subculture*, p. 29; Wendy Webster, 'The Empire Comes Home: Commonwealth Migration to Britain', in *Britain's Experience of Empire in the Twentieth Century*, ed. by Andrew Thompson (Oxford: Oxford University Press, 2011), pp. 122–160.
13 Parkes with Rafaeli, *Live at the Brixton Academy*, p. 130.
14 Stephen Brooke, 'Space, Emotions and the Everyday: An Affective Ecology of the 1980s', *Twentieth Century British History*, 28:1 (2017), p. 115.
15 bell hooks, 'Eating the Other: Desire and Resistance', in *Black Looks: Race and Representation* (New York: Routledge, 1992), p. 21.
16 Seth Koven, *Slumming: Sexual and Social Politics in Victorian London* (Princeton, NJ: Princeton University Press, 2006), p. 18.
17 Koven, *Slumming*, p. 9.
18 Stuart Hall, 'Cosmopolitan Promises, Multicultural Realities', in *Divided Cities*, ed. Richard Scholar (Oxford: Oxford University Press, 2010), p. 42.
19 Perry, *London is the Place for Me*, p. 48.
20 Paul Gilroy, *There Ain't No Black in the Union Jack: The Cultural Politics of Race and Nation* (Chicago, IL: University of Chicago Press, 1987), p. 104; Elizabeth Buettner, *Europe After Empire: Decolonization, Society and Culture* (Cambridge: Cambridge University Press, 2017), p. 365; Kieran Connell, *Black Handsworth: Race in 1980s Britain* (Berkeley, CA: University of California Press, 2019), p. 34.
21 Stuart Hall, Chas Critcher, Tony Jefferson, John Clarke and Brian Roberts, *Policing the Crisis: Mugging, the State, and Law and Order* (London: Palgrave Macmillan, 1978).
22 See Parkes with Rafaeli, *Live at the Brixton Academy*, p. 130.
23 For an exploration of Jazz Age Soho, see Judith Walkowitz, *Nights Out: Life in Cosmopolitan London* (New Haven, CT: Yale University Press, 2012) and Marc Matera, *Black London: The Imperial Metropolis and Decolonization in the Twentieth Century* (Berkeley, CA: University of California Press, 2015), chapters 1 and 4.
24 Val Wilmer, 'Rik Gunnell', *The Guardian*, 18 June 2007, www.theguardian.com/news/2007/jun/18/guardianobituaries.obituaries [accessed 13 September 2022].
25 Jeremy Marre, *Otis Redding Soul Ambassador* (London: BBC, 2013), BBC 4 documentary.
26 Dick Hebdige, 'The Meaning of Mod', in Stuart Hall and Tony Jefferson, *Resistance Through Rituals: Youth Subcultures in Post-War Britain* (London: Routledge, 2006), p. 72.

27 Hebdige, 'The Meaning of Mod', pp. 71–72.
28 Gilroy, *There Ain't No Black in the Union Jack*, p. 166.
29 Enamel Verguren, *This is A Modern Life: The 1980s London Mod Scene* (London: Shaman Books, 2012).
30 Hall et al., *Policing the Crisis*.
31 Otto Saumarez Smith, 'The Inner City Crisis and the End of Urban Modernism in 1970s Britain', *Twentieth Century British History*, 27: 4 (August 2016), p. 588.
32 Thomas Sugrue, *The Origins of the Urban Crisis: Race and Inequality in Postwar Detroit* (Princeton, NJ: Princeton University Press, 1995); Arnold Hirsch, *Making the Second Ghetto: Race and Housing in Chicago 1940–1960* (Cambridge: Cambridge University Press, 1983).
33 Kennetta Hammond Perry, ' "Little Rock" in Britain: Jim Crow's Transatlantic Topographies', *Journal of British Studies*, 51:1 (2012), pp. 155–177; Elizabeth Buettner, ' "This is Staffordshire Not Alabama": Racial Geographies of Commonwealth Immigration in Early 1960s Britain', *The Journal of Imperial and Commonwealth History*, 42:4 (2014), pp. 710–740.
34 For example, Tim Miles and Barry Baker, 'Race Murder in Suburbia', *Daily Mail*, 3 June 1981, p. 1. This article about a crime in a completely different London locale makes reference to how something like that might be expected in Brixton, but not the suburban neighbourhood referenced.
35 Hall et al., *Policing the Crisis*, p. 76.
36 Gilroy, *There Ain't No Black in the Union Jack*, p. 106.
37 Loretta Lees, 'Gentrification, Race, and Ethnicity: Towards a Global Research Agenda?', *City and Community*, 15:3 (September 2016), p. 210.
38 Simon Parkes, interview with the author, 7 June 2018.
39 Parkes with Rafaeli, *Live at the Brixton Academy*, pp. 11–19.
40 Parkes with Rafaeli, *Live at the Brixton Academy*, p. 57.
41 Simon Parkes, interview with the author, 7 June 2018.
42 Jacqueline Nassy Brown, 'Black Liverpool, Black America, and the Gendering of Diasporic Space', *Cultural Anthropology*, 13:3 (1998), pp. 291–325; Joe Street, 'Malcolm X, Smethwick, and the Influence of the African American Freedom Struggle on British Race Relations in the 1960s', *Journal of Black Studies*, 38:6 (2008), pp. 932–950.
43 Robin D. G. Kelley and Stephen Tuck, ed., *The Other Special Relationship: Race, Rights, and Riots in Britain and the United States* (London: Palgrave Macmillan, 2015).
44 Parkes, interview with the author, June 2018.
45 Parkes with Rafaeli, *Live at the Brixton Academy*, p. 59.
46 Clippings from *South London Press*, 1972, Lambeth Archive.
47 Leslie George Scarman, *The Scarman Report: The Brixton Disorders 10–12 April 1981: Report of an Inquiry* (Harmondsworth: Penguin, 1982).
48 Parkes with Rafaeli, *Live at the Brixton Academy*, p. 62.
49 *NME*, 12 November 1983, p. 41.
50 *NME*, 14 January 1984, p. 31.
51 Laurel Brake, ' "Gay Discourse" and The Artist and Journal of Home Culture', in *Nineteenth-Century Media and the Construction of Identities*, ed. by Laurel

Brake, Bill Bell and David Finkelstein (Basingstoke: Palgrave Macmillan, 2000), pp. 271–295.
52 For exploration of the 'Pink pound', see Justin Bengry, 'Courting the Pink Pound: *Men Only* and the Queer Consumer, 1935–1939', *History Workshop Journal*, 68 (Autumn 2009), pp. 122–148.
53 Parkes with Rafaeli, *Live at the Brixton Academy*, p. 101.
54 It should be noted that this iteration of The Clash was post-Mick Jones and Topper Headon's forced departures from the band. Their performances during this era were panned in the music press but, nonetheless, they remained a big name.
55 For an in-depth study of Rock Against Racism, see Ian Goodyer, *Crisis Music: The Cultural Politics of Rock Against Racism* (Manchester: Manchester University Press, 2009).
56 Paul Marko, *The Roxy Club W2: A Punk History* (London: Punk77 Books, 2007), p. 125.
57 'Then and Now: Palladium Cinema/Fridge, Brixton Hill, Photographic Comparisons of Old and Modern Views of Lambeth', Urban75 archive, n.d., www.urban75.org/brixton/history/fridge.html [accessed 2 September 2022].
58 Parkes, interview with the author, 7 June 2018.
59 Koven, *Slumming*, p. 20.
60 Parkes with Rafaeli, *Live at the Brixton Academy*, p. 97.
61 Parkes, interview with the author, 7 June 2018.
62 Parkes, interview with the author, 7 June 2018.
63 James Nott, *Going to the Palais: A Social and Cultural History of Dance Halls in Britain 1918–1960* (Oxford: Oxford University Press, 2015), p. 19.
64 Parkes with Rafaeli, *Live at the Brixton Academy*, pp. 159–160.
65 'Review of Gil Scott Heron at the Brixton Academy', *NME*, 24 March 1984, p. 45.
66 Parkes with Rafaeli, *Live at the Brixton Academy*, p. 34.
67 Parkes with Rafaeli, *Live at the Brixton Academy*, pp. 127–129.
68 Parkes with Rafaeli, *Live at the Brixton Academy*, p. 130.
69 In our interview, Parkes explained to me that he lived in a variety of North London locations during his tenure at the Academy, because he didn't want people at the club to know if his local home was unoccupied during peak work hours.
70 Parkes with Rafaeli, *Live at the Brixton Academy*, p. 237.
71 Parkes with Rafaeli, *Live at the Brixton Academy*, p. 414.
72 Perry, *London is the Place for Me*, p. 100.
73 Gilroy, *After Empire*, p. xi.

Bibliography

Bengry, Justin, 'Courting the Pink Pound: *Men Only* and the Queer Consumer, 1935–1939', *History Workshop Journal*, 68 (Autumn 2009), pp. 122–148.
Brake, Laurel, '"Gay Discourse" and The Artist and Journal of Home Culture', in *Nineteenth-Century Media and the Construction of Identities*, ed. by Laurel

Brake, Bill Bell and David Finkelstein (Basingstoke: Palgrave Macmillan, 2000), pp. 271–295.

Brooke, Stephen, 'Space, Emotions and the Everyday: An Affective Ecology of the 1980s', *Twentieth Century British History*, 28: 1 (2017), pp. 110–135.

Brown, Jacqueline Nassy, 'Black Liverpool, Black America, and the Gendering of Diasporic Space', *Cultural Anthropology*, 13:3 (1998), pp. 291–325.

Buettner, Elizabeth, *Europe After Empire: Decolonization, Society and Culture* (Cambridge: Cambridge University Press, 2017).

Buettner, Elizabeth, '"This is Staffordshire Not Alabama": Racial Geographies of Commonwealth Immigration in Early 1960s Britain', *The Journal of Imperial and Commonwealth History*, 42:4 (2014), pp. 710–740.

Bush, Barbara, 'The Dark Side of the City: Racialized Barriers, Culture, and Citizenship in Britain c. 1950-1990s', in *Rastafari: A Universal Philosophy for the Third Millennium*, ed. by Werner Zips (Kingston: Ian Randle, 2000).

Chambers, Eddie, *Roots & Culture: Cultural Politics in the Making of Black Britain* (London: I.B.Tauris, 2017).

The Clash, 'White Man (In Hammersmith Palais)', single, CBS Records, 1978, vinyl.

Connell, Kieran, *Black Handsworth: Race in 1980s Britain* (Berkeley, CA: University of California Press, 2019).

Gilroy, Paul, *After Empire: Melancholia or Convivial Culture* (London: Routledge, 2004).

Gilroy, Paul, *The Black Atlantic: Modernity and Double Consciousness* (London: Verso, 1993).

Gilroy, Paul, *There Ain't No Black in the Union Jack: The Cultural Politics of Race and Nation* (Chicago, IL: University of Chicago Press, 1987).

Goodyer, Ian, *Crisis Music: The Cultural Politics of Rock Against Racism* (Manchester: Manchester University Press, 2009).

Hall, Stuart, Brian Roberts, John Clarke, Tony Jefferson and Chas Critcher, *Policing the Crisis: Mugging, the State, and Law and Order* (London: Palgrave Macmillan, 1978).

Hall, Stuart, 'Cosmopolitan Promises, Multicultural Realities', in *Divided Cities*, ed. by Richard Scholar (Oxford: Oxford University Press, 2010).

Hebdige, Dick, 'The Meaning of Mod', in *Resistance Through Rituals, Second Edition*, ed. by Stuart Hall and Tony Jefferson (London: Routledge, 2006).

Hebdige, Dick, *Subculture: The Meaning of Style* (New York: Routledge, 1979).

Hirsch, Arnold, *Making the Second Ghetto: Race and Housing in Chicago 1940–1960* (Cambridge: Cambridge University Press, 1983).

hooks, bell, *Black Looks: Race and Representation* (New York: Routledge, 1992).

Kelley, Robin D. G. and Stephen Tuck, eds, *The Other Special Relationship: Race, Rights, and Riots in Britain and the United States* (London: Palgrave MacMillan, 2015).

Koven, Seth, *Slumming: Sexual and Social Politics in Victorian London* (Princeton, NJ: Princeton University Press, 2006).

Loretta Lees, 'Gentrification, Race, and Ethnicity: Towards a Global Research Agenda?', *City and Community*, 15:3 (September 2016), pp. 208–214.

Mare, Jeremy, *Otis Redding Soul Ambassador* (London: BBC, 2013), BBC 4 documentary.

Marko, Paul, *The Roxy Club W2: A Punk History* (London: Punk77 Books, 2007), p. 125.

Matera, Marc, *Black London: The Imperial Metropolis and Decolonization in the Twentieth Century* (Berkeley, CA: University of California Press, 2015).

Miles, Tim and Barry Baker, 'Race Murder in Suburbia', *Daily Mail*, 3 June 1981, p. 1.

Nott, James, *Going to the Palais: A Social and Cultural History of Dance Halls in Britain 1918–1960* (Oxford: Oxford University Press, 2015).

Parkes, Simon, interview with the author, 7 June 2018.

Parkes, Simon with J. S. Rafaeli, *Live at the Brixton Academy: A Riotous Life in the Music Business* (London: Serpent's Tail, 2014).

Perry, Kennetta Hammond, ' "Little Rock" in Britain: Jim Crow's Transatlantic Topographies', *Journal of British Studies*, 51:1 (2012), pp. 155–177.

Perry, Kennetta Hammond, *London is the Place for Me: Black Britons, Citizenship, and the Politics of Race* (Oxford: Oxford University Press, 2015).

Pratt, Mary Louise, 'Arts of the Contact Zone', *Profession* (1991), p. 34.

'Review of Gil Scott Heron at the Brixton Academy', *NME*, 24 March 1984, p. 45.

Saumarez Smith, Otto, 'The Inner City Crisis and the End of Urban Modernism in 1970s Britain', *Twentieth Century British History*, 27:4 (August 2016), pp. 578–598.

Scarman, Leslie George, *The Scarman Report: The Brixton Disorders 10–12 April 1981: Report of an Inquiry* (Harmondsworth: Penguin, 1982).

Schwarz, Bill, 'Claudia Jones and the *West Indian Gazette*: Reflections on the Emergence of Post-Colonial Britain', *Twentieth Century British History*, 14:3 (Autumn 2003), pp. 264–285.

Schwarz, Bill, 'The Only White Man in There: The Re-Racialision of England 1956–1968', *Race and Class*, 38:1 (July 1996), pp. 65–78.

South London Press, 1972.

Street, Joe, 'Malcolm X, Smethwick, and the Influence of the African American Freedom Struggle on British Race Relations in the 1960s', *Journal of Black Studies*, 38:6 (2008), pp. 932–950.

Sugrue, Thomas, *The Origins of the Urban Crisis: Race and Inequality in Postwar Detroit* (Princeton, NJ: Princeton University Press, 1995).

'Then and Now: Palladium Cinema/Fridge, Brixton Hill, Photographic Comparisons of Old and Modern Views of Lambeth', Urban75 archive, n.d., www.urban75.org/brixton/history/fridge.html [accessed 2 September 2022].

Verguren, Enamel, *This is A Modern Life: The 1980s London Mod Scene* (London: Shaman Books, 2012).

Walkowitz, Judith, *Nights Out: Life in Cosmopolitan London* (New Haven, CT: Yale University Press, 2012).

Webster, Wendy, 'The Empire Comes Home: Commonwealth Migration to Britain', in Andrew Thompson, ed., *Britain's Experience of Empire in the Twentieth Century* (Oxford: Oxford University Press, 2011).

Wilmer, Val, 'Rik Gunnell', *The Guardian*, 18 June 2007, www.theguardian.com/news/2007/jun/18/guardianobituaries.obituaries [accessed 13 September 2022]

12

Tribe Arts, Tribe Talks

Josh Doble, Liam J. Liburd, Emma Parker, Samran Rathore and Tajpal Rathore

Tribe Arts is a philosophically inspired, radical-political theatre, media and production company based in Leeds. Founded by Tajpal Rathore and Samran Rathore, its work aims to amplify the stories and voices of second- and third-generation black and Asian people in Britain, interrogating themes and issues such as race, belonging and identity. Tribe's previous shows have included Darokhand, *a reimagining of six Shakespeare plays amalgamated into an original story, set in a striking Gothic-Mughal world – stylistically a gothic landscape evoking Mughal India; and* Tribe Talks, *a radical format of participatory theatre in which a panel of speakers motivate the audience to discuss important topics around the history of black and Asian people as well as current socio-political issues affecting these communities. In describing the latter, Tribe Arts say: 'think the BBC's* Question Time, *but interspersed with live performance, music and film'. As the 2020/2021 Coronavirus pandemic closed many performance spaces across the UK, Tribe Arts launched* Off/Stage, *the only e-zine currently dedicated to black and Asian theatre and culture in the UK.*

As presenters at the 2018 'After Empire?' conference, Tajpal and Samran discussed decolonial theatre practice and, in October 2020, they reconvened with editors Josh, Liam and Emma to reflect on their origins as an organisation, exploring why decolonial theatre is necessary in modern Britain and how their work confronts the legacies of empire across our society.

Josh Doble: Hi guys, thanks for talking to us. To begin with, could you tell us how Tribe Arts started? What prompted the creation of your organization?

Tajpal Rathore: So I guess like many black and Asian artists, Tribe Arts was born out of a frustration that we all shared, being a group of actors who were usually cast as terrorists and taxi drivers and bus drivers.[1] As performers we speak other people's words, but we wanted to reclaim our part in the creative process. So we were black and Asian actors, in a room together, with this shared consciousness and although we didn't intend to set up a theatre company, it was kind of inevitable.

Strangely enough, the whole idea of Tribe Arts came about when we stood in line for the nationwide auditions for *Star Wars Episode VII* in 2013. We were actually in the queue. Well, Sam[ran] wasn't actually there...

Samran Rathore: I just got told later that we're in a theatre company now. I was like all right, cool.

Tajpal Rathore: We stood in that line for about eight hours and obviously none of us got cast. But yeah, that's the origin story of Tribe Arts – the concept, the name, everything was done in that line, which seems kind of fitting.

Josh Doble: When you actually started planning what you were going to do as a group, did you build upon or emulate specific ideas, intellectual traditions or theatre traditions?

Samran Rathore: Well, we were really anti-institutional when we first started up, we were trying to be as raw and individual as possible. We didn't want to emulate other theatre companies, although of course there were certain organisations like Tara Arts, Tamasha, Talawa, that we had heard about and, sure, we wanted to have their level of success. But it was never to emulate someone else's work. And as a cohort, we had a mix of performers, actors, dancers.

Tajpal Rathore: That's where our pride was, wasn't it? None of us were trained actors. But we had come into contact very early with Bertolt Brecht and [also] the Theatre of the Oppressed, so we were looking at theatre techniques that are politically informed. But instinctively we didn't want our theatre company to work through traditional, Eurocentric systems and processes. We were a very musical group, very lyrical group. We used to just sort of go out and spring out into song or dance. And we were all very brash as well, and I think some of these were the seeds of what became the thing that we ended up doing, which was looking at a decolonised theatre practice, what we call decolonial theatre.

Emma Parker: You've explained it to us that *Tribe Talks* initially took on a *Question Time*-style format; could you say a bit more about this performance and what it allowed you to do?

Tajpal Rathore: Yeah. Originally we wanted to make a show about the [British] Empire. It would eventually become a part-theatre show, part-symposium. We were a collective that included many disciplines, including actors and dancers, and this big cacophony of artistic practice wasn't very conducive to creating a coherent show. I used to work at the BBC, and I have worked on *Question Time* in the past, so the format was definitely in my head. Being in conversation, creating dialogue with our audiences, was key to what we wanted to do.

Samran Rathore: It initially developed from the idea of a kind of coffee morning with first-generation black and Asian elders in our communities. And we sort of talked about it, and it became a *Question Time*-style show.

Tajpal Rathore: We didn't want to find out about Britain's empire in museums and libraries and books. As a theatre company, Tribe had set out to work outside of institutions. We wanted to find out more about that true, hidden story that is still alive within that [older] generation, who had a direct connection with Empire. Tribe Talks was originally supposed to be a one-off, three-hour event. When we finished the first staging (which lasted four hours!) a lot of people came up to us afterwards, and they were like, 'This is fantastic, we've never been to anything like this before. When is it happening again?' We've been developing the show ever since and it's an amalgamation of many different things. We were due to stage an industry sharing at The Lowry in Salford shortly before the UK's first 2020 lockdown, but the pandemic delayed this, and we're actively working to make it happen again.

Josh Doble: It'd be good to find out a bit more about how exactly *Tribe Talks* worked as a format. Because it's clearly a show. But it also sounds like it has elements of subaltern or radical oral history practice by unearthing the stories of people who traditionally don't have voices within historical narratives. Where does the performance fit into this?

Tajpal Rathore: Well, actually, when we pitched the show to different places, that was one of the biggest hurdles. People said 'We don't understand how this is theatre'. It's basically about creating conversation with audiences. Decolonial theatre invites that interaction with the audience. For example, when you go to predominantly white-led institutions, there's this sort of decorum, a behaviour that's expected. The response of the audience is very much muted; you're supposed to clap at the right time. You have to laugh at the right time. And those kind of audience norms are completely thrown out the window when you look at the way many black and Asian people consume cultural outputs. I mean even if you look at Bollywood, the Hindi film industry, you go to any cinema in India, and forget about just laughing and clapping and joking. It's like a living room. People are putting out food, and they take off their shoes. It's a completely different atmosphere.

There are theatre companies in Britain, actually, that offer those kind of audience interactions. Blue Mountain Theatre being a prime example. For us, conversations with audiences was the way we could explain that very multilayered story of the British Empire. It's told through a little bit of spoken word, through a little bit of dance, through a little bit of music, through a little bit of talking and perhaps a little bit of intellectual work too.

Samran Rathore: I think this process came naturally as well because the question for us was, how do we engage with that audience made up of people from our black and Asian communities, with our generation? What and who do they listen to?

Josh Doble: I found it interesting that you framed *Tribe Talks* around different historical epochs; how did you bring this all together? How did it actually play out when the show starts, as it were?

Tajpal Rathore: We just wanted to talk. To talk about slavery, to talk about violence and difficult histories, to also have a conversation around race. We divided the programme into four epochs, beginning with an Origins tour focusing on prehistory and the origins of mankind. Following this is the Migration tour that includes forced migrations, slavery and the histories of the East India Company and the British Empire. The third one is the Empowerment tour, moving down the timeline to when many black and Asian people settled in the Western world and were actually asking for equal footing and representation and civil rights. And then the last epoch is called New Culture and Beyond, and that looks at black and Asian people now as British citizens, thinking beyond the present to what and where our futures will be. It's an expansive narrative that avoids being comprehensive and is instead inclusive, it's about igniting conversations.

Liam J. Liburd: What's the industry reaction been like? Has it been quite positive? Has there been any backlash? And on that note how do you apply for funding? It can be complicated to get financial backing for things that are seen as more overtly political than something a touch less confrontational.

Tajpal Rathore: I think the fact that we haven't actually done *Tribe Talks* fully since 2015 is telling about how problematic it's been to get that programme off the ground. Because we're trying to shift the power balance, strengthen our own theatre company, and our own decolonial practice. And it's made people uncomfortable, they don't always like what we're saying, there has been a lot of instances where we've felt like we're being shut down or coming up against gatekeepers who decide which shows get programmed or where resources are allocated.

For instance, I wrote a piece for *The Stage* around the time when the film *Black Panther* (2018) came out. And I asked: when is there going to be a *Black Panther* for the theatre sector? Theatre, especially in the UK, is definitely conservative but it's also elitist. I think there's a lot more gatekeeping in the theatre industry because of its status and focus on 'high art'.

Samran Rathore: In terms of the kinds of black and Asian stories that you do get on stage, there's an element of playing safe in the industry. There's a sense of only telling certain stories that won't really ignite any kind of passion between the communities, that are nicely contained. And the actors just happen to be black. I'm not saying these are the only narratives told on stage, but they are the ones most likely to get past gatekeepers. If a show is seen as 'radical' it's often shut down as 'not right for our venue or our audiences'. But that decision comes from one conversation with one person who will be on the senior leadership team in a particular venue. Why not actually engage the audiences to ask them if they'd be okay to see something like that?

Tajpal Rathore: Yeah, and I think also there are certain 'palatable' conversations around race which will be accepted, like it's okay to talk about representation, and giving more people opportunities. But when it comes to actually talking about the *problems* of race that continue to this day, both politically and socially, that's where you start feeling the brunt of the industry trying to stop you. I definitely think there's a push within the theatre sector to limit the ambition of many black and Asian artists through a slow and steady drip of resource which is enough to tick the boxes but never enough for those artists to realise their true ambition and to actually do what they really want to do.

It's important for artist collectives to be funded as well as commissions for individuals. Arts councils and other institutions [that provide funding] haven't really made provisions for artists to come together. But it's through collectives that that you actually get ambitious art, because you've got more people, more ideas in the pot. You've got more capacity. There are, of course, more white-led theatre companies than black and Asian theatre companies.

Emma Parker: Can collaborating with audiences, or challenging 'correct behaviour' in theatres, resist gatekeepers and allow you to develop a decolonial practice? I've read about Ngũgĩ wa Thiong'o staging plays in 1970s Kenya that demystified the process of rehearsals and performances. He suggested in *Decolonising the Mind* that drama should happen anywhere, not just in special buildings, that actors and audiences should be free to wander across the auditorium, sharing their knowledge communally. His decolonised theatre is specifically set in East Africa following colonial rule, but do some of these arguments chime with your own practice?

Samran Rathore: Definitely, Thiong'o's idea of actors walking across the auditorium, therefore breaking that fourth wall with audience members who are not following the traditional role of 'quiet and reserved' observers, is all part of the decolonising process. A similar concept can also be found among South Asian and Caribbean theatre audiences. While our decolonial practice has been informed by our histories and practitioners like Ngũgĩ, to truly execute this practice we would need to change the mindsets of gatekeepers in the buildings.

Emma Parker: I'm interested by the idea that the British stage, of all of Britain's major cultural sectors, is unready to tell stories about the British Empire, including the histories of migration to Britain in the twentieth century. From your perspective does that mean that decolonial theatre practice in Britain has to be a collective effort, it can't just be an individual given one opportunity, it has to be communities allowed to speak and explore together?

Tajpal Rathore: Yeah, I think that is definitely the case. I think a theatre is a lot stronger when people come together, when artists create bridges with communities and vice versa. I think that's actively discouraged now in the theatre sector. If you look back to the seventies and eighties it was very common, even encouraged, for groups or artists to have an all-black theatre group or an all-Asian theatre group or an all-black community centre. Now that's not the case. Now it's all about diversity and inclusion. It's all been driven by this sort of slow change in legislation with the Equalities Act, which [doesn't necessarily] progress any conversation when it comes down to race.

This is one of the biggest hurdles that we've had in [producing] any show that we do as a black and Asian theatre company is the whole idea of integration, because integration has to work both ways. When we were doing *Tribe Talks*, we used to get calls from white people asking whether it was okay to come and see the show, whether it was for them! And that really bowled me over, because that is similar to me calling a theatre up and saying, 'Hey, can I come and see *A Christmas Carol* or *Oliver Twist*? As a brown person, is that for me?' You'd never hear that, because the fact of the matter is that a lot of people who are not white have integrated into British society. They are British citizens. But integration has to work both ways. And so yeah, I think our work has been hindered by white people thinking that when they come to our shows, they will feel guilt. And I think a lot of white people are more scared of white guilt than they are of white supremacy.

Liam J. Liburd: I think you're right about the fragility over discussing the legacy of racism and colonialism and the real irritation that white people feel if they're being forced to confront their own complicity. In your attempts to deconstruct the legacy of colonialism and racism, have you encountered similar resistance from your audiences? You're making yourselves quite vulnerable through the *Question Time* format.

Tajpal Rathore: Yeah, completely. I actually remember an instance that happened with Sam. I think we were doing the lecture at Leeds Beckett University about *Tribe Talks*...

Samran Rathore: Yeah, so the comment that the guy in the audience was making – and I think he was of mixed black and European heritage – was, you can't really put the black and Asian experiences side by side, because the African experience is much harsher, and Africans were enslaved, and they were tortured. He thought that they [African people and their descendants] were oppressed and believed that didn't happen to people from South Asia. That was quite interesting for us because, for a start, we know that's not true. The reason there's so many South Asians currently living in the Caribbean is because once slavery was abolished, it was reinstated, in a sense, when South Asian [indentured labourers] were taken over to replace freed African slaves. So these histories and experiences are similar and very deep. And I think that was very telling for us. And we didn't expect that from someone we consider to be our target audience. We really thought everyone got it. And at that point we realised there's so much more work to be done with all our audiences, there's a lot of education that just isn't available for people.

Tajpal Rathore: We think it's important that *Tribe Talks* creates a 'safe space' to have these conversations. And that safe space isn't afforded just to black and Asian people. It's afforded to our entire audience. When white people are part of a *Tribe Talks* audience, we don't want them to feel like they have nothing to offer that conversation, no right to 'air time', or that their comments are not as valuable. On the contrary, for us, we think that the involvement of white people in the conversation about race is absolutely critical; otherwise it becomes an echo chamber. There's a lot of ignorance about certain aspects of history.

But if we're talking about ignorance in our audiences, it sometimes, unfortunately, goes into serious territory. Questions can drift into expressions of overt racism, either out of unconscious ignorance or a more wilful ignorance. But the *Tribe Talks* format allows for this. I think the only way that you can really have a proper, truthful conversation about race is when it's a non-politically correct environment. That's the only way we've found it to work. What we've tried to do within the *Tribe Talks* format is to dismantle the unfolding 'fourth wall' and make the audience an active participant within the story. And so we have to get them relaxed enough to shed their own sense of self or to find a different character through which they can take part in those conversations.

Josh Doble: It seems like you're saying that what you're talking about – decolonial theatre – is also kind of a form of education in a more explicit way than other forms for theatre are. So, I wondered if you could just explain a little bit more about what decolonised theatre looks like in Britain? Does it resemble a series of conversations, which have an educational purpose, and provide a space within which performers and audiences can have productive conversations in a theatre setting which would be difficult to have in the same way in another forum?

Tajpal Rathore: This might blow your mind, but we've had conversations with arts leaders, within the arts industry, who've asked us what decolonisation is. This is a real problem because when you're talking about anti-racism, or you're talking about living in a postcolonial society, a lot of people have no idea what that actually means. And a lot of people confuse it with the related but essentially different issues of representation or equality. Outside of the arts/academic circles, the idea of decolonisation as an ongoing process is not really fully understood. For me, this reflects how ingrained the legacy of colonialism is in British society and beyond. It's stamped into our past and our present.

It's hard to ask someone to start thinking in a way that jars with how they live on a day-to-day basis. Decolonisation aims to upset the established order of things, to turn the world upside down. The size and scope of decolonisation as a project reflects the earlier pervasiveness of colonialism and its legacy. It was and is impossible for people of colour not to be aware of the Empire, given that we lived under it, felt it and saw it, and live, feel and see its legacy now. In that sense, a lot of black and Asian people in Britain actually have knowledge from both sides of the fence. We're equally British, and we actually understand white people more than white people probably understand themselves. And I'm not talking about present-day British white people. I'm talking about historically in the way that certain systems have evolved through their thought. And we ourselves have had to do a lot of introspection to confront certain internalised aspects of colonial thought.

Emma Parker: Tell us more about *Tribe Arts*'s adaptations of Shakespeare. Given what you've mentioned about experiencing and observing Britishness and whiteness from a particular perspective, what was your experience of staging Shakespeare? Why were you drawn to these plays?

Tajpal Rathore: We had the idea of doing a Shakespeare-related show in 2016, which was the 400th anniversary of his death. We thought of it as just a bit of a joke, actually, saying: wouldn't it be really, really interesting for a couple of brown boys to get some funding to do a show about Shakespeare? And we did it in the way that we knew how, which was we took six of his plays, and mashed them together. If we told anybody in the Arts Council this, they would be raising eyebrows: 'You did what'? We mashed Shakespeare storylines into a new and original show. And then we set it in a Gothic-Mughal world, and it was just a really liberating performance. *Game of Thrones* was on at the time and a lot of people made comparisons to its look and feel. And I've always loved Shakespeare's work, Sam slightly less so.

Once we started making that show, which is called *Darokhand*, in 2016, we realised that we were starting to form a kind of 'decolonial' theatre practice. The idea was to question absolutely every single element in the creative process. It was staged in such a way as to confront the audience with a series of questions. Who's cast? Who's telling the story from which perspective? Where does the audience sit? What is the relationship with the audience and the actors? How can we create a format that challenges the etiquette and structure of conventional theatre settings? Things like audience interruptions and unexpected music became essential parts of the show.

There are clearly many forms of decolonial theatre. I'm sure that a lot of black and Asian performers up and down the country have developed their own 'decolonised' practices and techniques. What we're trying to propose with 'decolonial' theatre is a process for decolonising our own practice as performers. And, for us, the ultimate aim would be to decolonise theatre. But, within that broader project, there isn't one form of decolonial theatre, there are many.

Emma Parker: So you see decolonial theatre as an ongoing process, something in motion?

Tajpal Rathore: One hundred per cent, just like the process of anti-racism, it is an ongoing process. There's never going to be a time where we're going to be able to turn round and say, 'right, you're an anti-racist now', or 'we're a diverse society now'. It's not like making the Queen's Honours List! It's an ongoing process, we have to keep on our toes.

Josh Doble: You mentioned other practitioners of decolonial theatre. Have you found collaborators or perhaps allies within the theatre industry who've informed your practice, or whose practice you've informed? Within this, how do you see the future of decolonial theatre in Britain?

Tajpal Rathore: In terms of allies, it's a case of very few and far between. It's hard to be both critical and rewarded by a system or industry, which has been a bit of a blessing and a bit of a curse for us. We've always maintained a level of self-sufficiency in the way that we've operated at a certain distance from the theatre industry. We're rarely commissioned by white-led organisations or institutions or venues. A lot of the stuff that we create is all in-house. We've never really relied on other artists or other companies to be able to realise our vision.

Some of the stuff we are saying is quite heavy. Within the theatre sector, as I said earlier, there are palatable conversations to be had about race and critical conversations that tend to get censored. It has been very hard to find collaborators, even though behind the scenes we might have some really cool, honest conversations with people of colour who are absolutely on our wavelength. They understand what they're doing, but unfortunately their concerns and fears around the internal politics of the industry stop them from really, fully engaging with us. And that's been a big, big problem. Much like systems of power, racism and oppression in general, the system maintains itself by looking after itself first. Unfortunately, it's very difficult to break that cycle.

Liam J. Liburd: I was thinking about the way that the discussion of race by people of colour has tended towards comedy in the past, towards entertainment. Performed pieces that are politically engaged usually come from a satirical angle. And I wondered why you think that is and whether you think that the comedic approach is always the most effective genre for dissecting the legacy of colonialism and colonial racism in British society?

Samran Rathore: I think it's a very British thing to deal with these issues through comedy. American discussions of the same issues, for example, are much less accommodating and tend to be very serious, in its stories and themes. But in England, we need a joke or two in there. Even if you look at TV shows like *Goodness Gracious Me*, *The Real McCoy* and, more recently, *Famalam*. It's the same thing over and over again, where black or Asian people will use jokes to make serious points about their experiences. For me, it speaks to the fact that we're not at a point where we can start dealing with issues that we have as a society in serious terms. So we have to be smart in how we attempt to discuss those issues.

One of the shows we've developed is called *Jerk Chicken Samosa*. It looks at the legacy of colonialism though a Caribbean family and an Indian family next door to each other. Both have restaurants, and they compete for business. So, it was comedy, and we put in a lot of gags and a lot of jokes. But through that comedy, the two families start finding common ground based on their shared experiences as second- and first-generation migrants in Britain. They realise just how much the cultures have influenced one another. So, there are ways of doing it where it can be comedy, but when it gets real, it gets really real. You can be serious *and* really funny with some of those issues.

Tajpal Rathore: I saw Lenny Henry on a BBC *Imagine* documentary recently and he was explaining that a lot of comedy in Britain, historically, was done at the expense of people of colour. So, through

Goodness Gracious Me and a lot of Lenny Henry's material, we grew comfortable taking the piss out of ourselves as a way to enter white-dominated spaces. And at the time, it was okay. It was a sacrifice that we were willing to make because there weren't many black or Asian people on TV. Even for us back in the day as an Asian family, it was sheer excitement to see a black man on TV. We were just like wow, there's someone else there.

But I think the time is now right for us to have different kinds of conversations. Britain has been very slow getting on the bandwagon when it comes to this conversation. And maybe it's because they've got away with it, because they were strategically able to dodge the bullet, I guess, in terms of the slave trade, benefiting from it but at the same time keeping distant from it. Whereas in America, obviously the situation was very different. It was very much on the streets, and it was very overt. In the UK, racism has always been a little bit covert and behind the scenes, to an extent. So I'm so glad that, in the wake of BLM, there is a greater consciousness around social [and racial] issues. And I think theatre might be the way of pushing that forward, which brings me into that next point, which is what we've been doing recently. During the lockdown period, we've not had any theatres open, so we've had to think a little bit differently about how we continue engaging our audiences.

We have launched *Off/Stage*, an e-zine dedicated to black and Asian theatre and culture, it's the only magazine of its kind in the UK. It's available now on our website (www.tribearts.co.uk) and it aims to be a one-stop publication on all things black and Asian theatre and culture, while more generally reflecting some of the conversations that we're having as a society around representation and diversity. Another issue will, hopefully, drop in the next couple of months, so yeah, check out our website for that.

Emma Parker, Josh Doble and Liam J. Liburd: Thank you so much, guys.

Note

1 'Black' is not capitalised in this chapter at the request of Tribe Arts, who use the capitalised term only when referring to political Blackness.

Afterword: Disorder and displacement

Bill Schwarz

Decolonization ... is a programme of complete disorder.
Frantz Fanon, *The Wretched of the Earth* (1961)[1]

I've always been interested in ... finding music where music wasn't supposed to have been.
Brian Eno, *Melody Maker* (1980)[2]

In her Foreword to this volume, Elleke Boehmer retrieves Amos Tutuola's extraordinary 1954 novel *My Life in the Bush of Ghosts*. She explains that the story

> follows the pathway of a young boy into a dense African forest where he encounters terrifying composite beings drawn from Yoruba myth, Christian allegory, illusory colonial modernity and the writer's own fantasy. The structure is episodic; the boy spends twenty-four years wandering through the forest and, eventually, after meeting the 'television-handed ghostess', finds his way out. By then, however, his life has itself become phantasmagoric.

With the writings of Wole Soyinka and Ben Okri in mind, she notes that critics tend to take the forest to be 'an allegory of postcolonial Africa'. But Boehmer strikes out on a different path, which is both more demanding and more timely. In her view the forest 'oddly resembles Britain today'. In this reading we are living at a point when the old metropole has transmogrified from a site of enlightenment, in the eyes of its ideologues, to a disorderly emotional landscape where perpetual disorientation hovers on the horizon. The prospects of a failed state beckon. Britain, she continues, 'is a shadowy and confusing place in which nothing is quite as it seems, clown-politicians spread distorting and dangerous tales unchecked, and weird voices, presences and irruptions continually catch off-guard anyone trying to make their way through it'.[3]

This is an arresting, provocative interpretation which – as I see it – suggests how we can approach the larger question of Britain 'after empire'.

It is premised on the belief that the familiar spatial properties of the colonial system no longer hold. The given divisions between 'us' *here* and 'them' *there* do not reach the historical realities of contemporary times, if they ever did. As the dismantling of the settled divide between here and there gathers force – between metropole and colony – the erosion of the once-traditional verities of the old metropole accelerates. This can make things feel *as if* Britain has become one of its own colonies, where 'nothing is quite as it seems'. Everything slips out of place. The heart of empire becomes the heart of darkness, as Conrad, among others, anticipated. Or, to put it less programmatically, staying with Boehmer's formulation, the present-day metropole 'oddly resembles' its former colonies, although I wonder whether England, rather than Britain, is not the more appropriate focus.

The significance of this insight is huge. It properly positions the domestic metropole in the orbit of decolonisation – not only in terms of the commanding echelons of the state but also of those social relations which appear, at first sight, untouched by empire. The once-celebrated self-image of metropolitan England as a beacon of civilisation transmutes into a kaleidoscopic accumulation of shadows and half-truths, inflating mad-cap, extravagant stories of future redemption which is, we are promised, just around the corner. To those who believe, with good reason, that their lives have been expropriated by powerful, uncaring elites such desperate invocations of a glowing future have recast political sensibilities. Yet Boehmer's is an intransigent reading in which 'clown-politicians', in a Rabelesian gesture, gorge themselves on 'dangerous tales'. In a giddy spiral these tales are relayed to the electorate, the perpetrators no longer sure in their own minds where mendacity begins and where it ends. In these circumstances those who set out to comprehend the confusions find that they – we – are caught 'off-guard'. We live in unnerving times.

The last generations born as the colonised of Europe carried the presentiment that they were subject to a state of perpetual unreality. Reality, it appeared, was a privilege which belonged far away, to the modern peoples in the modern metropoles, while the lives of the colonised were experienced as threadbare fabrications. Yet convictions like these no longer maintain their authority. What once seemed the conditions of the colonised claim a broader reach. Apprehensions of unreality now periodically interrupt the governing pulse of the historic 'white' nations. The hegemony of the civilisation of the white man, once the symbolic nucleus of social classification, dissolves. The insistence on the totality of the divide between the white man and the 'native' no longer carries the power it once did, when all that was unruly could be projected onto the 'natives', leaving whites pristine and uncompromised, the embodiment of virtue and reason. Those days are past. White innocence, in which the English were excused from the darkness of the modern self, has lost its force. Now we all live in darkness. Yet in uncanny England the phantasmagoria of unreality does not operate out of sight, in the shadows or in the dark forest.[4] It hides in the clear light of day, for all to see.

My Life in the Bush of Ghosts evokes the condition of colonial nativehood, where the liberty to experience oneself as anything other than a native – as anything other than abject – is forcefully circumscribed. The entire cosmos of the forest induces strangeness, generating an arbitrariness so complete that it carries a continual menace. Elemental moral distinctions evaporate in a troubled miasma. The divide between good and bad marks the starting point for Tutuola's narrative. The opening chapter takes for its title, expressly, 'The Meaning of "Bad" and "Good"'. The emphasis falls on the social *meanings* at stake. The principal character of the story, the boy and then young man – such is the length of time he is condemned to the netherworld – who finds himself trapped in the disorientating darkness, discovers bad and good to be disconcertingly unpredictable. There is no knowing when either will descend or what either will bring. As he journeys further into the strangeness, the distinction between bad and good becomes fraught and difficult to disentangle. He can never be sure. His perceptions are ever more wayward. Meaning itself becomes a matter of heightened contention. He loses the capacity to decipher his world. In the forest meaning is forever on the point of collapse.

There are many ways to frame this interpretation. One is to suggest that the greater the refinement of the colonial order, the greater the burden of disorder for those who found themselves conscripted as natives. This is the position embraced by the Barbadian George Lamming, writing at the same time as Tutuola. Lamming was sure that a defining property of colonial power was that it worked to 'utterly disorganize' the subjugated 'in feeling'.[5] It is this insistence on the existential degradation of the colonial native which animates *My Life in the Bush of Ghosts*.

In the larger scheme of things, disorder works in a double register. On the one hand, for Tutuola and Lamming, as for many of their generation, disorder was a constituent of the lived relations of the colonial oppressed, radically undoing the integrity of the self. The racialised figure of the native could be nothing but the other. Frantz Fanon's *Black Skin, White Masks*, first published in 1952, is a philosophical elaboration of the foundational conception of the 'native'. However, on the other hand, Fanon also introduced an alternative reading of what disorder entails. Decolonisation, as a revolutionary rupture in the social world, he believed represented disorder of a radically different quality. On the very first page of *The Wretched of the Earth* he proclaims the necessary disorderliness which follows in the wake of the destruction of the colonial empires. 'Decolonization, which sets out to change the order of the world, is, obviously, a programme of completed disorder.' 'Obviously'. Drawing from the creolised Christianity of his Martinique childhood, he indicates that a precise explanation for decolonisation lies in the vision that ' "The last shall be first and the first last" '.[6] In all likelihood Fanon was thinking primarily of the disorder besetting the colony, not the metropole. But when he considered the fate of the '*Les damnés de la terre*' the metropole was consistently active in his mind. Towards the end of 1961, when he was being treated for leukaemia in Maryland, Paris became the scene of the officially sanctioned murder of scores of Algerians, the police assaults taking place in full sight, in familiar city-centre streets. Countless migrant bodies floated in the Seine for all to see.[7] For those who chose not to avert their eyes, disorder and darkness were all too visible in the City of Light.

Either way, disorder – and the disorderliness of meaning – turns on determinate histories. The job of the historian is to seek what the determinations look like and where they operate, working from the presupposition that disorder is the product of knowable forces. They may not be as we expect or work as we imagine. But they are there to be discovered.

In her understanding of 'after empire', Boehmer emphasises the determinacy of the symbolic world, highlighting how social relations are perceived and lived, and how they enter the inner life. She takes seriously phenomena which orthodox histories are liable to disregard, particularly when they do not fit with the conventional historiographical preconceptions. In doing this she turns the historic tables and views the metropole through the prism of the colony: through the eyes of the other. To suppose that the 'phantasmagoria' of an 'African forest' provides a rational means, perhaps even a privileged means, to interpret the postimperial metropole is, as it stands, scandalous, defying the mainstream protocols of formal, accredited history.

After the collapse of the colonial empires much appeared, and still appears, to be out of place when judged in terms of the hierarchical systems of knowledge bequeathed by the colonial imperative. Historical phenomena are not located where history – still disabled by the persistence of colonial sensibilities – tells us they should be. The dislocations of the African forest become a lens for comprehending the defamiliarised metropole of our own times.[8] This is history organised through a glass darkly, although historians are not well trained to think about the strangeness of reality. The palpable disorder which governs modern lives cannot be grasped only in its own terms. We need to reveal the determinate histories which lie behind disorder, alive to the many displacements which organise the historical world.[9] By shifting the field of vision, what initially appears chaotic acquires a measure of meaning. The social relations we inhabit are not arbitrary and infinitely liquid, as sometimes we are told. They are as material as ever. After empire, particularly, they are both determined (or overdetermined) and, *at the same time*, peculiarly out of place. In this lies the conceptual gravity of the term 'disorder', signifying the chaos of the phenomenal world, while the lens of 'displacement' acknowledges the unseen determinations which provide a degree of cohesion to the out-of-place social relations. In a tricky paradox, displacement moves to the centre of things.

As it does so, it assumes a measure of conceptual clarity. Displacement poses the question of how, in different conjunctures or epochs, histories are 'differently centred'.[10] To say this leaves plenty unresolved. Is displacement the means by which the postcolonial operates, in general, 'the last' becoming 'the first' signalling a decisive rearrangement of the historical order? Or, to follow a different line of argument at a lower level of abstraction, is there a quality in the postcolonial situation which organises particular forms of displacement, in the plural? These remain open questions.

There is a compelling anticipation of Boehmer's transplanting to the metropole of *My Life in the Bush of Ghosts*. Her act of relocation does not stand alone. In February 1981, as the Thatcherites were embarking on a single-minded struggle for political dominance by preparing a crazed deflationary assault on Britain's economy (stand up, Geoffrey Howe), Brian Eno and David Byrne released an album which took its title from Tutuola's novel and which paid homage to its author. Eno and Byrne were maestros in the unfolding rendezvous between the art-school avant-garde and popular culture: Eno with Roxy Music, Byrne with Talking Heads.[11] They were attuned to the frequencies – the 'weird voices, presences and irruptions' – which Boehmer identifies, and which they too understood as constituting a live current in their own experiences. The album is good to listen to, zipping along to what David Toop describes as its 'choppy reggae beat', with plenty of bass.[12] The result is a hybrid of Afro-futurism, touches of anglophone punk, old-school Ghanian High Life and what became known as World Music, *avant la lettre* – all mediated, inevitably, through the impress of metropolitan economies and institutions.[13] The entire album is composed from fractured samples. The spoken word, originating in any number of incommensurable settings in daily life, is set to scores deriving from an unlikely array of musics, producing a montage designed to testify to the radical pliability of meaning. In a spirited move, Eno and Byrne aimed to uncover the musicality of the everyday which in conventional interpretation, they claimed, is neither seen nor heard. They adhered to bafflement as a virtue. 'I like this, but I don't know why …'[14]

Knowledge for Eno/Byrne resides in the music, or in the forms of the music, and cannot be conflated with the intellectual disciplines represented by Boehmer-the-critic. Eno and Byrne inhabit distinct expressive aesthetic worlds, distinct modes of thinking and being, and no doubt distinct politics. This much is true. However, it is also the case that the Tutuola crossover signals a matter of importance. For all their differences, the Eno/Byrne and Boehmer appropriations of the phantasmatic African forest amount to an unexpected convergence. By way of Tutuola, they share a desire to excavate the unspoken, or the unspeakable, realities which now give meaning to the historic metropole, reading them through the predicament of the colonised.

Eno was captivated by the idea that he would find 'music where music wasn't supposed to have been'.[15] This prioritises displacement as way of comprehending the modern world. He looked for improvised musics in the practices of everyday life and, in the process, music itself took on new meanings. Conceptually, as a working method, his search for music-unheard, or music-unnoticed, may not be a million miles away from the questions which confront postcolonial historians. When we ask ourselves how empire's afterlives continue to shape the contours of the present, the mental journey may not be so very different. As we set out on this inquiry, there's no knowing where these traces will be located, nor that we will even notice them when we see them.

How, the authors of this volume ask, do we approach the metropole 'after empire'? To answer this each chapter draws from an appropriately eclectic range of conceptual perspectives. There is no need for me to rehearse them here. Yet perhaps this is an occasion to ask how it is that, in our own conjuncture, the erstwhile metropole seems so radically out of joint. Boehmer's emphasis on the epistemic disorientations of the metropole suggests a starting point. We are obliged to find the means to engage with the 'weird voices, presences and irruptions' which assail us – not as abnormalities, nor as historical exceptions, but as ever-present, determinate expressions of deep social forces.

This requires us to work analytically from the historical present. 'After empire', *in general*, is becoming an increasingly thin abstraction. For long the belief prevailed, or prevails, that the epoch of the European colonial empires has met its end, or is nearing its end. But notwithstanding the epochal significance of this long duration, each moment was, or is, specific in its historical configuration, and the end of colonial power structures remains a long way off. These days, the idea 'after empire' trips easily from the tongue. But the times of 'after empire' are varied, composed of a complex of plural histories. We have arrived at the point where we are obliged to heed these changing conjunctural phases. What does 'after empire' mean for us today? How are its specificities to be conceived? What can it – and what can't it – explain about the present? One thing, though, I think is clear. The disorderly wildness of Britain after empire, in our own times, touches a new nerve.

Notes

1 Frantz Fanon, *The Wretched of the Earth* (Harmondsworth: Penguin, [1961] 1971), p. 27. Thanks particularly to Josh Doble, Liam J. Liburd and Emma Parker.
2 Richard Williams, 'More Dark than Shark: Interview with Brian Eno', *Melody Maker*, 12 January 1980, a riveting conversation.
3 Amos Tutuola, *My Life in the Bush of Ghosts* (London: Faber and Faber, 1990).
4 I follow Ken Gelder and Jane M. Jacobs, *Uncanny Australia: Sacredness and Identity in the Postcolonial Nation* (Melbourne: Melbourne University Press, 1998).
5 George Lamming, *The Pleasures of Exile* (London: Pluto, [1960] 2005), p. 77. One can plot the emergence of the idea in Fanon in the recent collection of his writings, *Alienation and Freedom*, ed. by Jean Khalfa and Robert J. C. Young (London: Bloomsbury, [2015] 2018).
6 Fanon, *The Wretched of the Earth*, p. 28.
7 Jim House and Neil MacMaster, *Paris 1961: Algerians, State Terror, and Memory* (Oxford: Oxford University Press, 2006).
8 Earl Lovelace, 'Finding the Darkness in Which to Grow: The Journey Towards a Bacchanal Aesthetics', in *Growing in the Dark*, ed. by Funso Aiyejina (San Juan: Lexicon Trinidad, 2003); and for a celebrated reflection on 'bacchanal aesthetics', Carolyn Cooper, *Noises in the Blood: Orality, Gender and the 'Vulgar Body' of Jamaican Popular Culture* (London: Macmillan, 1993).
9 Bill Schwarz, 'Wild Power: The Aftershocks of Decolonization and Black Power', in *The Global History of White Nationalism: From Apartheid to Donald Trump*, ed. by Daniel Geary, Camilla Schofield and Jenni Sutton (Manchester: Manchester University Press, 2020).
10 'Displacement' was first elaborated by Sigmund Freud, *The Interpretation of Dreams* (London: Penguin, [1899] 1991), where the formulation 'differently centred' also appears; and, in a bravura move where displacement is recast in order to illuminate the historical world, Louis Althusser, 'Contradiction and Overdetermination' (first pub., 1962), in *For Marx* (London: Allen Lane, 1969).
11 For a wonderful discussion of this larger theme in the period, see Simon Frith and Howard Horne, *Art Into Pop* (London: Routledge, 1987), in which Eno plays a prominent role: pp. 116–119.
12 David Toop, 'Programme Notes' to Brian Eno and David Byrne, *My Life in the Bush of Ghosts*, album, Virgin Records, 2006.
13 Fela Kuti – the Nigerian trumpeter and saxophonist, fearless Pan-African activist who single-handedly declared war on the military state in Nigeria and all-round phenomenon – haunts the album, uncannily present in his absence. He was the progenitor of diasporic Afrobeat, which first came to life in Los Angeles. His gloriously funk album *Zombie*, released in 1977, ensured that in the eyes of the Nigerian authorities he was a marked man. Kuti was Wole Soyinka's cousin.
14 Williams, 'More Dark than Shark'.

15 Williams, 'More Dark than Shark'. Williams was far from an innocent party in this dialogue. For an indication of where *he's* coming from, his *The Blue Moment: Miles Davis's* Kind of Blue *and the Remaking of Modern Music* (London: Faber and Faber, 2010) is a revelation.

Bibliography

Althusser, Louis, *For Marx* (London: Allen Lane, 1969).
Cooper, Carolyn, *Noises in the Blood: Orality, Gender and the 'Vulgar Body' of Jamaican Popular Culture* (London: Macmillan, 1993).
Fanon, Frantz, *Alienation and Freedom*, ed. by Jean Khalfa and Robert J. C. Young (London: Bloomsbury, [2015] 2018).
Fanon, Frantz, *The Wretched of the Earth* (Harmondsworth: Penguin, [1961] 1971).
Freud, Sigmund, *The Interpretation of Dreams* (London: Penguin, [1899] 1991).
Frith, Simon and Howard Horne, *Art Into Pop* (London: Routledge, 1987).
Gelder, Ken and Jane M. Jacobs, *Uncanny Australia: Sacredness and Identity in the Postcolonial Nation* (Melbourne: Melbourne University Press, 1998).
House, Jim and Neil MacMaster, *Paris 1961: Algerians, State Terror, and Memory* (Oxford: Oxford University Press, 2006).
Lamming, George, *The Pleasures of Exile* (London: Pluto Press, [1960] 2005).
Lovelace, Earl, 'Finding the Darkness in Which to Grow: The Journey Towards a Bacchanal Aesthetics', in *Growing in the Dark*, ed. by Funso Aiyejina (San Juan: Lexicon Trinidad, 2003).
Schwarz, Bill, 'Wild Power: The Aftershocks of Decolonization and Black Power', in *The Global History of White Nationalism: From Apartheid to Donald Trump*, ed. by Daniel Geary, Camilla Schofield and Jenni Sutton (Manchester: Manchester University Press, 2020).
Toop, David, 'Programme Notes' to Brian Eno and David Byrne, *My Life in the Bush of Ghosts*, album, Virgin Records, 2006.
Tutuola, Amos, *My Life in the Bush of Ghosts* (London: Faber and Faber, 1990).
Williams, Richard, *The Blue Moment: Miles Davis's* Kind of Blue *and the Remaking of Modern Music* (London: Faber and Faber, 2010).
Williams, Richard, 'More Dark than Shark: Interview with Brian Eno', *Melody Maker*, 12 January 1980.

Index

Aboulela, Leila 9, 191, 195–198
  Minaret (2005)
Adams, Walter 65–70, 72–73, 77
Adegoke, Yomi 95
Aden 108–109, 111–114, 116–117
adoption 30, 32, 36
African American 207, 209, 211, 212
  beauty culture 211, 213, 218, 222
  literary culture 87
  music 232, 234, 237
  women 209, 212, 215
Akala 97–99
Ali, Mishti 89, 96
Alibhai-Brown, Yasmin 115
Amis, Martin 108, 115
anthropology 37, 46, 48–55, 57
  as a colonial science 7, 16, 47
  fieldwork 50, 53
Arnold, Matthew 15
Australia 9, 137, 166, 178
  and the 'White Australia' policy 133
Asquith and Elliot Commissions 66–67

Bailkin, Jordanna 47
Baldwin, James 87
Ballantyne, Tony 50
Ballard, James Graham 106
Barnes, Julian 107–108
Basu, Paul 35, 38, 42
Baudrillard, Jean 194
Bauman, Zygmunt 193, 201
Bean, John 131, 136–137
Bhopal, Kalwant 95
Biggar, Nigel 167–168, 170, 173–174, 176, 178–179
  and 'Ethics and Empire' 7, 167–168

Black Lives Matter 6, 11–12, 33, 96, 158, 166
Black Women's Action Committee 220–221
Boakye, Jeffrey 94
Boehmer, Elleke 10, 259–260, 263–264
Brexit xii, 2, 4–6, 8–10, 42, 138, 166, 179
  referendum 89, 96
Brinkhurst-Cuff, Charlie 95
British Department for Scientific and Industrial Research 53
British Museum 5, 14, 30–31, 34–35, 37–39, 41–42
British National Party 92, 127, 133, 138
British Union of Fascists 129
Brixton Academy, The 10, 231, 233, 235–236, 241
Brooke, Stephen 233
Bryan, Beverley 95
Bush, Barbara 232
Byrne, David 263–264

Caine, Sydney 72–73
Cameron, David 190
Cape Town, University of 6
  see also Rhodes Must Fall movement
Caribbean 67, 69, 132, 138, 166, 178, 252, 254, 256
Carr-Saunders, Alexander 67, 69–70
Central African Federation 67, 69, 132, 135

Chambers, Eddie 231
Chesterton, Arthur Kenneth (A. K.) 129–132, 134–137
  views on Commonwealth 134
  views on Powell 143
  Rhodesia 135
Churchill, Winston xii–xiii
Clash, The 230, 237–238
Clingman, Stephen 34
Colonial Office 46, 67, 69, 75
  Special Committee on the Higher Education for Africans 67
colourism 196, 214, 221–222
  see also pigmentocracy
Colston, Edward 3, 32, 87
Combahee River Collective 87–88, 96
Commission on Race and Ethnic Disparities: The Report 12–13
  see also Sewell, Tony
Commonwealth 1, 3, 8, 10, 12, 69, 72, 76–77, 127–128, 131, 133–136, 138, 150
  Commonwealth immigration 127–128, 131, 133–136
  Commonwealth literature 12
Communist Party 49, 53, 136
Conrad, Joseph 260
Conservative Party 3, 128, 131
  and the Monday Club 128, 135–136
Cooper, Anna Julia 87
Cousins, Susan 94
COVID-19 pandemic 9, 11
Cullors, Patrisse 96
culture wars 6, 33, 99, 166
Cunnison, Sheila 54, 56, 57

Dabbagh, Selma 9, 191, 202–203
  Out of It (2012) 200–201
Dabiri, Emma 94
Dadzie, Stella 95
Darwin, John 111
De Certeau, Michel 30
Decolonisation 2, 3, 5, 7, 8, 12, 47, 66–67, 76–78, 106–110, 117, 127–129, 133, 135, 138, 166, 231, 255, 260–262
  of Britain 518, 526
  of the curriculum 324, 327

  theory of 6
  of the university 6, 157, 162, 175
DiAngelo, Robin 90
Douglass, Frederick 87
Drayton, Richard 7
Driscoll, Lawrence 115

Eddo-Lodge, Reni 87–88, 95, 97, 100
  Why I'm No Longer Talking to White People about Race 89–94
Egypt 110–111, 202
  see also Suez Crisis
Elizabeth II, Queen 51
Empire 2.0 8
Empire Windrush 208, 233
  see also Windrush scandal
England 2, 4, 8–10, 49, 51, 106, 108, 110, 138, 194, 257, 260–261
English nationalism 138
Englishness 8–10, 49, 107, 108–109, 113, 117
Eno, Brian 259, 263–264
Esty, Jed 49
ethnic populism 3, 8, 129
European Union 4, 8
  see also Brexit

Falklands War 106, 107, 112, 168
Fanon, Frantz 209, 260, 261–262
  Black Skin, White Masks 261
  The Wretched of the Earth 260, 261
Farage, Nigel 8
Ferguson, Niall 7, 167, 169–170, 171–175, 177–178, 179
Finney, Brian 114
First World War 107
Flint, Kate 108
Floyd, George xiii, 11, 32, 87
Ford, Ford Madox 107
Forster, E. M. 36
Fowler, Corinne 1, 20, 32
Frankenberg, Ronald 49–53
Fryer, Peter 208

gal-dem 89, 96, 101
Gappah, Petina xv
Garvey, Marcus 209
Garza, Alicia 96
Gebrial, Dalia 6

Index

Gelfand, Michael 69
Gilley, Bruce 170
Gilroy, Paul 89, 91, 101, 110, 230, 242
   convivial cultures 230, 232–233, 242
Gluckman, Max 46, 48–49, 50–55, 57
Gopal, Priyamvada 5, 169, 172–173, 174, 177–178
Greater Britain Movement 128, 134, 136, 137
Grenfell fire xiii
Gulf War 190, 191, 193, 195, 197, 198, 199
Gunby, Ingrid 109

Hall, Catherine 14–15
Hall, Stuart 4, 14, 115, 117, 147, 214, 216, 233–234
   Familiar Stranger 95
   'The Great Moving Right Show' 99–100
   Policing the Crisis 96
   'Resistance through rituals' 96
Harlow, Barbara xv
hate crime 8, 161
Heart of the Race: Black Women's Lives in Britain, The 95, 208, 211, 215
Hebdige, Dick 232
Hirsch, Afua 94
historical amnesia 4, 8, 178–179
history wars 6, 8, 11, 168
Holland, Tom xiii
Hollinghurst, Alan 107
Homans, Margaret 32
Hostile Environment 9, 96
Hughes, Ted 109

imperial nostalgia xi, 8, 10, 13, 89, 96, 99, 110, 113
India 39, 111–112, 127, 130, 131, 166, 171, 249, 250
institutional racism 11, 12, 88–89, 90, 92, 93, 94, 96, 97, 101
Ireland 8, 137
Irwin-Zarecka, Iwona 168, 174
Ishiguro, Kazuo 109

Japan 29–30, 175
Jardine, Lisa 108

Johnson, Boris xii–xiii
Jones, Claudia 209, 211, 215, 219, 220, 221
Jones, Owen 114
Jordan, Colin 131, 134

Kassim, Sumaya 14
Kelley, Robin D. G. 236
Kennedy, Dane 8, 11, 168
Kenyatta, Jomo 134
Khan, Mariam 95
Kipling, Rudyard 111, 177
Koven, Seth 233, 236, 239
Kureishi, Hanif 106, 108–109, 115
Kwakye, Chelsea 95

Labour Party 17
Lammy, David 9
Lawrence, Stephen 92
League of Empire Loyalists 127, 129, 131–132
Lessing, Doris 2
Letts, Don 230, 238
Levy, Andrea 207, 213, 221
   Every Light In the House Burnin' 208, 213–214
   Never Far From Nowhere 208, 215
LGBTQI+ 100, 108, 232, 240
   AIDS crisis 239
Libya 111
Light, Alison 114
Livingstone, David xv
London xiii, 4, 9, 34, 65, 72, 77–78, 98, 109, 133–134, 191, 195–202, 208, 212–213, 218, 230, 232–233, 236–242
London School of Economics 65–67, 69, 71–78
   Agitator (student magazine) 73
   LSE student boycott 65
   university library 72
Londoners 231–234, 239, 241–242
Lupton, Tom 54–57

MacKay, Marina 107, 110, 54–57
MacKenzie, John 2, 15
Macmillan, Harold 120
MacNeice, Louis 37

MacPhee, Graham 111
Mahfouz, Sabrina 95
Mahjoub, Jamal 9, 191
    Travelling with Djinns (1993) 191–195, 197
Manchester Guardian 51
Manchester School 48, 52
Mandela, Nelson xiv, xv
Mantel, Hilary 106
Mbembe, Achille xiv
McClintock, Anne xii
McEwan, Ian 106
McLeod, John xvi, 21, 107, 119, 231
Metropolitan Police 234–235, 239, 240
Middle East 34, 43, 111, 114, 117, 191
migration 2–4, 9, 13, 99, 115, 127–128, 131, 133, 137–138, 148, 150, 152, 161, 189, 207, 216, 221, 251, 253
Ministry of Overseas Development 72, 75, 78
Mitchell, David 106
Monday Club 128, 135–136
    see also Conservative Party
Mosley, Oswald 129, 132
Mujinga, Belly 11, 13

Nagra, Daljit 14, 29, 31–42
National Front 127, 137–138
National Labour Party 127, 131
National Trust 12, 18, 32, 43, 166
National Union of Students (UK) 75
nationalism 2, 30, 89, 129, 134, 167, 200
    English 138
    white 96
Ndembu people 55
Nora, Pierre 171
Northern Ireland 9, 107
Northern Rhodesia 46, 48–49, 51–52, 55–56
Notting Hill Carnival 218–219, 221
    see also Jones, Claudia
Notting Hill race riots 75, 78, 132, 209
Nyasaland 65, 67, 69, 113, 135

Ogunbiyi, Ore 95
Okri, Ben xii, 259
Oluo, Ijeoma 90
Olusoga, David 95, 97, 156
Ondaatje, Michael 110
Oriel College 2–3, 6
Orientalism 111, 113
Osborne, Cyril 128
Owusu, Derek 95
Oxford, University of 2, 6–7, 11, 167, 169–170, 174–175

pan-African 99, 265
Parker, Emma 114
Parkes, Simon 232, 235–241
Patel, Priti 9
peripheries of empire 107
Perraton, Hilary 75
Perry, Kennetta Hammond 231, 242
Phillips, Caryl 108–109
pigmentocracy 214, 224
Pitts, Johny 94
populism 3, 8, 99, 129
    see also ethnic populism
postcolonial
    anthropology 100
    Britain 3, 9, 15, 77, 89, 230, 236, 241
    communities 234, 242, 255
    curiosity 31, 33
    histories xi, 65–66, 77, 263–264
    melancholia 13, 110
    nationalism 192
    present xiv, 11, 66
    studies xi, xiii, 12–13, 21, 40, 42, 101, 106–109, 115, 117, 168, 174, 208
Powell, Enoch 3–5, 8–9, 75, 78, 99, 127–129, 138–139, 143
Powellism 8, 75, 129, 138
    'Rivers of Blood' speech 3–4, 75, 99, 127, 138
Pratt, Mary Louise 231
Procter, Alice 33

Race Equality Charter 155
radical right 127–129, 132–138

Ram Jam Club 234, 237–239
Ramayana 36, 39
Ranger, Terence 69
Rhodes, Cecil 2, 170
Rhodes Must Fall movement 2, 6–7, 158, 166
Rhodesia 1–3, 16, 17, 65–67, 69–80, 128, 133–137
　Unilateral Declaration of Independence (UDI) 70
　see also Southern Rhodesia
Royal Anthropological Institute 53
Royal Historical Society 147, 151, 157, 162
　and the Past and Present Postdoctoral Fellowship: Race, Ethnicity and Equality in History 150
　'Race, Ethnicity and Equality in UK History' report 147–148, 151, 154
　'Roadmap for Change' 147, 153
Runnymede Trust 12, 150, 152, 161
Rushdie, Salman xiv, 21, 44, 106, 109, 190
Rutherford, Adam 94

Saad, Layla 92–93
Said, Edward xii, 15, 21, 37, 112, 202
Saini, Angela 95
Savage, Mike 47, 51
Scafe, Suzanne 95
Schwarz, Bill 3, 8, 13, 67, 75, 128, 230
Scotland 8–9, 107, 167, 195
　independence referendum 8
Second World War 29, 54, 69, 72, 107–111, 129–130, 171, 175, 233
settler colonialism 1–3, 8, 67, 69, 128, 130–133, 135–136, 166
Sewell, Tony 12–13
　see also Commission on Race and Ethnic Disparities: The Report
Shukla, Nikesh 95
slavery and the slave trade xii, 5–6, 9, 12–13, 148, 166, 171–173, 176, 220, 231, 251, 254
Smith, Ian 74, 78, 135
Smith, Otto Saumarez 235
Smith, Zadie 4, 106, 115

Socialist Party 49
South Africa xv, 6, 17, 48, 65, 67, 106, 128, 130, 132–137
　apartheid 17, 67, 72, 74, 128, 136, 238
Southern Rhodesia 1–2, 67, 134–135
　see also Rhodesia
Southrepps Hall 1–2, 16
Soyinka, Wole xii, 259, 265
Stockwell, Sarah 72, 80
Stormzy 95, 103, 152
Straw, Jack 75
Sudan 191–196
Suez Crisis 111–112
Swift, Graham 10, 106–117

Tatum, Beverly Daniel 90
Thatcher, Margaret 112, 114, 238–239, 263
Thomas, Nicholas 30–32, 34, 44, 100
Tilley, Helen 57
Tometi, Opal 96
trade unions 49, 53, 55
Trump, Donald 42
Tuck, Stephen 236
Turner, Victor 55
Tutuola, Amos xii, 259, 261, 263–264
Tyndall, John 134, 136–137

United Kingdom 8, 11, 65, 71, 75–78, 147, 167, 208
United Nations 75, 134
　UNESCO 75
United States of America 10–11, 41, 87, 108, 110, 130, 132, 134, 172, 199, 207, 211–213, 217–218, 221–222, 232, 234–237, 241, 257–258
　see also African American
Union Movement 132
　see also Mosley, Oswald
University College of Rhodesia and Nyasaland 65, 67, 69
University of Birmingham 15, 67, 76
University of London 65, 69, 70, 72, 76–77

University of London (*continued*)
  Inter-University Council for Higher Education in the Colonies 66, 70, 78
  special relations with colonial universities 65–67, 71, 74–75, 78
University of Manchester 53, 57
  Department of Social Anthropology 46
  see also Manchester School
Uviebinené, Elizabeth 95

Vinen, Richard 65

wa Thiong'o, Ngũgĩ xv, 252–253
Wales 7–9, 50–52, 107, 161
  relationship with Britain 8–9, 47, 50
  Welsh language 50, 51
War on Terror 39, 189
  and 7/7 191
  and 9/11 39, 191, 199–200, 203
Webster, Nesta 130
Webster, Wendy 15, 232

West Indian Gazette and Afro-Asian Caribbean News, The 208–221
  see also Jones, Claudia
West Indies 50, 74, 79
white
  innocence 260
  nationalism 89
  privilege 90, 94, 100
White Defence League 127, 131–132
White Dominions 116, 128, 134
Williams, Sophie 95
Wilson, Harold 112, 117, 135
Windrush scandal 9, 166, 202, 9
  see also Empire Windrush

X, Malcolm 87, 97, 209

Yassin-Kassab, Robin 9, 191, 197–201
  The Road to Damascus (2008) 197–201
Yeats, W. B. 36
Younge, Gary 5, 11
Yushukan military and war museum 29, 34

Zephaniah, Benjamin 95
Zimbabwe 79, 81

EU authorised representative for GPSR:
Easy Access System Europe, Mustamäe tee 50,
10621 Tallinn, Estonia
gpsr.requests@easproject.com